THE SEMINOLE NATION OF OKLAHOMA

American Indian Law and Policy Series
Lindsay G. Robertson, General Editor

The Seminole Nation of Oklahoma

A Legal History

L. Susan Work

Foreword by Lindsay G. Robertson

University of Oklahoma Press : Norman

Library of Congress Cataloging-in-Publication Data

Work, L. Susan, 1950–
    The Seminole nation of Oklahoma : a legal history / L. Susan Work ;
foreword by Lindsay G. Robertson.—1st ed.

        p.   cm. — (American Indian law and policy series ; v. 4)
    Includes bibliographical references and index.
    ISBN 978-0-8061-4089-6 (hardcover) ISBN 978-0-8061-9381-6 (paper)
    1. Seminole Indians—Oklahoma—History—20th century. 2. Seminole

Indians—Oklahoma—Government relations. 3. Seminole Indians, Oklahoma—
Legal status, laws, etc. 4. Seminole Indians—Oklahoma—Politics and government—20th century. 5. Seminole Indians—Land tenure—Oklahoma—History.
6. Tribal government—Oklahoma—History. I. Title.
    E99.S28W67 2010
    976.6004'973859—dc22

                                                                2009050411

The Seminole Nation of Oklahoma: A Legal History is Volume 4 in the
American Indian Law and Policy Series.

The paper in this book meets the guidelines for permanence and durability of
the Committee on Production Guidelines for Book Longevity of the Council on
Library Resources. ∞

To

my parents,

Hiahwahnah (Hudson) Work and John Henry Work, Jr.

and

my children,

Will, Kelli Brooke, and John Hudson Haney

and

my grandsons,

Jack Brady and Sam Haney

CONTENTS

Illustrations

Photographs

Maps

Series Editor's Foreword

L. Susan Work's *The Seminole Nation of Oklahoma: A Legal History* is a moving account of the successful struggles of the Seminole Nation to survive decades of fluctuations in federal policy—frequently hostile to its continued existence—from the late nineteenth century through the early years of the twenty-first century. Part of this story—the Seminole Wars in Florida, for example, and the removal to the Indian Territory—is well known. Much more of it is not.

The definitive account of the Seminole Nation's legal history, this book owes its authority to the author's long and deep connection with the Nation and its people, which afforded her extraordinary access to primary materials and oral tradition. The history of the modern Seminoles, while in some ways unique, shares much in common with that of other indigenous nations—especially the Cherokees, Choctaws, Chickasaws, and Muscogees (Creeks)—who were forced to deal with the United States. *The Seminole Nation of Oklahoma* offers readers a chance to experience that history from the inside, in sufficient detail that readers will be able to develop their own well-informed assessment of the legacy of two centuries of federal–tribal relations.

The Seminole Nation of Oklahoma is a remarkable work, and the University of Oklahoma Press and I are proud to offer it as the fourth volume in the American Indian Law and Policy Series.

Preface and Acknowledgments

The present book is intended to be a work of legal scholarship providing an aerial view of the history of the Seminole Nation of Oklahoma's survival and development in the twentieth century. It would take a book twice the size of this one to discuss this history in the broader context of the United States' general history or to focus on Seminole citizens instrumental in shaping the Seminole Nation's history. For that reason, this history is presented in the more limited context of the overall legal progression of federal–tribal relations, including important Supreme Court decisions and federal legislation affecting the Five Tribes (the Seminole, Choctaw, Cherokee, Muscogee (Creek), and Chickasaw Nations) specifically and Indian tribes generally.

My own perspectives are drawn from my thirty-year career as an Oklahoma attorney practicing federal Indian law and tribal law. Equally important, my perspectives are influenced by my membership in the Choctaw Nation and by the fact that I am a parent of children who are members of the Seminole Nation and who spent their younger years in Seminole, Oklahoma. Even though I have this personal affinity for the Seminole Nation's history, I have carefully documented my research and prepared a book that I hope can be used as a basic primer concerning not only Seminole legal history, but also federal Indian law and the shared legal histories of the Five Tribes as a group.

When I was growing up in Henryetta, Oklahoma, less than sixty miles from Seminole County, textbook descriptions of tribal histories fell far short of even touching the surface of events affecting Indian nations on the road to statehood. Proving that one person can change another person's life, at the urging of a friend, I took an Indian history course at the University of Oklahoma around 1970, only a year after the Seminole Nation had adopted its new 1969 constitution. This course sparked my interest in Indian law, and three years later, I participated in a summer law program that taught Native American law students basic Indian law principles and the importance of legal writing skills.

While attending the University of Oklahoma's College of Law, I was fortunate to find a job researching the histories of the Five Tribes. My first connection with the Seminole Nation also began at that time, when a few members of our Indian law student association, including myself, went to Seminole County to meet with Seminole members to discuss the possibility of providing legal research assistance to them. After I graduated from law school, I continued working on the Five Tribes research project. This work included reviewing files in Seminole that were made available by attorney Charles Grounds, a member of the Seminole Nation who played a significant role in the development of the Seminole Constitution and many other aspects of the Seminole Nation's affairs.

In the late 1970s I wrote a law review article summarizing the Seminole Nation's legal history and explaining why the Seminole Nation was not a "terminated" tribe. This work led to my meeting my future husband, a member of the Seminole Nation who visited my office in Oklahoma City as a result of reading the article. After our marriage, I had an office for a time in downtown Seminole, and our three children were born between 1980 and 1988. From 1991 through most of 1994, I had the honor and privilege of serving as attorney general for the Seminole Nation of Oklahoma. It was during my fifteen-year residence in Seminole that I saw firsthand the Seminole government and tribal politics in action. It was never dull, and it was a fascinating and rewarding experience.

I would like to express my appreciation for all of the people who assisted and inspired me, including the following members of the Seminole Nation: Eula Doonkeen, for contributing her papers to the Oklahoma Historical Society, serving as a strong role model for Native American women, and sharing her photographs with me; Charles Grounds, who provided access to his tribal files in the 1970s; Jerry Haney, former principal chief, who shared both his recollection of events that occurred during his first term of office and his personal collection of files reflecting the Seminole Nation's history; my ex-husband, Kelly Haney, who served as principal chief from 2005 to 2009, for providing interviews and sharing reports that were prepared when he served as tribal planner for the Seminole Nation in the 1970s; the Seminole Nation Code Development staff of 1991 to 1993, including project director Leonard M. Harjo (son of former chief Floyd Harjo), secretary Renae Larney, volunteer legal consultant Yvette Harjo (daughter of former Chief Harjo), and research analyst Leonard Gouge, a member of the Muscogee (Creek) Nation; the Terry Walker family (Larry Walker, Jerry Walker, Harry Walker, Gary Walker, Susie McNeal, Terri Jackson, Beatrice Walker, Shirley Scott Walker, and Anna Romeo), for sharing memories and photographs of their father, former chief Terry Walker, and for providing access to his invaluable papers; Lewis Johnson, assistant curator of the Seminole Nation Museum in Wewoka, who provided assistance in my review of papers there; newly elected in 2009 chief of the Seminole Nation Leonard M. Harjo, who reviewed my manuscript; Terry Spencer, chairman of the Seminole Nation Education Committee, who reviewed my manuscript; Glenn Sharpe, a Seminole attorney, who also reviewed my manuscript; Ted Underwood, for providing photographs; and Loretta (Burgess) Finkenberg, former general council secretary, for her assistance and encouragement in my efforts involving the Seminole Nation.

There are many other Seminoles who have inspired me by zealously developing the Seminole Nation's government and working to better the lives of Seminole citizens. Although in this book I do not attempt to credit all of the many tribal members who gave of themselves to the Seminole Nation, their own family members and others know of their contributions. Their work has been meaningful, and I hope it will serve as an inspiration to younger Seminole members in years to come.

I would also like to extend my appreciation to attorney William Wantland, who preserved papers concerning the development of the Seminole Nation Constitution of 1969 and gave his time for an interview concerning that topic. In addition, I would like to thank Mary McCormick, former chief of the Sac and Fox Nation, both for sharing memories of her Seminole father, Thomas Coker, who played a critical role in the development of the 1969 Constitution of the Seminole Nation, and for contributing his papers to the Oklahoma Historical Society. Former chief of the Cherokee Nation Wilma Mankiller has also graciously given time to review the manuscript.

I am also thankful for the encouragement that Sharon Blackwell and Charles Wilkinson provided in my legal writing class at the University of New Mexico American Indian Pre-Law Program in Albuquerque, New Mexico; for the assistance of paralegal Vanessa Mankiller, a Cherokee member who compiled many of the legal histories of federal legislation discussed in this book; and for help from many Native American attorneys, including the following: Vincent Knight, former Oklahoma coordinator for the Native American Legal Defense and Education Fund, who employed me to work on the Five Tribes legal research project; Rennard Strickland, for encouraging my desire to write a book involving Oklahoma Indian law and for serving as a reader of the manuscript for the University of Oklahoma Press (OU Press); David A. Mullon, Jr., for encouraging me to finally start on this work and for working tirelessly to try to repair federal land laws involving the Five Tribes; my friend and fellow Choctaw member Douglas Dry, who served as an inspiration in his efforts concerning the civil rights of tribal members; and all of the other Native American attorneys, many of whom are mentioned in this work, who achieved legal victories on behalf of the tribes in Oklahoma during the last few decades. I also thank the law firm of Hobbs, Straus, Dean & Walker, LLP, for its many contributions to the development of Indian law nationwide and for its financial support to the production of this book.

The staff of the OU Press has, of course, been instrumental in completing this book project, and I would like to give special thanks to acquisitions editor Alessandra Jacobi Tamulevich, special projects editor Alice Stanton, editorial assistant Ashley Eddy, production coordinator Julie Rushing, and copyeditor Kimberly W. Kinne for their assistance in review and publication of this book. I also appreciate the work of attorney Curtis Berkey and OU law professor and series editor Lindsay Robertson for reviewing the manuscript and providing insightful comments and encouragement. I also appreciate assistance of the following persons who assisted me during my research: Oklahoma History Center staff, particularly Chester Cowan, who assisted with my review of photographs, and Jennifer Silvers, who assisted in retrieval of Seminole documents for my review; Jeffrey Wilhite, Government Documents, OU Bizzell Library; and the staff of the OU Western History Collections.

Finally, I appreciate not only my three children's enthusiastic support, but also their more concrete contributions to this effort. My older son, William, proofread the final manuscript for me. My daughter, Kelli Brooke, listened to my venting when I was frustrated with my work on the book. My younger son, John Hudson, took photographs at Mekusukey for the book. I hope they, and other young Seminole adults, are pleased with the final result.

Abbreviations

AIM	American Indian Movement
BCR Commission	Business and Corporate Regulatory Commission
BIA	Bureau of Indian Affairs
CDIB	certificate of degree of Indian blood
CETA	Comprehensive Employment and Training Act
C.F.R.	*Code of Federal Regulations*
CFR Court	Court of Indian Offenses
CHR	Community Health Representative
Cong. Rec.	*Congressional Record*
Fed. Reg.	*Federal Register*
F. Supp.	*Federal Supplement*
GAO	General Accounting Office
HHS	U.S. Department of Health and Human Services
HUD	U.S. Department of Housing and Urban Development
IBIA	Interior Board of Indian Appeals
ICRA	Indian Civil Rights Act
ICWA	Indian Child Welfare Act
IGRA	Indian Gaming Regulatory Act
IHS	Indian Health Service
ILCA	Indian Land Consolidation Act
IRA	Indian Reorganization Act of 1934
IRS	Internal Revenue Service
JOM	Johnson O'Malley Program

LEAA	Law Enforcement Assistance Administration
NA NRD	National Archives, Natural Resources Division
NIGC	National Indian Gaming Commission
OBA	Oklahoma Bar Association
OICWA	Oklahoma Indian Child Welfare Act
OIPA	Oklahoma Independent Petroleum's Association
OIWA	Oklahoma Indian Welfare Act of 1936
Pub. L. No.	Public Law Number
SEDA	Seminole Economic Development Authority
SITBA	Seminole Intra-Tribal Business Association, Inc.
SNEDA	Seminole Nation Economic Development Authority
Stat.	*United States Statutes*
TERO	Tribal Employment Rights Office
WHC	University of Oklahoma Western History Collections

The Seminole Nation of Oklahoma

INTRODUCTION

This is the story of the legal relations between the Seminole Nation, the smallest and fiercest of the so-called Five "Civilized" Tribes, and the federal government during the twentieth century. These relations were defined to a large extent by the impact of federal laws on tribal and individual land ownership, federal administrative repression of the Seminole government, the Seminole Nation's efforts to recover damages against the United States in claims cases that spanned decades, and the Seminoles' determination in accomplishing a remarkable redevelopment of their government after adopting a new constitution in 1969.

Federal–Seminole relations can be best understood only with reference to the events of the nineteenth century. The Five Tribes—the Seminole, Cherokee, Choctaw, Chickasaw, and Muscogee (Creek) Nations—were originally from the Southeast. In the 1830s the Cherokee Nation secured Supreme Court decisions that recognized Indian tribes as sovereign "domestic dependent nations" and established solid legal principles that have assisted Indian tribes in their relations with the federal government for almost two centuries. President Andrew Jackson nevertheless immediately disregarded those decisions and enforced an executive policy of forced removal, a decision that resulted in several years of war with the Seminoles in Florida and the removal of the majority of Seminoles to lands west of the Mississippi River.

The Five Tribes acquired fee simple deeds to their new lands in Indian Territory with the intention, clearly stated in their respective treaties, that they would each enjoy separate tribal communal ownership of the new lands and would continue government operations that were to remain forever untouched by territorial or state governments. This plan soon backfired when the Five Tribes were forced after the Civil War to cede large portions of their domains back to the United States and were again faced with non-Indian encroachment on their remaining lands. Their struggle for autonomy occurred in an environment that eventually moved from earlier genocidal policies to a more "benevolent" policy advocating the allotment of tribal lands and the assimilation of Indians into mainstream society.

The push for the fragmentation of tribal lands was an especially ugly development for the Five Tribes, which had continued to have faith in the strength of their unique treaties. There was an increasing recognition by many federal officials that, because the Five Tribes owned their lands in fee, the federal government lacked legal authority to deed those lands to allottees—unlike its ability to dispose of other tribes' reservation lands owned by the United States and held in trust for the Indians. The federal government's pretense of protecting Indian interests by forced allotment of other tribes' trust lands developed into to a much more serious situation for the Five Tribes: If they refused to deed the lands to individual Indians and enable their lands to be subject to eventual non-Indian ownership, then Congress would threaten the Five Tribes' governments with total destruction in order to force the issuance of deeds, or it would attempt to completely crush them so that the United States could step in and assume sufficient control to move the lands to non-Indian hands.

The Five Tribes steadfastly refused to submit to the division of their lands into separate Indian ownership or to subject tribal citizens to local, non-Indian territorial or state governments. In response, Congress enacted special federal laws in the 1880s and 1890s that were applicable to the Five Tribes as a group and were designed to place increasing pressure on them to deed their communal lands to tribal members—a prelude to "legitimizing" the presence of thousands of non-Indians who were pouring into Indian Territory. These laws included an 1898 law known as the Curtis Act that threatened the existence of their governments, particularly the tribal court systems that they held so dear, and each of the Five Tribes eventually capitulated to the pressure. When the Five Tribes' governments were on the brink of annihilation in 1906, Congress enacted a law that continued the tribes' governments indefinitely. If tribal leaders gave some sighs of relief, they must have been short-lived. Almost immediately, Congress enacted a series of laws that disregarded protections in the allotment agreements, resulting in the rapid loss of individual Indian lands and the destitution of once prosperous Five Tribes citizens.

These events set the stage both for the enactment of a myriad of federal laws that were applicable only to the Five Tribes as well as for destructive actions by federal officials who once again stepped in to try to finish off the Five Tribes. Federal officials advanced the legal fictions that the Curtis Act's most damaging provisions had become law (when, in fact, they had not), that the Five Tribes were effectively terminated, and that only chiefs appointed by federal officials could act on behalf of the tribes for the limited purpose of signing deeds. As so plainly stated by a federal court in 1976, the Bureau of Indian Affairs engaged in practices that could only be characterized as "bureaucratic imperialism" in its treatment of the Five Tribes in the twentieth century. The leaders and citizens of the Seminole Nation, like those of the other four nations, dug in their heels, continued their determined efforts to secure changes in their treatment by the federal government, and waited for a miracle, which eventually occurred when federal policy shifted toward favoring tribal self-determination.

Seminole leaders were the first of the Five Tribes to strengthen their government in this new era, through a new Seminole Constitution approved by the Seminole people in 1969. After the Seminole government was organized according to the new constitution, it suffered growing pains as Seminole leaders worked to strike a balance of power between the Nation's chief and its council members, who were each elected by their own respective bands. By 1969 Seminole citizens were inherently distrustful of having a chief with significant executive powers, in light of past precedence of federal officials insisting that they had the sole power to appoint the chiefs and control their actions. The Nation's internal conflicts after adopting the new constitution were fueled by interference from the Bureau of Indian Affairs—a situation exacerbated by the lack of a Seminole court system.

Counterbalancing these problems, the 1970s, 1980s, and 1990s marked a new period in the history of the United States' relations with Indian tribes, as reflected by federal laws that were increasingly advantageous to tribes. During this time, tribes in Oklahoma began challenging state authority and were rewarded with federal court decisions that repeatedly found that the state of Oklahoma did not possess the type of governmental authority over Indians and tribes that it had exercised since the 1907 formation of the state. In this new environment, the Seminole Nation was able to strengthen its governmental infrastructure, provide services to tribal members, acquire land, construct governmental and community facilities, and engage in economic development activities, while continuing to maintain cultural integrity. The Nation also improved relationships with the federal and state governments, resulting in the betterment of not only its tribal citizens, but also the non-Indian community in Seminole County and in the state of Oklahoma. Although the Seminoles experienced difficult political upheavals after embarking on their new governmental journey, their history is one of cultural, governmental, and social survival; the Seminole people withstood a battery of federal laws and administrative actions that could have destroyed them if not for their remarkable courage and determination.

CHAPTER 1

FORCES OF FEDERAL LAW IN
INDIAN TERRITORY, 1831–1898

At the close of the twentieth century, the capital complex of the Seminole Nation was located just east of the small town of Wewoka, the county seat of Seminole County, Oklahoma, approximately seventy miles southeast of Oklahoma City. The Seminole Nation capital complex included an office building for the executive branch, a community building, a gas station and tobacco store, and nearby property leased by the Nation to the federal government for the offices of the Bureau of Indian Affairs and for a health clinic. The Housing Authority of the Seminole Nation, also located in Wewoka, was providing federally funded housing services to tribal members. The National Council of the Seminole Nation continued to function at the Nation's council building at Mekusukey, located south of Seminole, Oklahoma, at the former site of a school operated by the Seminole Nation in years gone by. By the early twenty-first century, the Seminole Nation's population of more than 15,000 members far exceeded the population of 2,567 shown by the 1890 census.

The continued vitality of the Seminole Nation in the twentieth and twenty-first centuries could not have been foreseen at the close of the nineteenth century. By 1897, the existence of the Seminole government was severely threatened. The Seminole Nation was not alone. As in past decades, the U.S. government viewed the Seminole, Cherokee, Choctaw, Chickasaw, and Muscogee (Creek) Nations as a unique group of "civilized" Indians and was attempting to address unique "problems" caused by their political and legal strength. By 1897, little more than sixty years after the Five Tribes had been forced to give up most of their homelands in the southeastern portion of the United States, the tribes' newer lands in Indian Territory were overrun by non-Indians, and they were again faced with a federal government prepared to accommodate the unrelenting demands from settlers who coveted their rich lands.[1]

Throughout the nineteenth century the Five Tribes demonstrated their strength, tenacity, and unique reliance on the federal legal system in their battle for survival. The Cherokee Nation was instrumental in early landmark Supreme Court decisions in the 1830s that recognized the special legal status of Indian tribes, including *Worcester v. Georgia* and *Cherokee Nation v. Georgia*.[2] Although these early decisions, which have served as an important legal foundation in the development of federal Indian law for almost two centuries, seemed to validate tribal reliance on the federal courts, the Five Tribes quickly learned that court victories would not help them defeat the executive office's resolve that they be removed to Indian Territory. Following President Andrew Jackson's decision to ignore the Supreme Court rulings in the Cherokee cases and to use military force against the Five Tribes, the Choctaws, Chickasaws, Cherokees, and Creeks entered into treaties with the United States and took the harsh and often deadly Trail of Tears to Indian Territory in the 1830s. The Seminole Nation, the smallest of the Five Tribes, had been displaced from a huge area of land in Florida under the Treaty of Camp Moultrie in 1823 (an event that finally lead to a multi-million dollar federal award to the Florida and Oklahoma Seminoles almost a century and a half later) and subsequently entered into treaties for removal to Indian Territory in 1832 and 1833.[3] Many Seminoles resisted, and a violent and bloody war was waged as Seminoles defended their homes in Florida from 1835 through part of 1842.[4] An army of 41,000 soldiers was required to subdue the fierce tribe, costing the United States more than ten million dollars and the death or wounding of 765 soldiers. A large number of Seminoles perished in the battle to save their homeland, and only about 3,000 members survived.

Many of the surviving Seminoles began forced emigration to Indian Territory in 1839 as the Seminole war wound down. The Seminoles traveled mostly by boat to destinations in or adjacent to Indian Territory, and they walked the remainder of the way. Over their objections, the Seminoles were required by the 1832 treaty to settle among the Creeks in Indian Territory. In an attempt to induce more Seminoles to migrate to Indian Territory, in 1845 the United States agreed to a new treaty that allowed the Seminoles to settle apart from the Creeks. The 1845 treaty permitted the Seminoles to make their own town regulations but provided that they would continue to be subject to the general control of the Creek Council. This tactic did not prove to be persuasive, and as a result the Seminole Nation was permanently split. As many as 500 Seminoles retreated into the swamps and remained in Florida. Approximately 2,800 Seminoles settled in Indian Territory, and a few hundred African Americans settled among them. Some African Americans were free persons and some were slaves, but eventually they became referred to collectively as "freedmen."[5]

The Seminoles in Indian Territory did not own lands of their own at first and settled on lands owned by the Muscogee (Creek) Nation, as required by the 1845 treaty. Under the leadership of head chief Micconapy, the Seminole Nation finally acquired and communally occupied a tract of land from the Muscogee (Creek) Nation in 1856 after negotiating a new treaty with the Creeks and the United States that was approved by Seminole representatives John Jumper, Tuste-nuc-o-chee, Pars-co-fer, and James Factor.[6] Under the 1856 treaty, the Seminoles also achieved independence from authority of the Creek Council and established a separate government and separate educational institutions in Indian Territory comparable to those of the other four nations, though smaller in size.

Unlike the other four nations, the Seminole Nation did not have a written document identified as a constitution, although it may have operated under written bylaws adopted in 1856 defining the general governmental structure.[7] The Seminole government operated for the latter half of the nineteenth century in accordance with Seminole law, which was based on Seminole traditions, some of which were written.[8] The Seminole Council consisted of *tustenugees* (subchiefs) who were elected by loosely organized groups of Seminoles, known as bands. In the early nineteenth century, the bands regulated most areas of Seminole life, and council authority was limited to inter-band relations and foreign affairs. The balance of power began shifting more in favor of the council after the Civil War. By the 1880s the council was responsible for supervising the bands and serving as legislators and courts for the Nation. However, band chiefs retained significant control over tribal resources. By 1890 the number of bands represented on the council decreased from twenty-five to fourteen, two of which were African American. The principal chief served as head of the executive branch. The Seminole laws were enforced by a Seminole police force known as the "Lighthorse," which had increased to fourteen men by the 1880s.[9]

The Five Tribes possessed a remarkable ability to survive the outside pressures on their self-government, in large part because of their sophistication in legal matters. This sophistication was demonstrated in the wording of treaties negotiated at the time of removal and following the Civil War. Their treaties contained unique provisions expressly protecting tribal governmental powers and authority. The 1856 treaty between the United States, the Seminole Nation, and the Muscogee (Creek) Nation stated that to the extent compatible with the U.S. Constitution and federal laws regulating trade and intercourse with Indian tribes, "the Creeks and Seminoles shall be secured in the unrestricted right of self-government within their respective limits." The treaty excepted tribal authority over white persons who were not, by adoption or otherwise, members of either the Muscogee or Seminole Nation; those white persons were to be "removed from and kept out of the same by the United States agents for said tribes, respectively; (assisted, if necessary, by the military)." The 1856 treaty also contained a provision by which the United States solemnly agreed "that no state or territory shall ever pass laws for the government of the Creek or Seminole tribes of Indians" and that no portions of the tracts described in the treaty and owned by those tribes "shall ever be erected into a territory without the full and free consent of the legislative authority of the tribe owning the same."[10]

The United States forced new treaties on the Five Tribes in 1866 based on their support of the Confederacy, whether real or perceived. Although some of the tribes had officially supported the Confederacy, it is debatable whether the Seminole Nation had entered into a formal government-to-government relationship with the South during the Civil War. Some Seminoles had actively supported the Confederacy, and others, who became known as the "Loyal Seminoles," had remained loyal to the Union. The Seminole Nation's 1866 treaty continued the protections established in the earlier treaties by specifically reaffirming previous treaty obligations "not inconsistent" with the new treaty. It included a provision in which the Seminole Nation agreed to "such legislation as Congress and the President may deem necessary for the better administration of the rights of person or property within the Indian Territory" but added the proviso that "said legislation shall not in any manner interfere with or annul their present tribal organization, rights, laws, privileges, and customs."[11]

The Five Tribes did not fare as well in protecting their land holdings in their 1866 treaties. The Seminole treaty, signed by John Chup-co as the head chief and John F. Brown as special delegate for the Seminoles who had supported the Confederacy (known as the "Southern Seminoles), required the Seminoles to sell their land in the central and western parts of Indian Territory back to the United States and purchase a smaller area from the Muscogee Nation. That smaller portion of land consisted of approximately 200,000 acres located to the east of the area they were forced to sell. The Seminole Nation acquired a deed to the tract so that it was held in fee by the Nation as a separate legal entity and was occupied by tribal members in a communal fashion, with no individual ownership. The Seminoles paid fifty cents an acre for the new lands, compared with fifteen cents an acre they received for the lands sold. The Muscogee Nation later sold the Seminoles another tract of 175,000 acres, resulting in the Seminole Nation's fee ownership of a total of 375,000 acres. The new Seminole domain, which was hilly and bounded in part by portions of the Canadian River, covered a rectangular area about thirty-five miles long from north to south and about ten miles wide. It was very small in comparison with the approximately twenty-five million acres still owned by the other four of the Five Tribes after the Civil War. By the end of the nineteenth century, almost the entire domain of the Seminole Nation would be removed from tribal ownership and chipped into fragments ripe for the taking by non-Indians.[12]

The Five Tribes recognized that the large land cessions required by the post–Civil War treaties meant that they must reinforce their political and legal strength. As a result, they included provisions in their 1866 treaties that authorized establishment of a council of Indian tribes residing in Indian Territory.[13] The Five Tribes lost little time in organizing the council to safeguard against future encroachments on their sovereignty. A general council of delegates representing each of the Five Tribes began meeting in 1869. In December 1870 council delegates developed for the Indian Territory a constitution, known as the "Okmulgee Constitution," and submitted it to each of the tribes. The *New York Sun* criticized these efforts in 1872, characterizing organization of an Indian state as a "plausible but injudicious scheme" and "one open to many serious objections." In response, W. P. Boudinot, editor of the *Cherokee Advocate*, stated that the opposition to an Indian territorial government reflected the wishes and expectations of the mass of the American people, "that is that our little nationalities as they are, must in time go down . . . Hence, every action taken by the Indian Nations in concert, is narrowly watched; because there is the general apprehension that they might by some action of their own, ward off for a long period the extinction of their nationalities."[14]

The Five Tribes efforts to close ranks and develop their own Indian state was reasonable in light of congressional action to weaken the sovereign status of Indian tribes nationwide. In 1871, two years before the development of the Okmulgee Constitution,

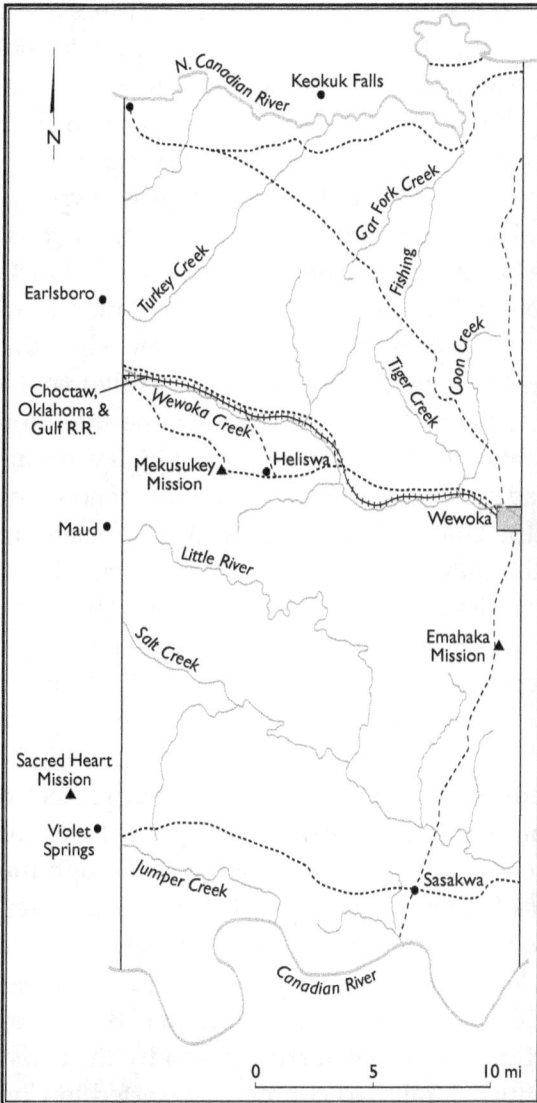

The Seminole Nation, 1901. Reproduced by permission from Edwin C. McReynolds, *The Seminoles* (Norman: University of Oklahoma Press, 1957, 1972), 271.

Congress enacted a law abolishing the right of Indian tribes to enter into treaties with the United States. The 1871 law established new parameters for the relationship between tribes and the federal government. Up until that time, the executive branch had the authority to negotiate treaties and the Senate had the power to ratify them. The purpose of the 1871 act was to include the U.S. House of Representatives in federal policymaking regarding Indian affairs. As a result, the entire Congress assumed authority over the regulation of Indian affairs, including matters involving the Seminole Nation and the other four nations. This act weakened the Five Tribes ability to resist the fragmentation of tribal lands into individual allotments thirty years later when the Supreme Court declined to review tribal challenges to allotment legislation; the Court cited the 1871 act as voicing the intention to make tribes amenable directly to congressional legislative authority.[15]

The railroad companies were natural allies of non-Indian settlers throughout the United States, and railroad officials significantly influenced the outcome of the ongoing struggle by non-Indian intruders for Indian lands in Indian Territory. The federal government began to offer special protection to the railroad interests in Indian Territory as early as 1866 when each of the Five Tribes treaties included specific, although not identical, language concerning railroad rights of way. In the case of the Seminole Nation, the railroad interests were more than sufficiently protected by treaty provisions allowing excessively wide rights of way along tracks that would eventually cross the Nation. Although the railroads did not cross Seminole lands until thirty years later, the 1866 treaty marked the beginning of a bitterness toward the railroads that would lead, more than a century later, to charges that a group of Seminoles burned a railroad bridge. By 1872 one railroad crossed portions of Indian Territory, and by the early 1880s the powerful influence railroad companies exerted in Congress had become even stronger.[16]

The Cherokee Nation fought back by challenging the legality of an 1884 law that granted rights-of-way through Indian Territory to the Southern Kansas Railroad, with compensation to be paid to the tribes whose lands were crossed. In 1889 the Supreme Court ruled that Cherokee treaty protections did not render the 1884 act invalid. The Court found that the lands owned in fee by the Cherokee Nation, like the lands held by private owners nationwide, were subject to federal government eminent domain powers. The exercise of eminent domain enabled the government to acquire private property for certain necessary purposes, such as transportation needs, subject to payment of just compensation to the property owner. The Court stated that it would be "very strange" if the United States could exercise the power of eminent domain within states but not within a Territory occupied by Indian tribes. At the time of the decision, Congress had enacted numerous additional laws authorizing railroad construction in Indian Territory, and there were already more than one million miles of railroad tracks in Indian Territory. The decision was quickly followed by even more congressional enactments authorizing railroad construction there.[17]

In part because of the establishment of railroad towns in Indian Territory, the desire for town property became an important force during the push for the forced division of the Five Tribes lands into individual allotments in the 1880s and 1890s. The Department of the Interior apparently did not understand that the power of eminent domain allowed the federal government to take private property only for certain necessary purposes and argued that such power could be exercised to acquire tribal lands. According to one Interior report,

> Congress should pass a town site act for The Five Tribes, forcing their consent, if necessary, to the end that valuable accrued property rights shall be protected. . . . Railroads are chartered through The Five Tribes, and cities, towns and villages grow up along them in aid of their operation. Congress should incorporate these towns and provide for a legal method of registering and passing title to these various properties or adjuncts of railroad trade and commerce . . . In any view of Five Tribe affairs, town sites are the serious problems. They should be settled first, and at once, by Congress exercising its

right of eminent domain and in aid of internal commerce. The Five Tribes will probably never pass an incorporative law by which whites or colored, so-called intruders, can get title to lots. Congress will have to do this.[18]

The Seminole Nation's capital in Wewoka and the other towns in the Seminole Nation, such as Konawa, Wolf, and Sasakwa, were different from towns in the other four nations. By 1890 Wewoka had a population of twenty-five and consisted of one store, a post office, the council house, a small steam corn mill, and a cotton gin. Towns in the other four domains were served by railroads, were much larger than the Seminole towns, and included significant numbers of non-Indian intruders. Even though there were few intruders in the Seminole Nation and no railroads crossed the Seminole Nation in 1890, the problems caused by railroad towns in other parts of Indian Territory had a negative impact on the Seminole Nation's struggle to retain ownership of its lands. Congress was intent on treating the Five Tribes as a group, and the fates of all Five Tribes were closely intertwined.[19]

The railroads did not limit their efforts to taking only those Indian lands that were needed for railroad purposes. In the 1896 case of *Atlantic and Pacific Railroad v. Mingus*, the U.S. Supreme Court ruled against the railroad company, which was claiming certain land in New Mexico. The Court found that the railroad's claim had been forfeited under federal law. Although the case did not involve lands in Indian Territory, the Court discussed the railroad's position that it was entitled to lands that were set aside for the construction of railroad tracks across Indian Territory, even though it did not use those lands. The Court stated, "Under these circumstances it could scarcely be expected that the United States should be called upon to extinguish, for the benefit of a railroad company, which had chosen to locate its route through this Territory, a title guaranteed to the Indians by solemn treaties and which had been possessed by them for upwards of forty years with the powers of an almost independent government."[20]

Immediately following the *Mingus* decision, Congress allowed railroad construction in Indian Territory by special enactments granting rights of way to specific railroads. In 1899 Congress eliminated the need for special enactments by including Indian Territory in a law that authorized railroad rights of way through Indian lands nationwide, subject to requirements related to compensation, limitations on the width of the rights of way, and other matters. Only three years after that, in 1902, Congress repealed the 1899 law to the extent that it applied to Indian Territory and replaced it with a law that empowered railroad companies to exercise the power of eminent domain to take lands in Indian Territory, including lands owned by tribes. Eventually, the grasp of the railroad interests took hold of the Seminole Nation: in 1895 the Choctaw, Oklahoma and Gulf Railroad was constructed across Indian Territory in an east–west direction. The railroad passed through the Seminole Nation, connecting the Seminole town of Wewoka with Shawnee, Oklahoma City, and El Reno on the west and McAlester and Wister Junction on the east. Shortly after that, the Oklahoma City, Ada and Atoka Railroad crossed the Seminole Nation's eastern border at Maud and extended through Konawa, also in the Seminole Nation, to towns in the Choctaw and Chickasaw Nations.[21]

The interests of the railroads and intruders had already prevailed in the western portion of Indian Territory and other locations across the United States a decade earlier, when Congress enacted the General Allotment Act of 1887, also known as the Dawes Act. The Dawes Act empowered federal officials to establish tribal citizenship rolls, to divide lands owned by the United States in trust for the tribes into tracts known as trust allotments, and to assign the beneficial ownership of the allotments to tribal members, with the United States retaining title. The tribes affected by the Dawes Act were unable to stop allotment because the United States held legal title to their lands. The federal government, purportedly acting under the auspices of its guardianship relationship with its tribal wards, could therefore dispose of the lands without having to obtain the execution of deeds by tribal officials.[22]

The Dawes Act eventually resulted in the division of tribal lands of the Kiowa, Comanche, Apache, Cheyenne and Arapaho, Sac and Fox, and Potawatomi tribes into trust allotments assigned to individual members in western Indian Territory. The passage of the Dawes Act enabled non-Indian settlers in Indian Territory to finally achieve their two primary objectives: ownership of the unallotted land in the western portion of Indian Territory and, only a few years later, establishment of a non-Indian territorial government there. Most of that area had been owned by the Five Tribes from removal until the ratification of the post–Civil War treaties. It had taken less than fifty years for the United States to violate the treaty promises it had made to the Five Tribes related to those lands. Seminole chief John F. Brown characterized the Dawes Act's assimilation policy as a "fatal policy, fraught with so much misery, suffering and death."[23]

The Seminole Nation, along with each of the other four nations, owned its lands in fee and thus was in a unique legal position that at least temporarily protected it from the devastating effect of the Dawes Act. Although the Five Tribes lands were subject to railroad takings through eminent domain, which was arguably consistent with some treaty provisions concerning railroad use of the lands, the United States still did not own the Five Tribes lands and therefore had no legal authority to execute allotment deeds or deeds to non-Indian settlers. However, the victory of non-Indian settlers in securing legislation for the allotment of lands in western Indian Territory and other locations across the country, together with the non-Indians' hunger for lands in eastern Indian Territory, increased the pressure on Congress to fashion a method of forcing allotment of the Five Tribes lands. A congressional solution that was even more drastic than the Dawes Act would be needed to free the Five Tribes land for non-Indian settlers— as a result, Congress came up with a plan to destroy the Five Tribes governments. According to views expressed by the Department of the Interior,

The allotment of Five Tribes lands can not be proceeded within the manner that lands of the reservation or wild Indians are allotted . . .

The necessary action to dismember The Five Civilized Tribes as nations and put them into citizenship must be taken cautiously . . . The small actual Indian population would be absorbed and hardly noticed in the population, which would soon utilize the lands and other resources of the territory.[24]

The Five Tribes ability to resist allotment was also weakened by the federal government's ongoing failure to comply with treaty provisions that required the federal government to remove non-Indian intruders and that restricted the ability of the Five Tribes to enforce their laws against the non-Indian occupants of their lands. The 1856 Seminole and Creek treaty expressly excepted white persons who were not members of either tribe by adoption or other means from tribal governmental authority and provided that they would be considered intruders and be removed by U.S. agents, "assisted, if necessary, by the military." The 1866 Seminole treaty guaranteed the Seminoles "quiet possession of their country." The delegation of responsibility to the United States for the removal of intruders placed the Seminole Nation—as well as the other four tribes, which had similar treaty provisions—in the position of being entirely dependent on the United States to keep intruders off their lands, to remove intruders, and to prosecute non-Indian criminals who were beyond the reach of tribal law enforcement even when they committed crimes on the lands owned and governed by the Five Tribes.[25]

Rather than using federal military force to eject the intruders, Congress instead began a slow legislative process to expand federal law enforcement for protection of the intruders. Two decades before passage of the Dawes Act, the Five Tribes had each agreed in their 1866 treaties that courts could be established in Indian Territory, "with such jurisdiction and organized in such manner as Congress may by law provide." By 1877 Congress had included Indian Territory within the jurisdiction of the U.S. federal court for the eastern district of Arkansas in Ft. Smith but had not specified types of matters or persons in Indian Territory subject to that court's jurisdiction. Congress enacted a law in

1883 that gave federal courts in Wichita, Kansas, and Paris, Texas, jurisdiction over other portions of Indian Territory but left the federal court in Ft. Smith with jurisdiction over the portion of Indian Territory occupied by the Five Tribes. According to debate, keeping the Five Tribes lands separate was for "convenience and economy." At that time John Jumper, who took office after the death of "Long John" Chupco in 1882 and served until 1885, was the leader of the Seminole Nation.[26]

The expansion of federal court authority in Indian Territory was in keeping with Congress' enlargement of federal judicial authority over tribal and individual Indian lands nationwide during the last two decades of the nineteenth century, which began after the Supreme Court recognized tribal judicial powers over tribal members in 1883 in *Ex Parte Crow Dog*. In that case, the Court determined that a tribal court was the proper forum for prosecution of an alleged murder of an Indian by another Indian on the Sioux Reservation. The Court recognized that the United States had always left the tribes to their own rules, traditions, and customs in their exercise of governmental powers, including jurisdiction over crimes involving only Indians. Congress quickly responded to *the Ex Parte Crow Dog* decision by enacting in 1885 the Major Crimes Act, which extended federal jurisdiction over seven major offenses, including murder and manslaughter, committed by one Indian against another within Indian reservations located in territories and states. The tribal courts retained authority over lesser crimes committed by Indians. The Major Crimes Act was the most significant congressional move away from recognition of tribal autonomy since the enactment of the 1871 law that had ended treaty making.[27]

In recognition of Congress' expanding authority over Indian affairs, in 1886 the Supreme Court determined in *United States v. Kagama* that the Major Crimes Act was a valid exercise of congressional authority over Indians. Ironically, part of the Court's rationale for this decision was based on its perception that because of "local ill feeling, the people of the States where they [Indians] are found are often their deadliest enemies." The Court reasoned that the United States had a duty "and with it the power" to protect Indians because of "their very weakness and helplessness, so largely due to the course of dealing of the Federal Government with them." The *Kagama* case marked the beginning of a battle by Indian tribes to maintain their precious judicial powers—a battle that lasted beyond the nineteenth century and continued throughout the twentieth century. The Cherokee Nation won a temporary victory in that battle in 1896, when the Supreme Court found that the Major Crimes Act was inapplicable to major offenses committed by members of the Five Tribes.[28]

The congressional threat of federal legislation that would limit or destroy the Five Tribes judicial powers was a focal point in the mounting onslaught of federal legislation that eventually forced allotment of the Five Tribes lands. Because of railroad expansion and an increasing non-Indian population in Indian Territory, the number of federal cases arising there grew dramatically in the latter part of the nineteenth century. According to the Department of the Interior, intruders committed 80 percent of the murders. Partly in response to concerns about the increasing burden on the federal district court in Arkansas, Congress established on March 1, 1889, a federal court in the city of Muskogee in Indian Territory. The establishment of this court was an implicit recognition by the federal government that it had no intention of treating non-Indians in Indian Territory as "intruders" subject to removal, as required by the treaties of the Seminole Nation and the other four nations. To add insult to injury, one congressman even remarked during debate of the 1889 act that the new federal court would have a "civilizing" effect on the Indians.[29]

Under the 1889 act, the federal court in Ft. Smith, Arkansas, maintained criminal jurisdiction over the more serious criminal offenses committed by Indians against non-Indians or committed by non-Indians without regard to race. The new federal court in Muskogee assumed exclusive criminal jurisdiction over lesser offenses—including obstruction of railroad tracks, assault, and arson—involving such defendants. The new court was also given jurisdiction over certain civil cases between U.S. citizens and Indian Territory residents.[30]

The 1889 act placed Indian defendants tried in the Muskogee federal court at a distinct disadvantage as compared with their non-Indian counterparts. Trials were to be conducted in English only, and jurors were required to be residents of Indian Territory over the age of twenty-one and "understanding the English language sufficiently to serve as jurors" in the court. These requirements reduced the odds that Seminole defendants charged with any of the covered crimes against non-Indians would be tried by their own peers, because the Mvskoke language was the primary language of most Seminole members. The 1889 act also required that only U.S. citizens could serve as jurors in cases involving non-Indian defendants, thus preventing Five Tribes members, none of whom were U.S. citizens, from serving as jurors in those cases. In other words, as a matter of law, Indian defendants before the Muskogee federal court on charges of crimes against non-Indians were almost certainly tried by non-Indian jurors, whereas non-Indian defendants, even those charged with crimes against Indians, were rarely tried by Indian jurors.[31]

Because of congressional recognition of Five Tribes courts' ability to settle issues involving only Indians, the 1889 act protected tribal judicial authority over Indians in Indian Territory by specifically withholding civil jurisdiction "over controversies between persons of Indian blood only" from the federal court. The act also provided that the federal offenses described in the act did not apply to "offenses committed by one Indian upon the person or property of another Indian." These protections of tribal court jurisdiction were appropriate, because tribal authorities promptly punished Indian defendants, and the defendants honored tribal decisions. For example, when a member of the Five Tribes was condemned to death by shooting, he was given a period, usually thirty days, in which to go home without guard and settle his affairs and bid farewell to family and friends. As of 1890, it was reported that every Indian condemned by tribal authorities and permitted to go home returned at the time appointed for execution.[32]

By 1890 there were 561 dwellings in the Seminole Nation's domain as established by the 1866 treaty, and there were eight Christian church buildings and four post offices. The Seminole Nation, unlike the other four nations, did not own or have a newspaper within its small domain. However, the Nation did have four neighborhood schools, two of which were set apart for education of African American children. Approximately 160 students attended the four schools annually. In addition, the Wewoka Presbyterian Mission School served up to fifty students annually, and the Seminole Female Academy, which was located in Sasakwa and was placed under the control of the Seminole Council in 1887, averaged thirty students annually. Later, in 1891, the Mekusukey Academy for boys was constructed three miles southwest of the town of Seminole. In 1893 the Emahaka Academy for girls was constructed five miles south of Wewoka, and it soon replaced the female academy in Sasakwa.[33]

The Five Tribes lands were among the most valuable in the United States, with extensive water resources. There were no applicable federal public land laws, and persons entering as settlers in the 1890s were still trespassers and intruders. The United States made only weak attempts to protect the Five Tribes ownership interests in their lands, such as posting notices stating that non-Indians were required to obtain permits from the tribe in order to reside there and that they must follow the laws of the tribe in which they resided. Some of the tribes gave citizenship status to non-Indians who married tribal citizens, and some used a permit system authorizing non-Indians to occupy their lands. In the end the tribes' generosity worked against them, making it more difficult to protect their lands from allotment.

On May 2, 1890, Congress enacted the Organic Act in response to increasing pressure for a non-Indian government in Indian Territory. The Organic Act provided for the creation of a territorial government in the western part of Indian Territory, which had been opened for settlement following the passage of the 1887 Dawes

Mekusukey Mission Academy, circa late nineteenth or early twentieth century. (Photograph courtesy of the Western History Collections, University of Oklahoma Libraries, Norman)

Act.[34] At the time the Organic Act was passed, there was pressure to place the whole of Indian Territory under a territorial government. It was difficult for Congress to legally accomplish that goal, in part because virtually all of the lands in eastern Indian Territory were still held in fee ownership by the Five Tribes, with the exceptions of Osage Nation lands west of the Cherokee Nation and a small area occupied by the Peoria, Quapaw, Ottawa, Shawnee, Modoc, Wyandotte, and Seneca tribes in the northeastern corner. During debate of the Organic Act, Senator Matthew Butler of South Carolina complained, "We yielded then and we are yielding now to an unreasoning and unreasonable clamor from the outside made by people who are anxious to get these public lands. There is great force and great truth in what the Indian says, that the white man wants his land and he will have it at all hazards, right or wrong."[35] This opposition to placing the Five Tribes under a territorial government prevailed. The new territory on the west side was named Oklahoma Territory and was subject to a territorial government. The area occupied by the Five Tribes on the east side constituted most of the diminished Indian Territory but was never subject to a territorial government.

The Organic Act gave the federal courts an even larger presence within the domains of the Five Tribes. The act authorized the federal court in Muskogee to be operated as separate divisions in different portions of Indian Territory. The third division was held in Ardmore and served the people of the Seminole and Chickasaw Nations. The act gave the federal court in Indian Territory exclusive jurisdiction over all civil cases, except cases over which the tribal courts had exclusive jurisdiction. It extended a number of Arkansas laws over Indian Territory, including marriage laws as well as laws concerning descent and distribution, contracts, wills, and basic procedures. It also gave the federal court in Indian Territory jurisdiction over cases involving contracts between tribal members and U.S. citizens, provided that such contracts were entered into in good faith, for consideration and in accordance with tribal laws.[36]

The Organic Act broadened the criminal jurisdiction of the federal court in Indian Territory by placing in effect Arkansas criminal laws and all criminal federal laws that were generally applicable to other locations within the sole jurisdiction of the United States. The federal courts in Arkansas and Texas retained exclusive jurisdiction over the more serious crimes committed by Indians against non-Indians as well as those committed by non-Indians regardless of the race of the victims. As a result, undue hardships were placed on criminal defendants, police officers, and witnesses, who were forced to travel long distances for court proceedings. During this time the U.S. Indian agent for the Five Tribes oversaw a U.S. Indian police force of forty officers who traveled about the territory to assist tribal police in keeping the peace. The agent's police force dealt mainly with non-Indians, with an emphasis on enforcement of federal laws prohibiting introduction of liquor into Indian Territory. This force was in addition to the U.S. marshals and the Fives Tribes police.[37]

In spite of the Organic Act's extension of federal court jurisdiction in Indian Territory, the act protected both tribal civil and criminal jurisdiction over tribal members. At the insistence of the Cherokee Nation, the Organic Act provided that nothing in the act should be interpreted to interfere with the power of the Five Tribes to punish their members for violation of tribal laws. The act also provided that the tribal judicial tribunals would keep exclusive jurisdiction in all civil and criminal cases occurring in their domains if the only parties were members "by nativity or by adoption," and that Arkansas law would not apply to those cases. The Supreme Court found in 1896 that this protection of tribal jurisdiction over tribal members did not apply to an African American freedmen defendant who resided in Indian Territory, because he was not a tribal citizen. A year later a federal appeals court found that the Organic Act's protection of tribal jurisdiction over tribal members did apply with respect to a civil divorce action between a Cherokee by blood and a non-Indian who had been adopted as a Cherokee citizen.[38]

The purported reason for the Organic Act's expansion of federal jurisdiction was to protect the occupants of Indian Territory by prosecuting and removing non-Indian criminals who, before passage of the 1889 act, were amenable to neither tribal nor federal criminal laws. According to the House report on the Organic Act, Indian citizens were "especially interested in the suppression of lawlessness in their midst," and there could be no security to their persons or property "so long as they are in contact with the criminal classes of all other nationalities, who commit crimes and depredations and in many cases escape without punishment." However, Congressman Isaac S. Struble of Iowa recognized that the Organic Act protected non-Indian intruders and trespassers; he remarked that the act's jurisdictional provisions affecting Indian Territory were for the purpose of "promoting the peace, the order, and the prosperity of the people in that Territory, especially those who are not subject to the laws of the Indian Tribes."[39] By protecting the non-Indian intruders and trespassers from the non-Indian criminal element, the Organic Act implicitly legitimized their illegal presence in Indian Territory.

Some congressmen challenged the legality of the Organic Act. Senator John Ingalls of Kansas questioned whether the government had the right to organize the courts in Indian Territory or the right to erect a territorial government in Oklahoma Territory, given past federal pledges not to erect a territorial government except by the consent of the Indian tribes. Senator Ingalls also stated that the tribes in Indian Territory had "solved the problem of civilization, with their own laws and jurisdiction, with their own literature, with their own civil and educational institutions," and he asked, "[A]re we to be told that because we are 65,000,000 and they are 15,000 or 20,000 we have a right to take possession of their property because white men want it?" Senator Butler complained that there were no less than 16,000 squatters in the Cherokee Nation, and that the Five Tribes had "no power to exclude them, and they have never been able to get the Government to drive them out." He succinctly summarized the trespass problem as follows: "Of course, while they [the squatters] are not amenable to Indian law, and they are outside of the jurisdiction of the laws of the States or of the United States, but the solution of that problem would be very easily made by the Government simply sending a force of troops there, if necessary, and driving them out of the Indian Territory. That is what ought to be done. Now we practically recognize their right to be there by extending the laws of the State of Arkansas over the Territory."[40]

The Organic Act permitted tribal members to apply to the federal court to become U.S. citizens and provided that in doing so they would not forfeit or lose any rights or privileges they enjoyed as tribal members. The Five Tribes viewed this action as an attempt to undermine their governments, and their members were generally not interested in applying. At the time the Organic Act was enacted, the United States was conducting the 1890 census, including a census in Indian Territory. The Five Tribes often took their own census, mainly for the purpose of resisting the claims of persons who sought tribal citizenship status in an effort to participate in land and funds division in the event of allotment. The Seminole and Creek authorities supported the 1890 census, but the other three nations opposed it. The unsettled condition of the Indian Territory and the constant clashing between the Indians and intruders produced a prejudice against the census efforts that was hard to overcome, and census takers found it difficult to obtain statistics beyond population statistics.[41]

The increasing numbers of non-Indians in Indian Territory inevitably led to outside demands to open the portion of Indian Territory owned by the Five Tribes for non-Indian ownership. According to the 1890 census, out of a total population of 178,097 people occupying the domains of the Five Tribes, 128,042 were non-Indians (109,393 whites, 18,636 African Americans, and 13 Chinese), and 50,055 were identified as Indians. At that time, Indians in three of the nations were the minority population: Only 9 percent of the people in the Chickasaw Nation, 25 percent of the people in the Choctaw Nation, and 39 percent of the people in the Cherokee Nation were identified as Indians. Only the Creek and Seminole Nations had populations with Indians as the majority race. Almost 56 percent of the people in the Creek Nation were Indians, and more than 64 percent of the people in the Seminole Nation were

Indians by blood. The large numbers of non-Indians in Indian Territory resulted in claims to tribal membership by persons who were not acknowledged by the Five Tribes as citizens.[42]

In 1893 Congress created a commission, sometimes known as the "Dawes Commission" but more formally referred to as the Commission to the Five Civilized Tribes (or Five Tribes Commission), in response to non-Indian demands for ownership of lands in the Five Tribes. The commission was authorized to negotiate with the Five Tribes "for the purpose of extinguishment of the national or tribal title" to their lands and "to enable the ultimate creation of a State or States of the Union which shall embrace the lands within said Indian Territory." Congressional debate of the 1893 act showed an increasing willingness on the part of Congress to violate the treaties, if necessary, for the acquisition of the land. According to Senator Bishop Perkins of Kansas, an attorney whose clients included the Missouri, Kansas & Texas Railroad, "There are 6,000,000 acres of land and more, rich and beautiful, waiting to be occupied by people who are living upon its borders, and who have been living there for months waiting for Congress by its enactment to give them authority to go to, to possess, and to occupy it." Senator James Berry of Arkansas stated, "I believe, sir, that the time has come for the Congress of the United States to lay bold hands upon the Indian Territory and upon the people there" to allow the selection of allotments, and "without any preparatory treaty or without any preparatory proceeding beyond the simple mandate of the Government, throw open all the rest of the land of every character and description to homestead settlement by the people."[43]

The federal policy of assimilating Indians into the mainstream, as established by the 1887 Dawes Act only six years earlier, also played a major role in the passage of the 1893 act. As expressed by Senator Platt of Connecticut, "The Indians constituting these independent governments must be absorbed and become a part of the United States . . . The real question which should interest the American people is the question of whether we can longer endure five separate, independent, sovereign, and almost wholly

foreign governments within the boundaries of the United States."
Senators also expressed concern about the presence of criminals
in Indian Territory, lamenting the expense of maintaining the
federal courts in Indian Territory, and criticizing the tribal courts.[44]

During the political maneuvering to force the allotment of Five
Tribes lands, politicians also sharply criticized tribal members'
communal use of tribal lands, claiming it resulted in an unequal
distribution of land. Tribal members could, by occupancy, secure
possessory rights to tracts of tribally owned lands. Failure of a
tribal member who had possessory rights of a tract to use the
tract for a period of time, usually two years, constituted abandon-
ment, and other tribal members could then claim occupancy rights.
However, members who had possessory rights sometimes mono-
polized large areas of land, sold their occupancy rights to other
tribal members, or entered into "pretended leases" with non-
Indian intruders, even though such practices were prohibited by
tribal law. Those people who sympathized with non-Indians in
Indian Territory censured the Indian system of land ownership,
characterizing it as contrary to the sanctity of private ownership—
a characterization that is ironic as it actually helped non-Indian
trespassers occupy tribal lands.[45]

The commission established by the 1893 act originally consisted
of three members, Henry L. Dawes of Massachusetts, Meredith H.
Kidd of Indiana, and Archibald S. McKennon of Arkansas. It was
later expanded to include two additional members. After visiting
Indian Territory at the direction of Congress, the commission
issued a report in the mid-1890s that described the manner in
which the tribes administered use of their lands: "The lands of
The Five Tribes are known among them as 'public domain,' and
are held in common. Occupation of lands for any purpose gives
a possessory or occupancy title, which can be defended in the
tribal courts. A person running a furrow with a plow around a
tract of land holds all within the same, and in case it covers a road
or public highway the road must be changed and pass around
the tract . . . No titles are recorded." The commission concluded
that this system of landholding was wrong, stating, "It is apparent

to all who are conversant with the present condition in the Indian Territory that their system of government cannot continue. It is not only non-American, but it is radically wrong, and a change is imperatively demanded in the interest of the Indian and whites alike, and such change cannot be much longer delayed. The situation grows worse and will continue to grow worse. There is no modification of the system. It cannot be reformed. It must be abandoned and a better one substituted."[46] The commission, which characterized the Five Tribes governments as corrupt and irresponsible, was apparently unperturbed by the unequal distribution of wealth in non-Indian society in the United States.

In May 1894 Seminole chief John F. Brown wrote a letter to Henry Dawes and other members of the Five Tribes Commission, summarizing some of the commission's arguments in favor of allotment and stating that the Seminole people had replied at various public meetings on the subject with "a firm declination to agree to any of the propositions presented by the Commission." Chief Brown explained why the commission's proposals would not protect the Seminole Nation, accurately predicting that allotment would soon result in loss of the allotted lands to "the sharp speculator, with money and friends." He discussed treaty protections and stated, "If these solemn pledges are to be broken at last, with or without the Indians' consent, for no apparent reason given except that the Supreme Court of the United States has decided that this can be done with an Indian Tribe, and because it is inconvenient to observe them any longer—it is idle for us to refer to them, though they are the bulwarks of our faith. If we have worshiped an idol, then, indeed, are we lost." In his letter, Chief Brown also answered allegations that the laws in Indian Territory were not enforced and that the local judiciary was a farce, stating, "So far as the Seminoles are concerned, we know this is not true, and believe it is slanderous of the other Nations as well; we challenge truthful contraction and invite the closest inspection."[47]

As it became more clear that negotiation alone would not be sufficient to achieve allotment, Congress began increasing pressure on the Five Tribes to force them to acquiesce. This pressure included enacting an 1895 law that implicitly validated the presence of non-Indians in Indian Territory by expanding federal court authority there. The 1895 act repealed earlier laws that had given the federal court in Arkansas jurisdiction over certain felonies in Indian Territory. It conferred that authority on the federal court in Indian Territory. The 1895 act also extended Arkansas criminal laws over Indian Territory, established appellate courts, and allowed construction of prisons. It replaced the three divisions of the federal court in Indian Territory previously established by the 1890 Organic Act with three judicial districts—identified as the northern, central and southern districts—and designated the towns in which each district's court would be held. It moved the Seminole Nation from the former third division of the federal court, which heard Seminole cases in Ardmore, to the new northern district, which heard Seminole cases in Muskogee, about ninety miles from the Seminole capital in Wewoka.[48]

The stated purpose of the 1895 act was to control the non-Indian lawless element in Indian Territory. During debate, Rep. Charles Curtis of Kansas explained, "I understand from what the Dawes Commission said that it was not the Indians who were committing the crimes but the white people and criminals who had fled there from other states and who have taken up their crimes there. If that is the case, and we establish these courts extending the jurisdiction of the law, these people can be punished." As demonstrated by Representative Curtis's comments, the 1895 act was not intended to have any effect on crimes and controversies involving only Indians. Congressman David Browning Culberson of Texas remarked that the bill gave the federal courts "no right of jurisdiction over controversies which arise between the Indians themselves. They are taken care of by the tribal courts."[49]

Congress failed to approve a proposed amendment of the 1895 act that would have allowed an Indian defendant charged in tribal court with a crime against another Indian to remove his case to federal court. This proposed amendment was an apparent attempt to address the Supreme Court's decision four years earlier in *In Re Mayfield* that the federal courts had no authority to try a tribal member accused of adultery. Shortly after the enactment of the 1895 act, the Supreme Court in *Talton v. Mayes* again recognized the unique strength of the Five Tribes treaty provisions and upheld the 1895 act's protection of the Five Tribes courts' jurisdiction over murders committed by tribal members against tribal members. The Court found that Cherokee Nation treaty provisions protecting tribal self-government recognized the Nation's power to enact and enforce criminal laws governing offenses committed by members of the tribe against other members within the Nation's domain. This ruling implicitly recognized that the 1885 Major Crimes Act, which gave federal courts jurisdiction over certain major crimes committed on Indian reservations, did not apply to the Five Tribes, each of which had treaty guarantees concerning tribal self-government. The decision in *Talton v. Mayes* was followed in 1897 by the Supreme Court's ruling in *Nofire v. United States* that a white man adopted as a Cherokee citizen by marriage and exercising tribal voting rights was also subject to the exclusive jurisdiction of the tribal courts.[50]

In the latter part of the 1890s, Congress directed the Five Tribes Commission to make determinations of citizenship for the Five Tribes. This task was performed in order to establish rolls for allotment purposes. During a visit from the Five Tribes Commission in 1896, Chief Brown told the commission that he recognized that changes were not far off, and he requested its members to give special consideration to the Seminoles because they were "less than any other nation responsible for the condition that is to bring these changes about or make them necessary." In a continuing attempt to separate the Seminole Nation from the other four tribes, Chief Brown, unlike the Cherokee and Creek leaders, did not call a council meeting to advocate resistance to negotiations following the Five Tribes Commission visit in 1896.[51]

In 1897, close on the heels of the 1895 act, Congress enacted yet another law to extort the Five Tribes into negotiating allotment agreements. Although it did not expressly abolish tribal courts, the 1897 act threatened tribal courts by giving federal courts in Indian Territory "exclusive jurisdiction" to try all civil and criminal cases, and it extended Arkansas and federal laws over everyone "irrespective of race." This law was a ploy to force the Five Tribes to negotiate allotment agreements that would, as stated in the act, "operate to suspend any provisions of this Act if in conflict therewith as to said nation." Senator Berry stated, "As I said before, if this provision is retained in regard to the courts, I have no doubt but what within six months or one year treaties will be made in regard to allotments and all the rights of the Indians will be protected; but if this legislation be defeated, the Senator will find that there will be no agreement of any kind with the Dawes Commission."[52]

Some senators were outraged by the threatened annihilation of the tribal court systems as a method of forcing allotment. In an impassioned speech during debate of the bill, Senator William Bate of Tennessee stated,

> One of the ugly features in this—and I know no man here appreciates it more sensibly or highly than the Senator from Missouri—is that while we are holding out to them the hand of negotiation we hold in the other hand a bludgeon with which to brain the Indian. Shame upon us! That is the situation, or at least that is the force and meaning of this amendment when taken in connection with the Dawes Commission. I say this is unmanly; it is cowardly in the Government of the United States thus to extend negotiations to these Indians, and while that negotiation is pending and being considered, that we strike them down with a blow . . . The Indians have exclusive jurisdiction, where Indians alone are concerned, in both criminal and civil suits. This amendment takes the jurisdiction away from those Indians and gives it exclusively to the white man.[53]

The 1897 act was hotly debated in Congress. Several senators asserted that the tribal courts were corrupt and should be abolished. Other senators responded with disbelief. Senator William Vilas of Wisconsin stated that a recent report from the Five Tribes Commission gave only a "single side of the picture, and they are presenting it as darkly as possible." He stated that other information had been provided to the Senate, including statements of clergymen, agents, and persons of excellent character, "just as much character, just as good judges, as those gentlemen [the Dawes Commission], who say the Indians are doing well in many respects." In a statement that was particularly insightful—in light of the non-Indian mob burning of two Seminole men later that year for a crime they did not commit—Senator Bate argued that tribal courts were not the real problem, stating,

> But, Mr. President, we are told that there is a nest of robbers in this Territory. Well, if so, who makes it so? Is it not the white men who go there; and very likely while there they perform some very evil deeds. They form organizations that perhaps ought not to exist and are unlawful; but the United States Government is to blame for it. For the treaties say the Government shall keep whites from molesting them. White people have gone there and outnumber the Indians, and they control to a great extent the government of that country. Because these lawless bands of white men—not Indians—are there, is no reason why we should go and take away from the Indians the right which we have solemnly granted to them.[54]

Senator Vilas emphasized that greed was the true motive for enactment of the 1897 act. He stated,

> But when the United States bargains with a tribe of Indians that if they will surrender their homes and their lands for a new home and a patent in fee, with the right of absolute government by themselves, is the United States by and by, when greedy citizens thrust themselves unbidden upon them and have destroyed or disturbed their comfort in defiance of the engagement of the United States to protect them to turn around and say, "We will ravish the rest from you of what is yours; will kick our engagement under foot, not because we want it, but in tender consideration of you poor people."[55]

Chief Brown recognized the inevitability of allotment and focused his efforts on negotiating an allotment agreement with the Five Tribes Commission that would protect the Nation's powers of self-government, including its judicial powers. Under his leadership, the council enacted resolutions in the spring of 1897 that resolved that no allotments would be accepted unless additional lands were secured for the Nation, that no territorial organization would be accepted, no additional railroad charters would be given without the Seminole Council's advance consent, and that the council would not be subject to presidential change or supervision. The Seminole Nation was the first of the Five Tribes to ratify an allotment agreement. The agreement was executed in 1897 by the Five Tribes Commission and Seminole representatives John F. Brown, Okchun Harjo, William Cully, K. N. Kinkehee, Thomas West, and Thomas Factor. Although the agreement did not contain most of the provisions desired by the council, it did contain several important protections of Seminole governmental powers, including limitations on federal court jurisdiction and protection of tribal judicial authority.[56]

The Five Tribes Commission was unable to negotiate and secure tribal ratifications of allotment agreements with the other four nations in 1897. As a result, Congress devised a plan to force the Choctaw, Chickasaw, Muscogee, and Cherokee Nations to enter into allotment agreements, using the threat of a new federal law that would expressly abolish tribal courts and end enforcement of tribal laws. Congress introduced the bill that would become known as the Curtis Act on February 24, 1898, two weeks after the Seminole Nation allotment agreement was introduced in Congress for federal ratification. According to a later Five Tribes Commission report, Congress was "confronted with the alternative of either abandoning its policy and abolishing the Commission, or else of converting the commission from merely a negotiating body into also an executive and semi-judicial body, and of proceeding with the work under the constitutional power of Congress, and largely, at least regardless of the will of the tribe."[57]

The Curtis bill referenced the "Five Civilized Tribes" as a group. The bill provided for the compulsory allotment of occupancy rights of the tribal lands, granted territorial towns the right to

KANSAS

Kansas &
Arkansas
Valley RR

Nowata

Neosho
River

Miami

1
2
5
3 4
6
7

MISSOURI
ARKANSAS

Verdigris River

Vinita

Arkansas River

St. Louis & San Francisco RR

Claremore

Grand River

Salina

St. Louis & San Francisco RR

Chicago, Rock Island & Pacific RR

Santa Fe RR

OKLAHOMA
TERRITORY

Tulsa

CHEROKEE

N

Cimarron River

Sapulpa

Wagoner

Tahlequah

Park Hill

Kansas City, Pittsburgh & Gulf RR

CREEK

Muskogee

Fort Gibson

North Canadian River

Oklahoma
City

★Okmulgee

Webber's
Falls

Sallisaw

Ft.
Smith

Arkansas River

Minco

SEMINOLE

Wetumka

Eufaula

Chickasha

★Wewoka

Canadian River

Sans Bois Cr.

Poteau

Washita River

Purcell

Emahaka

McAlester

Choctaw, Oklahoma & Gulf RR

Wister

Rush Springs

Pauls Valley

Ada

Muddy Boggy River

Talihina

Marlow

Blue River

Clear Boggy

Tuskahoma ★

St. Louis & San Francisco RR

Kiamichi River

CHICKASAW

Duncan

Davis

Missouri, Kansas and Texas RR

Comanche

Woodford

Tishomingo
★

Boggy
Depot

Atoka

CHOCTAW

Antlers

Little River

Ardmore

Ryan

Red River

Marietta

Durant

Bokchito

Red River

TEXAS

OKLAHOMA
TERRITORY

INDIAN
TERRITORY

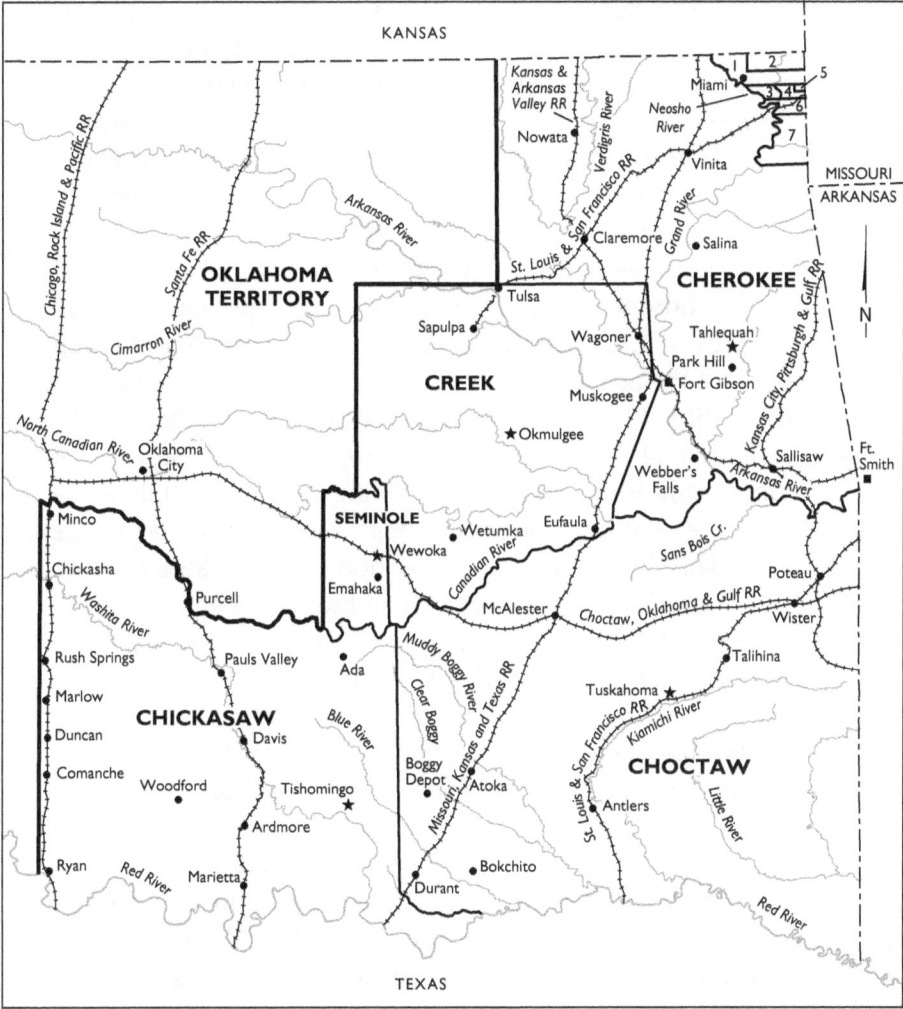

● Early settlements
★ Indian National Capital
■ Military Forts

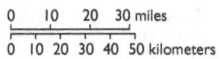

0   10   20   30 miles

0 10 20 30 40 50 kilometers

1. Peoria
2. Quapaw
3. Modoc
4. Ottawa
5. Shawnee
6. Wyandotte
7. Seneca

Political districts of Indian Territory, 1907. Reproduced by permission from
Clara Sue Kidwell, *The Choctaws in Oklahoma: From Tribe to Nation, 1855–1970*
(Norman: University of Oklahoma Press, 2007), 172.

establish municipal governments under Arkansas laws, and prohibited payments by the United States to tribal officers for disbursements to tribal members. Other damaging sections would have prohibited enforcement of Five Tribes laws "at law or equity by the courts of the United States of Indian Territory" and would have abolished all tribal courts in Indian Territory effective July 1, 1898. Two sections of the act incorporated the tentative agreements made earlier with the Muscogee (Creek), Choctaw, and Chickasaw Nations and provided that if the agreements were ratified by those tribes, the agreements would control conflicting provisions of the act. This action was intended to be an incentive for tribal ratification of agreements that preserved tribal courts. Because the Seminole Nation had already ratified its agreement and federal ratification was already pending as a separate bill before Congress, the Seminole agreement was not incorporated in the Curtis bill. The Curtis bill did not mention the Cherokees because they had refused to negotiate even a tentative agreement.[58]

Throughout the early months of 1898, Chief Brown and other delegates of the Seminole Nation were present in Washington to urge Congress to ratify the Seminole allotment agreement. Many federal leaders conceded that the Seminole Nation should be allowed to close up its own affairs, but some unsuccessfully objected to ratification of the Seminole agreement because the manner of settling the affairs of the Seminole Nation would be different from the other four nations and would cause confusion. The Curtis Act was enacted on June 28, 1898, and the Seminole Nation's allotment agreement was ratified by Congress two days later on July 1, 1898. The ratified Seminole agreement, which included provisions that protected Seminole governmental authority, provided that all laws and parts of laws inconsistent with the agreement were repealed. In this way, the Seminole Nation avoided the provisions in the Curtis Act that would have eroded its governmental authority and abolished its courts.[59]

The Creek Nation refused to ratify an agreement before the December 1, 1898, deadline established by the Curtis Act. The 1901 Creek agreement stated that none of its provisions would be construed as reviving the Creek courts. There was a similar stipulation in an unratified 1901 version of the Cherokee agreement, but that provision was not included in the ratified 1902 agreement. The Choctaws and Chickasaws approved their allotment agreement before the deadline; thus, along with the Seminoles, they avoided the provisions in the Curtis Act that were most damaging to their governmental authority, as a matter of law.[60] However, in spite of the nations' efforts to protect their governmental authority through their allotment agreements, as a practical matter in the following century, federal officials treated all Five Tribes as if the Curtis Act applied to them. Congress continued to enact a labyrinth of federal laws that were difficult to comprehend and that resulted in it being virtually impossible for the Seminoles to protect their government as specified by their allotment agreement.

CHAPTER 2

ROAD TO STATEHOOD

The Impact of
Federal Allotment Legislation, 1897–1907

The Five Tribes governmental infrastructures changed drastically in the short ten-year span between 1897, when the Seminole Nation negotiated its allotment agreement under duress, and 1907, when the state of Oklahoma was established. Many of these changes occurred as a result of federal approval of the tribes' allotment agreements, including the Seminole allotment agreement approved by Congress in 1898 (the Seminole Allotment Act), and federal misinterpretation of the 1898 Curtis Act. Other changes occurred as a result of several new federal laws that established more uniform requirements concerning the Five Tribes allotment process, included provisions that ignored the rights that Seminole leaders believed they had secured in the Seminole Allotment Act, and eventually allowed the merging of Oklahoma and Indian Territories into a state. During this decade, the Five Tribes Commission prepared citizenship rolls and divided tribal lands into allotments, the non-Indian population continued to grow, and the Five Tribes persisted in their battle to maintain government operations.[1]

The Seminole Allotment Act was the first federal law specifically governing division and distribution of the Seminole Nation's communally owned lands into individual allotments for its members. It provided for the division of Seminole lands into allotments for use by tribal members, but it required the principal chief to deliver deeds to them only when the tribal government ceased to exist. According to the Allotment Act, each allottee would select forty acres as a homestead (an amount that was later increased), which would be inalienable and nontaxable "in perpetuity." Because the Seminole land acreage was not sufficient to assign adequate allotments for tribal members, the United States agreed to purchase from the Creek Nation 200,000 acres immediately adjoining the eastern boundary of the Seminole Nation and to convey it to the Seminoles for allotment purposes, upon reimbursement by the Seminole Nation.[2]

The Seminole Allotment Act contained important protections of tribal governmental rights. It repealed the 1897 act "in any manner affecting the proceedings of the general council of the Seminole Nation," effectively repealing the 1897 act's jurisdictional provisions that interfered with the judicial powers exercised by the Seminole Council over crimes or disputes involving only tribal members. The Allotment Act also eliminated the 1897 act's requirement for presidential approval of all laws enacted by the Seminole Council, and the council's legislative authority was to be recognized as long as the Nation continued in existence. Consistent with Seminole leaders' insistence that the Seminole Nation be protected from future territorial or state authority, the Allotment Act specifically provided for exclusive federal court jurisdiction over controversies growing out of the title, ownership, occupation, or use of real estate owned by Seminoles and over the crimes of homicide, embezzlement, bribery, and embracery (attempting to influence a jury through improper influence) committed in the Seminole country, without reference to race or citizenship of the person charged. It also provided that the Seminole courts would "retain all the jurisdiction which they now have, except as herein transferred to the courts of the United States." In addition, the Allotment Act provided that it would "in no wise affect the provisions of existing treaties between the Seminole Nation and the United States, except in so far as inconsistent therewith."[3]

According to A. S. McKennon—one of the members of the Five Tribes Commission), who later served as an attorney for the Seminole Nation—the Seminole Allotment Act protected Seminole authorities' "full jurisdiction in all other matters the same as theretofore exercised by the tribe." In later years, McKennon described the Seminole system of justice, in which the Seminole Council served as the judicial arm of the Nation. There were only two offenses punishable by death: homicide and a fourth offense of larceny. When a person was convicted of homicide and sentenced to be shot, family members of the deceased prepared and loaded two guns with which the condemned was to be executed and delivered them to two Lighthorsemen. According to McKennon, if the guns "failed to fire," the man was set free, perhaps implying that the victim's family members could make the final decision concerning the death sentence.[4] McKennon knew of no cases in which anyone was ever put to death for larceny, which was punished by whipping. In accordance with the Allotment Act's protection of Seminole authority over crimes involving its citizens, the council continued to hear criminal cases, including cases involving freedmen defendants, at least as late as October 1905, but probably until statehood in 1907.[5]

The Seminole Allotment Act acknowledged continued Seminole control over at least a portion of the Nation's natural resources. The act required the principal chief's approval of all surface leases of allotted lands, subject to the allottee's consent. It also recognized the Seminole government's sole authority to lease mineral rights with the allottee's consent, providing that one-half of any royalties from coal, minerals, coal oil, or natural gas "discovered on any allotment" would be paid to the allottee and one-half would be paid into the Nation's treasury "until extinguishment of tribal government." The Allotment Act required the disposition of the townsite of Wewoka according to an act of the Seminole Council approved April 23, 1897, and excepted from allotment one-half-acre tracts for the use and occupancy of each of twenty-four churches, with the consent of the Seminole Council.[6]

Demonstrating the significance of education to the Seminoles, the Allotment Act set aside $500,000 for a permanent school fund for the support of the Mekusukey and Emahaka Academies, and the Seminole district schools and excepted from allotment 320 acres for each academy and 80 acres each for eight district schools in the Seminole Nation. It also excepted one acre in each township from allotment to be purchased by the federal government to establish schools for the education of non-citizens' children.[7]

In 1899 the Five Tribes Commission secured a supplemental allotment agreement approved by tribal representatives, including Chief John F. Brown. The Supplemental Seminole Allotment Act, ratified by Congress on June 2, 1900, contained only a few substantive provisions. It enabled children born to Seminole citizens as of December 31, 1899, along with all Seminole citizens "then living," to be placed on the Seminole citizenship rolls. It stated that when approved by the Secretary of the Interior, the final citizenship rolls would be used for the allotment of lands and distribution of money and other property belonging to Seminole citizens. Finally, it provided that the property of Seminole citizens who died after 1899 would descend to those heirs who were Seminole citizens in accordance with the laws of Arkansas, with a few limited exceptions.[8]

Less than a year after the Supplemental Seminole Allotment Act was ratified, Congress approved the Creek Nation allotment agreement, which included provisions that Seminoles located on Creek lands could take allotments within the Creek Nation, and Creeks on Seminole lands could take allotments within the Seminole Nation.[9] During this same time period, Congress enacted a law that imposed criminal sanctions on any person who unlawfully cut timber on Five Tribes lands and allowed the Secretary of the Interior to establish regulations for obtaining timber and stone from Five Tribes' lands for domestic and industrial purposes, including railroads and highways.[10]

It was estimated that by 1900 there were at least 350,000 white people who were not citizens of any tribe living in Indian Territory. Some were there with consent of tribal members; others were not. They had established farms and in some instances erected substantial residences and business blocks in many towns throughout the territory. During the 1900 fiscal year, the Union Agency of the U.S. Indian Service, located in Muskogee, Indian Territory, reported that it had received more than 2,000 complaints filed by Five Tribes citizens against noncitizens. The majority of these were complaints against white men "who in the past had intruded themselves upon the Indians and gained their confidence to a sufficient degree to secure possession of their prospective allotments" and after having secured possession refused to pay rent or to vacate the land. The non-Indians conducting farming and business activities in the domains of the Five Tribes were required to pay permit taxes or license fees under tribal laws recognized in 1900 as valid by the Court of Appeals for Indian Territory.[11] The non-Indians benefited from the many roads and highways used by the general public and by the mail service but had no representation in the governments of the Five Tribes. At that time there were twenty-eight Indian police officers employed by the Union Agency, only one of whom was stationed in the Seminole Nation. These police officers were almost constantly employed in investigating complaints by tribal citizens against intruders, "many of whom the police were obliged to remove from the territory."[12]

As the allotment process moved forward, the Five Tribes Commission faced two major tasks: the inventory of the properties to be divided and the identification of the citizens of each of the nations. The Five Tribes Commission began appraising and classifying tribal lands in Indian Territory on June 30, 1890, so that the allotments within the domain of each nation would be roughly equal in value, though not necessarily equal in size. The appraisal of the Seminole Nation's lands was completed in November 1899. Seminole lands were classified according to three grades: first, second, and third, respectively valued at $5, $2, and $1.25 per acre (compared with nineteen different grades used to classify Choctaw, Chickasaw, Creek, and Cherokee Nation lands). The appraisers conducted field appraisals of the Seminole lands and also considered the location and proximity of the lands to market. The average value of a Seminole allotment was $308.76. It took longer to complete the enrollment process, which included working with the Seminole Nations' fourteen town chiefs, who were responsible for protecting the interests of the people in their communities. By 1903 the commission had considered numerous applications for tribal citizenship, had classified and platted hundreds of thousands of forty-acre tracts, and had almost completed the allotting of Seminole and Creek lands. Notwithstanding these efforts, some delays were caused by the refusal of many Seminole freedmen, along with some Seminole citizens by blood, to select their allotments.[13]

While the Five Tribes Commission worked on the allotment of Seminole lands, Congress continued enacting laws aimed at eventual statehood for Oklahoma and Indian Territories. In 1901 U.S. citizenship was automatically conferred on members of the Seminole Nation and other Indians in Indian Territory. That same year, Congress made Arkansas laws governing corporations applicable in Indian Territory "so far as they may be applicable and not in conflict with any law of Congress applicable to said Territory heretofore passed." This law granted the federal courts in Indian Territory the same jurisdiction over corporations that the Arkansas courts exercised over Arkansas corporations. Two years later, Congress enacted the Act of February 19, 1903, which provided that the federal court clerks of the four judicial districts in Indian Territory would be responsible for recording all deeds, mortgages, leases, and other land records at the place where court proceedings were held for the district where the property was located. This law established twenty-five locations for the conduct of court proceedings, including District 13, which served citizens of the Seminole Nation and was located in Wewoka. Wewoka was still a small town, with a cotton mill and cotton seed oil mill, and it continued to serve as the capitol of the Seminole Nation.[14]

By 1904 the estimated population of Indian Territory was between 500,000 and 700,000. The tribal courts exercised jurisdiction over only Indian and freedman citizens, and the explosion of the non-Indian population caused a practically insurmountable burden on the federal courts there. The four federal district courts in Indian Territory, each having only one judge, handled thousands of cases, compared with the hundreds of cases handled by other district courts in the northern and western states. The circuit locations served by the federal court in Muskogee included Wagoner, Sapulpa, Eufaula, Okmulgee, and Wewoka. According to a federal judge in the Muskogee district, he had made it a rule to finish a murder case in a day, even if it took past midnight to do so. He stated that over a two-year period he had tried 103 murder cases and 75 cases of assault with intent to kill, "and in not a single instance has the trial in any of these important cases exceeded a day." Fortunately for criminal defendants, capitol punishment was rarely approved by the jurors.[15]

In order to address these problems, as well as the purported concern that the property interests of minor Indian allottees would not be protected unless guardians were appointed to handle their affairs, Congress enacted the Act of April 28, 1904. The 1904 act provided for the appointment of four additional judges in Indian Territory, gave federal courts "full and complete" jurisdiction over the settlement of estates and the guardianship of minors and incompetents, and extended all Arkansas laws "heretofore put in force in Indian Territory" to "all persons and estates" in Indian Territory, "whether Indian, freedman, or otherwise." This extension of Arkansas law apparently was intended only to establish laws governing estate and guardianship matters in Indian Territory. During debate of the 1904 act, members of Congress expressed no intent to subject tribal citizens to all Arkansas laws and, in fact, recognized the continued existence of the tribal courts. In any event, the 1904 act's provisions concerning Arkansas laws were short-lived because of later federal enactments.[16]

While Congress was busy debating and enacting laws concerning jurisdiction within the domains of the Five Tribes, Seminole governmental operations continued. In 1902 John F. Brown, the well-educated half-blood son of a physician, was defeated in the election for chief by Hulbutta Micco, a leader reported to have less educational background than Brown and described as belonging to the "ultra full blood element."[17] The following year, the Seminole Council approved a compilation of Seminole laws entitled *1903 Revised Statutes*, which demonstrated the Seminole people's determination that their government would survive the allotment process. The revised statutes recognized that the Seminole government was based on the fourteen tribal towns, each having a town chief "of inestimable value and benefit to the Nation being . . . in close touch with the people." The town chiefs had authority to enact rules and regulations and to assess fines for the regulation of immediate local affairs; they also served on the Seminole Council, along with two elected representatives from each town. The Seminole Council, led by the council chairman, enacted laws, was generally responsible for decisions concerning tribal affairs, and also served as the Nation's court in civil and criminal cases.

According to the *1903 Revised Statutes*, the principal and second chief possessed broad executive powers, including the power to "carry on the government in strict accordance of the law," to recommend to the Seminole Council those measures in the best interest of the nation, and to veto council actions, subject to council override if no legal objections were given and the council reaffirmed its action. The chief exercised semi-judicial and prosecutorial functions as well, having authority to issue arrest warrants, to use tribal funds for law enforcement, to present cases to the council for judicial decisions, and to serve as an appellate court and disapprove the council's judicial decisions. The Seminoles clearly intended to continue exercising law enforcement functions, as reflected in chapters concerning the Lighthorsemen, who served as tribal police, and chapters defining crimes such as wrongful lies, theft, arms violations, breaking and entering, and rape. The revised statutes also covered civil areas, including marriage, sales, hiring property, establishment of businesses by noncitizens, taxation, public roads, estates and wills, and divorce.[18]

The Seminoles' belief that their nation would continue to exist as a governmental entity collided with the path that Congress was taking to force the break-up of Five Tribes lands and to enable the non-Indian intruders to finally achieve land ownership and a non-Indian government. By being the first to enter into an allotment agreement, the Seminoles avoided having to include in the agreement a March 4, 1906, deadline for the dissolution of their tribal government—a deadline that was placed in the other four nations' allotment agreements.[19] However, after the U.S. Department of the Interior received a letter from Seminole chief Hulbutta Micco arguing that the dissolution of Seminole government was not required under the Seminole Allotment Act, federal officials recommended that this situation be addressed. As a result, in early 1903 Congress enacted a law providing that the Seminole government also would not continue longer than March 4, 1906, which reflected a federal policy increasingly aimed at uniform treatment of the Five Tribes.[20]

Notwithstanding congressional intent to end the governments of the Five Tribes, the federal courts continued to recognize the validity and enforceability of the Five Tribes laws.[21] The Seminole Council also continued to meet as allotment progressed, in spite of complaints by federal administrative officials that the council meetings were "at considerable expense," and that the federal government had no control over Seminole expenditures because the Seminole Allotment Act had repealed provisions in the 1897 act that would have required federal approval of council legislation.[22] In 1904, federal officials questioned the legality of the Seminole townsite commission and its sales of townsite lots under the Seminole Allotment Act. This issue was later resolved in favor of tribal action, when Congress enacted a law in 1905 confirming a sale of unsold lots in Wewoka to Chief John F. Brown for $2,000, as permitted by a 1900 Seminole Council resolution that required distribution of the sale proceeds to tribal members.[23] Federal officials also expressed concern in early1905 that Chief Micco, who reportedly could not read or write the English language, had executed by his mark the approval of "irregular leases" that had not been approved, as had been the customary practice, by the Nation's attorney. It was recommended that a special agent be sent to the Seminole Nation to investigate the matter.[24] Notwithstanding federal complaints regarding the Seminole government, in 1905 the Seminole Council addressed matters such as selecting a tribal trustee to be responsible for handling tribal affairs in the event the tribal government was dissolved, selecting an attorney to serve as the Nation's legal counsel, and hearing criminal cases in its judicial capacity.[25]

In 1905, the Indian inspector for Indian Territory estimated that the population in Indian Territory totaled 700,000 people, the majority of whom were non-Indian. That year Congress enacted a law authorizing the Five Tribes Commission to consider applications for enrollment of infant children born to enrolled Seminole citizens before March 4, 1905 (referred to as "afterborn children"), and to make allotments to them. The Five Tribes Commission ended on June 30, 1905, but its work was continued by the commissioner of the Five Civilized Tribes. When Seminole enrollment was completed, 2,138 Seminoles by blood had been placed on the Seminole Indian roll and 986 freedmen had been placed on the Seminole freedman rolls, each roll including afterborn children.[26]

Only two days before the deadline set for the end of the Five Tribes governments, Congress enacted a joint resolution on March 2, 1906, that continued the "tribal existence and present tribal governments" of the Five Tribes in "full force and effect for all purposes under existing laws until all property of such tribes, or the proceeds thereof shall be distributed among the individual members of said tribes, unless hereafter otherwise provided by law." In debating the resolution, Congress discussed two primary reasons for the continuance of the Five Tribes governments. First, it was feared that if tribal government was discontinued before the disposal of tribal property, then tribal lands would become part of the public domain and would be subject to claims by railroads. This concern was based on statutory land grants providing that railroads would acquire title to strips of land along railroad rights of way in the event that title passed from the tribes to the United States. Second, there was concern that termination of the tribal governments would make the maintenance of law and order even more difficult. In addition, Congress feared that the tribal schools would cease to function, and that the absence of principal chiefs would interrupt the allotment process. During debate of the resolution, at least one congressman questioned whether the Seminole Nation's government should be continued given that the Seminole allotment had been completed, but the Seminoles were included anyway.[27]

The following month, on April 26, 1906, Congress enacted the Five Tribes Act. The act dealt with the Five Nations as a group, notwithstanding specific points they had negotiated independently in their separate allotment agreements with the United States. The act's primary focus was on Five Tribes property, but it also contained a few provisions concerning their governments. The act continued the existence of the Five Tribes "in full force and effect for all purposes authorized by law until otherwise provided by law" in order to safeguard against railroad claims to tribal lands. However, the act limited council sessions to thirty days annually and required that all council legislation and contracts affecting tribal property be approved by the president of the United States. These requirements were opposed by the Seminole Council on the grounds that they were contrary to the Seminole Allotment Act's repeal of similar provisions in the 1897 act. Federal officials relied on the Five Tribes Act to support their interference with tribal governmental operations through most of the twentieth century, even after the 1934 shift toward federal policies favoring tribal self-government.[28]

Section 6 of the Five Tribes Act also involved the Five Tribes' governmental authority. It was used as a significant federal tool throughout much of the twentieth century both to complete allotment and to support federal agency refusal to recognize the chiefs elected by the Five Tribes. Designed to ensure that allotment deeds were issued to allottees, section 6 authorized the president of the United States to appoint a citizen by blood to serve as principal chief in the event of the removal, disability, or death of an incumbent chief and to remove from office any chief who refused or neglected to perform his duties. This authority was eventually delegated to the Secretary of the Interior by executive order in 1951. Section 6 also authorized the secretary to execute and record instruments conveying legal title to lands if the Chief failed, refused, or neglected to execute a document within thirty days after notice that the instrument was ready for his signature. Congress included a separate provision in section 6 authorizing the Seminole Nation's principal chief to execute the deeds to allottees before the Seminole government ceased to exist. This provision was designed to circumvent the Seminole Allotment Act, which provided for execution of allotment deeds only when the tribal government ended.[29] It was reported in late September 1906 that the deeds would soon be provided to Chief Brown for signature.[30]

Up until enactment of the Five Tribes Act, there was no question that the Seminole people controlled selection of the chief. Thus, a 1905 opinion by an assistant attorney general for the Department of the Interior recognized that the Nation had an autonomous government and concluded that the May 5, 1905, election by the Seminole Council of John Brown as the new chief after the death of Chief Hulbutta Micco was within its powers.[31] Regrettably, soon after that federal officials seized on section 6 of the Five Tribes Act to justify their efforts to prohibit tribal elections of principal chiefs and to withhold recognition of any elected chief absent a federal appointment. This interpretation and practice continued for decades and did not change until enactment of a 1970 law that provided for the "popular selection" of the governor of the Chickasaw Nation and the chiefs of the Seminole, Creek, Cherokee, and Choctaw Nations.[32] A few years after that, a federal court decided that federal officials had misapplied section 6 of the Five Tribes Act, and that it was only intended to ensure that the allotment process would not be disrupted under limited circumstances.[33]

Other provisions in the Five Tribes Act that involved tribal governmental affairs included the required transfer of records from Indian Territory land offices to federal court clerks' offices and the abolition of tribal taxes imposed on non-Indians using tribal fee lands. The act directed tribal officers to make a full accounting of all tribal money and other tribal property in their custody upon dissolution of the tribal government and to pay such money and deliver such tribal property to the secretary. The act also permitted the Secretary of the Interior to collect tribal revenues and pay lawful claims against the Five Tribes and to bring suit in the name of the United States on behalf of any of the Five Tribes for the collection of money or recovery of land claimed by that tribe in federal court, with costs and expenses of any such suit to be paid from tribal funds.[34]

Several provisions in the Five Tribes Act concerned restrictions on use of allotments, disposition of tribal lands, and disposition of other tribal property. The act allowed the secretary to take possession of and sell buildings used for governmental, school, and other tribal purposes and to deposit the proceeds in the U.S. Treasury for the benefit of the respective tribes, less expenses related to appraisal and sale of the lands. Tribal lands reserved from allotment were to be held in trust by the United States for the use and benefits of tribal citizens after dissolution of tribal governments. The act also required the secretary to sell any tribal lands remaining after allotment "not reserved or otherwise disposed of."[35] A proposed amendment that would have limited sales to no more than 160 acres to any one person or individual failed. The congressman who offered the amendment stated that a surplus of six million acres, much of which was valuable, remained for sales in Indian Territory "in unlimited quantities by the Secretary of the Interior," and asked, "[W]hy should we permit corporations that have been existing there for years, organized for that very purpose, to beat these very Indians . . . and if you pass this bill you will give these men the benefits for which they have plotted and schemed for years."[36]

The Five Tribes Act began the process of expanding educational services to all inhabitants of Indian Territory by authorizing the Secretary of the Interior to assume control and direction of tribal schools until such time as a public school system was established under a territorial or state government and to use tribal funds for that purpose.[37] When the act was approved, the Seminoles already had fourteen day schools for white and Indian children and two day schools for freedmen children. The Seminole annual school maintenance cost was $5,000,[38] which was a relatively small portion of the $422,000 expended on schools in 1905 by the Five Tribes.[39] At that time, the Seminole general fund reportedly exceeded two million dollars, a larger amount than the funds of each of the other four tribes, except the Cherokee Nation.[40]

Some of the other requirements in the Five Tribes Act that were particularly beneficial to non-Indian residents involved streets, highways, utilities, and towns. The act authorized the establishment of section line roads in the Choctaw, Chickasaw, and Seminole Nations. Allottees who had allotments along section lines took title subject to this authorization, and tribal funds were to be used for highway construction costs and for payment of any damages caused by highway construction. The act also permitted municipalities with a population over 2,000 to order improvements of streets and alleys and to assess property owners for the costs of those improvements.[41]

Seminole Chief John F. Brown disputed the validity of several provisions in the Five Tribes Act that modified certain terms of the Seminole Allotment Act. He challenged the Five Tribes Act's provision authorizing the delivery of deeds to allottees before the expiration of Seminole government; the distribution of tribal trust funds by the Secretary of the Interior, rather than the tribal treasurer; and the use of tribal funds for purposes not specified in the Allotment Act. The Secretary of the Interior forwarded the issues presented by Chief Brown to the U.S. attorney general in March 1907 and received a response five months later. The attorney general opined that the Seminole allotment agreements were "not really treaties" and were of legal force and effect only because ratified by act of Congress. He noted that the Supreme Court had upheld congressional authority over tribal property in *Cherokee Nation v. Hitchcock*, a 1902 decision involving the Cherokee Nation's challenge to the validity of the 1898 Curtis Act, and stated that there was "nothing to differentiate the case of the Seminoles from that of the Cherokees." He also stated that the Five Tribes Act did not involve any federal taking of tribal property, that it "merely" made "somewhat different provisions" for the allotment of lands and distribution of tribal revenues, and that "the measures provided are all for the benefit and protection of the Seminole Nation and its members."[42]

The protection of tribal coal resources was the subject of a great deal of attention during debate of the Five Tribes Act. The

U.S. Geological Survey had directed a survey with respect to coal deposits and determined that there were 437,734 acres of coal lands in Indian Territory. The coal resources were valued at more than 4.3 billion dollars. As of 1906, a little more than one-fourth of the coal interests had been leased. The railroads had acquired fifty-three coal mining leases out of a total of 113 leases located on Choctaw and Chickasaw lands, aggregating 49,460 acres and running for thirty years. Some argued during debate that these long-term leases were equivalent to the sale of the coal resources, and that the government should proceed with "extreme caution" in dealing with property "of this immense value." Some congressmen suggested an increase in coal royalty payments to Indian owners, but such suggestions were to no avail. In the end, the Five Tribes Act's only protection of the tribal coal resources was a provision that there would be no sale of these resources until the existing leases for coal and asphalt lands expired or until otherwise provided by law.[43]

Although the coal situation affected the Choctaw and Chickasaw tribes more than the others, it demonstrated the government's awareness of the rich natural resources of the Five Tribes, the continuing role of the railroads, and the prevailing forces that resulted in loss of those resources to the Five Tribes. By 1905 the *Oklahoman* was reporting that the "world has never seen anything to compare with the development of the oil fields of Kansas and Indian Territory." Oil and gas deposits were being developed in Indian Territory "in abundance and of the highest quality," and Congress had approved a law authorizing the Secretary of the Interior to grant rights of way for oil and gas pipelines through Indian Territory. Although oil development had not yet spread to Seminole lands as of that time, oil speculators believed that there were oil resources there—based on an 1892 U.S. Geological Survey—and soon bought up large amounts of mineral rights in the Nation.[44]

The Five Tribes Act included requirements for the finalization of both Indian and freedman citizenship rolls in order to identify the recipients of allotments. By 1906 the Five Tribes Commission had considered 135,000 applications for Five Tribes citizenship, approved 90,000 applications, prepared freedman rolls and Indian rolls specifying degree of Indian blood for each enrollee of each tribe, and determined the interests of enrollees in twenty million acres of land.[45] Applications for enrollment in the Five Tribes were received until March 4, 1907, when the rolls were closed in accordance with the Act of March 3, 1905, and section 2 of the Five Tribes Act.[46]

The Five Tribes Act was one of the most important in a series of federal laws affecting tribal and individual Indian property and other rights throughout the twentieth century. The act caused a uniquely complicated maze related to the legal rights of the Five Tribes and their members. Shortly before passage of the act, a senator commented, "One day we provide one thing; in the next Congress we provide another. So we have gone on. It would take a Philadelphia lawyer, with all the acumen they are supposed to possess, to determine what the present status is." This statement proved prophetic as to the future multitude of oversimplified and detrimental federal agency interpretations of the Five Tribes' legal status by persons who usually lacked any legal training at all. Congressional debate of the Five Tribes Act also included discussion of the morality of congressional actions concerning the Five Tribes and other Indians. According to Senator Clark, "[W]e have taken upon ourselves to violate year after year, by our legislation, every solemn covenant that we have entered into with the Indians. It is a breach of morality, but we seem to have the power to make that breach." Senator John Spooner responded, "We have done that with all Indians," to which Senator Clark rejoined, "We have done that with all Indians; and I think it is time to stop."[47]

One month after the Five Tribes Act was ratified, Congress approved the Oklahoma Enabling Act—over protests by the Five Tribes—in order to merge Oklahoma and Indian Territories into a state. Two earlier attempts to pass legislation to create Oklahoma had failed. During debate, the resources of Indian Territory were repeatedly discussed. As noted by one congressman, "Their climate is delightful; their soil is most productive; their rainfall abundant. They have coal and iron and oil." Another stated that "The abundant deposits of coal in Indian Territory, with gas, oil, timber, and stone, coupled with the great agricultural possibilities of Oklahoma will make it a great Commonwealth from the very day that it is admitted into the Union, if such good fortune shall ever come to its people." Some congressmen viewed with skepticism the desire of many Indians in Indian Territory to have a separate state, called the State of Sequoyah. One noted that the request for an Indian state was "not to assist the Indian Territory to statehood, but to throw every possible obstruction and impediment in the way of statehood of any kind or character." According to one opponent of joining Indian Territory and Oklahoma Territory into a state, statehood would be "the last sod that is to be put on the political coffin of these people." He noted that "Many eloquent and wise remarks had been made in this Chamber by men who have passed away to honor and to glory in defense of the propositions contained in the treaty. And here we are, Democrats as well as Republicans, shoveling them into a coffin and burying them out of sight forever."[48]

The Enabling Act placed the laws of Oklahoma Territory in effect "as far as applicable" until changed by the state legislature, and it designated the state courts, when established, as successor of all courts of original jurisdiction in the Oklahoma and Indian territories. The Enabling Act protected Indian rights to some extent by providing that nothing in the state constitution could be construed to limit or impair the rights of person or property pertaining to the Indians of Oklahoma and Indian Territories so long as such rights remain unextinguished. It further provided that the Oklahoma Constitution could not be construed to limit or impair the authority of the federal government to make any law or regulation respecting such Indians, their land, property, or other rights that it would have been competent to make if the Enabling Act had never been enacted. The Enabling Act required that the state disclaim any rights to unappropriated public lands and to all lands owned or held by any Indian, tribe, or nation, and it provided for federal jurisdiction over those lands until the title should be extinguished by the United States.[49]

Slightly more than a year after the Enabling Act was approved, the constitution of the state of Oklahoma was ratified on September 17, 1907.[50] Within a few years after statehood, most of the Five Tribes lands were allotted and deeded to individual Indians and freedmen. By the time allotment of Five Tribes lands was completed, approximately 225,000 separate allotments had been made; about 275,000 homestead and allotment certificates had been prepared and delivered; and about 250,000 homestead and allotment patents had been executed by the respective principal chiefs, approved by the Department of the Interior, and recorded. This transfer of tribal ownership to individual ownership set the stage for non-Indian intruders to acquire the lands—intruders who had prevailed in convincing Congress to ignore the Five Tribes treaty guarantees of self-government and absolute tribal ownership of tribal lands.

CHAPTER 3

FEDERAL STRANGLEHOLD ON SEMINOLE LANDS AND MINERALS, 1904–2002

The forced allotment of Seminole lands marked the beginning of a rapid decline in Indian property ownership within the Seminole Nation, quickly taking the former communally owned tribal lands out of the hands of the individual Indian allottees, who were supposedly the intended beneficiaries of the allotment policy, and making them available to the true beneficiaries: the non-Indian population in Indian Territory. This process was expedited by congressional treatment of Five Tribes lands that was markedly different from its treatment of other tribes' allotted lands and that afforded Five Tribes members far less protection in many respects.

Only a few years after Congress enacted allotment acts approving the separate Five Tribes agreements, it began to approve numerous laws applicable only to Five Tribes allotments. Contrary to the 1898 Seminole Allotment Act, which recognized that the Seminole Nation would maintain land ownership and that allottees would have only possessory rights to their allotments, these laws required the land to be deeded outright to allottees while federal officials continued their efforts to finish off the tribal governments. They described various statutory requirements, known as "restrictions," on the lease and sale of the allotted lands, supposedly for the protection of Five Tribes citizens. Uniquely, these laws designated the Oklahoma state courts, rather than the Secretary of the Interior, to serve as the Indians' protectors.[1]

The restrictions, which often required different treatment of homestead and surplus allotments, were based on the blood quantums of the allottees, so that allottees with greater Indian blood quantums were subject to more restrictions regarding their lands.[2] This process caused the following classification of Five Tribes Indian allottees and their heirs: (a) mixed-blood Indians having less than half Indian blood, (b) mixed-blood Indians having half or more Indian blood and less than three-quarters Indian blood, (c) mixed-blood Indians having three-quarters or more Indian blood, and (d) full-bloods. Allottees listed on the tribal freedmen rolls were not subject to this classification.

This mixture of state court implementation of federal laws and the need to define the blood quantums of Five Tribes allottees and their heirs contributed to great confusion regarding the ownership status of restricted Five Tribes lands. It eventually became necessary for title examiners to use complicated charts to determine the validity of Indian land titles, and Congress periodically enacted laws validating questionable sales of Five Tribes allotted lands and inherited allotments.[3] To make matters more complicated, most of the federal Five Tribes land statutes were not codified in the *United States Code*, unlike the laws generally governing trust allotments of most other tribes' members. The many issues that arose in interpretation of these laws resulted in extensive litigation in federal court and in Oklahoma state courts.[4]

The reduction of lands subject to federal statutory protection had a detrimental impact on Five Tribes governments in the latter part of the twentieth century. Many tribes in other parts of the country occupied recognized reservations, all of which constituted "Indian country" for governmental purposes. Those tribes enjoyed governmental authority not only over trust lands, but also over fee (non-trust) lands, at least for some purposes. In contrast, as of the end of the twentieth century, there were no judicial decisions addressing whether unrestricted lands within the Five Tribes original boundaries also possessed Indian country status. Instead, federal and state authorities recognized that smaller checkerboard areas of restricted Five Tribes lands had the legal status of Indian country and took the position that only those lands, plus tribal trust lands, were subject to tribal governmental authority.

Thus, reductions in the amount of Five Tribes restricted allotted lands reduced the amount of lands generally recognized as being subject to Five Tribes' governmental authority.

Congress began reducing the Five Tribes allotment acts' federal protection of Indian owners of allotted lands in the appropriations Act of April 21, 1904, the first of the uniform laws governing Five Tribes allotments. The 1904 act, which had no effect on homestead allotments, removed restrictions on the conveyance of surplus lands held by non-Indian allottees (the intermarried whites of the Choctaw and Chickasaw Nations and the freedmen). It also allowed, on a case-by-case basis, removing restrictions on the sale of surplus lands held by Indian allottees, except minors, with the approval of the Secretary of the Interior.[5]

Congress's uniform treatment of Five Tribes allotments continued with passage of the Act of April 26, 1906. During debate, Congress wrestled with the extent to which individual Indian ownership of allotments should be protected. Although some congressmen argued that, absent statutory protections, Five Tribes citizens would soon be parted from their allotments, others asserted that tribal citizens were no longer distinguishable from non-Indians and did not need to be protected. Some opponents of federal protection even questioned whether limitations could be placed legally on the sale or leasing of allotments, given the U.S. citizenship status of Five Tribes members.[6]

In the end, Congress imposed uniform restrictions on Five Tribes allotments in the 1906 act relating to the sale and lease of the allotments, some of which were not as protective as the allotment acts. The act prohibited half-blood allottees from deeding their homestead and surplus allotments to third parties for twenty-five years after passage of the act. It provided that removal of restrictions as to half-bloods could be done only by an act of Congress, thus repealing the 1904 act's provisions that had allowed the Secretary of the Interior to remove restrictions on surplus lands. It required leases of half-blood allottees' lands to be in writing and approved by the Secretary of the Interior, except agricultural leases of surplus lands for less than one year. The 1906 act also placed restrictions on sales of lands inherited by half-blood heirs by making such sales subject to the secretary's approval.[7]

In order to prevent a full-blood Indian from being induced to disinherit close family members by trickery or for inadequate payment, the 1906 act required a territorial federal judge or a U.S. commissioner to approve a will disinheriting certain family members. The act provided that restricted lands would remain untaxable so long as title remained with the original allottee, but that they would become taxable when restrictions were removed. It included a provision invalidating every contract for the execution of a deed to restricted land and invalidating every deed executed before the removal of restrictions, which was later found by the Supreme Court to be a lawful exercise of the guardianship power of the United States over the Five Tribes.[8]

The Indian blood quantums of allottees became an important factor in determining restrictions on Five Tribes allotments under the 1906 act and was unique to the Five Tribes. On the one hand, titles to individual Indian allotted trust lands of other tribes were held in the name of the United States in trust for the Indian beneficiaries, regardless of their degree of Indian blood. On the other hand, titles to Five Tribes allotments were held in the name of the allottees but were subject to federal statutory restrictions concerning sales and leases if the Indian owner had the required degree of Indian blood. The 1906 act provided that, for all purposes, an allottee's Indian blood quantum would be determined by the rolls approved by the Secretary of the Interior. This statutory presumption as to blood quantum was continued in later federal laws regarding restricted Five Tribes land. There was no need for such presumptions for members of other tribes, as blood quantum had no relationship to the protection of their trust lands.[9]

The allotment process for dividing Seminole lands resulted in the establishment of Seminole allotments consisting of approximately forty-acre homestead allotments and 120-acre surplus allotments, depending on the value assigned to the allotments. In 1907, 3,124 allotments were deeded to Seminole and freedman allottees, with the freedmen receiving 986 of those allotments. Homestead and surplus allotments of varying sizes, depending on valuation, were also made for the other four tribes during this period.[10]

The continued break-up of Indian lands in eastern Oklahoma accelerated after statehood was established in 1907 as a direct result of additional federal legislation. By December 1907, restrictions had been removed from more than three million acres of the original 19.6 million acres formerly owned by the Five Tribes up until allotment, leaving approximately sixteen million acres, most of which were allotted in restricted and tax-exempt status. This situation gave rise to complaints that Five Tribes members, mischaracterized as "the most wealthy of the people in the State," were relieved from tax burdens. There was increasing congressional concern that there was little taxable property in eastern Oklahoma to support the new non-Indian government, and that the cities were required to bear most of the expenses of county and state government.[11]

This concern led to the enactment of the Act of May 27, 1908, which removed restrictions on large quantities of Five Tribes allotted lands and placed those lands on the tax rolls. Removal of restrictions on all Five Tribes lands, except certain lands of Five Tribes citizens of one-half or more Indian blood, would remove restrictions from an estimated 8,434,948 acres, thus exposing those lands to taxation and easy sale. In dealing with Five Tribes land issues, Congress rationalized that the 1908 act would enable a large number of Indian allottees, deemed by Congress as "capable of managing their affairs," to sell the portion of their lands "not required by them" and to improve the lands that they retained. Supporters of the 1908 law believed that it would enable "the large portion of Oklahoma occupied by the Five Civilized Tribes [to become] the property of the men who till the soil."[12]

Congress's decision in 1908 to enable the swifter transfer of Indian lands to non-Indians was, at least in part, due to the fact that Five Tribes allotment legislation initially did not result in opening of large areas of lands for immediate non-Indian ownership. In contrast, tribes in western Oklahoma and other regions nationwide had been divested of large portions of their reservations within established non-Indian territories and states following the 1887 passage of the General Allotment Act. Many of those tribes' lands were then opened to non-Indian settlement, leaving the Indian populations in smaller segregated areas within organized territories and states. Members of Congress rationalized the decision to remove restrictions on Five Tribes allotments by arguing that most mixed-blood Indians of the Five Tribes were educated and capable of transacting their own business.

In deciding where to draw the line in removing restrictions with the 1908 act, Congress considered a statistical breakdown of tribal enrollment based on degree of Indian blood for each of the Five Tribes. This breakdown included findings that out of 3,124 adult and minor enrollees in the Seminole Nation, 1,399 Seminoles were full-blood Indian, 180 were more than half, 394 were one-half, 165 were less than one-half, and 986 were freedmen. Federal statutory restrictions and tax-exempt status imposed by earlier tribal allotment acts on the sale and leasing of large amounts of Five Tribes allotted lands were removed by the 1908 act. The act removed restrictions on all allotments of all freedmen and on all allotments of Indian allottees of less than one-half Indian blood, and it removed restrictions on the surplus allotments of allottees of half or more Indian blood but less than three-quarters blood. As a result, the allotments of 1,151 allottees in the Seminole Nation became open to taxation and sale. Hence, the act eliminated restrictions on the lands of almost 37 percent of the Seminole allottees and on the lands of a significant percentage of the other four tribes' allottees. It caused land loss and the impoverishment of the affected freedmen and Indian allottees and their heirs, and it contributed to the growing disregard state and local officials paid to the existence of the remaining territorial area subject to the Five Tribes governmental authority.[13]

Under the 1908 act, the Secretary of the Interior's approval was required for sales of homesteads of allottees who were one-half or more Indian blood, sales of both surplus and homestead allotments of allottees who were three-quarters or more Indian blood, certain surface leases, and all oil and gas leases. However, the act enabled state courts to assume the role of protector, acting as a federal instrumentality, with regard to Indians who inherited restricted lands from original allottees. Thus, under the 1908 act, if an allottee died still owning restricted lands, his half-blood heir could sell his inherited allotment if approved by a state court. The 1908 act also required state court approval of the will of an Indian of half or more Indian blood in cases where the will disinherited certain family members. State court involvement in Seminole land matters was contrary to Seminole chief John Brown's request to have all cases affecting Seminole lands removed to the federal courts, as required by the Seminole Allotment Act. Titles to land in the Seminole Nation were reportedly "in a peculiar tangle, owing to the general diversity of opinion relative to the law laid down in the Seminole treaty and the subsequent acts of congress, the long delay in receiving patent after allotment and other complications."[14]

Even more devastating to the Seminole Nation, the 1908 act targeted the regulatory and property interests of the Seminole Nation as a governmental entity. It ended the Seminole Allotment Act's requirement that all mineral leases be entered into with the Seminole Nation and provided that only the allottee or owner could make oil and gas leases after June 30, 1908. It also ended, effective June 30, 1908, the Seminole Allotment Act's provision that one-half of any oil and gas royalties produced from Seminole allotments would go to the tribe. Thus, the act eliminated the huge financial rewards that the Nation would have received from the production of the immense oil reserves underlying the lands within its boundaries. Oil exploration in Seminole lands had started as early as 1902, when Chief Brown's Wewoka Trading Company unsuccessfully drilled for oil; in 1907, only one year before the enactment of the 1908 act, an oil well in Wewoka produced oil that overflowed into a nearby stream. By 1913 speculators had secured oil and gas leases on most available lands in Seminole County, although the real oil boom did not start until 1923. Congress's failure in the 1908 act to honor the Seminole Allotment Act's guarantee of oil royalties to the Seminole Nation resulted many years later in an unsuccessful tribal claim against the United States.[15]

The 1908 act required that all royalties arising from leases of Five Tribes allotments were to be paid to the U.S. Indian agent of the Union Agency, which was located in Muskogee, for the benefit of the Indian lessor "or his proper representative." These "proper representatives" included state-court-appointed guardians because the 1906 act authorized the sale of Five Tribes minors' allotments by court-appointed guardians, and the 1908 act authorized the Oklahoma probate courts to exercise jurisdiction over minors' property. Congress simultaneously permitted the Secretary of the Interior to appoint local representatives, later referred to as "district agents," to investigate the conduct of those guardians. These district agents were required to report any negligence to the probate court and to the secretary for further investigation and remedial action. The establishment of this convoluted system suggests that Congress was doubtful that state guardianships would truly protect Indian interests. Such doubts soon proved to be well-founded.[16]

The passage of the 1908 act was resisted by persons who correctly predicted that it would lead to the separation of Five Tribes members from their allotments, including M. L. Mott, who served as attorney for the Creek Nation at that time. Mott maintained that the act's establishment of state jurisdiction over the restricted lands of Five Tribes minors was inadvisable because the federal government's past experience "disclosed conclusively that no local control should be granted over the affairs of the Indians" because of an "unbroken record of oppression, robbery and plunder." Mott predicted that "such local control was not only directly opposed to the Indian's best interest but would inevitably lead to his impoverishment."[17]

In 1912, after the 1908 act had been in effect for only a few years, Mott prepared a report that was funded with Creek tribal funds. The report was based on an examination of the files in pending guardianship cases in several counties. Mott's detailed report concluded that the average cost of a guardianship was "the unprecedented" sum of 19.3 percent of the value of an estate for Indian guardianships, compared with 2.3 percent of the value of non-Indian guardianship estates. The report found that a large number of the Indian guardianship costs ran from 30 percent to 60 percent, and that these "unconscionable and unjustified" costs resulted exclusively from the state courts' allowance of attorney and guardian fees. Mott's report also determined that in a great number of instances large sums of Indian minors' money were being loaned by guardians with totally inadequate securities, and that these loans were made to the guardians themselves and their family members. The unsavory practices involving restricted lands included forgeries of deeds to Seminole allotments as well as a scandal involving a Seminole County judge alleged to have repeatedly approved a specific guardian's sales of Seminole minors' lands at substantially less than their value.[18]

During a 1912 debate on an appropriations bill, South Dakota congressman Charles H. Burke discussed the Mott report at length. Congressman Burke, who was a former chairman of the Indian Committee, criticized the treatment Five Tribes members received because of federal legislation influenced by the Oklahoma congressional delegation. Congressman Burke discussed an earlier federal law that had given the Department of the Interior exclusive authority over the administration of estates of deceased Indians from other tribes, and he noted that "when the law was being considered our friends from Oklahoma, always alert to protect what they believe to be in the interest of their State," excepted from its application the Indians in Oklahoma. Congressman Burke noted that the 1908 act was enacted instead, placing jurisdiction over the persons and property of minor Five Tribes allottees in the Oklahoma probate courts. Not mincing words, Congressman Burke stated that in eastern Oklahoma, where Five Tribes members resided, "some of the judges are corrupt and dishonest and a large number of them are indifferent to the discharge of the duties of their office, so far as the affairs of Indian minors and Indians generally are concerned, and particularly in guardianship matters."

Congressman Burke supported his accusations with statistics from the Mott report.[19]

In response, Oklahoma congressman Scott Ferris, who had ties to the oil industry, insisted that the costs of Indian guardianships were higher than non-Indian guardianships because of numerous unauthorized conveyances of small portions of allotments by Indian allottees that caused clouds on the land titles that had to be cleared by quiet title actions at additional expense. At least one Oklahoma congressman, James Davenport, challenged Mott's character and described him as a "carpetbagger."[20]

Principal Chief Moty Tiger of the Creek Nation defended Mott in a letter describing a number of times that Mott had protected Indian interests, including favorable decisions in the U.S. Supreme Court that were contrary to Oklahoma Supreme Court decisions against Indian interests. The Oklahoma delegation subsequently joined in a telegram to Lee Cruce, governor of Oklahoma, who initiated an investigation by the state examiner and inspector. After the state investigation, the governor announced to the press and the state legislature that the investigation disclosed that the facts as set out in the Mott report were true. Although efforts were made to secure state legislation to correct the situation, those efforts failed.[21]

Congress eventually responded to the Five Tribe allottee land issues in a very limited manner in 1914, by appropriating $175,000 for expenses of the administration of the Five Tribes affairs and $85,000 for salaries and expenses of attorneys and other employees deemed necessary by the secretary in connection with state court probate matters affecting individual allottees. It also appropriated $25,000 for salaries and expenses of oil and gas inspectors to supervise oil and gas mining operations on leased restricted Five Tribes lands and to conduct investigations related to the prevention of waste. The 1914 act abolished the office of the commissioner of the Five Civilized Tribes, and it replaced the position of Union Agency superintendent with the new position of superintendent for the Five Civilized Tribes. The Five Civilized Tribes superintendent's office remained in Muskogee and was the predecessor of the Muskogee Area Office, later designated the Eastern Oklahoma Regional Office, of the Bureau of Indian Affairs (BIA).[22]

The more substantive laws governing Seminole allotted lands, including the 1908 act, continued relatively undisturbed until passage of the Act of June 14, 1918. That act provided that decisions of the Oklahoma probate courts identifying heirs of deceased Five Tribes members were conclusive, and it authorized those courts to determine the heirs of deceased members when the time for filing a probate case established by state law had passed. The act also made the Oklahoma partition laws applicable to Five Tribes restricted lands. Under the partition laws, when more than one person owned only a percentage (known as an undivided interest) in an entire tract of land (as opposed to each separately owning a defined parcel of land within a larger tract), any one of them could file a partition suit. After considering recommendations by court-appointed commissioners who examined the land, the court could approve division of the tract into smaller parcels so that each owner of an undivided interest in the tract would become the sole owner of a parcel within that tract. However, the courts more often ruled that the lands could not be practically divided (even in documented cases where that was not accurate), in which case the court would order a sale of the entire tract at public auction, with the sale proceeds divided among the undivided interest owners.[23]

The application of the state partition law was an unprecedented attack on the ability of Five Tribes members to retain their restricted lands, and it expedited the loss of restricted lands. It was not uncommon for a non-Indian to purchase an undivided interest in a tract from one willing Indian seller and then file a partition action in order to force the sale of the entire tract. If an Indian owner either did not bid or bid unsuccessfully, he would lose his ownership interests and be paid a share of the proceeds of the auction, often for an inadequate price. Even if an Indian owner was able to buy the entire tract at auction, the restricted and tax-exempt status of that percentage of the lands purchased at auction was subject to challenge, and the land could later be lost at tax sale. In contrast, trust lands of members of tribes in western Oklahoma and elsewhere within the United States were not subject to state partition laws or state court jurisdiction, and thus those tribal members did not lose their land holdings in this manner.

Predictably, the loss of lands by Five Tribes allottees continued at a rapid rate, aided in part by corrupt practices involving guardianships in the state probate courts. At its annual meeting in 1923, a committee of the Oklahoma Bar Association approved a resolution criticizing the dissipation of estates by the appointment of one or more guardians or administrators "wholly incapable of handling business affairs, many of them graduates of the bankruptcy court," and by appointment of attorneys "on fat salaries" to aid them and keep them "at large while the widows, orphans and wards go hungry and poorly clad." The resolution stated that the Oklahoma probate practice was so essentially political that the "the better class of lawyers are seldom found connected with it except in contested cases, or in winding up estates of former clients." The resolution wryly concluded that this state of affairs "causes one to wonder why he should die and leave an estate in Oklahoma."[24]

In another attempt to secure reform of Five Tribes land laws, in early 1925 M. L. Mott again corresponded with members of Congress, reminding them of his 1912 report. Mott noted that although Congress had taken steps in 1914 and subsequent years to fund probate attorneys to protect the restricted property interests of Five Tribes members, the funding had dwindled to an amount sufficient to fund only eight of the twenty attorneys originally funded by the 1914 appropriations act. Mott also described a similar survey of state court records conducted in 1923 by S. E. Wallen, superintendent of the Five Tribes. Wallen provided examples of cases in which Indian interests were not protected in state court proceedings and concluded that the investigation made it clear "that there are many cases in which bad management and great waste of the estates have been the rule; that there are extravagant and unwarranted allowances for maintenance and personal expenses of the wards; that guardians' and attorneys' fees are excessive, and in many cases unconscionable; and that the costs of administration through the Probate Courts of Oklahoma constitute an unfair tax upon the estates." Wallen concluded that the laws relieving the Secretary of the Interior of the supervision and control of Five Tribes restricted property caused, to a large extent, the "grafting on and plundering" of Indian estates.[25]

In his 1925 correspondence, Mott stated that Wallen's report showed conclusively that the use of federal attorneys to participate in or monitor state court proceedings involving restricted Five Tribes lands in the past decade had been "wholly inadequate" and had "not resulted in the correction of the evils which it was hoped it might correct." Mott rhetorically asked why federal probate attorneys were needed at all, if the Indian wards were being accorded full protection by the state courts. He noted that the records were replete with cases where adult Indians, upon coming suddenly into large incomes by reason of oil or mineral development of their property, were taken into court and declared incompetent, guardians were appointed, attorneys and guardians fees were allowed on a liberal scale, and court orders were issued to the superintendent for the payment of the fees out of restricted funds in his hands. Mott stated that a new legal maxim had been established in Oklahoma: "that an Indian becomes incompetent simultaneously with the acquisition of wealth." Mott stated that Wallen's report established "such a wanton disregard of the interests of the Indian as to leave no doubt of the attitude of the courts toward him and his property and no hope that where full power is vested his interests [would] be conserved and protected." He suggested that Congress could continue funding this "futile remedy," could stop funding altogether, or could withdraw jurisdiction over restricted Indian properties from the Oklahoma probate courts and place it exclusively with the Indian Bureau "where it formerly rested and from which experience has demonstrated it should never have been taken."[26]

The following year, Congress passed the Act of April 12, 1926, primarily for the purpose of providing more certainty for non-Indian purchasers of restricted lands. The act required that notice be given to the Five Tribes superintendent in cases claiming an interest in allotted Five Tribes lands, and it allowed federal intervention and removal of the case to federal court. Although these practices were somewhat beneficial to Indian owners of restricted lands, the act further provided that if the United States failed to remove the case to federal court within a specified time, then the state proceedings and judgment would bind the United States and the parties to "the same extent as though no Indian land or question were involved."[27]

The 1926 act contained another provision that resulted in more serious consequences for Five Tribes owners of restricted lands. It made the Oklahoma state statute of limitations applicable to all restricted Five Tribes members and their heirs. This enabled persons who were in possession of restricted Indian lands, but who had not acquired valid title because of a failure to comply with applicable federal law, to perfect title through a state court quiet title action proving the claimant's adverse possession of the land for the time period specified in the state statute of limitations. The Secretary of the Interior protested at the time of the 1926 act's passage that although the application of the state statute of limitations could grant relief in deserving cases, it could also "create machinery whereby titles without merit would also be validated," a prediction that later proved true. This provision was also later interpreted as allowing a non-Indian purchaser to establish title to restricted land acquired in violation of federal statutory requirements if a court found it would be inequitable to enforce an Indian seller's legal rights because of the passage of time.[28]

Two years after approval of the 1926 act, Congress enacted the Act of May 10, 1928, which extended the restrictions on allotments of members of the Five Tribes of one-half or more Indian blood for an additional twenty-five-year period commencing on April 26, 1931, thus carrying restrictions forward until April 25, 1956. The courts broadly interpreted the statute as including inherited lands and lands purchased with restricted funds, if owned by persons of one-half or more Indian blood. The 1928 act permitted Indian land owners to apply to the Secretary of the Interior for removal of restrictions, and it expressly authorized the secretary to remove the restrictions "wholly or in part." This permission to remove restrictions from only parts of allotments was intended to end the unrequested and unnecessary wholesale removal of restrictions from entire allotments occurring in past transactions.[29]

At the same time that it extended the restricted status of individual Five Tribes land, the 1928 act also eroded the tax-exempt status of that land. This erosion of tax-exempt status was apparently in response to representations that Oklahoma's revenue was insufficient for state purposes, that large areas of allotted Indian lands within the state were tax exempt, and that Indian citizens were enjoying the benefit of local government without taxation. The erosion was accomplished in two ways. First, the 1928 act provided that all minerals produced after April 26, 1931, from restricted lands of Five Tribes members would be subject to state and federal taxes. This requirement applied "only" to taxation of minerals produced, not to gas bonus and delay rentals paid before oil production. Second, the act limited tax exemptions to 160 acres of land to be selected by the Indian landowner, who was to receive a certificate designating the exempt acreage. The exemption, which was found to include an exemption from state estate taxes, was to continue so long as the title remained with the Indian owner who had obtained a certificate or any half-blood heir or devisee of the land. Restricted lands in excess of the 160 acres designated as tax-exempt were taxable and subject to sale for non-payment of state ad valorem taxes. The act further provided that nothing in the act could be construed to exempt from taxation any lands already subject to taxation under existing law.[30]

The imposition of taxes on large quantities of restricted Five Tribes lands was not consistent with the Senate report accompanying the 1928 act, which stated that it would be "unsafe" for Five Tribes owners of restricted lands "to be turned loose, free from governmental supervision after April 26, 1931." This statement was made after the report described the rapid loss of Five Tribes allotments as follows: The enrolled members of the Five Tribes "at one time" (in other words, only about twenty years earlier) had owned approximately nineteen million acres of land in eastern Oklahoma within a forty-county area. The allottees received 15,794,218 acres. The restrictions on 14,050,244 acres were removed by order of the Secretary of the Interior or by act of Congress, "but mostly by the act of May 27, 1908." The allottees and their heirs owned 1,743,974 acres of restricted land in 1928, only 1,000,000 of which would remain non-taxable after April 26, 1931, under the terms of the 1928 act, and "the acreage of exempt land [would] be reduced from year to year as restrictions [were] removed by the Secretary of the Interior" and by death if the decedent's heirs were of less than one-half Indian blood.[31]

That same year, in 1928, the Brookings Institute issued its report entitled "The Problem of Indian Administration," popularly referred to as the "Merriam Report." The report contained a separate section that addressed the manner in which Five Tribes members were losing their lands. According to the report, the deviation of special federal laws regarding Five Tribes lands had resulted "in a flagrant example of the white man's brutal and unscrupulous domination over a weaker race." The report found that the 1908 act's authorization of surface leases of Five Tribes restricted homesteads for limited terms without federal approval led to "great abuses," including the payment of inadequate rentals. The authors of the report noted that conditions involving corrupt state court judges seemed to be improving following their exposure and replacement, but there were still problems protecting restricted lands. The report noted that the federal probate attorneys who participated in Five Tribes land matters were hampered by lack of adequate supervision and leadership, absorption in administrative details, and the necessity for the constant reference to higher authority before taking decisive action. The report also criticized the conduct of court approvals for sales of restricted lands, finding that the presence of the Indian seller was not required, and that the discretion of the state court judge was absolute and unappealable. It described the 1918 act's application of Oklahoma laws to the partition of individual Five Tribes lands as yet "another way" for "the Indian to lose title to his lands." The report recommended that restrictions on inherited lands not be limited to Indians of one-half or more Indian blood, but that recommendation was never followed.[32]

A few years after the Merriam Report was published, Congress enacted the Act of March 2, 1931. The 1931 act provided that lands purchased with the proceeds from the sale of non-taxable lands of a restricted Five Tribes member sold to the state, a county, or a municipality for public improvement purposes, or sold to any other person for any other purpose, would also be restricted if approved by the Secretary of the Interior. The following year, Congress enacted legislation extending this benefit to members of all tribes. That legislation allowed use of proceeds from sales of nontaxable Indian lands to acquire substitute restricted lands and required that the restrictions be stated in the deed. Congress later enacted a law in 1937 that provided that these lands were nontaxable until otherwise provided by Congress.[33]

In 1933 Congress enacted a law concerning conveyance of restricted lands owned by Five Tribes citizens of half or more Indian blood.[34] Three years later, Congress passed three more laws involving individual Five Tribes restricted lands. The first of these was the Act of February 11, 1936, which allowed individual Five Tribes owners of restricted lands to lease surface lands for farming and grazing for periods not longer than five years, with the approval of the Secretary of the Interior. The second was the Act of June 20, 1936, which appropriated money so that the Secretary of the Interior could pay taxes on restricted Five Tribes lands that previously had been bought with restricted funds by Indians who believed that the purchased lands would be nontaxable. This law expressly provided that such lands were to be nontaxable until otherwise directed by Congress.[35]

The opportunity for increasing the non-taxable Indian land base was seemingly enhanced by enactment of a third 1936 law, the Oklahoma Indian Welfare Act, known as the OIWA. The OIWA was enacted two years after the Indian Reorganization Act of 1934, popularly known as the IRA. The IRA allowed the Secretary of the Interior to purchase lands, with title to be held by the United States in trust for tribes and individual Indians nation-wide. Although many sections of the IRA were expressly made inapplicable to tribes in Oklahoma, the IRA section permitting such land acquisitions was applicable. Nonetheless, the OIWA also included a section allowing the Secretary of the Interior to buy lands and to hold title to those lands in trust for Oklahoma tribes and individual Indians. The OIWA provisions concerning land acquisitions were less protective than similar provisions in the IRA, which provided that the purchased lands were to be tax exempt, without any exceptions. The OIWA stated that the pur-chased lands were to be free from "any and all taxes," except the state gross production tax on minerals.[36]

The Department of the Interior made little effort to acquire and place lands into trust for Oklahoma tribes under either the IRA or the OIWA. Instead, as a general rule lands were acquired and accepted by the United States in trust for one of the Five Tribes only when the tribe took the initiative and performed the work required to qualify for federal approval. Although that proved to be a workable solution later in the twentieth century for the other four tribes, which contracted realty functions from the BIA and set their own priorities, it was not as useful for the Seminole Nation, which remained dependent on realty services provided by the BIA Wewoka Agency. The Department of the Interior also rarely, if ever, exercised its right to preferential purchase of restricted lands on behalf of the Five Tribes established by the OIWA, and a later law provided for an automatic waiver of that right when not exercised. In eastern Oklahoma, the placement of restrictions on lands acquired by Five Tribes members with restricted funds under the 1931 act was the more common method of adding restric-tions to unrestricted land, but this method failed to adequately remedy the continuing loss of individual restricted lands.[37]

The OIWA, at least theoretically, was enacted in order to place Oklahoma tribes on a more equal footing with other tribes in various respects, and it applied to most, if not all, federally recog-nized tribes in Oklahoma. John Caesar, chairman of the Seminole

Nation General Council, and others communicated their support of most of the provisions in the 1935 version of the bill. At that time, Congress recognized that many Indians in Oklahoma suffered extreme poverty and owned no property at all. Nonetheless, members of Congress were unwilling to approve a bill to reform the federal laws that had led to this problem, and many proposed measures to reform federal legislation governing Five Tribes restricted lands did not survive in the final version of the OIWA. For example, the 1935 version included provisions that would have eliminated the use of state courts for probates and sale approvals concerning restricted Five Tribes lands and would have returned probate and other protective functions involving such lands to the Secretary of the Interior. Congress did not approve these provisions, even though the secretary already possessed that authority over Indian trust lands in western Oklahoma. Congress instead chose to maintain separate sets of laws concerning individual lands in eastern and western Oklahoma. Thus, Indian trust lands in western Oklahoma remained protected regardless of the owner's Indian blood quantum, whereas restricted lands in eastern Oklahoma were protected only if the owner was at least one-half Indian blood.[38]

A few opponents of the 1935 draft of the OIWA testified at hearings on the bill. The bill's detractors were adamantly opposed to that portion of the bill that would give the Secretary of the Interior exclusive jurisdiction to determine heirs; to divide lands, funds, or other restricted property among the heirs; and to settle claims against the estates. Oklahoma congressman Jack Nichols complained that such a measure "strikes at the very heart of the sovereignty of the State of Oklahoma and lays down a blanket indictment against the courts of the State of Oklahoma and the legal profession." Opponents attempted to discredit the earlier Mott report advocating legislative reform by assailing the characters of Mott and former superintendent S. P. Wallen and by questioning the track record of the Department of the Interior based on reports of mishandling of Indian funds. Opponents also argued that to "take away the rights" of Five Tribes members to use state courts would deny them essential citizenship rights and would establish an autocratic and bureaucratic power in the Secretary of the Interior.[39]

In their 1935 testimony before Congress, the commissioner of Indian Affairs, John Collier, and the Secretary of the Interior, Harold Ickes, were strong advocates of federal legislation that would end state court authority over restricted Five Tribes lands. Collier rejected the notion that removal of state court jurisdiction would take away a "privilege" given to Five Tribes owners of restricted lands. He emphasized that no Oklahoma tribe requested or endorsed placement of Indian lands under the "protection" of the state courts when the jurisdictional acts (the 1908 and subsequent federal laws) were first enacted. According to Collier, the 1908 act resulted in the loss of 14,300,000 acres of land by the Five Tribes, and by 1935 they only possessed 1,500,000 acres.[40]

Collier's testimony strongly rebutted the insinuations of the bill's opponents that the Mott report was not valid. Collier discussed a number of cases handled by the state courts resulting in property losses to Indian owners of restricted Five Tribes allotments, including cases involving Seminole members in Seminole County. For example, in one 1933 case the attorneys arranged for the Seminole spouse of a deceased Seminole to receive an undivided interest in restricted oil producing lands, then purchased the interest for $2,500 from the Seminole spouse, and soon sold the oil royalties alone for $33,500, making a profit of $31,000. In another case a state court approved a conveyance of valuable oil lands by a Seminole heir for $50,000, which was less than the value of the property. After the Department of the Interior learned of the sale, suit was filed and, after protracted litigation, the heir received an additional $30,000 and an undivided one-half interest in the lands involved. In another case involving a Creek–Seminole, the guardian of a blind Seminole could not account for $1,800 of his ward's funds that the guardian had received. The Seminole County Court "positively refused" to charge the guardian for that sum and instead approved a large fee for him. In a fourth Seminole case, a Seminole county judge "virtually forced" the guardian of a Seminole minor to purchase property valued at $750 from a friend of the judge for $5,000. In a fifth Seminole case, a Seminole county judge did not approve a deed after the federal probate attorney objected that $175 offered for purchase of a property interest valued at $500 was insufficient. After a few months passed, the same judge approved a deed to the same property for the price of $25, without giving notice of the proposed sale to the probate attorney. Collier discussed many other cases, which he characterized as only a few of the state cases involving injustices to Five Tribes members.[41]

Collier testified that local courts approved large attorneys' fees and that a practice had developed by which third parties made claims against valuable Indian estates in the hope that they could acquire something through compromise settlements, regardless of the merit of the claims. He stated that the 1935 version of the bill would eliminate that problem by placing authority over heirship determinations in the Department of the Interior, where the proposed charge against the Indian estate would be small as compared with the amounts allowed by the state courts. Collier acknowledged that the Department of Justice could already intervene in state proceedings under existing law but noted that "intervening in a court that does not want you to get results is not of much use."[42]

Secretary Harold Ickes noted in his 1935 testimony before Congress that there had been some opposition to the 1935 version of the bill but stressed that it had "come almost exclusively from white business and professional groups of those Oklahoma localities in which the exploitation of Indians and of Indian estates has long been a leading industry so well established that it is considered a vested right." He stated, "What happened? Oil came in and now we are trying to exploit those Indians who were sent down there without any volition on their part. We are trying to take away from them the profit which they are making out of the property which we in all deliberation gave them to possess." He emphasized that he was not attacking Oklahoma judges and attorneys and that his criticism was directed to a few individuals who took advantage of a "bad legal situation," which he described as "a crazy quilt of divided administrative and judicial responsibility for Indian property peculiar to the State of Oklahoma."[43]

Ickes stated in his testimony that the 1935 draft bill would reverse the "heartless policy established by Congress in 1908" by clearly directing the secretary to save what was left of Five Tribes property and enabling him to resist local Oklahoma pressure on the basis of congressional policy. He noted that eastern Oklahoma was the only place where this type of situation existed and that it was time for it to be completely eradicated, "regardless of the wishes of those who selfishly profit by it." He argued that the bill was more than a local bill affecting Oklahoma, and that Congress had a national responsibility. Ickes addressed concerns that "vast quantities of land [would be] purchased and made nontaxable," stating that less than 8 percent of property in Oklahoma would remain free from local taxation, compared with more than 30 percent of federal-tax-exempt lands in the western states. He also pointed out that the federal government had consistently provided funds to Oklahoma to take the place of revenue that might be derived from tax-exempt Indian lands and property.[44]

Opponents of the OIWA as drafted in 1935 eventually won, and the final revised version did little to improve the status quo with regard to Five Tribes individual restricted lands. The protection of non–Five Tribes individual trust allotments in western Oklahoma remained under authority of the Secretary of the Interior, regardless of the blood quantum of the Indian beneficial owners. In eastern Oklahoma deed approvals, partitions, guardianships, determination of heirs, and probate of estates involving Five Tribes restricted lands were left under the jurisdiction of the Oklahoma courts acting as federal instrumentalities. However, Congress did not remove the Secretary of the Interior's oversight and control over restricted funds accrued from the sale and leasing of restricted Five Tribes lands—apparently Congress did not agree with opponents' claims that the Department of the Interior had failed to protect Indian trust funds.

More than a decade after approval of the 1936 OIWA, Congress enacted the Act of August 4, 1947, which was the last federal law in the twentieth century to comprehensively address the disposition of Five Tribes restricted lands. The 1947 act, also known as the Stigler Act, affected most transactions involving those lands throughout the remainder of the century. The act expressly repealed all prior inconsistent laws but did not contain any provisions inconsistent with the 1918 act's provisions allowing state court determinations of Five Tribes members' heirs, the 1918 act's applicability of state partition laws, or the 1926 act's imposition of the state statute of limitations on Five Tribes individual restricted lands. The 1918 and 1926 acts thus continued to be implemented along with the 1947 act through the remainder of the twentieth century.[45] Strangely, the 1918, 1926, and 1947 acts, unlike federal land laws concerning other tribes, were never codified in the *United States Code*, making them somewhat obscure to persons otherwise unfamiliar with federal laws concerning the Five Tribes.

Under the 1947 act, if a Five Tribes member inheriting property from a deceased owner of restricted and tax-exempt property was one-half or more Indian blood, the property remained restricted and tax exempt. Mineral leases and sales of restricted lands remained subject to state court approval. The act also provided that all funds and securities held by the Secretary of the Interior for Five Tribes members of one-half or more Indian blood remained restricted until otherwise provided by Congress. Like earlier laws, the act provided that the final rolls of the Five Tribes were "conclusive" as to the blood quantum of un-enrolled heirs or devisees. It continued earlier rules allowing lands purchased with restricted funds for a Five Tribes member of one-half or more Indian blood to have restricted status, but it added the requirement that the deed must state that the purchase had been made with restricted funds.[46]

The 1947 act granted exclusive jurisdiction to the Oklahoma courts over all guardianship and probate matters involving Five Tribes restricted property. It also required that notice of these cases be served on federal probate attorneys and authorized them to represent restricted Five Tribes members in state court matters in which the restricted Indians had an interest. The 1947 act ended the 1926 act's authorization of the United States to remove guardianships and probates involving restricted lands from state to federal court. The U.S. attorney retained the authority to remove other types of state court cases to federal court, such as actions to clear title to restricted lands.[47]

The 1947 act contained several provisions concerning the tax-exempt status of the restricted lands of individual Five Tribes members. Tax exemptions of restricted tax-exempt individual Five Tribes lands were continued "during the restricted period" and also during the life of a Five Tribes member if that member was of one-half or more Indian blood and had acquired such lands by descent, devise, gift, exchange, partition, or purchase with restricted funds. Consistent with earlier laws, the 1947 act limited tax-exemptions to 160 acres of restricted lands per owner. Because some restricted Five Tribes lands were accordingly not tax-exempt, the 1947 act afforded an opportunity for the federal government to assist individual Indians threatened by loss of restricted lands through tax sale: county treasurers were required to send the Five Tribes superintendent a list of restricted tracts included in proposed delinquent tax sales at least ninety days before the date of the proposed sale. In theory, the federal government could use these notices to ensure that the individual Indian landowners knew about the upcoming sale of their lands and could use available restricted funds, if any, to pay the delinquent taxes. The 1947 act also included some record-keeping provisions, which, as later amended by the Act of August 12, 1953, required the Secretary of the Interior to file an annual list of Five Tribes non-taxable lands sold during the year.[48]

Congress made Oklahoma oil and gas conservation laws applicable to Five Tribes restricted lands in the 1947 act. The effect was that non-Indian oil interests, which had strong ties with the Oklahoma Corporation Commission, again gained a greater measure of influence in oil and gas matters affecting restricted Five Tribes lands. Although the act provided that no order of the Oklahoma Corporation Commission affecting restricted Indian land would be valid until submitted to and approved by the Secretary of the Interior, it was not atypical for the commission to issue administrative orders affecting restricted mineral interests, with little federal involvement. The 1947 act also failed to address the lack of federal oversight of oil and gas production after the state court approved mineral leases of inherited restricted lands, which left many Five Tribes heirs with no federal agency to assist them in seeking damages or overdue royalties or to conduct investigations of lease agreement violations. In contrast, federal agencies monitored and maintained production records from mineral leases of original Five Tribes allottees and mineral leases of trust lands of members of other tribes, a function that was eventually performed by the Minerals Management Service of the Department of the Interior.[49]

The Act of August 11, 1955, continued restrictions on Five Tribes restricted lands. During consideration of the act, it was reported that approximately 12,000 Indians of the Five Tribes owned restricted lands, most of them original allottees. It was estimated that 4,800 of these persons lived on their restricted lands, and many of them were the older and non-English-speaking Indians. Congress responded by extending the restriction period beyond April 26, 1956, for the lives of Five Tribes members of half or more Indian blood who owned or inherited restricted lands. According to the accompanying Senate and House reports, this extension was intended to clarify that the restricted lands owned by original allottees and the restricted lands inherited by heirs of half or more Indian blood were to be continued in restricted status indefinitely. The 1955 act also provided that any existing exemption from taxation "that constitutes a vested property right" was to continue in force and effect until it terminated by virtue of its own limitations.[50]

According to the 1955 act's legislative history, a large number of restricted landowners were capable of handling their own affairs without federal assistance. Congress accordingly followed a recommendation that the act should include a procedure for terminating the restrictions on the property owned by members who did not need assistance, by authorizing the Secretary of the Interior to remove restrictions with or without application from the owner of the land. This authorization included provisions for a state court hearing in those situations where an application had been denied or where restrictions were removed without application and against the will of the owner. This hearing procedure appears to have been rarely used, if ever, in the twentieth century. The 1955 act explicitly continued in effect provisions of the 1906 and 1908 acts that required state court approval of wills of Five Tribes owners of restricted lands who wished to disinherit their spouses or certain other listed relatives. According to accompanying reports, this requirement needed to be continued in order to circumvent an Oklahoma probate law that prohibited the disinheritance of a spouse. Congress recognized that other Indians in the United States were not prohibited from disinheriting a spouse and believed that Five Tribes members should also be allowed to disinherit spouses with appropriate approval, given "the fact that some marriages with members of the Five Civilized Tribes have been motivated by a desire to inherit the Indians' property."[51]

In 1970 Congress enacted the last law of the twentieth century concerning individual restricted Five Tribes lands. This law, narrow in scope, addressed the disposition of restricted land in situations where it was finally determined after a period of five years from the death of a Five Tribes member that he had died without a will and without heirs. The act provided that in such instances, any interest in and any rents and profits from trust or restricted lands in Oklahoma would become the property of the tribe from which title was derived. Titles to lands acquired by the Five Tribes in this manner were to be held in trust by the United States for the tribe.[52]

In sum, Congress never granted the state complete legislative or judicial authority over Seminoles and their lands. Instead, Congress made only the following few, but devastating, state substantive property laws applicable to the restricted lands of Seminoles and the other four tribes' members: partition, statute of limitations, guardianships, inheritance, probate, and oil and gas conservation laws. Congress afforded Oklahoma state courts a significant role in protecting Five Tribes restricted lands, but such courts were acting only as federal, rather than state, instrumentalities. In the

absence of a federal statute expressly making a state law applicable, the state could not enforce a state statute that disregarded
federal statutory requirements concerning the use and disposition
of individual restricted Five Tribes lands.[53]

The use of federal government representatives to monitor the
protection of Indian interests in state court proceedings—a practice that had been started in 1908—eventually evolved into the
establishment of an office known as the Office of the Tulsa Field
Solicitor, which was part of the Department of the Interior's Office
of the Solicitor. That office was originally located with the BIA
offices in Muskogee, but it was eventually relocated to Tulsa,
Oklahoma. The work force at that office included the field solicitor
and several other attorneys, originally called "probate attorneys"
and later known as "trial attorneys." One of the most costly and
time-consuming functions performed by the trial attorneys involved
representing the Secretary of the Interior in state courts to protect
Indian interests concerning Five Tribes deed and mineral lease
approval cases. Unfortunately, as demonstrated by the 1987
federal court decision in *Walker v. United States*, the deed approval
system established for Five Tribes lands by Congress created some
inherent attorney conflicts that were difficult to surmount.[54]

The *Walker* case was filed in federal court against the United
States by a Cherokee–Creek Indian landowner named Austin
Walker after he learned that there were already producing oil
wells on his property at the time that his lease was approved by
a state court. Rex Herren, who held the position of associate solicitor at the time (a position that was later replaced by the position
of the Tulsa field solicitor), had failed to tell Walker of an earlier
lease approval in state court that was based on fraudulent testimony by a person with the same name and had failed to advise
Walker of the significant value of the lease. Instead, Herren allowed
the attorney representing the oil company to act as Walker's
counsel at the hearing, did nothing to secure an appraisal, did
not insist that the lease be offered for competitive bidding, and
did not advise Walker as to the best possible price. The federal
court found that this inaction constituted malpractice by Herren,

and it found that the deed approval process established by the 1947 act was "fatally flawed" because of a "procedural masquerade wherein the government's trial attorneys know first-hand that the private attorneys filing these petitions are bought and paid for by the Indian's adversary," the oil company seeking approval of the leases. The court admonished that federal trial attorneys "cannot and must not solely rely upon representations made to them by private attorneys to the exclusion of their independent judgment and responsibilities."[55]

It is not clear from the *Walker* decision whether that was an exceptional case, or whether the probate attorneys had abandoned an earlier reported practice of providing appraisals to Indian sellers of restricted property.[56] In any event, after *Walker* the Tulsa Field Solicitor's Office standardized guidelines for representation in Five Tribes lease and deed approval proceedings in state court, under the leadership of a new field solicitor, Tim Vollmann. After notice was provided to the field solicitor's office, the trial attorneys from that office secured an appraisal of the value of the land and minerals from a BIA, Bureau of Land Management, or tribal appraiser. They also determined whether any producing oil or gas wells were located on property in cases involving leases or sales of mineral interests in order to ensure that the Indian owner was fully advised regarding the value of the property. The federal trial attorneys consulted with the Indian owner to ensure that the owner understood that the private attorney who filed the approval proceedings was representing the proposed purchaser of the property. The trial attorneys also confirmed that the Indian owner was fully advised as to the value of the property before he or she made a final decision concerning the sale or lease.[57]

Under the new standardized guidelines, the trial attorneys attended each deed or lease approval hearing and took an active role in representing the federal government's interest in protecting the Indian owners of restricted property. In most cases, there were multiple Indian owners of the property. The trial attorneys made routine inquiries of the Indian owners present at the approval

proceedings, including questions intended to conclusively identify the person testifying as the actual owner of the property, or
in some cases, as the undetermined heir of a deceased owner of
the property. The trial attorney insisted that the sale be opened
for public bid during the hearing and required testimony that the
purchaser would pay the costs of filing and handling the deed
approval case. In cases in which the amount offered for the property was less than the appraised value, the trial attorney objected
to the sale at the lower price. Such objections sometimes prevented
sales desired by Indian landowners, but probably more often it
resulted in higher bids and greater benefits to them. As additional
protection, a court reporter prepared a transcript of the proceedings that was maintained as part of the permanent court file.[58]

As allowed by the 1947 act, the trial attorneys of the Tulsa
Field Solicitor's Office played a similar protective role in quiet
title actions and actions to partition-restricted Five Tribes lands.
In quiet title actions, the trial attorneys considered the allegations and facts and recommended that the U.S. attorney remove
certain cases having little merit to federal court, particularly cases
in which correct application of federal law by the state court
seemed doubtful. In partition cases involving restricted lands,
the trial attorneys sometimes tried to facilitate agreement among
multiple Indian owners regarding the division of the land into
separate tracts in order to avoid court-ordered sale of the entire
tract. If the court ordered a sale, the trial attorneys obtained an
independent appraisal for submission to the court and objected to
any proposed partition that would result in payments to Indian
owners in an amount less than the appraised value of the property.

The Tulsa Field Solicitor's Office often filed and provided representation in state probate proceedings of deceased Five Tribes
members who had restricted land, but over the years a large
backlog of cases developed, and the field solicitor's office eventually stopped providing probate assistance because of funding
constraints. This lack of federal legal services for the probate of
Five Tribe members' estates was inconsistent with the federal
probate assistance in cases involving Indian trust lands of members

of other tribes. Most Five Tribes Indian heirs could not afford to hire an attorney to probate family members' estates; hence, the backlog of unresolved estates in eastern Oklahoma grew until there were hundreds of unresolved estates involving the ownership of thousands of acres of restricted lands. By the 1990s the field solicitor's responsibilities concerning probates of restricted Five Tribes lands were limited to monitoring probates filed at the expense of Indian heirs and monitoring the reasonableness of fees charged by private attorneys for that service.

In 1989 a group consisting of leaders and employees of the Cherokee, Creek, Choctaw, Chickasaw, and Seminole Nations, as well as experienced employees of the BIA Muskogee Area Office, began developing draft legislation that would increase federal protection and place Five Tribes restricted allotments on a more even footing with Indian trust allotments. Some of the tribal leaders who led this effort, supported by tribal realty staff, included Chickasaw governor Bill Anoatubby, Cherokee chiefs Wilma Mankiller and Chad Smith, Muscogee (Creek) chiefs Claude Cox and Perry Beaver, Choctaw chief Greg Pyle, and Seminole chief Jerry G. Haney. David A. Mullon, Jr., a Cherokee Nation member; Leah Harjo Ware, a member of the Muscogee (Creek) Nation; and Susan Work, a Choctaw Nation member, were tribal attorneys who played an active part in drafting the bill. Sharon Blackwell, a Muscogee (Creek) citizen who served as Tulsa field solicitor and later as commissioner of Indian Affairs, was also active in this effort.

After six years of work, the first official version of the draft law was approved by the Executive Committee of the Inter-Tribal Council of the Five Civilized Tribes by resolution approved on October 12, 1995. The following spring, the Inter-Tribal Council submitted it to the assistant secretary of the Interior. In response to suggestions and comments provided by Interior staff, congressional staff, and others, Five Tribes attorneys continued to make changes for several more years, with the ongoing support of tribal leaders. During this time, tribal attorneys obtained statistics from the Tulsa Field Solicitor's Office, which Five Tribes officials later used in congressional testimony to demonstrate the need for legislative reform. According to these statistics, between 1995 and 2000, five or six attorneys in the Tulsa Field Solicitor's Office were involved in hundreds of expensive and time-consuming state court probate, quiet title, partition, guardianship, mineral lease approval, and deed approval cases. The statistics also revealed that, although most of the Five Tribes land losses had occurred during the first part of the twentieth century, a steady loss had continued in later years. Between 1978 and 1998, 2,695 acres of restricted Seminole lands were lost, leaving only 26,430 aces of restricted lands in the Seminole Nation. The total combined loss of restricted acreage for all Five Tribes members was much greater: in the twenty-year period between 1978 and 1998, the amount of individual restricted lands decreased from 510,706 acres to 392,011 acres—a loss of 118,695 acres.[59]

The draft Five Tribes land reform bill finally was submitted to Congress at the end of the 106th Congress in 2000, but it was not enacted into law. The proposed bill was designed to unify revised Five Tribes land laws into a single law, to be placed in the *United States Code*. The bill eliminated the Indian blood quantum requirement for continuation of restrictions for persons who would inherit restricted lands after a specified date. As recommended by Commissioner Collier back in 1935, the 2000 bill replaced state court authority with federal agency administrative approval of sales, partitions, leases, and mortgages of restricted land as well as management of leased mineral interests; in addition, it transitioned probate and heirship determinations and other proceedings that affected title to Five Tribes restricted and trust property from state courts to the Department of the Interior. It also continued the secretary's trust responsibility, made technical amendments to a few existing federal Five Tribes land laws, and repealed the rest.[60]

The Five Tribes relied on Oklahoma members of Congress to sponsor the bill, anticipating that other members of Congress would defer to the Oklahoma delegation. Congressman Wes Watkins introduced the bill in the House in September 2000, and Senator

Jim Inhofe introduced an identical bill in the Senate the following month. The House quickly passed the bill, but the only action in the Senate in 2000 was referral to the Senate Committee on Indian Affairs. Further congressional action was delayed for two years. During that time, tribal attorneys met and corresponded with members of the Oklahoma Bar Association (OBA) Probate Committee and the OBA Real Property Section and made a number of technical changes to the bill. In that manner, they secured the unofficial support of the OBA groups and eliminated the prospect of any official OBA opposition.[61]

The revised bill was re-introduced as H.R. 2880 in the House of Representatives in early 2002, and it was approved by the House on June 11, 2002. After conducting a hearing in September 2002, the Senate Committee on Indian Affairs reported the bill favorably to the full Senate. It appeared that the bill was on a fast track to final enactment, but that event never occurred because of the sudden opposition by the Oklahoma Independent Petroleum's Association (OIPA) and by Denise Bode, commissioner of the Oklahoma Corporation. Despite tribal attorneys' efforts to provide changes to H.R. 2880 to satisfy the concerns of OIPA members, the OIPA decided that it preferred continuation of the status quo regarding restricted Five Tribes lands.[62] As a result, Senator Inhofe called a halt to proceeding with the legislation, which died in the Senate.

After the failed tribal attempt at legislative reform, the federal protection of allotted Five Tribes lands—or lack thereof—continued to be based on aberrant and outdated federal laws that, except in limited instances, remained uncodified in the *United States Code,* which made the laws difficult to find and apply. The lack of legislative reform resulted in the continuing loss of individual restricted lands and decreased much of the geographic area recognized by federal and state agencies as subject to tribal government authority. Some of the tribes more aggressively sought federal approval to place purchased tribal lands into trust status, in part to preserve a tribal jurisdictional area, increase federal protection, and reduce state interference. The Seminole Nation succeeded in obtaining federal approval of trust land acquisitions in a few instances, but the acreage of those new Seminole tribal trust lands was significantly less than the large trust acquisitions of the other four tribes. This disparity was probably at least partly the result of the Nation's inability to free itself of a realty office that was, unlike with the other four tribes, operated and controlled by the BIA. [63]

Although the federal system governing most other Indian lands nationwide was much better than the maze of federal laws affecting the Five Tribes and their members, that system was also far from perfect. The federal mismanagement of Indian resources was historically a significant problem that was the subject of public attention as early as the 1920s during the highly publicized "Teapot Dome" scandal. That incident involved the bribery of high-level federal officials, including the Secretary of the Interior, Albert B. Fall, in the leasing of federal oil and gas reserves in western states. The scandal occurred during the same time that the Seminole Nation's Mekusukey Mission minerals were leased. The fractionation of non–Five Tribes Indian trust lands owned by multiple Indians also became a widespread problem that the federal government belatedly tried to remedy by approving the Indian Land Consolidation Act in 1983 and subsequent amendments, including the Indian Probate Reform Act of 2004, which was inapplicable to Five Tribes probates.[64]

At the close of the twentieth century, the U.S. Department of the Interior was embroiled in *Cobell v. United States*, a class action suit seeking an accounting of funds held by the department in trust for individual Indian landowners throughout the United States. These funds were generated from revenues from Indian restricted and trust lands, including revenues from oil and gas leases. Because, in some limited circumstances, the United States held in trust the revenues generated from individual restricted Five Tribes lands, the *Cobell* suit's allegations of federal mismanagement of trust funds included the interests of some Five Tribes members. Thus, members of the Five Tribes suffered ill effects not only from the special federal laws affecting only their property, but also from the detrimental effects of the imperfect federal agency system that governed most Indian restricted lands and trust lands throughout the United States.[65]

CHAPTER 4

OVERVIEW OF SEMINOLE CLAIMS
CASES AGAINST THE UNITED STATES
1929–1990

For at least half of the twentieth century, the Seminole Nation joined other tribes nationwide in litigating suits authorized by acts of Congress, seeking damages for losses that had resulted, or that had allegedly resulted, from federal actions affecting them. Most of the Seminole claims cases were filed in the Court of Claims in the late twenties and early thirties, with final decisions issued in the forties. Several of these cases were re-filed in the Indian Claims Commission, and a few new cases were also filed there, with resulting decisions in the fifties, sixties, and seventies. After considerable expenditure of time, money, and effort by Seminole leaders, their attorneys, the Indian Claims Commission, the Court of Claims, and the U.S. Supreme Court, the Seminole Nation lost most of its claims cases. After litigation of the Seminoles' most successful claims case, which concerned Florida lands, the Nation still had to wait until 1990 for congressional approval of the distribution of the award.

The attorneys who were principally responsible for representation of the Seminole Nation for its claims cases were Oklahoma City attorney Roy St. Lewis, who originally served as the lead attorney but died before all cases were finally resolved, and Washington, D.C., attorney Paul M. Niebell, who represented the Nation in the claims cases for nearly four decades. Some of the other attorneys on record as counsel for the Nation in claims cases included Cherokee member Frank J. Boudinot; W. W. Pryor, an attorney from Wewoka; E. J. Van Court, an attorney from Eufaula, Oklahoma;

and John Campbell. As allowed by the 1924 act, Congress approved various payments from Seminole Nation funds held in the U.S. Treasury to tribal claims attorneys for reimbursement of proper and necessary expenses incurred in the investigation of records and the prosecution of the Seminole Nation's suits. The claims attorneys or their estates were also paid fees for legal services in the few successful claims cases[1]

The first Seminole claims cases were brought under a 1924 special federal jurisdictional act that conferred jurisdiction on the Court of Claims to adjudicate legal and equitable claims arising from any treaty, agreement, or other federal law that the Seminole Nation might have against the United States and that had not previously been litigated on the merits in the Court of Claims or Supreme Court. The 1924 act authorized the court to adjudicate any claims that the United States might have against the Seminole Nation, allowed offsets against any payment made by the United States for a Seminole claim, and authorized appeals to the Supreme Court. Congress approved a joint resolution in 1926 that permitted the Seminole Nation to bring separate suits on one or more causes of action. In 1929 Congress passed a joint resolution extending the 1929 deadline (established by the 1924 act) for beginning a suit to June 30, 1930. In 1937 Congress enacted another law that had the effect of extending filing deadlines further, by affording the Five Tribes the right to amend, prior to January 1, 1938, their petitions in cases before the Court of Claims, even if the amended petitions presented new claims.[2]

The Seminole Nation's later claims cases were brought in accordance with the federal 1946 Indian Claims Commission Act, which established the commission and broadened the grounds on which relief might be granted in tribal claims cases, including "claims which would result if the treaties, contracts, and agreements between the claimant and the United States were revised on the ground of fraud, duress, unconscionable consideration, mutual or unilateral mistake, whether of law or fact, or any other ground cognizable by a court of equity," and "claims based upon fair and honorable dealings that are not recognized by any existing rule of law or equity." The act also eliminated, for the most part, the use of "gratuitous offsets," which were credits given to the United States for past federal appropriations beneficial to a tribe and its members and used in Court of Claims cases to reduce or eliminate damages awards to tribes.[3]

One of the most important claims cases asserted the Seminole Nation's rights to one-half of the royalties from oil and gas underlying allotted lands, as promised in the 1898 Seminole Allotment Act. Seminole member John Burgess and others originally filed the case in the late twenties. In a letter in 1929, C. J. Rhoads, commissioner of Indian Affairs, opposed the Nation's desire to hire attorney Frank Boudinot to pursue those claims, stating his position that the Seminoles were not allowed by federal law to elect tribal leaders with authority to hire an attorney. He was unresponsive to Seminole concerns that a 1925 contract with attorney John Campbell had been assigned to other attorneys with conflicts of interest in their representation of the Nation. Some of the new attorneys allegedly represented individual claimants to oil and gas underlying Seminole allotments and did not advocate the validity of the Seminole mineral claim.[4]

The commissioner also discouraged the Seminoles' pursuit of the mineral claim because the 1908 act contained provisions eliminating the Seminole Nation's one-half interest in royalties from all allotted lands effective June 30, 1908. His position was supported by a 1928 U.S. attorney general opinion that the proposed mineral claim was without any substantial basis in law or equity. The previous year more than 347 new wells were being drilled, and the population of Seminole County neared 40,000. Oil companies in the county were producing the largest number of barrels of high-grade oil of any county in the world, averaging a total of 400,000 barrels daily.[5]

In 1930 Senator Blaine of Wisconsin introduced a bill seeking to revert all royalties to the Seminole Nation; the bill was opposed by a non-Indian group called the Seminole Royalty Owners' Association, and it never became law. The early mineral claim was apparently abandoned at some point, but in 1951 the Seminole Nation filed its Docket 204 claim with the Indian Claims Commission. The commission issued a decision favorable to the Oklahoma Seminoles in 1966 on the grounds that the United States did not have "fair and honorable dealings" with regard to the Nation's mineral rights; however, the commission noted that the Seminole government would need to attempt to establish a "viable theory of recovery and measure of damages at a future date." The decision paved the way for the Nation to prove the amount of actual damages. According to Roy St. Lewis, the Nation's longtime attorney in the claims cases who died before all of the claims cases were finally completed, such a process might require another length of time comparable to the years during which he had spent "days and weeks and months in the archives, the Library of Congress and the Indian department" going through files.[6]

The hearing on damages in the minerals claim case was held three years later, in 1969. The Seminole attorneys presented evidence of damages in excess of $95 million on the basis of royalties from 1923 to 1968. The United States argued that the Nation should recover nothing. According to the United States, any damages would have arisen at the time that the 1908 act effectively repealed the Seminole Allotment Act's reservation of the Nation's one-half interest in royalties underlying allotments, almost fifteen years before any significant production of the huge oil resources underlying Seminole County began and made many non-Indians, and a few Indians, rich. Additional briefs and motions were filed, and six years passed without a determination of the damages amount. In 1972 the Indian Claims Commission, which was no longer composed of the same individuals who had served on the commission in 1966, decided to reconsider the entire record in its determination of the damages issues. Remarkably, the new commission vacated the Nation's favorable 1966 ruling altogether. Seminole attorneys appealed that decision to the Court of Claims, which affirmed it in 1974. After the U.S. Supreme Court denied review of the case, some believed that federal legislation referring

the case to the Court of Claims might result in reinstatement of the
earlier decision and a determination of damages, but that avenue
was not actively pursued by the Nation.[7]

In another case filed in the late twenties or early thirties, the
Seminole Nation unsuccessfully claimed that for many years the
federal government had disbursed tribal annuities for various
purposes in violation of its duty as trustee and without congressional authorization. After the United States appealed a Court of
Claims award to the Seminole Nation in the amount of $1,317,087
in the annuities case, the Supreme Court reversed the award in
1937. The Court found that the Court of Claims had no jurisdiction
as to most of the claims, because they had been filed by amended
petition after a statutory deadline for the filing of claims. The
Court disallowed most of the remaining claim. After passage of
the 1937 law that conferred jurisdiction on the Court of Claims
to reinstate and retry untimely claims of the Five Tribes that had
been previously dismissed, the Court of Claims considered a
second amended petition by the Seminole Nation concerning the
annuities claims. The court disallowed half of the claims, awarded
the Nation $18,388.30 for the other claims, and found that the
United States was entitled to gratuity offsets in the amount of
$705,337.33, resulting in dismissal and no monetary award to
the Nation.[8]

The Seminole Nation appealed, and the annuities case went
to the Supreme Court again. In 1942 the Supreme Court upheld
the Court of Claims' disallowance of most of the claims. The
Supreme Court found that the federal government properly diverted
and disbursed a large portion of the annuities for clothing and
feeding refugee and destitute Indians driven from their homes
during the Civil War because of their loyalty to the Union; that the
post–Civil War 1866 treaty contained a release of federal liability;
that there had been no treaty violations; and that the gratuity off-sets
in favor of the United States were proper. The Court remanded
two issues to the Court of Claims for further material findings
of fact: whether "the Seminole tribal officers were mulcting the
Nation from 1899 to 1907" with the knowledge of federal officials,

and whether the Seminole Nation received the benefit of the annuities received and expended by the treasurer. In remanding those claims, the Supreme Court emphasized the United States' fiduciary responsibility to Indians, stating that the federal government's conduct, as disclosed in the acts of those who represent it in dealings with the Indians, should be judged by the most exacting fiduciary standards.[9]

After the Supreme Court's remand of the annuities case, in 1944 the Court of Claims again ruled in favor of the United States, finding that the Seminole Nation received the benefits of the annuity payments in the total amount of $66,422.64 made to the Seminole treasurer for the time period from 1870 to 1874 and received the benefits of annuity payments in the total amount of $864,702.58 made from 1899 through 1907. The Court of Claims made detailed findings of fact concerning allegations that Chief John Brown and his brother, Jackson Brown, who was the Nation's treasurer, misappropriated tribal funds through their personal business operations. The brothers owned trading posts in Wewoka, where Treasurer Brown resided, and in Sasakwa, where Chief Brown resided. The allegations focused primarily on the practice of providing credit to Seminole members at the Wewoka Trading Company by issuing a form of scrip known as "chokasutka," which was redeemable as merchandise at the store and which Treasurer Brown paid off when the federal government made annuity payments. The Court of Claims stated its "suspicion" that the prices of goods at the Wewoka Trading Company were higher than the prices of similar goods at other stores, but it found that there was little, if any, creditable evidence that exorbitant prices were charged for the merchandise. The court concluded that it was not shown that the tribal officers were "mulcting" the Nation.[10]

During the same period that the annuities case was being litigated, the Seminole Nation was also pursuing a separate land takings case involving erroneous surveys that established the eastern and western boundaries of the Seminole Nation after the Civil War. Under the 1866 Creek treaty, the Muscogee Nation had agreed to cede 200,000 acres of land to the Seminole Nation.

Boundary issues surfaced in 1871 when a survey known as the Bardwell survey placed the dividing line between the Seminole Nation and the Creek Nation seven miles west of the Seminole Nation's eastern boundary line established by the earlier 1868 Rankin survey. This boundary line decreased the Seminoles' land area along its eastern boundary, a considerable portion of which had been occupied and improved by Seminoles. As a result, the United States had purchased lands in that area from the Creek Nation, with the intention that the boundary would be drawn so that the newly purchased tract would include 175,000 acres in addition to the original 200,000-acre tract. Suspicions arose years later, in 1900, that there was another deficiency in the original 200,000-acre tract, this time on the western portion of the Seminole Nation, where lands had been allotted to members of the Potawatomi Tribe.[11]

The Seminole Nation filed the survey claims case in 1937, alleging a deficiency of 11,550.54 acres with regard to the original 200,000-acre tract and seeking compensation for the value at the time of the taking, plus interest. Without determining damages arising from a shortage, the Court of Claims concluded that the Seminole Nation was more than compensated for any shortage by the purchase of the additional 175,000-acre tract from the Creek Nation and that an offset for the value of that acreage would exceed the value of the land shortage. In 1942 the Supreme Court reversed and remanded the case on the basis of its conclusion that the Court of Claims should have determined whether money was due from the United States before considering offsets. The Court of Claims reconsidered the survey case and the annuities case jointly in 1944, because it was required to consider all federal offsets to the extent the Nation was found to be entitled to damages in either or both cases. Although the Court of Claims found that the Nation was not entitled to any damages in the annuities case, it ruled that the Seminole Nation was entitled to compensation in the land survey claim in the amount of $202,678. However, it awarded nothing to the Nation, finding that the United States' payment of "gratuities" for such purposes as clothing, education, delegation expenses, livestock, medical attention, agricultural implements and equipment, farmers' expenses, presents, provisions, and other rations, in the total amount of $221,569, entirely offset the compensation for the land.[12]

Another claims case, this one involving the Seminole freedmen, was litigated over the span of many years and ended in another failure for the Seminoles. The Seminole Nation first filed the claim in the Court of Claims in 1930, asserting that during allotment, the United States distributed a vast acreage of tribal lands and tribal funds to at least 986 Seminole freedmen without authorization from the Seminole Nation. In 1933, the Court of Claims rejected this claim and dismissed the case, on the basis of article 2 of the Seminole Nation's 1866 treaty, the Seminole allotment agreement, and the supplemental Seminole allotment agreement. Article 2 of the treaty provided that persons of African descent and blood "among the Seminoles," and their descendants, would "have and enjoy all the rights of native citizens," and that the Nation's laws would be "equally binding upon all persons of whatever race or color, who may be adopted as citizens or members" of the Nation. The Court of Claims ruled that in the 1866 treaty the Seminole Nation had granted all the rights of native members or citizens to the freedmen, including both civil rights and property rights. The court rejected the Nation's argument that article 2 granted Seminole freedmen only the political rights and immunities enjoyed by all the members of the Seminole Nation, not any interest in or title to Seminole communal lands and tribal funds. The court noted that the 1866 treaty did not free Seminole slaves—that action had already been accomplished by Seminole law three years before the tribe entered into the 1866 treaty. The court found that the treaty was to be construed in light of conditions as they existed in 1866 and reasoned that at the time the treaty was made, the question of allotments in severalty was distant, lands were of comparatively little value, vast acreages of Indian reservations were set aside, and the question of the number of individuals composing the Seminole Nation "was in no sense so important or acute as it subsequently became when the date of allotment arrived and the lands had materially increased in value."[13]

In other words, in the Court of Claims' view, in 1866 native Seminoles had no reason to consider that they might have more at stake sometime in the future and therefore did not consider expressly protecting their future property interests when negotiating the 1866 treaty. Ironically, and although not noted by the court, Congress itself targeted the freedmen to be the first to lose federal protections of their allotments shortly after allotment in the early twentieth century, a process that quickly resulted in the sale of much of their lands to non-Indian settlers. It was those non-Indian settlers who ultimately ended up being the true beneficiaries of the 1866 treaty as interpreted by the court. After the Nation amended its petition, the Court of Claims found no new issues, adopted the 1933 opinion, and again dismissed the case.[14]

A similar claim concerning freedmen acquisition of tribal assets during allotment was heard almost thirty years later by the Indian Claims Commission in Docket 152. The commission considered new arguments by the Seminole Nation that were based on new grounds for relief under the 1946 Indian Claims Commission Act. The Nation contended that the 1866 treaty, the Seminole allotment agreement, and the Seminole supplemental allotment agreement were tainted by unfair or dishonorable dealings by the federal government. Although the commission found that it could not reconsider any factual issues previously decided by the Court of Claims, it nonetheless produced an additional detailed description of negotiations of the 1866 treaty. The commission rejected Seminole arguments that only a few leaders had signed a treaty with the Confederacy—not the Seminole government. The commission accordingly found that there was no duress or intimidation in federal threats during the 1866 treaty negotiations and that, because of the Seminole "treaty" with the Confederacy during the Civil War, the federal government could require the forfeiture of all of the Nation's previous treaties if it wished. The commission, like the Court of Claims in the earlier freedmen case, dismissed the suit in 1962, finding that the Nation had failed to present a case upon which relief could be granted. Although the freedmen claims cases were determinative of the Nation's claims to damages against the United States for loss of tribal property distributed to freedmen members, they were not determinative of the Nation's right to establish new requirements restricting tribal membership to members with Indian blood, which continued to be an issue in the Seminole Nation in the late twentieth century.[15]

The Seminole Nation also lost claims before the Court of Claims and the Indian Claims Commission involving the value of the townsite of Wewoka. The Oklahoma Seminoles took the position that the sale of more than 3,100 Wewoka town lots to Seminole chief John F. Brown in 1900, which had been specifically approved by the Seminole Council, was the result of an unconscionable contract. The Seminoles also argued that the United States failed to protect the Seminole Nation when it enacted a 1905 law that ratified and confirmed the Nation's sale of the townsite to Chief Brown. The Court of Claims dismissed the suit in 1941 after ruling that the court's jurisdiction to render judgment "in any and all legal and equitable claims" could not be construed to embrace a claim founded upon an allegation that a former act of Congress was fraudulent. The court also noted that the United States did not appropriate the land for its own benefit or for the benefit of another, and it further stated that any mere inadequacy of payment was not sufficient to establish fraud. The Nation later filed the claim before the Indian Claims Commission as Docket 53, but in 1952 the commission also rejected the claim. The commission found that there was insufficient proof of fraud, that when the deed was issued in 1900 the Seminole Nation was a self-governing tribe, that the United States was honoring what the Nation wanted, and that the United States did not benefit from the transaction.[16]

In 1958, five years after the final resolution of the Wewoka Townsite case, the Indian Claims Commission rejected claims concerning a group known as the "Loyal Seminoles" in Indian Claims Commission Docket 121. These claims were filed by three members of the Seminole Nation—Lincoln Burden, Willie Haney, and Buddig Little—on behalf of themselves and the "Loyal Group of Seminole American Indians," who sought an award based on a "fair and honorable dealings" theory. They claimed compensation arising from a federal promise to compensate Seminoles who had remained loyal to the United States for their losses during the Civil War. The Indian Claims Commission dismissed their case, finding that it had previously been settled when Congress appropriated $186,000 for the loyal Seminole claim in 1900. The Indian Claims Commission ruled that the Senate was acting as an arbitrator in 1900, that its decision determined the rights of the parties just as effectively as a judgment by a court, and that Seminole claimants were barred from recovery on a claim that was already subject to final judgment. In 1963, the Indian Claims Commission rejected a similar claim filed by the Seminole Nation (identified as Docket 205) after the commission concluded that there were no violations of fair and honorable dealings in negotiation of the 1866 treaty and the 1900 payments made for the loyal Seminoles. In 1965 the Court of Claims affirmed that decision.[17]

In 1926 the Seminole and Creek Nations filed claims before the Court of Claims involving railroads; these claims were consolidated. The tribes sought payment from the United States on the basis of the federal government's failure to enforce treaties and statutes concerning railroad use of lands within their domains, alleging that the railroads had taken and held certain station reservations unnecessary for railroad purposes for their own benefit, that the railroads had received rents and profits from the use of those lands, and that the railroads failed to pay the annual mileage charge. The Court of Claims dismissed the cases in 1942, ruling that the special jurisdictional acts did not permit suits based on alleged federal fiduciary duties to tribes. On appeal, in 1943 the Supreme Court affirmed the Court of Claims decision, holding that the United States had not assumed treaty or statutory obligations that required it to indemnify the Seminole and Creek Nations for injuries alleged to have been suffered by them as a result of the seizure and use of their land by private railroad companies. The Court found that the guarantee of the right to quiet possession in the Creek Nation's 1866 treaty, although not an "empty promise," did not obligate the United States to compensate the tribes for the encroachments by railroads. The Court stated that in view of "the pressures of the time," the federal government appeared "to have treated its obligation with real care." In considering a 1902 act requiring an annual charge to the railroads, the Court further stated, "No word was said indicating that the United States, acting as a voluntary tax collector for the tribes, meant to guarantee to the tribes that the taxpayers would make their payments when due."[18]

Many years later, in the seventies, the Seminole Nation also lost similar railroad takings claims in Indian Claims Commission Docket 247, which was based on the fair and honorable dealings clause of the 1946 Indian Claims Commission Act. There was, however, one case the Seminole Nation won: a finding by the Court of Claims on appeal that it was not fair and honorable for the 1906 act to vest in municipalities the title to lands that were the sites of abandoned railroad stations. The Seminole railroad claim was eventually settled in 1980 for $100,000.[19]

The Seminole Nation also succeeded in three other claims against the federal government. Two of these claims resulted in relatively small awards. The first such claim resulted in a 1958 decision of the Indian Claims Commission in Docket 150, affirmed by the Court of Claims in 1959, related to the federal government's 1924 sale of the 320-acre Emahaka Mission lands. The sale had been protested by John Burgess and other Seminole members, and tribal leaders refused to sign the deed. The Secretary of the Interior eventually signed the deed over the Seminoles' protests. Under the terms of the sale, the government was authorized to cancel the deed if the buyer failed to make all of the required installment payments, which, as the Court of Claims stated, "lodged in the Secretary a high degree of responsibility to the Seminole Nation." Although the value of the property had increased because of the discovery of oil, when the buyer failed to make all of the payments the Secretary gave an extension to the buyer for payment, rather than cancelling the deed as requested by Seminole Nation leaders. The commission ruled that the Secretary of the Interior had not discharged a duty owed by the government to the Seminole Nation, because it had not cancelled the sale and resold the Emahaka lands for the benefit of the Nation at its enhanced value. The commission awarded $34,213.66 to the Seminole Nation for the claim on the basis of the $64,000 value of the tract, deduction of $29,786.34 for payments already made, and deduction of an off-set of $160. Congress appropriated funds to pay the Emahaka judgment in 1959.[20]

The second claim that resulted in an award involved the federal government's approval of the Gypsy Oil Company's 1926 lease of the oil and gas underlying the Seminole Nation's 320-acre Mekusukey Mission School lands. In 1964 the Indian Claims Commission ruled in Docket 248 that the lease violated fair and honorable dealings under the Indian Claims Commission Act. The commission found that the persons responsible for the lease were remiss in their duties, and the sale was not conducted in accordance with statutory regulations and procedures approved by the commissioner of Indian Affairs, such as advertising at least thirty days prior to the lease sale. The commission further found that oil was discovered in Seminole County in 1923, just two miles southeast of Wewoka, known as the "Wewoka Field." The commission determined that by December 1925 wells in the area were producing a higher yield and that in 1926 and 1927 the area known as the Greater Seminole Area underwent substantial growth. The commission concluded that the amount paid for the lease was considerably less than the fair market value at the time of the sale. The commission awarded $63,680 to the Seminole Nation on the basis of the $96,000 lease value, less $32,320 paid for the lease. Congress appropriated funds to pay the Mekasukey judgment in 1966.[21]

A third successful case, and the one that was most beneficial to the Seminole Nation, was a consolidation of Indian Claims Commission Docket 73, filed by the Seminole Tribe of Florida, and Docket 151, filed by the Seminole Nation of Oklahoma. In the consolidated case, the two tribes sought compensation for the 1823 loss of Seminole aboriginal lands in Florida under the Treaty of

Camp Moultrie. In 1964, the Indian Claims Commission ruled that the tribes had satisfactorily established their Indian title, at the time of the loss, to all of the state of Florida, with a few specific areas excepted. The United States appealed that decision to the Court of Claims, which affirmed the decision in 1967 after review-ing in some detail the record in the case concerning the history of the occupancy and use of the land from 1512 until 1819.[22]

The Court of Claims returned the case to the Indian Claims Commission for further proceedings, and the commission awarded $12,262,781 to the tribes in 1970, after deducting an offset in the amount of $84,719 for certain federal land expenditures. The award figure was significantly less than the valuation of almost $48,000,000 by the tribe's expert, and it was somewhat higher than the valua-tion of $5,500,000 by the United States' expert. After both parties appealed, the Court of Claims found in 1972 that the commission had not provided sufficient discussion of the basis for its value determination. The Court of Claims stated that it was "unable to say" whether the commission's ultimate conclusions on valuation were adequately supported by substantial evidence, and it remanded the case back to the commission. The Court of Claims also ordered that an overlapping Creek claim to a portion of the Florida lands be consolidated with the Seminole claims, but the Creek claim was later dismissed.[23]

The Seminoles and the United States eventually agreed on a final settlement of the case four years later that required the United States to compensate the tribes in the amount of $16,000,000, with no offsets. The Indian Claims Commission made detailed findings and issued an order approving the settlement on April 27, 1976. Congress appropriated funds to satisfy the award in June 1976. However, because of disagreement between the two tribes regarding the division of the award, the tribes did not have access to the funds until they reached agreement and Congress enacted a law in 1990 governing the use and distribution of the funds. The 1990 law allocated 75.404 percent of the award to the Seminole Nation and 24.596 percent of the award to the Seminole Tribe of Florida, the Miccosukee Tribe of Indians of Florida, and the independent

Seminole Indians of Florida, with specified percentages to be distributed to them. By that time, because of accrued interest on the judgment funds, the total Seminole claims award had increased substantially, and the Seminole Nation of Oklahoma's share had grown to approximately $42.2 million. After enactment of the 1990 law, the leaders of the Seminole Nation were tasked with developing a plan to govern the use of the funds, which were held in trust by the United States on behalf of the Seminole Nation. Thus, more than a century and a half after the Seminoles lost their Florida domains, the Seminole Nation was finally granted restitution in an amount sufficient to provide significant interest income, which boosted the Nation's ability to provide services and benefits to Seminole members.[24]

CHAPTER 5

ENDEAVORING TO PERSEVERE

Continuance of Seminole Government, 1906–1968

In the face of almost overwhelming adversity, including poverty, a cultural clash with the flood of non-Indians coming into the Seminole Nation, imposition of state court involvement in individual restricted allotment matters, interference in tribal affairs by federal officials, and lack of control over tribal resources, Seminole citizens nevertheless maintained a strong cultural and governmental identity during the era that began at the time of statehood and lasted through the 1960s. The Seminoles' strong identity was reflected by their continuing use of the Mvskoke language, involvement in native religious activities at ceremonial grounds, maintenance of a governmental structure, and participation in communal social activities, including stickball, baseball, and church functions. During this era when the Seminole Nation was maintaining its cultural and governmental identity, it was also biding its time, waiting for an improvement in the national political climate regarding Indian affairs. When such changes did arrive, including transformations in federal policy that resulted in the availability of federal funding for tribal governmental operations, the Seminoles began to see more hope for reorganizing their tribal government and achieving some measure of success in their litigation of tribal claims against the United States.

Before Oklahoma statehood in 1907, Seminole government operations were funded by the sale of hay, a foreign tax for cattle grazing, and interest on tribal funds invested by the federal government.[1] After statehood, tribal leaders found it increasingly difficult to maintain government operations because of federal officials' grip on tribal funds and resources. While Seminole citizens steadfastly exercised their right to act as a government to the greatest extent possible without access to funding, federal administrative officials refused to recognize their governmental status, in spite of federal court decisions that the Five Tribes still existed.[2]

Federal interference contributed to confusion, dissatisfaction, and dissent within the Seminole Nation for decades. Occasionally individual tribal members requested federal intervention in governmental matters, but more often than not, federal officials leapt into action on their own. Federal officials' unwarranted involvement in Seminole affairs began as early as 1907, when the Seminole Council enacted legislation continuing incumbent officers in their positions. This action was opposed by many Seminole citizens, who correctly believed that the Five Tribes Act's express continuation of the Five Tribes existence entitled the Seminole Nation to elect new officers. Agreeing with that view, F. E. Leupp, the commissioner of Indian Affairs from 1905 until 1909, recommended to the Secretary of the Interior in 1907 that an election be called for the purpose of electing tribal officers in accordance with Seminole laws. In 1908 he also recommended that Congress pass legislation to pay salaries to Seminole Council members. However, the acting secretary declined to follow these recommendations, based on his belief that Congress "intended that the existing status of the Five Civilized Tribes, so far as their officials were concerned, were not to be disturbed during the short remaining period of tribal existence." The incumbent chief, John Brown, continued to serve in office until his death in 1919.[3]

Federal officials used a number of tactics to keep the leaders of the Five Tribes in check. One early method of doing so was to restrict the tribes' freedom to select legal counsel. For example, in 1915 Cato Sells, the commissioner of Indian Affairs from 1913 until 1921, sent a letter to John F. Brown, noting that the Seminole Nation needed a tribal attorney. The commissioner suggested that Chief Brown call a meeting of the Seminole Council, limited to a one- or two-day session, to authorize the employment of the attorney. The commissioner stated that the council should leave the federal government a free hand in drafting the contract and refrain from designating a particular person.[4]

More often, federal officials preempted the tribal government's use of tribal funds, determining on their own how tribal funds should be spent. Congress permitted this practice to some extent but eventually began placing legislative restrictions on federal officials' control and use of tribal funds. In 1916, Congress included a provision in appropriations legislation that no moneys could be expended from tribal funds belonging to the Five Tribes without specific congressional appropriations, except for certain purposes listed in the act, including per capita payments, certain attorney contracts, funding for tribal and other Indian schools, and salaries and expenses for governors, chiefs, assistant chiefs, secretaries, interpreters, and mining trustees. This limitation on federal officials' control and use of tribal funds was continued in subsequent appropriations acts and was made permanent by legislation in 1922 that prohibited federal expenditures of Five Tribes funds without specific appropriations.[5]

Congress occasionally appropriated Seminole tribal funds for per capita payments to tribal members at times when the Seminoles were facing the most severe hardships. Such times included the decade immediately following enactment of a 1908 law that resulted in the rapid loss of Seminole lands, causing great poverty. During part of this period, World War I was fought by many patriotic Seminoles, including those serving as Indian codetalkers who radioed messages in their native tongues to avoid enemy interception. In 1913 Congress directed the Secretary of the Interior to make a per capita payment of $200 from Seminole tribal funds to each enrolled tribal member, "to relieve the distressed condition at present existing among the allottees of that tribe." In 1916 Congress allowed the secretary to make per capita payments of $300 from Seminole tribal funds to members and their lawful heirs but provided that the Secretary of the Interior could withhold those payments from tribal members "who belong to the restricted class" and use it for their benefit. In 1917 Congress approved another per capita payment, not to exceed $200. Because the larger part of the Seminole funds had been previously set aside in a school fund, the per capita payment amount was reduced to $34. The following year, Congress approved payments not to exceed $100 per capita and specified that payments should be made from the Seminole school fund or other money belonging to the Seminole Nation. These per capita payments were apparently not always distributed to tribal members' satisfaction, resulting in 1919 legislation that authorized members to file claims for unpaid per capita money, to be adjudicated in accordance with secretarial rules and to be paid from tribal funds.[6]

In 1921 Congress ratified the Snyder Act, which was subsequently relied on by the Indian Office—later renamed the BIA in the late forties—as a source of broad BIA administrative and regulatory powers and functions. The act authorized the Indian Office to direct expenditures of congressional appropriations for the "benefit, care, and assistance of the Indians throughout the United States" under the supervision of the Secretary of the Interior.[7] This strengthening of federal administrative power over Indian affairs contributed to federal officials' belief that they had a free rein with regard to the affairs of the Five Tribes, which a federal court characterized in later years as "bureaucratic imperialism."[8]

It is not surprising that the Seminoles did not react favorably to the Indian Office's attempts to take over their government functions, as demonstrated in the early 1920s by a group of Seminoles who visited Coahuila state in Mexico to investigate whether tribal members should move to Mexico. A small group of Seminole and blacks had located in Mexico almost a century earlier, in 1849, making their more permanent settlement in the 1850s at a site called El Nacimiento, where a group of Kickapoos also settled. Coacoochee, a Seminole leader also known as Wild Cat, had led this eighteenth-century exodus from Seminole lands in Indian Territory. Coacoochee and his followers had exchanged military services to the Mexican government for land. Within a few years after Cooacoochee's death in 1857, the Seminoles had returned to Indian Territory. The objectives of the new potential move in the 1920s were based on a similar desire to escape federal oppression by returning to the Seminole practice of owning tribal property in common and to be free of federal laws imposed on Seminoles in Oklahoma. However, members of the group who visited Mexico in the 1920s, as well as others who had visited at various times after allotment commenced, did not relocate there. Years later, in 1938, the ambassador to Mexico informed the U.S. Department of the Interior that the Mexican government wished to send representatives to Oklahoma to determine living conditions of the Seminoles. Mexico had reportedly offered to settle forty-eight Seminoles in Coahuila state. Later that year, John Collier, the commissioner of Indian Affairs from 1933 until 1945, reported that the proposed migration of Oklahoma Seminoles to Mexico was "very definitely dead." However, for many years some Seminoles maintained an interest in the possibility of Seminole rights to lands in Mexico.[9]

The twenties were a time of struggle for Seminole citizens. There was a huge influx of non-Indians in the twenties because of the oil boom; for example, Wewoka's population rose from 1,520 in 1920 to 10,401 by 1930, and Seminole's population increased from 854 to 11,459 during that same time span. While Seminoles struggled with impoverishment resulting from the rapid loss of their lands, conflicts between the federal government and Seminole citizens also occurred. For example, Seminoles wanted to elect their own chief, but federal officials asserted that section 6 of the Five Tribes Act afforded the U.S. president the exclusive authority to select the chiefs of the Five Tribes; hence, federal officials periodically obtained appointments in order to secure execution of deeds to Seminole lands. In early 1922 federal officials wanted a Seminole chief to sign papers, and Thomas McGeisey, who had been the chairman of a Seminole mass meeting, sent a telegram to Charles H. Burke, who served as the commissioner of Indian Affairs from 1921 until his resignation in early 1929. In the telegram McGeisey protested the federal appointment of Alice B. Davis, sister of the late Chief John F. Brown, as principal chief. The telegram stated that the people desired to select their own chief and asked that the commissioner withhold further consideration of the matter until receipt of a letter from the Seminole Nation. Two days later a petition was sent to the commissioner and the Secretary of the Interior requesting them to explain the necessity for federal appointment of a chief and asking them to withhold action until tribal members had an opportunity to submit recommendations.[10]

President Harding ignored these requests and appointed Alice B. Davis to be chief for thirty days in 1922, and she signed forty documents as requested by federal officials. After she was appointed again in 1923 to sign deeds, she refused to sign some of the deeds because the land had been occupied for many years by Seminole members and had often been used for religious purposes. She also refused to sign a deed to the Emahaka academy land, an eighty-acre tract west of Holdenville and a few miles from Wewoka. The federal government had already auctioned the land in July 1920 without providing a deed to the purchaser. In notifying the Indian Office of her refusal to sign the deed, she said that tribal members were poverty stricken and "The price is so inadequate for this property as to shock the conscience of a court of equity, and I feel at this time, to sign this instrument, would be a great injustice to my people, and not in keeping with the trust they have reposed in me."[11]

There was an ongoing struggle between Seminoles and federal officials, as the Seminoles continued to seek federal acknowledgment of their right to select their own chief and continued to protest the proposed sale of the Emahaka Mission lands. In 1924 George Jones, chairman of the Seminole Council, sent a letter to the Secretary of the Interior notifying him of a Seminole protest against the conveyance of the Emahaka Mission property, stating that the land was needed for educational purposes, noting that the underlying minerals were worth more than the purchase price, and requesting that no deed be issued and that payment be returned to the purchaser. In 1925 George Jones was federally appointed to serve as chief for the purpose of executing more deeds. In late 1925, Jones met with Seminole members to obtain instructions regarding execution of the deeds. It was agreed that he should execute all church deeds, all cemetery deeds, and all deeds to unallotted lands, but that he should not sign deeds to lands set apart for specific purposes by the Seminole Allotment Act. Thus, he signed all the deeds federal officials presented to him except for the one to the Nation's Emahaka Mission lands. Federal officials desired execution of the Emahaka deed by a tribal official even though the Secretary of the Interior had already approved the deed in December 1924 under the 1906 Five Tribes Act, which purported to allow federal officials to sign documents when tribal officials refused to do so. In 1926 Harry Tiger notified Commissioner Burke about the Seminole Nation's desire to take legal action to cancel the deed. The following year, the Emahaka Mission building burned in a "mystery fire." Although the Seminole Nation never recovered possession or title to Emahaka, in 1959 it was successful in securing a judgment in its favor against the United States for additional compensation.[12]

In 1924 Congress enacted a law that made all non-citizen Indians born within the territorial limits of the United States American citizens. This law did not affect members of the Five Tribes, including the Seminole Nation, who had already acquired citizenship in 1901. By the time of the 1924 enactment, the Supreme Court had already issued a decision that citizenship was not incompatible with tribal existence or continued federal guardianship and could be conferred without completely emancipating the Indians or placing them beyond the reach of congressional regulations adopted for their protection.[13]

Although continued federal guardianship proved to be beneficial to the preservation of tribal governmental authority in later years, the manner in which federal officials exercised control over tribal affairs continued to be heavy-handed and not protective of tribal interests. In 1927 Seminole members organized a council with the structure described in the Seminole Nation's 1903 revised statutes, and they elected Harry Hully Tiger as the council chairman. After being advised of this matter, Commissioner Burke sent a letter to Tiger, stating that the federal government had not recognized any elections of Five Tribes chiefs since 1906. Burke stated that on July 13, 1927, the president had appointed Tiger to serve as chief for one day for the purpose of signing deeds, and that Tiger would be notified of the date that he was to "report for duty."[14]

The following year, the 1928 Merriam Report concluded that the two most serious deficiencies in federal administration of Indian affairs were the exclusion of Indians from managing their own affairs and the poor quality of public service provided by public officials. This message went unheeded in Oklahoma. In 1929 C. J. Rhoads, the new commissioner of Indian Affairs, declined a request by Seminole representatives for federal recognition of the Seminole Council as the Seminole people's mouthpiece and recognition of Chili Fish as the newly elected chief. Commissioner Rhoads refused to acknowledge the need for a chief, reasoning that "there are now no tribal deeds or any other unfinished business requiring action by a Principal Chief at this time."[15]

Regardless of federal officials' attempts to interfere with their government, Seminoles demonstrated their own respect for Seminole culture and other Indian cultures by hosting a gathering of tribes on July 3 and 4, 1931, with a grand parade led by Chili Fish, followed by the chiefs of other Indian nations and a few state officials. This was the first, or one of the first, of the annual events later known as "Seminole Nation Days."[16] Seminole leaders also persisted in their efforts to obtain restitution for the past losses the Nation had suffered at the hands of the United States. Those efforts included a plan in 1931 for a Seminole delegation to go to Washington to examine certain records related to their claims. Predictably, Commissioner Rhoads refused their request for release of tribal funds to pay the train fare, noting that they did not state their objectives, "nor does it appear what good purpose would be served." Commissioner Rhoads misinterpreted the 1916 act's prohibition against tribal fund expenditures without specific congressional appropriations as a mandate to block payment of the expenses because the most recent federal appropriations act made no appropriations for salaries and expenses of a Seminole delegation to Washington. That view was contrary to the true purpose of the 1916 act, which was to protect the Five Tribes from federal mismanagement of tribal funds.[17]

In 1931 the Department of the Interior continued the practice of securing appointment of a Seminole chief for the limited purpose of performing acts desired by the department. The president appointed Chili Fish to serve as chief to sign a deed to the Nation's last tract of tribal land: the 320-acre site of the Mekusukey School. Fish declined the appointment, stating, "Consistent with the attitude of the members of the Seminole group in connection with the arbitrary closing of the [Mekusukey] Academy, the property of the Seminole people, we look askance upon the policies of the Department with reference to matters pertaining to our properties and interests."[18]

It was in this climate that Seminole leaders began planning in the summer of 1931 to circulate a petition seeking permission to file suit against the federal government and seeking an accounting of both the $500,000 held in trust for the Seminoles and the royalties on the 1926 lease of the Mekusukey Mission minerals. Seminole leaders also discussed inviting members of the Oklahoma congressional delegation to address a gathering of Seminoles concerning potential legislation that would allow the Nation to file the claims suits.[19]

In early 1932 a delegation of five Seminole members, including Chili Fish, visited Washington in connection with the proposed legislation. The delegation requested Congress to investigate the Secretary of the Interior's 1926 oil and gas lease of the Mekusukey Mission to the Gypsy Oil Company. The Seminole delegation charged that although Congress had made an appropriation to support the Mekusukey Mission school the previous fiscal year, the Department of the Interior closed it without warning and leased the property to the oil company for less than the true value of the lease. The delegation requested that school operations be continued, and that federal officials be stopped from continuing with plans to sell the land.[20]

Soon after that, Congress passed the Act of April 27, 1932, which made all sales, leases, encumbrances, or other dispositions of tribal lands subject to the approval of the Seminole General Council "selected in pursuance of Seminole customs." This legislation prevented federal officials from signing a deed to Mekusukey without tribal approval, as had previously been done in 1924 with the deed to the Emahaka lands. Although the legislation did not restore school operations or provide any monetary relief, the Nation eventually filed suit and was awarded compensation in 1964. Even though the 1932 act clearly reflected congressional recognition of the importance of the Council's general authority over tribal affairs, Commissioner Rhoads chose to interpret it as somehow limiting council authority to only those matters involving disposition of tribal property. During this time, the commissioner also refused to recognize elections for chief that had been held by two factions of the tribe, based on the longstanding federal administrative position that there was no legal authority for such election by the Seminoles.[21]

The Seminoles, led by George Jones, the elected chief, held a council meeting and hosted their second annual hospitality day in July 1932. Jones expressed the Seminoles' hope that they could prove to the federal government, by conservative and constructive progress, that they should be permitted to use their tribal assets, land, and money as their council deemed best for tribal members.[22] Jones expressed this optimism during the Great Depression, shortly before Congress again approved in 1933 per capita payments of Seminole tribal funds to enrolled members of the Seminole Nation or their lawful heirs. The per capita payments were not to exceed $35, and the Secretary of the Interior was given authority to withhold payments from tribal members "who belong to the restricted class" and to use it for their benefit. At a meeting in 1933, Seminole members discussed a notice by Commissioner John Collier concerning the per capita appropriation, with some favoring the per capita payment and others favoring a lump sum payment to the Nation to be expended for emergencies. The issue of whether it was best for the tribal government to control lump sums of tribal funds or for individual member to receive small per capita payments was one that continued to

1930s meeting. *Eighth from left*: Alice Brown Davis, chief in the 1920s and early 1930s); *6th from left*: George Jones, chief in the late 1930s and early 1940s. (Photograph courtesy of the Western History Collections, University of Oklahoma Libraries, Norman)

be a controversial subject in Seminole affairs throughout the twentieth century.[23]

In the early thirties, all three branches of the federal government took actions recognizing the sovereignty of Indian tribes. In 1933 the Supreme Court recognized the significance of treaties with Indian tribes, finding in the landmark case of *Cook v. United States* that a treaty would not be deemed abrogated or modified by later statute unless such purpose had been clearly expressed by Congress.[24] In 1934 Nathan Margold, acting on behalf of the executive branch as the solicitor of the Department of the Interior, issued an opinion popularly referred to in Indian law practice as the "Margold opinion." The Margold opinion recognized that

Indian tribes possessed governmental authority in numerous areas, including the right to determine form of government; power to determine membership; power of taxation; right to exclude non-members from tribal territory; authority over tribal property and rights of occupancy in tribal lands; jurisdiction over members' property; authority in administration of justice; and power to apply Indian customs, laws, and jurisdiction regarding domestic relations and descent and distribution of property. This opinion was not inconsistent with past judicial decisions, but it was a significant reversal of the Department of the Interior's oppressive policies concerning Indian tribes in earlier years.[25]

That same year, a new federal legislative policy favoring tribal self-government for Indian tribes nationwide emerged when Congress enacted the Indian Reorganization Act, also known as the IRA or the Wheeler–Howard Act of 1934. Enacted almost a half a century after the 1887 General Allotment Act, which had started the allotment period for tribes throughout the United States, the IRA explicitly prohibited allotment. In discussing the application of the failed allotment and assimilation policies, Representative Howard, one of the primary authors of the act, stated that those policies had "not stopped with the mere destruction of the material assets of the Indians." He described the federal government's application of these policies as "an extraordinary example of political absolutism in the midst of a free democracy . . . which caused methods of repression and suppression unparalleled in the modern world outside of Czarist Russia and the Belgian Congo."[26]

Most of the IRA applied to tribes in Oklahoma, including authorization of the Secretary of the Interior to acquire lands for individual Indians and Indian tribes, authorization to restore surplus reservation lands to tribal ownership, and establishment of an Indian preference in federal employment. However, six sections of the IRA were not applicable to twenty-eight listed Oklahoma tribes, including the Seminole Nation. This exclusion was requested by Senator Thomas of Oklahoma, chairman of the Senate Indian Affairs Committee, who promised that he would conduct studies with regard to the need for such provisions in Oklahoma. Three of the inapplicable IRA sections included protecting Indian lands by extending the trust periods "until otherwise directed by Congress," imposing restrictions on transfer of Indian lands, and allowing the establishment of new reservations. Two other inapplicable sections concerned tribal government and business activities. These sections authorized two distinct types of tribal organization: organization of a tribal government for its common welfare by adoption of "an appropriate constitution and bylaws" and organization of a tribal business entity by tribal ratification of a charter of incorporation subject to federal approval. The final IRA section that was inapplicable to Oklahoma tribes allowed "any reservation" to vote against application of the IRA to that reservation in an election to be called within a year of enactment of the IRA.[27] Apparently finding no need for a federal law authorizing tribal reorganization, Seminole citizens drafted a brief Seminole organizational document a few days before the IRA became law.[28]

In 1936, two years after enactment of the IRA, Congress passed the Oklahoma Indian Welfare Act, also known as the OIWA or the Thomas–Rogers Act. The OIWA was designed to meet the special needs of Oklahoma Indians, with the exception of the Osage Nation. Although Congress recognized that the federal laws applicable in eastern Oklahoma with respect to the Five Tribes were distinct from the federal laws applicable in western Oklahoma with regard to other tribes, it chose not to make any distinction in the OIWA's treatment of the tribes in eastern and western Oklahoma. This uniform treatment demonstrated a congressional view that the Five Tribes and other Oklahoma tribes possessed the same governmental status as other tribes nationwide. Consistent with that view, the OIWA specifically recognized the right of Oklahoma tribes to organize for their common welfare and to adopt a constitution and bylaws under rules and regulations prescribed by the Secretary of the Interior. The OIWA, unlike the IRA, further strengthened tribal sovereignty by repealing all prior inconsistent laws. Although this action did not result in a wholesale repeal of past federal laws interpreted by federal officials as limiting the Five

Tribes home rule, it was indicative of Congress's intent to establish a new policy for Oklahoma tribes and was later interpreted
as repealing provisions in the Curtis Act that had abolished the
judicial authority of some of the Five Tribes.[29]

Commissioner of Indian Affairs John Collier, who was labeled
by past Commissioner Burke as a "notorious Indian agitator,"
was extremely supportive of facilitating tribal self-government in
Oklahoma through enactment of the OIWA. According to Collier,
self-government was "enormously important," because Congress
and the Supreme Court had "clothed the Interior Department with
almost czar-like powers, plenary and substantial unreviewable
powers, and it is that peculiar fact which leaves the Indians bereft
of essential citizenship rights." He noted that there were repeated
experiences in the past thirty years of "having a department wan-
tonly, just tear to pieces an Indian tribal organization . . . outlaw
it, shatter it, tell it to go to hell, and, of course under those conditions Indians are not going to get very far in organizing for mutual
benefit." Collier stated that after a tribe adopted and secured
secretarial approval of a constitution under the OIWA, the secretary would be bound by that and would not be able to change the
constitution except with the tribe's consent through a majority
vote. He stressed that this was "merely the right of the people
who have a common interest to unite and to hold themselves
together, even if the Interior Department does not want them to."[30]

The OIWA also contained provisions intended to foster tribal
economic development. The act allowed the Secretary of the
Interior to issue a charter of incorporation to tribes organized
under the OIWA, which would become operative when ratified
by a majority vote of the adult members who voted, provided that
at least 30 percent of those entitled to vote actually voted. The
OIWA provided that the charter might convey, in addition to any
powers that might properly be vested in a body incorporated
under the laws of the state of Oklahoma, the right to participate
in a revolving credit fund and to "enjoy any other rights or privileges secured to an organized Indian tribe" under the IRA. It also
allowed the creation of cooperative associations by Indian groups,

authorized loans to individuals or corporate groups, and entitled Oklahoma Indians to a "fair and just share" of funds thereafter appropriated under the IRA. The OIWA required that any royalties, bonuses, or other revenues derived from mineral deposits underlying lands purchased in Oklahoma under authority of the OIWA or IRA be deposited in the U.S. Treasury, and that they be used by the secretary for the acquisition of lands and for loans to Oklahoma Indians as authorized by the IRA. The act also authorized the Secretary of the Interior to make any necessary rules and regulations.[31]

Enactment of the OIWA did not improve relations between federal officials and the Seminole government. The Seminole Council reelected George Jones as chief in July 1937, and tribal leaders drafted a resolution charging that federal, state, and Seminole County officers had been negligent and requesting establishment of a special U.S. marshal's office to protect the general welfare of tribal members.[32] In 1938, the superintendent of the Five Tribes Agency viewed Seminole activities as a display of "interest" in organization as a tribe but believed that there were "a number of hurdles to jump before any effective action" could be taken. According to the superintendent, the principal issue involving Seminole organization under the OIWA was whether the Seminole freedmen would share in any tribal assets or tribal organization. The superintendent felt that organization should not be "pressed."[33]

Possibly unaware of federal officials' belief that their governmental activities merely expressed an "interest" in tribal organization, the Seminole Council met in 1938 and 1939 to address a variety of matters, including the appointment of a committee to help indigent members, insurance for the Mekusukey Mission buildings, a protest against the location of an Indian Office agency at Wewoka, and construction of a tribal building.[34] The Seminoles' desire for a tribal building was heeded by Congress, which, in 1939, approved an expenditure from tribal funds in the amount of $7,787 for the construction of a community house for the Seminoles.[35]

Most of the federal legislation enacted after the IRA and the OIWA were passed did not distinguish Oklahoma tribes from other tribes. Nonetheless, misunderstandings about the status of the Seminole Nation and other Oklahoma tribes caused them to lose some advantages—including federal funding for housing assistance—that were enjoyed by other tribes. After Congress enacted the 1937 Housing Act, non-Oklahoma tribes received federal funding to be administered by tribal housing authorities established under tribal law. Oklahoma tribes were not afforded this opportunity, because the U.S. Department of Housing and Urban Development relied on the Department of the Interior's unofficial opinion that Oklahoma tribes did not possess the authority to create their housing authorities under tribal laws. Oklahoma tribes, whose members were in dire need of housing, received no direct federal housing funding until a state law was enacted in 1965 that enabled Oklahoma tribes to establish their housing authorities under state law.[36]

The Seminole Nation continued to elect its chiefs in the 1940s. In May 1940, the Seminoles held an election for chief and assistant chief. George Jones, known as Estahakee, was up for reelection as chief for a third term, running against Alex Harjo. Willie Haney and Buddy Little were candidates for assistant chief, a position held at that time by Chili Fish. The election was held at the Meku-sukey Mission grounds near Seminole, with votes cast by male Seminole Indian and male freedmen. Willie Haney and Jeffie Brown also held the office of Seminole chief in the mid-to-late forties. George Harjo served in the late forties and early fifties.[37]

In the forties, the Seminole Council increased its efforts to secure more federal support of its various governmental objectives.[38] In late 1944, council members repeated requests that the Seminole representatives had made five years before, including the following: construction of a clinic and council house on Mekusukey land, appropriations to finance local government, continuation of the federal prohibition of liquor for the tribe (to be enforced by tribal officers), continuation of certain restrictions, approval of the school system, and creation of a special commission to hear claims by the Seminole Nation against the United States.[39] That same year, the council also passed a resolution requesting the president to appoint Waddie Gibbs to serve as chief. The Seminole Nation's Railroad and Attorneys Committee, which handled appropriation requests for tribal operational expenses for 1946 and 1947, also requested assistance with matters such as health needs and maintenance of the Mekusukey Mission property, and it sought a report from attorney Paul Niebell in 1946 regarding the Nation's claims cases.[40] The Indian Credit Association, which was organized in 1938 to provide a loan program to benefit persons of at least one-fourth Indian blood for livestock, farming implements, housing repairs, and home furnishings, continued to meet in the forties as well.[41]

After World War II, in which many Seminoles fought for their country, the Five Tribes returned to their past practice of combining resources to attempt to achieve common objectives, including lobbying Congress to address educational and social welfare issues. Leaders of the Five Tribes, including Seminole attorney Charles Grounds, formed the Inter-Tribal Council of the Five Civilized Tribes on October 20, 1949, following a period in which tribal leaders met regularly as a group with the BIA Muskogee Area director, W. O. Roberts, to discuss congressional activities and protection of the tribes. After its formation, the Inter-Tribal Council acted as an important unified tribal force both in negotiating, litigating, and otherwise dealing with state opposition to tribal governmental authority through the remainder of the twentieth century and in seeking and obtaining congressional legislation for the betterment of tribal members.[42]

In 1948 Congress enacted a law defining the term "Indian country" for implementation of the Major Crimes Act, which required federal prosecutions of certain major crimes involving Indian victims and Indian offenders on Indian country.[43] The definitions in the 1948 act were based on Supreme Court decisions rendered in 1913, 1914, 1936, and 1938, finding that Indian reservations, restricted and trust allotments, and dependent Indian communities were all Indian country and, as such, were all subject to federal, rather than state, court authority over certain federal crimes committed there. Those decisions each applied the same basic test for Indian country: whether lands had been validly set apart for the use of Indians as such, under the superintendence of the federal government.[44] In codifying the definition of "Indian country," Congress expanded the reference to "Indian reservation" to include all lands, whether Indian trust lands or non-Indian fee lands, within an Indian reservation. This expanded definition was significant, because it recognized the Indian country status of larger areas of lands for federal law enforcement purposes and, in many cases, for purposes of tribal governmental authority, rather than limiting federal and tribal jurisdiction to parcels of trust and restricted lands.[45]

The importance of the definition of Indian country with regard to the exercise of tribal governmental powers became more clear when the Supreme Court issued a landmark decision in 1959 in *Williams v. Lee.* In that case, the Court ruled that the Arizona state courts had no authority to hear a suit by a non-Indian storekeeper on the Navajo reservation to collect a debt owed by a Navajo Indian living on the reservation, because that would undermine the authority of the tribal courts over reservation affairs and would be an infringement of the Indians' right to govern themselves.[46]

The 1948 law defining Indian country went unremarked in Oklahoma for many years, in spite of earlier federal court decisions recognizing continued federal jurisdiction over certain activities on Five Tribes Indian country. For example, in 1911 the Tenth Circuit held that Indian Territory did not cease to be Indian country upon statehood and that statehood did not affect the applicability of federal liquor laws there. The Supreme Court reached a similar conclusion in 1913, finding that the Oklahoma Enabling Act and statehood did not repeal pre-statehood federal laws governing the introduction of alcohol in what was then known as Indian Territory. Although a 1934 law was eventually enacted specifically ending applicability of Indian liquor laws in the former Indian Territory, these early decisions reflected federal court recognition of the continued federal, as opposed to state, jurisdiction over Five Tribes members in Indian country, absent express federal legislation to the contrary. Consistent with that view, the Supreme Court issued decisions in 1916 and 1918 recognizing that no territorial government was ever created in the reduced Indian Territory, and that certain matters in the territory remained directly subject to federal governance.[47]

Notwithstanding these court decisions, somewhere along the way, a general belief that the state had acquired jurisdiction over Five Tribes members' activities on restricted lands became the prevailing view of federal and state officials. As a result, throughout most of the twentieth century the Oklahoma state courts heard cases arising on Indian trust and restricted lands in the state, including major crimes involving Indian offenders and Indian victims. In 1936, before enactment of the 1948 law codifying the definition of Indian country, the Oklahoma Court of Criminal Appeals ruled in *Ex Parte Nowabbi* that an individual restricted Choctaw allotment was not an Indian reservation, and it concluded that a murder of an Indian by another Indian on the allotment was subject to state jurisdiction, rather than federal jurisdiction under the Major Crimes Act. The court failed to consider previous Supreme Court rulings that trust and restricted Indian allotments constituted Indian country, including the Supreme Court's 1926 ruling in *United States v. Ramsey* that a restricted Osage allotment in Oklahoma was Indian country and that crimes by Indians against Indian victims on such allotments were subject to federal prosecution under the Major Crimes Act. The *Nowabbi* case, and other federal and state cases resulting in similar rulings with regard to Indian trust allotments in western Oklahoma, remained unchallenged for more than four decades, until distinguished, and in some cases overruled, by federal and state cases findings in the late seventies and later years that Indian trust allotments and tribal trust lands in both eastern and western Oklahoma constituted Indian country.[48]

The *Nowabbi* case and other early erroneous decisions concerning Indian country in Oklahoma affected the ability of Oklahoma tribes, including the Seminole Nation, to exercise governmental authority over a geographical land base through much of the twentieth century. Oklahoma tribes were characterized as "non-reservation" tribes with no jurisdiction over individual and tribal trust lands. State and federal officials accordingly took the position that crimes and other activities on trust and restricted lands were subject to exclusive state authority in most instances, except for the actual disposition and use of restricted and trust lands, which were governed by federal laws. Thus, although numerous other tribal governments nationwide exercised civil regulatory authority described in the 1934 Margold opinion, such as authority over domestic relations and taxation, the Seminoles and many other Oklahoma tribes faced an uphill battle in exercising governmental powers. Unlike tribes in other parts of the country, most tribes in Oklahoma did not exercise law enforcement powers over tribal members for the greater part of the twentieth century, until tribal courts were established under tribal law or until BIA courts— known as "Courts of Indian Offenses" or "CFR Courts"—were established by amendment of the *Code of Federal Regulations*.[49]

There was a slight improvement in federal legislative policies with regard to the Five Tribes governments in the fifties. In 1952 Congress enacted legislation that amended 1906 act provisions that had required presidential approval of Five Tribes contracts involving the expenditure of money. The 1952 act authorized the Five Tribes to enter into contracts for the expenditure of any money or affecting any tribal property, subject to the approval of the Secretary of the Interior. This authorization included tribal contracts for legal services, except those involving the prosecution of claims against the United States. That same year a small budget was approved by the BIA for the operation of Seminole government in fiscal year 1953.[50] Unfortunately, this slight policy improvement did not curtail the BIA's paternalistic treatment of the Seminole government during the early fifties. The BIA continued its historic refusal to recognize the elected chiefs as valid representatives of the tribe. In response to rumors that the BIA was maneuvering to eliminate the chieftainships altogether, the Inter-Tribal Council fought back, adopting a resolution in 1954 that advocated the continuance of these Five Tribes offices.[51]

As the Seminole people continued their efforts to maintain a functioning tribal government, federal officials began a new strategy to try to continue their control of tribal affairs: they made decisions as to the validity of elections for the chief and council, particularly when internal tribal election disputes arose. Federal officials refused to recognize actions of those persons they deemed not to have been validly elected, withholding tribal funds to pay their salaries and refusing to recognize their authority. For example, Marcy Cully claimed to be the validly elected chief and was given a certificate of appointment by the Secretary of the Interior in 1952. The secretary later revoked Cully's certificate of appointment after receiving a petition signed by 300 people protesting Cully's appointment, and federal officials refused to pay his salary. Although council members expressed concern that the BIA was impairing their efforts to operate as a tribal government, in 1954 Paul Fickinger, the area director of the Muskogee Area Office, refused to approve an attorney's contract authorized by Cully. In late 1954 the area director met with Seminole groups to discuss who should be appointed chief by the federal government, but no new appointment was made. Instead, Cully served out his term, which ended in 1956, in accordance with tribal laws. Cully was the last Seminole chief appointed by the Department of the Interior, and the Seminole people continued to choose their own leaders throughout the twentieth century and beyond, including Phillip Walker in the late fifties and John A. Brown in the sixties.[52]

During Cully's term, the area director met with the council on some occasions. This action may have been intended to divide the Seminole government, in light of the area director's refusal to recognize the authority of the elected chief. At least some Seminole citizens viewed the area director's activities as a means of acquiring control over the tribal government. In 1958 a group of tribal members formed a committee for reorganization and discussed the problems they had been having. They concluded during one of their meetings that the federal government viewed the chief as having primary authority, with the council in a strong advisory capacity, yet the federal government refused to recognize a chief who had been elected by the people. The committee members also complained that the council consisted of persons who were self-appointed or appointed by the Indian Office, and that the Indian Office was acting in collusion with the council and its chairman to fraudulently and wrongfully spend Seminole funds. They felt that some immediate action was necessary to prevent irreparable injury to the Seminole Nation, but such action apparently did not occur. After the 1958 meeting, the Seminole Council continued to meet to discuss tribal matters, and at least one mass meeting of tribal members occurred in 1961.[53]

The historic federal bureaucratic misperception that the Five Tribes had been terminated and that there was no Indian country in Oklahoma actually worked to the benefit of the Five Tribes and other tribes in Oklahoma in one instance. This belief enabled Oklahoma tribes to escape application of a law popularly referred to as Public Law 280. As originally enacted in 1953, Public Law 280 required some states to assume civil and criminal jurisdiction over Indians and Indian activities in Indian country, and it allowed other states to voluntarily assume such jurisdiction by affirmative legislative action. Oklahoma was classified in the group of states that could voluntarily assume jurisdiction. However, Public Law 280 required that Oklahoma, and other states with constitutional disclaimers of state jurisdiction over Indian lands, could not assume jurisdiction unless they amended their constitutions and enacted affirmative legislation. After Public Law 280 was enacted, the Oklahoma governor took the position that there was no need for Oklahoma to take any action to activate Public Law 280 by constitutional amendment and affirmative legislative action, based on the long-standing belief that there was no Indian country in Oklahoma and that Oklahoma already possessed general criminal and civil jurisdiction over Indian activities on Indian lands. This erroneous belief resulted in inaction on the part of the state with regard to Public Law 280.[54]

Fifteen years later, Public Law 280 was amended by the Indian Civil Rights Act of 1968 to require tribal consent (by tribal referendum) to state civil and criminal jurisdiction before the state could acquire jurisdiction. That tribal consent was never requested of Oklahoma tribes, nor was it given by them. More than a decade after that amendment, state and federal courts ruled that the Oklahoma courts had no jurisdiction over criminal cases and civil disputes involving Indians and arising on Indian restricted and trust lands. The courts also determined that restricted and trust lands constituted Indian country subject to tribal and federal jurisdiction. These later developments strengthened the governmental authority of tribes in Oklahoma and weakened state authority over activities in Indian country.[55]

While the Five Tribes were still struggling in the fifties to overcome misperceptions that their governments were terminated at statehood, a number of other tribes were targeted for real termination. In 1954 and 1956 Congress enacted legislation terminating the governments of more than a dozen tribes, most of which were located in the Northwest, including the Menominee and Klamath tribes. These enactments were experimental efforts to subject Indians to state control without federal support, and to eliminate federal health, education, and general assistance programs to the terminated tribes. Unlike the federal laws that had forced the allotment of Five Tribes lands by threatening tribal governmental existence—which federal officials erroneously characterized as termination legislation—the federal termination laws in the fifties purported to end the trust relationship between the United States and the affected tribes. The termination experiment was not a success, and Congress eventually enacted legislation restoring most of the affected tribes to their status as federally recognized tribes, but it did so only after great hardship to the affected tribes and their members.[56]

Although not subjected to actual termination, the Five Tribes continued to struggle in the sixties with misperceptions that their tribes had been terminated. In 1964, Congress enacted the Economic Opportunity Act, which provided funding for community action programs to be operated by the states, political subdivisions of the states, and tribal governments. The benefits of that law were not immediately available to the Seminole Nation and other Oklahoma tribes, because, as originally enacted, it appeared to restrict its tribal benefits to "a tribal government of an Indian reservation." Federal administrators did not provide funding to Oklahoma tribes under the act for years, because of administrative decisions that there were no Indian reservations in Oklahoma and the belief that Oklahoma tribes did not possess the necessary governmental authority to charter community action programs. Oklahoma tribes faced similar problems in obtaining funding through the Public Works and Economic Development Act of 1965. That law allowed direct funding to Indian tribes that obtained recognition as redevelopment areas by the secretary of labor. Tribes in Oklahoma had difficulty achieving that recognition partly because of that law's focus on areas recognized as Indian reservations and the federal administrative position that there were no reservations in Oklahoma.[57]

Unaided by the federal government, the Seminoles attempted to engage in economic development activities of their own in the sixties. The Seminole Nation invested $85,000 of tribal funds in the early sixties to fund the Plasteck Central Manufacturing plant, which manufactured lighted panels, dials, and electronic circuits for aircraft, as a subcontractor to larger manufacturing companies. This investment was opposed by some Seminole members. The plant opened in 1961 in Wewoka with twenty-two employees. In 1962 it was predicted that forty-one Indians who had vocational training from the BIA would be employed there by July 1962, and that an additional fifty-one Indians would be employed there by 1963. The company name was changed to Wewoka Plastics, Inc., in the summer of 1962, and the company eventually merged with System Engineering Electronics, Inc., in mid-1964. By that time, the plant had only five employees and was close to being shut down; however, it regained strength in 1965, maintaining thirty employees, two-thirds of whom were Seminole members.

In 1966, it was reported that more than one-half of the sixty workers were Creeks and Seminoles.[58]

The Seminole people had demonstrated remarkable persever-ance in battling the many forces working against them and their culture. Their determination to survive as a government remained strong from statehood through the sixties. The Seminoles continued to have ceremonial dances, known as stomp dances, at various ceremonial grounds in the Seminole County area. The native Mvskoke language was still spoken by tribal members, most of whom were bilingual. There were a number of Indian churches in Seminole County, where sermons were delivered and songs were sung in the native language. The importance of the Five Tribes cultures was also finally beginning to be recognized in the main-stream. In 1966, not long after renovations of the old nineteenth-century building that had housed the Union Agency in Muskogee were completed, that building became the site of the Museum of the Five Civilized Tribes. The museum became a repository for various tribal records and other historical documents and items, and it also served as a gallery that showcased the art of Five Tribes members.[59]

In the late sixties, the Seminole Nation's government began to regain some control over tribal funds. In 1968, only a few months before the Seminoles approved a constitution in early 1969, Con-gress approved a law related to its 1959 and 1966 appropriations for awards to the Seminole Nation in its claims cases concerning the sale of the Emahaka Mission lands and the Mekusukey Mission lease. The 1968 law specified that unexpended funds from those appropriations were to be used for the benefit of the Seminole Nation as a whole, rather than for per capita payments to indi-vidual tribal members. The 1968 law specified that those funds, and any interest on those funds (less payment of attorneys' fees and expenses), together with tribal school funds held in the U.S. Treasury, "may be advanced, expended, invested, or reinvested for any purpose that is authorized by the General Council of the Seminole Nation of Oklahoma or other recognized governing body of that tribe and approved by the Secretary of the Interior."[60]

Hitchitee Owls ball team, mid-twentieth century. *Middle row, far left*: Richmond Tiger, chief from 1977 to 1978; *back row, far right:* Charles Grounds, attorney. (Photograph courtesy of Enoch Kelly Haney)

More than twenty more years would pass before the Seminole Nation would be able to achieve even greater economic independence through the use of the much larger award in its last successful claim, which involved the taking of Seminole lands in Florida. Nonetheless, the Seminole government's ability to determine the use of its Emahaka and Mekusukey judgment funds marked a new beginning for the Seminole Nation to act as a government in determining its own destiny with regard to its economic resources. This milestone was particularly significant because the Seminole people were on the threshold of approving a new constitution, electing tribal officials, and reducing, however slightly, federal officials' interference in tribal affairs.

CHAPTER 6

Seminole Nation Constitution, 1964–1969

Notwithstanding the adoption of the IRA in 1934 and the OIWA in 1936, none of the Five Tribes reorganized and adopted new constitutions until more than thirty years later. The Cherokee, Muscogee (Creek), Chickasaw, and Choctaw Nations approved new constitutions in 1976, 1979, 1983, and 1984, respectively. As a result of tribal leaders' tireless efforts, the Seminole Nation approved and secured federal approval of its new constitution several years earlier, in 1969.[1]

Although the delay in the Five Tribes reorganization may seem surprising given the strength that the Seminole Nation and the other tribes demonstrated in the nineteenth century and the tenacity their members continued to show throughout the twentieth century by maintaining their own governments, the delay is not so surprising when one considers the domination that federal agencies exerted over the Five Tribes. The federal agencies, most notably the BIA, treated the tribes as if they had been terminated prior to statehood. BIA officials consistently took the erroneous position that the Curtis Act had eliminated the tribes' judicial powers and that the Act of April 26, 1906 (hereafter referred to as the 1906 act) had greatly diminished tribal legislative powers. In taking that position, the BIA failed to take into account a number of important factors: the inapplicability of the Curtis Act to the Seminole Nation and some of the other four tribes, because of superseding allotment agreements; the fact that the Curtis Act's more damaging provisions were based on the anticipated dissolution of the governments of the Five Tribes in 1906, which never occurred; and the fact that the allotment era ended in the 1930s, when the policy of Indian self-determination began.[2]

The Seminole Intra-Tribal Business Association, Inc., played an important role in securing the adoption of the 1969 constitution for the Seminole Nation. The association was formed on February 22, 1962, for the protection of Seminole citizens' general welfare, advancement of the Seminole Nation's business, preservation of tribal customs, and promotion of good government. Every Seminole Indian by blood who paid annual dues was eligible for membership. Control of the association was vested in a board of trustees composed of eleven members. Many of the association's leaders, all of whom were tribal members, also served as their band's representative on the Seminole Nation General Council. Floyd Harjo, who had attended Seminole Junior College, was the first association president, and Terry Walker, a minister, was its first vice president. Effie Kivett served as secretary. Charles Grounds, a life-long attorney in Seminole County, was the association's legal counsel. Thomas Coker—whose efforts for the Seminole government's reorganization began as early as the forties, continued in the fifties, and finally reached fruition in the sixties—was also one of the first association board members, along with James Cully, Louis King, Billie Palmer, Solomon Fish, Jimmie Harjo, Cecil Narcomey, and Joe Powell.[3]

In 1964 John A. Brown, great-grandson of former chief John F. Brown and the chief from 1960 until 1969, was reelected to serve as chairman of the Seminole Nation General Council. That same year the Seminole Constitution Committee was formed, with Floyd Harjo, Effie Kivett, Charles Grounds, Glenn Factor, James Cully, Pete Miller, and Flora Short serving as its first members.[4] A general council resolution appointing one member from each band to serve on the committee was later approved on March 28, 1964.

Even though the constitution committee had been formed, the Intra-Tribal Business Association continued to meet independently to discuss the development of the constitution and other issues.

In May 1964 attorney Charles Grounds and other association members met to discuss the BIA's encouragement of the tribe to reorganize and adopt a new constitution. Association leaders stressed the need to protect the Nation's interest in future federal payments of damages resulting from successful tribal claims against the United States, known as "judgment funds." They also expressed their view that tribal members would be happier if they could vote on tribal matters, including the election of the tribal chairman, and stated that after tribal reorganization the association would be dissolved. Because of issues concerning disbursements of the Nation's funds, the association requested the BIA to instruct the general council to hold tribal business in abeyance until after approval of the new constitution, but the BIA declined. The association subsequently reviewed the draft constitution developed by the constitution committee, recommended a few changes, and endorsed it.[5]

Joseph Frank served as chairman of the constitution committee, Terry Walker served as vice chairman, and Effie Kivett served as secretary. Constitution committee members met with Leslie Gay, head of the BIA Tribal Government Section, who traveled from Washington, D.C., to meet with them. They met at least six times in June 1964 in a concentrated effort to develop a constitution to be submitted to the people for a vote. The push for development of the constitution was spurred somewhat by judgment in favor of the Florida and Oklahoma Seminoles in their claims case involving thirty million acres of Seminole lands in Florida taken by the United States under the 1823 Treaty of Camp Moultrie. Only twelve Indian bands—the Rewalke, Ocese, Mekusukey, Tom Palmer, Nurcup Harjo, Tusekia Harjo, Tallahassee, Hecete, Eufaula, Ceyvha, and Hvteyievlke (Newcomer)—were represented at the meetings. The committee members, each of whom was fluent in the Mvskoke language or had a competent grasp of the language, voted to conduct all committee business in English. Committee members and their alternates who attended the meetings included Thomas Coker, Terry Walker, Charles Grounds, Jonah Charty, Solomon Fish, Roy Cosar, Benjamin Johnson, James Tiger, Cecil Narcomey, James

Fife, Louis King, and Joseph Frank. Council chairman John Brown and a few other tribal members also attended at least one of the June meetings.[6]

During the first meeting on June 8, Virgil Harrington, the BIA Muskogee Area director, told the group that Leslie Gay was present to give advice and direction, rather than to dictate anything to the committee, but this assurance was not entirely accurate. One of the more important examples of BIA pressure in the constitutional process was its disagreement with Seminole leaders' proposal to exclude freedmen members from tribal membership. Some BIA representatives insisted on freedmen membership and representation of the two freedmen bands, the Dosar Barkus Band and the Bruner Band, on the general council. This insistence was inconsistent with a 1941 commissioner of Indian Affairs opinion that the Five Tribes had full authority to exclude freedmen from their membership through a new constitution under the 1936 OIWA, provided that the freedmen were allowed to vote on the new constitution. Although it is possible that some BIA officials still held that opinion in the sixties, the Seminoles nevertheless declined to develop an OIWA constitution. They chose instead to rely on the Nation's sovereign tribal status as underlying authority for their government, and they acquiesced to BIA instructions to include constitutional provisions for freedmen membership and freedmen council representation.[7]

Several other items were the subject of special interest and discussion during the June 1964 meetings. One of the more important items included a provision that the constitution's requirements for the election of officers could not to be construed as limiting the president's authority to appoint the principal chief; this provision was based on the misconception that the 1906 act required presidential appointments of the chiefs. Other items included decisions to require officers to have at least one-quarter Indian blood, to remove the Okfuskee Band from the list of bands, and to require that the constitution be submitted to Secretary of the Interior for approval. Other items of interest (which were later changed before the constitution was submitted to Seminole citizen vote) included provisions permitting tribal members to select the band to which they wished to belong, establishing a higher voting age for men than women, and designating the courthouse in Wewoka as the council's official meeting place.[8]

The committee worked rapidly in June to produce a constitution for submission to the council, which then would be responsible for approving the final document and submitting it to the Seminole people for a vote. The draft constitution was in the form of a true governmental document, in contrast with many of the western Oklahoma tribes' OIWA constitutions, which were based on corporate organizational models provided by the BIA. The constitution committee submitted a draft constitution and bylaws to the general council on June 19, 1964, but the council did not approve it.[9] A few months later, the council again considered the draft constitution at an October 31 meeting. In early November, council chairman John Brown wrote a letter to the council, stating that band representatives who had not already done so should meet with their bands to decide whether their bands desired any changes to the draft constitution and should be prepared to discuss the changes at an upcoming December 5 council meeting. He noted that considerable time and expense had gone into preparation of the June draft for council consideration.[10]

The Seminole General Council took no action on the draft constitution for almost a year after the June 1964 draft was completed. The Seminole Intra-Tribal Business Association continued meeting in late 1964 and throughout 1965, and the constitution was a frequent topic of discussion. On February 26, 1965, a group of Seminoles requested that the BIA Muskogee Area Office facilitate action on the June 1964 draft constitution. The following month, Thomas Coker and Effie Kivett met with Marie Wadley, the tribal operations officer from the BIA Muskogee Area Office, to discuss a special council meeting scheduled for the following day. They were informed that the BIA could not push action on the draft constitution because it would be accused of injecting itself into tribal affairs. Yet Wadley somewhat inconsistently interjected BIA views by reiterating that the freedmen could not be left out of the constitution, based on the BIA's interpretation of the 1866 treaty. A few weeks later, on April 8, 1966, council chairman John Brown issued a notice of a special council meeting to be held on April 17, 1965, to address the Seminole claims cases and the pending constitution. However, no approval action resulted at the council meeting.[11]

In May 1965 the Seminole Intra-Tribal Business Association decided to seek additional legal counsel, in part because of mounting concern related to the expenditure of tribal funds for the Seminoles' plastics business venture. The association contacted William Wantland, an attorney who had graduated from law school only a few years earlier and returned to Seminole in 1962 to practice law, to discuss the possibility of obtaining his services to work with attorney Charles Grounds to try to suspend all tribal business and stop the expenditure of tribal funds until adoption of the new constitution.[12] In June, Wantland met with the association board and agreed to assist in getting the constitution to a vote and obtaining federal appointment of a Seminole chief. His plans included contacting Oklahoma State senator Fred Harris and traveling to Washington, D.C., later in the summer.[13]

The Intra-Tribal Association continued to press for adoption of a new constitution after the general council voted on June 5, 1965, to postpone discussion of the constitution until the next regular meeting.[14] The association, having no success in obtaining the active support of the BIA Muskogee Area Office, contacted Senator Mike Monroney, Senator Fred Harris, and Congressman Tom Steed. In reply, the area office sent a letter to Senator Monroney in June, characterizing the association as "a dissident group" made up of tribal members "who make it a practice to oppose most of the actions of the General Council." This characterization was offensive to association members, many of whom also served as band representatives on the Seminole Nation General Council and also on the constitution committee.[15]

The association sponsored a meeting of tribal members held on September 14, 1965, in Seminole. At the meeting, attorney William Wantland provided a report concerning his recent trip to

Washington, D.C. He informed those present that he had contacted various BIA officials in Washington to discuss the need to bring the constitution to an election and the need for the appointment of a new chief. During Wantland's meeting with Philleo Nash, commissioner of Indian Affairs, Nash advised Wantland—with little or no explanation for his position—that he did not intend to call an election for the adoption of a new Seminole constitution unless federal law required it. He further advised that federal officials would supervise an election only if requested by the general council, or if the general council became hopelessly dead-locked. Nash also informed Wantland that the BIA felt that tribal members could select the Seminole Nation chief after approval of a new constitution. According to Nash, whose service as commissioner ended only a few months later in March 1966, the BIA did not want to seek a federal appointment of the chief before adoption of the new constitution, because that could result in the Seminole Nation having two chiefs after adoption of the constitution. The BIA preferred to continue to recognize John Brown, who was apparently opposed to the 1964 draft constitution, as the Seminole Nation's leader.[16]

At the September 14, 1965, meeting, Wantland also stated that he had learned that the federal government had the authority to expend tribal funds, and the general council had no voice in the matter.[17] Although the minutes of the meeting contain no detailed explanation related to this statement, it was apparently intended as a description of the BIA's position, which had historically relied on allotment legislation as authority to prevent the Five Tribes from controlling and using tribal funds for any purpose. That position was ruled invalid by the federal courts several years later in *Harjo v. Kleppe*, a suit involving BIA interference with the government of the Muscogee (Creek) Nation.[18]

The general council continued to delay submitting the proposed 1964 constitution to a vote of the people through 1965 and 1966. The proposed constitution was objectionable to some tribal members for various reasons. For example, some objected to a provision that required that council members be able to read and write the

English language. This provision was eventually deleted from the final 1969 version. There were also objections to the band membership provisions in the Bill of Rights in the 1964 draft, which were later significantly revised.[19] Other provisions in the 1964 draft of special concern would have established the office of treasurer; these provisions were eventually eliminated in the final approved constitution.[20]

The Seminole Intra-Tribal Business Association persevered in its push for approval of the constitution in 1967. The association finally began to see progress as the result of a 1966 meeting between members of the constitution committee and Bob Bennett, the new commissioner of Indian Affairs, who had taken office in April 1966 after the resignation of Philleo Nash. At their meeting with Bennett, members of the constitution committee requested federal assistance in calling an election for the approval of the proposed constitution. Bennett was a member of the Oneida Nation and the second Native American commissioner in history, taking office almost a hundred years after the 1869 resignation of the first Native American commissioner, Ely S. Parker. Bennett was sympathetic to the legal rights of Indian tribes and took the opposite view of his predecessor. Bennett's basic philosophy was that tribes should set their own priorities and the BIA should help them accomplish their goals. He advised the committee that unless federal law prohibited it, he would call an election for adoption of the proposed Seminole constitution, if a petition requesting an election was signed by at least 250 members of the Seminole Nation.[21]

There being no federal law prohibition, the association proceeded to seek the required signatures on a petition. On January 7, 1967, attorney William Wantland met with leaders of the Seminole Intra-Tribal Business Association, including Floyd Harjo, Terry Walker, Thomas Coker, and Effie Kivett, to discuss the circulation of petitions for an election on the constitution. They discussed the Mekusukey Mission claim award in the amount of $64,000 and the Emahaka claim in the amount of $68,000, which had not yet been appropriated by Congress for the Nation—a situation that,

in the eyes of many, increased the urgency of securing reorganization of the Seminole government. They discussed expenses
related to a constitutional election, noting that no tribal money
was available because the council had not reconsidered the draft
constitution. Wantland informed the group that Bob Miller, a
tribal member with a degree in journalism and a position at the
University of Oklahoma, had made some suggested changes on
the proposed constitution, and the group agreed that the draft
would be reviewed by the constitution committee before being
submitted to a vote.[22]

The group scheduled a special association meeting to discuss
the proposed constitution. The meeting was held on January 12,
1967, with forty-five association members attending. At the meeting,
William Wantland discussed the history of the Seminole Constitution and informed the group that supporters of the constitution
finally had an opportunity to obtain a federally assisted election
through petitions signed by tribal members. He read the petition
aloud and distributed copies to twenty-one meeting attendees,
who were asked to obtain signatures and return the signed petitions by February 24, 1967.[23]

During this same time period, the constitution committee, with
Terry Walker as chairman, revised the 1964 draft. One of the most
significant changes was the separation of provisions concerning
the chief and assistant chief from provisions concerning the council. Other changes included moving provisions concerning oath
of office, duties of office, meetings, and order of business from the
1964 draft's bylaws to the body of the constitution and eliminating
the bylaws altogether. During the revision process, members of
the constitution committee traveled to meetings with each of the
bands and explained the constitution's purpose and provisions
to them. On February 25, 1967, the committee approved a new
draft of the proposed constitution, which was signed by acting
chairman Terry Walker and Effie Kivett as committee secretary.[24]

The revisions apparently did not satisfy all concerns, some of
which were political in nature. On March 25, 1967, the Seminole

General Council rejected calling an election on the proposed constitution. On May 9, 1967, acting deputy commissioner William E.
Friole notified Terry Walker that the BIA was considering the
petition's request that the Secretary of the Interior call an election
on the constitution, if one was not called by the council.[25] More
than six months later, during an October 20, 1967, meeting, BIA
Muskogee Area director Virgil Harrington told Intra-Tribal Business Association members that the proposed constitution was in
the solicitor's office in Washington. He advised them that there
was no need to make a new roll for Oklahoma Seminoles until
Congress appropriated funds to satisfy their claims awards and
authorized the making of a new roll.[26]

On November 2, 1967, the associate solicitor of Indian Affairs
issued a written opinion finding that the commissioner of Indian
Affairs possessed authority to call an election to determine whether
a new constitution would be adopted by members of the Seminole Nation.[27] At its November 21 and 28 meetings, the board of the
Intra-Tribal Business Association discussed the need to revitalize
the association and seek additional members. The association also
passed a resolution recommending that the Seminole Nation join the
National Congress of American Indians, an organization that emphasized tribal government unity and worked to inform the public
and Congress on Native American governmental rights issues.[28]

At a meeting of the association early in 1968, it was reported
that John Brown, general council chairman, had written a letter to
the Secretary of the Interior appealing the commissioner's decision
to allow the Nation to hold a constitutional election. However,
on March 2, 1968, after more than 600 citizens petitioned for an
election on approval of the proposed constitution, the general
council authorized an election on the 1967 draft and requested
the BIA to call a special election on the proposed constitution.
After some changes requested by general council members were
made to the proposed constitution, on May 3, 1968, the council
approved a revised draft at a special council meeting, as attested
by John Brown, chairman of the general council, and Wisey
Cully, secretary.[29]

The BIA became involved again in the constitutional drafting process in 1968. Leslie Gay met again with the committee on at least one occasion. The BIA employees had their own ideas about what should and should not be in the constitution. They informed the constitution committee that the BIA would not approve provisions for a treasurer in the constitution, which was likely based on the BIA's erroneous belief that federal allotment legislation restricted tribal authority over expenditure of tribal funds. BIA representatives also vetoed the committee's proposal to require all candidates for chief to be bilingual. The BIA advised that the constitution could provide for an elected "chief" but not an elected "principal chief," because of the BIA's incorrect view that the 1906 act required that the "principal chief" be appointed by the president of the United States. BIA employees also expressed displeasure with the proposed constitution's prohibition against dual enrollment in the Seminole Nation and other tribes. Proposed eligibility requirements based on blood quantum for citizens and elected officers were also discussed by the committee and federal employees. The membership eligibility provisions, which included freedmen citizens at the BIA's insistence in 1964, remained in the revised drafts.[30]

On September 16, 1968, Clyde Busey, tribal operations officer of the BIA Muskogee Area Office, sent a copy of the proposed constitution containing changes requested by the commissioner of Indian Affairs to attorney William Wantland. The Muskogee Area Office director, Virgil Harrington, worked with the committee to resolve the issues raised by the BIA. The committee found Harrington, who was the adoptive father of a Florida Seminole child, to be helpful in finalizing the proposed constitution. Another BIA official located in the Muskogee Area Office, Dennis Springwater, was instrumental in assisting the Nation with election issues. The general council refused to approve some of the changes proposed by the BIA but eventually approved a revised draft developed by the committee dated December 9, 1968.[31]

The Seminole Nation Election Committee worked with the BIA in the latter part of 1968 and early 1969 to develop and implement procedures for ratification of the constitution. Election committee members included Bennie Johnson as chairman, Effie Kivett as secretary, and members Thomas Coker, Terry Walker, John Larney, Wesley Tanyan, Amos Tiger, and Louis Harjo.[32] According to news articles, one of the unusual features of the election was that women would be allowed to vote for the first time in the Nation's history. On March 8, 1969, the constitution was submitted to voters and approved by vote of 637 for and 249 against. The certificate of adoption of the 1969 constitution was executed by John Brown, general council chairman; Bennie F. Johnson, the chairman of the Seminole Nation Election Committee; and Effie G. Kivett, the general council secretary, on March 12, 1969. The constitution was approved by Commissioner Robert L. Bennett on April 15, 1969.[33]

Throughout the constitutional development process that finally resulted in the approved 1969 Constitution of the Seminole Nation of Oklahoma, the constitution committee held community meetings, not only within the Seminole Nation, but also in Oklahoma City, where a significant number of tribal members worked and resided. Floyd Harjo, Thomas Coker, Terry Walker, and others played significant roles in organizing and attending these meetings. The dissemination of information concerning the proposed constitution included discussions at the First Annual Seminole Nation Days celebration in October 1968, a celebration at which Commissioner Robert Bennett served as the main speaker.[34]

During one of these meetings, comments by Thomas Coker's daughter, Mary McCormick, who later became the second female chief of the Sac and Fox Nation, prompted a discussion regarding the ability of women to serve on the general council. The matter of women serving on the council may not have been an issue by that time, because none of the constitution drafts developed in 1968 and 1969 expressly authorized or excluded women from serving in the Seminole government. Regardless, the first council elected under the new 1969 constitution included women within its membership. The first women serving on the council included Jane McGeisey, Alice Kernell, Irene Bemo, Effie Kivett, and Shirley Scott, who was Terry Walker's daughter. Later, in 1972, Eula

Doonkeen became the first female assistant chief.[35] Doonkeen and other female tribal members served on the council for many years.

The approved 1969 constitution was the result of a metamorphosis of the 1964 draft as it evolved into the 1967 draft, the two 1968 drafts, and the final 1969 draft, and it was a reflection of hard work and a cooperative spirit of those who worked so diligently to achieve its approval. The constitution established the name of the tribe as the "Seminole Nation of Oklahoma." The use of "Nation" was consistent with the Nation's treaties, and, together with the reference to Oklahoma, distinguished the Nation from the Seminole Tribe in Florida. The constitution stated that members of the Seminole Nation ordained and established the constitution for various described purposes, including promotion of social, educational, and economic opportunities, and it included language added in the May 1968 draft referencing "democracy and self-government."[36]

Several changes were made in the membership provisions during finalization of the constitution. The February 25, 1967, draft based membership on all citizens on the 1906 rolls as well as their descendants and legally adopted children. There was no distinction made between the Indian and freedmen rolls, the issue of freedmen membership having already been resolved in favor of such membership at the BIA's insistence. In the May 1968 draft the reference to adopted children was deleted, and a new requirement was added limiting membership to descendants "according to mother's enrollment only." The committee removed this requirement in the December 1968 draft, so that the final version simply based membership on all persons whose names appeared on the 1906 rolls and their descendants. The December 1968 draft also added a prohibition against dual enrollment by providing that a member of another tribe was not eligible for membership in the Seminole Nation.[37]

The 1969 constitution established two branches of government with executive and legislative functions, but it did not establish a judicial branch. Although the federal government and Indian tribes outside Oklahoma exercised law enforcement and judicial functions over matters arising in Indian country, in Oklahoma the belief—fueled largely by erroneous federal administrative opinions—persisted that Oklahoma tribes had no territorial areas subject to tribal or federal control. There was also a widespread belief that the 1898 Curtis Act had forever abolished the tribal courts of the Five Tribes, a belief that was not dispelled until issuance of a federal court decision in 1988, *Muscogee (Creek) Nation v. Hodel*, almost twenty years after the adoption of the 1969 Seminole Constitution.[38]

The two branches established in the constitution were not exclusively executive or legislative branches. Instead, the constitution established a structure that intertwined executive functions with legislative functions. This structure afforded the general council greater control over governmental affairs than that usually afforded a legislative branch in federal and state government, and it gave the chief no veto power. However, the constitution gave the chief a prominent role in the council by authorizing the chief to appoint committees (subject to council approval), preside over council meetings, act as chairman of the council, vote in case of a council vote tie, generally supervise the affairs of the council, and execute official papers when directed by the council.[39]

The chief and assistant chief were to be elected for four-year terms or until successors were elected and installed. In order to be qualified for the positions, candidates were required to be at least thirty-five years of age and no less than one-quarter Indian blood. Any person who had been convicted of a felony was required to have been pardoned or released from confinement for at least five years in order to be eligible. The constitution provided that election of the chief would not be construed as limiting the authority of the president to appoint the chief, pursuant to the 1906 act. The assistant chief was empowered to assist the chief, preside in the absence of the chief, and succeed to office of chief upon death or resignation of the chief, subject to general council approval and confirmation.[40]

Some of the requirements concerning the general council changed during the revision of the 1964 draft, whereas others remained the same. The approved constitution established a forty-two-member council, consisting of three band representatives from each of the fourteen bands. It required that council members be at least eighteen and required that council members must have no less than one-fourth Indian blood, except representatives of freedman bands. Although earlier draft constitutions required an at-large election in which all qualified electors would be entitled to cast one vote for each council seat, the final constitution provided that election of council members "shall be by band and all qualified electors shall be entitled to cast one vote for each seat his band has on the general council to be filled." Council members were to serve for four years or until successors were elected and installed, and they were to be paid in accordance with a duly adopted council ordinance.[41]

Under the new constitution, the council had the power to speak and act on all matters of the Nation; promote health, education, and charity and other services that might contribute to the social and economic advancement of tribal members; negotiate with federal, state, and local governments; prevent the sale, disposition, lease, or encumbrance of the Nation's land; manage, lease, or otherwise deal with tribal lands and resources; prepare budgets; approve expenditures; enter into contracts on behalf of the Nation; employ legal counsel; borrow money and pledge future tribal income; and exercise other powers that might be delegated to the council. Council enactments were to be valid only if approved by a majority of those voting in a legal meeting. The secretary of the general council was to be selected from within or without council membership, and council records were to be maintained at the tribal office in Wewoka.[42]

Under the approved constitution, the general council possessed authority to remove any officer or band representative from office by affirmative vote of twenty-two of the forty-two members. The grounds for removal included failure to carry out responsibilities, a finding of guilty by a court of competent jurisdiction of a misdemeanor involving dishonesty, and gross neglect of duty or misconduct reflecting on the integrity or dignity of the general council. The constitution also authorized the council to automatically declare vacant the seat of any member who died, resigned, was found guilty of a felony, or failed or refused to attend two successive council meetings unless excused by the general council. The bands were authorized to fill any vacancy that might occur in their council representation for the remainder of the term, pursuant to Seminole tribal custom—a practice that apparently eliminated the need to follow the Nation's general election procedures.[43]

The constitution established several special requirements concerning selection of candidates and oversight of the first election. It created other requirements, including establishment of an election board, for all subsequent elections. The election board was charged with maintaining the list of registered and qualified voters, conducting all regular and special election, checking credentials of candidates, passing on the validity of petitions for nomination submitted, and counting ballots. It was also given the responsibility of determining the number and location of voting places. The final constitution established eighteen as the voting age, in contrast to earlier drafts that would have required male voters to be older. The election procedures required voting by secret ballot, election of candidates by a majority of votes cast, and a run-off election between the two candidates with the highest number of votes if no candidate received a majority of the votes cast in an election. The constitution authorized the council to enact an ordinance setting the dates of elections and any additional rules and regulations not inconsistent with the constitution.[44]

The constitution contained a bill of rights, including provisions concerning band membership. It also guaranteed members equal economic opportunities and freedom of association and assembly, and it provided that individual property rights of any member could not to be affected by the constitution without consent of the individual member. The constitution contained no reference to the Indian Civil Rights Act (ICRA), which was enacted in 1968, the year before approval of the 1969 constitution. The ICRA enumerated specific individual rights that could not be abridged by tribal governments. These rights included due process, equal protection, right to religious freedom, freedom of speech, right of peaceable assembly, and a prohibition against taking private property without just compensation. The ICRA also afforded various protections in tribal criminal proceedings, such as the right to a speedy trial, which applied only to tribes that, unlike the Seminole Nation in 1969, exercised law enforcement and judicial functions. The Seminole Nation Constitution does not list all of the rights enumerated in the ICRA, but those rights nevertheless apply as a matter of federal law; however, federal courts have found that the ICRA rights may be interpreted, as a matter of tribal law, differently from their counterparts in the U.S. Constitution.[45]

Elections on constitutional amendments were held in 1989, 1991, 2000, and 2008. The more significant amendments included eliminating the Secretary of the Interior's authority to appoint the principal chief, reducing the size of the council, and finally, in 2008, establishing a separate judicial branch for the exercise of tribal court functions. These amendments refined the Seminole Nation's 1969 Constitution, which has remained a viable, solid organizational document through the latter part of the twentieth century and into the twenty-first century. The adoption of the 1969 Constitution was a true turning point for Seminole citizens, leading to federal funding opportunities, greater provision of services to tribal members, and, beginning in 1969, the election of tribal leaders who would be recognized as officials of the Seminole Nation by the federal government—at least in most cases.[46]

CHAPTER 7

New Beginnings

Administrations of Chiefs Terry Walker (1969–1972),
Floyd Harjo (1972–1973), and Edwin Tanyan (1973–1977)

The leaders and other citizens of the Seminole Nation faced many
challenges in the late sixties and in the seventies. In spite of some
setbacks, most notably delays in the Seminole Nation's access to
its Florida claim award and obstacles to Oklahoma tribes' eligibility for certain federal programs available to other tribes, Seminole leaders made great progress during the first eight years of
Seminole government under the 1969 constitution. They developed
a sound legal infrastructure for the Nation's government, acquired
additional land, and established government, recreation, health,
and federal administrative facilities. They established new programs
to provide services to tribal members. In addition, Seminole leaders
began rebuilding community relations with other tribes and local
governments and strengthening relationships with Congress.

In the late sixties and seventies federal administrative and legislative policy increasingly emphasized tribal self-government; hence,
the timing was right for the Seminoles to revitalize their government. In 1969 Louis Bruce, a Mohawk–Oglala Sioux, was appointed
as commissioner of Indian Affairs. During his tenure, Bruce sought
input from young Indian activists, worked closely with the National
Tribal Chairman's Association, and advocated tribal contracting
of federal programs through the "Buy Indian Act."[1] His efforts
contributed to a policy shift toward stronger Indian self-determination, which Congress began to more actively endorse. In
1974 Congress enacted the Indian Financing Act, which allowed
the Secretary of the Interior to guarantee or insure loans by private

lenders to Indians in order to provide capital to help develop Indian physical and human resources.[2] In 1975 Congress enacted the Indian Self-Determination and Education Assistance Act, which strengthened the ability of Indian tribes to assume responsibility for federally funded programs. This new law, popularly known as "Public Law 638," established a federal policy to enable the transition from federal domination of Indian programs and services to meaningful participation by Indians in the planning, conduct, and administration of those programs and services. It clarified the authority of the Secretary of the Interior and the Secretary of Health and Human Services (formerly the Department of Health, Education and Welfare) to contract with and make grants to Indian tribes and organizations to operate federal programs, including education, child welfare, and other social services programs.[3]

Tribal self-government was also strengthened by several U.S. Supreme Court decisions in the early seventies, including the 1973 decision *McClanahan v. Arizona State Tax Commission*. In that case, the Court ruled that the state of Arizona had no jurisdiction to impose a tax on income derived from reservation sources and earned by Navajo Indians residing on the Navajo Reservation. Although Navajo treaties and laws did not expressly free the Navajos from state taxation, the Court considered Navajo treaty language similar to Seminole treaty language, finding it persuasive that the treaty expressly "set apart Navajo" lands for their "permanent home." The Court also rejected the state's argument that Arizona was expending tax monies for education and welfare within the reservation, finding that the federal government had defrayed eighty percent of Arizona's ordinary Social Security payments to reservation Indians and had approved the expenditure of millions of dollars for programs for Navajos and Hopis living on the reservation.[4]

A year later in another landmark decision, *Morton v. Mancari*, the Supreme Court held that the Indian hiring preference for BIA jobs established in the 1934 Indian Reorganization Act did not constitute unconstitutional invidious racial discrimination. The Court found that the hiring preference applied only to members of federally recognized tribes and was accordingly political rather than racial in nature. The Court also noted that the hiring preference was an "employment criterion reasonably designed to further the cause of Indian self-government and to make the BIA more responsive to the needs of its constituent groups."[5]

Although these new federal legislative and judicial decisions were on the near horizon, they had not yet occurred at the time that Seminole leaders first began operations under the newly reorganized government in 1969. Seminole leaders faced a daunting task in their effort to improve the lives of Seminole citizens. There were more than 5,000 members of the Seminole Nation, including a service population in Seminole County of 3,115. The Oklahoma Seminoles were outnumbered by non-Indians, and many lived on ever-decreasing restricted lands scattered throughout the relatively small area within the Nation's domain, which was eighteen miles wide and thirty-six and one-half miles long, occupying Seminole County. More than 41 percent of Indians in Seminole County had incomes below the poverty level in 1975. The county itself, located in a rural area, had been on a downward spiral for some time. The transformation of the county's predominate farming and mining occupations to include secondary activities, such as manufacturing as well as professional and service-oriented occupations, reduced the availability of unskilled jobs.[6]

Those Seminole members who no longer lived within the Seminole boundaries, particularly those who had moved to urban areas as part of the federal government's relocation experiment in the fifties and sixties, also faced problems. The relocation experiment had been a failure, in part because there were no orientation programs for those Indians who relocated to cities, there were insufficient opportunities for work, and city and state governments offered no services specifically designed for the needs of relocated Indians. Many Seminoles returned home, and many of those who remained had to contend with inadequate job opportunities and problems assimilating into large urban populations.[7]

The 1969 constitution was approved and the election of officers was held within this environment. Candidates for chief included

Swearing-in ceremony of Chief Terry Walker, 1969. *Left to right*: William Carmack, assistant commissioner of Indian Affairs; Eliza Walker; Chief Terry Walker. (Photograph courtesy of Walker family)

John A. Brown and Terry Walker. On July 11, 1969, Terry Walker was elected chief, and Floyd Harjo was elected assistant chief. On September 6, 1969, an inauguration ceremony was held in Wewoka as part of the Second Annual Seminole Nation Days. William Carmack, assistant commissioner of Indian Affairs, administered the oath of office to the chief and assistant chief in the morning and gave the principal address that afternoon. The program for this event listed the new council members (see the appendix for a complete list), some of whom were replaced with new band representatives during the first term of office.[8]

Only a year after the new Seminole government officials were seated, Congress passed the Act of October 22, 1970. The primary purpose of that law was to confirm authority of the Five Tribes

Five Tribes Inter-Tribal Council, 1970s. *Left to right*: Terry Walker, chief, Seminole Nation; Harry J. W. Belvin, chief, Choctaw Nation; Claude Cox, future chief, Muscogee (Creek) Nation; Dode McIntosh, chief, Muscogee (Creek) Nation; Floyd Harjo, assistant chief, Seminole Nation; and Overton James, governor, Chickasaw Nation. (Photograph courtesy of Walker family)

to elect their chiefs and to eliminate past BIA interference with selection of tribal officials. The act provided that "notwithstanding any other provision of law," the principal chiefs of the Seminole, Creek, Cherokee, and Choctaw Nations and the governor of the Chickasaw Nation "shall be popularly selected by the respective tribes in accordance with procedures established by the officially recognized tribal spokesman and/or governing entity." The 1970 act's authorization of "popular selection" rather than "election" reflected congressional concern "that it would be unwise to impose on the tribes by statute or mandatory requirement that the principal officers must be popularly elected"; instead, Congress thought that the "choice of the method of selecting the principal officers should be left to the tribes themselves." The act somewhat inconsistently subjected the tribes' "established procedures" to approval by the Secretary of the Interior.[9]

Although the 1970 act was generally positive, its inclusion of a provision requiring selection of a chief within twelve months threatened to disrupt the new Seminole government, because there were still three years of the current chief's term remaining. In order to avoid holding new elections prematurely, the Seminole Council enacted a resolution requiring that steps be taken to "insure the uninterrupted four year term of all elected officials of the Seminole Nation, including the Chief," and stating that the Seminole Nation should be exempted from the 1970 act's new selection deadline. In the spring of 1971, the council approved another resolution reciting that Chief Walker had been elected in 1969 by the adult citizens of the Nation to serve as principal chief for a four-year term, and that the council also selected him to serve as chief, "with future selections, beginning in 1973, to be pursuant to the provisions of the Constitution of the Seminole Nation of Oklahoma." Although an initial solicitor's opinion stated that the Nation's election procedures could not be retroactively approved for purposes of maintaining Walker in office for the full four-year term, the assistant secretary of the Interior subsequently acknowledged receipt of the 1971 council resolution and stated that he approved the method of popular selection of the chief, thus eliminating the need for another election.[10]

In late 1971, a dispute involving Chief Terry Walker occurred that led to his leaving office the following year. The events involved in this dispute marked the beginning of a historic power struggle between elected Seminole chiefs and council members—a power struggle that continued into the twenty-first century. The controversy centered on Chief Walker's alleged failure to communicate with claims attorney Paul Niebell and the council regarding pending Seminole claims cases. In September 1971 the council had approved Thomas Coker, Ishmael Tiger, Assistant Chief Harjo, and Effie Kivett to go to Washington to meet with Paul Niebell regarding the claims cases. Without express council approval,

Chief Walker made a similar trip on his own in order to meet with Interior officials; he was accompanied by local attorneys Charles Grounds and James Rodgers, whom the council had hired in 1970 to work on the mineral claims. At the December council meeting, Chief Walker and the four approved delegates gave reports about their separate trips to Washington. The delegates reported that Niebell had corresponded with Chief Walker about his work and about BIA disapproval of the attorney contracts with Grounds and Rodgers. The latter point became a controversial issue, because some council members apparently were unaware that the BIA disapproved of the Grounds and Rodgers contracts. The council confirmed the existing contract with Paul Niebell for all of the remaining claims work, effectively invalidating the contracts with Grounds and Rodgers.[11]

After Chief Walker, Assistant Chief Harjo, Councilman Ishmael Tiger, and Secretary Effie Kivett made another trip to Washington to attend a hearing in the Florida claims case on January 11, 1972, as approved by the council, they made a report to the council on January 15, 1972. Only days later, on January 29, 1972, the council met to discuss the potential removal of Chief Walker from office, with twenty-five council members present. Chief Walker had earlier announced the cancellation of the meeting because of bad weather, but the council met anyway. Chief Walker was telephoned from the meeting, but he declined to attend. The following month, the council enacted a resolution to remove Terry Walker as chief. The resolution claimed that Chief Walker was uncooperative when general council members attempted to resolve a dispute between him and the assistant chief, that Walker had attempted to obtain BIA approval of Grounds and Rodgers's claims attorney contract without council authorization, that there was lack of coordination in the operation of some of the tribal programs, and that Walker had made various trips without providing a report to the council. The resolution recited that a copy of the resolution was to be provided to Chief Walker, as required by Article IX, section 1, of the Seminole Constitution.[12]

At some point during this time, Chief Walker filed suit against Assistant Chief Harjo, alleging slander and seeking a restraining order. In April 1972 the council approved a resolution requesting the Secretary of the Interior to withdraw his recognition of Terry Walker as chief and to recognize Floyd Harjo as acting chief. Floyd Harjo was recognized by the general council as acting chief on March 4, 1972, with the concurrence of the BIA. Terry Walker attended the March 4 meeting, but he left after a BIA representative made statements in support of the removal procedures used by the council. This BIA involvement in disputes between the council and chief also became a common practice throughout the next several decades, an involvement that sometimes caused more problems for the Seminole government than it solved. On April 22, 1972, the general council confirmed Floyd Harjo as chief. Harjo, a member of the Tusekia Harjo Band, served as acting chief at the June council meeting, and by the July 1972 council meeting, he was serving as chief. Eula Doonkeen, a member of the Mekusukey Band who was also a business owner, an artist, and a graduate of the University of Central Oklahoma, was elected by the general council to serve as the first female assistant chief of the Seminole Nation on April 22, 1972.[13]

Chief Harjo and Assistant Chief Doonkeen served for a little more than one year, which completed the first four-year term for chief and assistant chief under the new constitution. Near the end of that term of office, in August 1973, Edwin Tanyan, Floyd Harjo, and John Brown ran for chief, and Thomas Palmer, George Bemo, and Joe Spain ran for assistant chief. Thomas Palmer won the assistant chief position. Seventeen incumbent council members were elected at the August election, and the number of female members on the forty-two-member council increased to seven: Jennie Rice, Lucy Lena, Susie Periote, Corena England, Jane McGeisey, Mandy Wise, and Beulah Jones. The new council included longtime tribal leaders Charles Grounds and Thomas Coker as well as future chiefs Richmond Tiger and Enoch Kelly Haney, both Mekusukey Band members. There was a run-off election for chief on September 1 between Edwin Tanyan and John Brown. The winner was Edwin Tanyan, a Seminole County high school graduate who attended Oklahoma City University, received a Purple Heart and three Bronze Stars for his service in World War II and the Korean Conflict, and was employed by the U.S. Army Corps of Engineers in Tulsa and by the Federal Aviation Administration in Oklahoma City prior to becoming chief. Although there was an election dispute during the course of the election, the elections of Chief Tanyan and Assistant Chief Palmer were certified on September 4, 1973, and they took office that month. Like Chief Walker and many of the later principal chiefs of the Seminole Nation, Chief Tanyan's authority was sometimes severely challenged, but he survived his first four year term of office without suffering removal.[14]

The general council secretary was responsible for recording votes on all measures, numbering resolutions and ordinances (most of which were in writing), and keeping the written minutes of the council meetings. During the terms of Chief Walker and Floyd Harjo, Effie Kivett, who had played an important role in the process for development of the 1969 constitution and was also a council member, served as council secretary. On at least one occasion, early in Chief Walker's administration, Ella Mae Pennokee and Jane Northcutt executed council resolutions in the capacity of council secretary. During Chief Tanyan's first term, Corena Mae England, who was also a council member, served as general council secretary.[15]

The general council held quarterly meetings from 1969 through 1971, with few, if any, special meetings. Council meetings were conducted in both the Mvskoke and English languages, with bilingual members providing translations when needed. Less than a third of the council members spoke only English, and the rest were bilingual or spoke only the Mvskoke language. As efforts to rebuild the Nation accelerated, the council soon began meeting more often. The council met at different churches, including Ciaha, Hichitee, Hilltop, and Mekusukey, and sometimes met at the courthouse in Seminole. Later it met at a new building constructed at the Mekusukey Mission grounds south of Seminole. The council took action at a minimum of eight meetings in 1972, six meetings in 1973, eight meetings in 1974, thirteen meetings in 1975, ten meetings in 1976, and ten meetings in 1977.[16]

Council meetings in the seventies were sometimes dramatic. During an argument at one meeting, a fight occurred and a council member pulled a knife. At another meeting, members of the council requested the attendance of an employee to answer questions they had concerning his work. As he stood up to address questions from the council, a gun dropped to the floor. He bent down, picked up the gun and stuck it back in his belt. No one had any questions for him. Another, perhaps more subtle, method of intimidation used on occasion at council meetings involved activities by Seminoles in the audience, who blew smoke, presumably doctored by someone trained in Native medicine, at the council member intended to be affected by it.[17]

Council members and their constituents were actively involved in the progress of the Seminole Nation outside of the council meetings. The general council structure was built around the fourteen bands, including the two freedmen bands: the Bruner Band and the Dosar Barkus Band. Throughout the Nation's history, the band chiefs, some of whom did not serve on the council, also provided leadership to each of their respective bands. It was a common practice for council members to discuss important measures with their band members and to secure directions from them before voting. This process, described by the Indian Claims Commission in 1976 as "an effective two-way communication between the tribal membership and the tribal governing body," did not reflect the "one-man one-vote" principles of the United States' governmental structure, in part because the bands varied in size. Smaller bands had the same number of council representatives as the larger bands, effectively giving members of smaller bands greater representation than members of larger bands. This disproportion was particularly significant in situations where a smaller band was controlled by a small group of close-knit family members, sometimes resulting in the disenfranchisement of other band members, particularly those who did not live in Seminole County and who could not easily attend band meetings.[18]

Seminole leaders in the seventies recognized that establishment of a sound legal, organizational, and economic infrastructure for the government of the Nation was crucial to the success of the Seminole government. Under Chief Walker's leadership, the general council enacted several measures in 1969 related to maintenance of an organized government. One of the more significant laws enacted by the council governed the presentation, numbering, enactment, and approval of "resolutions," which was the term used for legislative actions governing specific matters, such as budget approvals and committee appointments. That law also governed the presentation, numbering, and enactment of "ordinances," which was the term used for general laws of a permanent nature. The law governing ordinances required that all ordinances be presented to the council in writing, that they be presented on the council floor with an opportunity for debate, and that after council approval they be executed by the chief, who chaired council meetings. That law also required approval by the BIA Muskogee Area director, a requirement believed to be mandated by federal law and that was not eliminated from tribal law until several years later.[19]

In 1969 the council enacted a resolution establishing salaries and expenses for members of the general council and other elected officers, including $5,000 for the chief's salary and a total of $5,040 for general council expenses. These salaries and expenses were increased five years later to $7,000 for the chief's salary, $4,000 for the assistant chief's salary, $4,000 for the treasurer's salary, and $20 per diem for council member for each council meeting attended (unless he or she left early, in which case a smaller amount was paid).[20]

Other efforts concerning the tribal government infrastructure involved financial management, elections, tribal personnel, membership rolls, and the Nation's legal affairs. In June 1970 the council approved a law establishing the office of treasurer, but that law was rejected by the commissioner of Indian Affairs and was revised later in the year. The main difference in the two laws was that the revised version did not define the duties of the treasurer but instead provided that the treasurer's duties would be as defined by council resolution from time to time. In the fall of 1972, the council enacted a law describing the election procedures for the Seminole Nation; in subsequent years the council continued to enact laws replacing previous election laws. In 1974 the council established a personnel board to develop, maintain, and control written policies and procedures to govern tribal employees. By 1975 plans were underway to work on the Seminole Nation's membership rolls, and in 1977 the council enacted a law establishing the Office of Tribal Enrollment to update tribal rolls and officially verify the memberships of individual Seminole citizens.[21]

The development of laws concerning the Nation's legal counsel was also a priority for the general council. In December 1969 the council appointed William Wantland to serve as the Oklahoma Seminoles' first attorney general and specified that his duties included advice to the council, the principal chief, the assistant chief, and all committees established by the constitution or approved by the council. The following summer, the council enacted a permanent law defining the duties of the attorney general. In 1972 the council accepted the resignation of Wantland, who had decided to dedicate his time and effort to the Oklahoma Indian Rights Association, an Indian advocacy organization that focused on civil rights and economic development issues. In July 1975 Wantland was again appointed to serve as attorney general for the Seminole Nation. The council later approved a resolution restricting the legal services of the attorney general only to work that was specifically requested and prohibiting use of tribal trust funds for legal services unless properly appropriated by the general council.[22]

Seminole leaders recognized the importance of maintaining a good relationship with the local, state, and other tribal entities. They worked more closely with the Inter-Tribal Council of the Five Civilized Tribes and obtained greater shares and benefits from federal grants obtained through that organization. Representatives of the Seminole Nation participated in numerous other activities that increased the Nation's voice in matters affecting tribal members, by serving on boards such as the Sasakwa Water District Board and the Oklahoma City Area Indian Health Board, participating in the Congress of American Indians and the Indian Tribal Chairman's Association, meeting with federal officials in Washington on matters such as housing, and supporting the work of the Seminole County commissioners for the improvements of roads in rural parts of Seminole County. The Seminole Nation also continued its annual Seminole Nation Days activities, an important Seminole County event. One indication of the Seminole Nation's importance in local affairs was that in 1973 the Seminole Nation Historical Society, which was not an agency of the Seminole Nation, established the Seminole Nation Museum in Wewoka and opened it to the public in late 1974.[23]

The hundreds of thousands of federal dollars that Indian tribes in Oklahoma, including the Seminole Nation, obtained and infused into local communities had a significant positive impact on the state's economy—a fact that is often overlooked by detractors of Indian tribes. Before tribal reorganization in 1969, the principal sources of tribal income were small amounts from leases, rentals, royalties, and interest on deposits in the U.S. Treasury. The Oklahoma Seminoles also participated in a few federally funded programs, such as Head Start, and had the use of a small amount of proceeds from the Emahaka and Mekusukey claims cases for tribal government expenses, investments, and any other purposes approved by the council from time to time.[24] During the terms of Chief Walker, Chief Harjo, and Chief Tanyan, from 1969 through 1977, Seminole leaders obtained significantly larger amounts of federal funding for government operations and services to Seminole Indians. Included was funding for various programs through the U.S. Department of Health, Education and Welfare (HEW; later reorganized into the Department of Health and Human Services, or HHS) as well as BIA funding for tribal planning activities and an Indian Action Team related to employment and education. The programs funded by the BIA did not benefit freedmen members because the BIA's position was that eligibility was based on Indian blood.[25]

Seminole leaders' efforts to increase tribal resources were aided by the 1974 establishment of a planning department, which was responsible for strategic planning and development of tribal objectives, goals, and policies. The Nation contracted with the Oklahoma Indian Affairs Commission in early 1974 in order to evaluate the tribal organizational structure and to make recommendations to help strengthen the tribal government. The Seminole Nation Planning Department also used a comprehensive planning grant from the BIA and a 1975 grant from the HEW Office of Native American Programs for the purpose of developing long-range plans for the Nation. A number of tribal members were active in this endeavor, including Enoch Kelly Haney, director of the planning department (who was elected chief thirty years later); Bertha Tilkens, Community Health Representative (CHR) Program director; Margarette Vietta, director of the Seminole Nation Housing Authority; and Jess Johnson, Robert Kernell, Jr., Charles Grounds, Tom McGeisey, Sr., and V. V. Harjo, who comprised the Tribal Land Acquisition Committee.[26]

In June 1975, the planning department provided interim comprehensive and economic development plans to the council. The interim plan noted that, in spite of the many obstacles faced by the Seminoles, "the people of the Seminole Nation have remained remarkably unscarred, independent, and distinct as a people, able to accept . . . and to adjust to extremely difficult circumstances in ways that not only preserve to a great extent Seminole customs, traditions, and life-styles, but often making those characteristics stronger and more functional." The 1975 interim plans focused primarily on the need for developing job- and income-producing activities, increasing the Nation's base for community and economic development purposes, providing a good health facility for Indians in the area, caring for elderly citizens, and developing transportation opportunities for those who could not afford private or public transportation. The interim plans also discussed the need for community development relating to housing, roads, meeting places, education, social services, and recreation. In late 1975 the council established a tribal planning commission whose purpose was to act in an advisory capacity to support and assist the planning department with achieving tribal goals and developing codes and ordinances to maintain the orderly construction of buildings on tribal lands.[27]

The management of tribal property was an important task for Seminole leaders and included the 1970 cancellation of the Systems Engineering Electronics, Inc., business lease, approval of oil and gas and grazing leases, and development of the Mekusukey Mission lands.[28] The council began its development of Mekusukey (south of Seminole) by constructing a recreation center there that was dedicated on July 1, 1970. The council soon enacted a permanent law that established a board of directors for the management of all recreation areas under the jurisdiction of the Nation. It also endorsed the work of the building committee, which was planning for the development of the Mekusukey property, and authorized it to obtain all possible resources for that purpose. That same year, the council approved the construction of a community building at Mekusukey. The first floor of the Mekusukey academy, which by that time was all that was left of the building, was torn down when the new building was constructed; only the school's old laundry building, which was later used for tribal offices, remained. The council began meeting at the newly constructed building at Mekusukey in 1973. In early 1974 the council approved the construction and location of tribal office buildings at the Mekusukey Mission site. By 1975, the development at Mekusukey included offices, meeting space, and two softball diamonds, and plans were underway for additional improvements to prepare the site for industry and other uses, including water and sewer facilities.[29]

Because Seminole leaders wanted to improve members' access to health care, they acquired and developed additional tribal lands south of Wewoka, approximately fourteen miles east of Mekusukey. Decades earlier, the Seminole government had rejected BIA plans to build a hospital within the Nation's boundaries, but that decision was reconsidered in the seventies because of the serious health problems of Seminole people, many of whom suffered from hypertension and diabetes. The inadequate health system for tribal members was reflected in statistics indicating that the life expectancy for Indians in the United States was 64.9 years in 1970, compared with 70.4 years for all races in 1969. Health services were not easily accessible to Seminole citizens. The nearest Indian Health Service (IHS) clinic was in Shawnee, Oklahoma, thirty-two miles from Wewoka. The Shawnee clinic was staffed by two physicians, three nurses, and one public health nurse, and it served members of several tribes in the area, with approximately 70 percent of the clinic's patient load coming from Seminole County. The nearest IHS hospitals were located 119 miles away in Pawnee, Oklahoma, 121 miles away in Claremore, Oklahoma, and 141 miles away in Lawton, Oklahoma. An IHS hospital was later built in Ada, about thirty-five miles southwest of Wewoka.[30]

In addition to establishing the CHR program to aid tribal members in traveling to the IHS clinic in Shawnee, the council took immediate steps toward improving sanitation facilities and establishing a clinic in Wewoka. During Chief Harjo's term the council requested the Public Health Service to assist the Nation in establishing permanent sanitation facilities at the Mekusukey Mission Recreation Area, and it established that project as its top priority. Later, in 1973, the council approved the construction of a health clinic in the Wewoka area to serve Indian people and to relieve some of the work load of the IHS clinic in Shawnee. By 1975 the Seminole Nation had established a health committee to work closely with the CHR program director and the planning department to develop health programs, and the Nation had received a grant from IHS to develop a department within the Seminole government to deal with health issues. In the spring of 1975, Seminole delegates testified before U.S. House and Senate committees to support a request for funding to staff an IHS clinic to be constructed in Wewoka. The council also authorized the chief to negotiate with the IHS for coordination of an effective tribal and community development program. The Nation eventually obtained funding for the clinic, with the assistance of Carl Albert, speaker of the House, and Oklahoma U.S. senator Henry Bellmon.[31]

At the same time that Seminole leaders were working on obtaining funding for the clinic, they were also working on acquiring separate tracts of land for each of the following: the clinic site, a site upon which offices were to be constructed and leased to the BIA's Wewoka Agency, and a site for a new tribal office building. Seminole leaders had originally planned to locate most of the Nation's facilities at the Mekusukey site. However, in 1975 the council approved an agreement between the Seminole Nation and Wewoka Industries, Inc., in which that corporation agreed to give to the Seminole Nation a forty-acre tract of land south of Wewoka for the clinic site and for the BIA's agency offices. The council rescinded all past resolutions that had called for the relocation of the BIA agency to Mekusukey.[32]

In the fall of 1975, the council authorized the principal chief and staff to take necessary steps to establish a Seminole Nation nonprofit corporation and a Seminole Nation construction corporation for profit. As a result, the Seminole government established a nonprofit corporation named Seminole Nation Enterprise, whose primary purpose was to manage federal leases of the sites for the planned clinic and BIA agency building. Consistent with that plan, in late 1976 the general council empowered the principal chief to execute leases of the clinic and BIA office sites to Seminole Nation Enterprises, which in turn leased those sites for use by the IHS and the BIA. The Seminole government continued to operate its executive offices in a renovated house in Wewoka while development of the new tribal land south of Wewoka progressed. Finally, in 1977 the Seminole Nation received a grant to build a tribal headquarters and approved a bid for construction costs in the amount of $347,000. The site of the tribal complex was south of Wewoka, north of the site of the Wewoka BIA Agency and the IHS clinic. The headquarters site was purchased from a member of the Creek Nation, Isaac Walker, on the boundary between the Seminole and Muscogee (Creek) Nations. Dedication ceremonies for the clinic, BIA office building, and tribal headquarters were held in May 1979.[33]

Improving Seminoles' basic living conditions was a high priority of Seminole leaders and other citizens. In the mid-1970s large numbers of Seminoles lived in substandard housing. Seventy-five percent of the Indian homes within the Seminole service area did not have sewage and sanitation facilities, and fifty-five percent did not have individual water facilities. In the late sixties the Nation had established the Housing Authority of the Seminole Nation under an Oklahoma public housing law. By the fall of 1969, there were plans to build one hundred new homes with federal funding through the U.S. Department of Housing and Urban Development (HUD). The housing authority had three projects funded by HUD in 1972, numbered Projects 93-1, 93-2, and 93-3. These projects included a leasing program that was not limited to Indian participants, with 176 out of 200 leased homes occupied. The projects also included a Mutual Help home owner-ship program, with 159 homes already constructed, and construction planned or underway for an additional ninety-one units. In 1974 the council approved a resolution requesting continued HUD funding for tribal housing programs. It was determined during this time that at least 320 additional housing units were required to meet Indian housing demands in Seminole County. To address these needs, in 1975 and 1976 the council authorized the housing authority director to submit an application for construction of additional homeownership units, to acquire low-rent housing units for handicapped and elderly persons, and to apply for a HUD loan for surveys and planning.[34]

Education was another important challenge facing Seminole leaders in the seventies, when less than 29 percent of adult Indians in Seminole County had completed high school. Seminole leaders and federal officials recognized a need for special federally funded programs for schools with higher Indian student populations in Seminole County, where Indian students comprised 30 percent of the total county enrollment. The Johnson O'Malley Program was one such federally funded program. It enabled the Secretary of the Interior to contract with states for educational services to Indians, and it required local school administrators to obtain input concerning education needs from Indians in the community. The Indian Education Act of 1972, which established a comprehensive program of federal aid for special education needs of Indians, was also in effect. In 1973 the council established an education committee to serve as a liaison with state officials, local school administrators, and parents to improve relations involving education. In 1974 the council approved having the Nation contract for the Johnson O'Malley Program in order to enable Seminoles to have more input into the educational programs in Seminole County. Oklahoma benefitted from the 1976 award of nearly $22.6 million in federal education grants that were made to Indian tribes, organizations, and institutions of higher education in Oklahoma, including an adult education award to the Seminole Nation.[35]

Seminole leaders were also concerned about law enforcement and fire protection issues throughout the seventies. The fire departments of Seminole and Wewoka provided fire protection services on tribal and individual restricted Seminole lands. The Wewoka and Seminole police departments, the Seminole County sheriff, and the Oklahoma Highway Patrol performed law enforcement functions on tribal and individual restricted lands. Seminole leaders questioned these activities, correctly believing that Congress had not conferred law enforcement authority in Indian country on the state. In 1973 members of the general council discussed problems that Indians were having with the police. Chief Tanyan was particularly critical of the police chief of Seminole, Oklahoma, charging that the rate of arrests for Indians far exceeded that for non-Indians. The council recommended seeking financing from the Law Enforcement Assistance Administration (LEAA) to establish its own law enforcement agency and hiring three law enforcement officers within the next ten years to provide necessary police protection for all tribal assets. Founded in 1968, the LEAA established federal grants to be awarded to states and "units of local governments," including tribes, that performed law enforcement functions, as determined by the Secretary of the Interior, to improve law enforcement and criminal justice systems. Unfortunately, the Department of the Interior did not recognize the authority of the

Seminole Nation and other tribes in Oklahoma to perform law enforcement functions at the time the LEAA was established or, indeed, for many years after that.[36]

Oversight of the Seminole claims cases was another important matter addressed by the Seminole Council in the seventies. By 1970, with Paul Niebell serving as the Nation's attorney, only three claims cases remained pending: the mineral claims case, which the Nation finally lost in 1974; the Florida lands claim, which was settled with the federal government in 1976; and the railroad claim, which was finally settled in 1980. The Florida claims case proved to be a particularly time-consuming and lengthy endeavor for Seminole leaders. In 1970 the Indian Claims Commission issued a decision in consolidated Dockets 73 and 151 finding that the Oklahoma and Florida Seminoles were entitled to damages for the federal government's taking of Seminole lands in Florida in 1823. Seminole leaders tried to negotiate a settlement that year with the Seminole Tribe of Florida regarding the division of the award between the tribes. The Florida Seminoles met with the council at the Mekusukey Church near Bowlegs in June 1970 to discuss a proposed division of the award, and several Seminole delegates later traveled to Hollywood, Florida, for additional discussions. Representatives of the two tribes discussed a split of 75 percent for the Oklahoma Seminoles and 25 percent for the Florida Seminoles. After returning to Oklahoma, the Seminole Nations' delegates met with the council to discuss the proposed split, but the Florida Seminoles decided that they wanted a larger share, and the settlement was not finalized that year.[37]

In 1972 the Court of Claims reversed the Indian Claims Commission award and remanded the case for further consideration of the amount of damages. The Oklahoma Seminoles and Florida Seminoles worked hard to negotiate a settlement with representatives of the United States. This was a complicated process, because it required securing a consensus among three groups of Seminoles in Florida, the Seminole Nation of Oklahoma, and the federal government. In 1975 the council directed its attorney to settle the Florida land claims case for a total sum not less than $16,000,000, with no off-sets in favor of the United States. In early 1976, Chief Tanyan testified at a hearing on the proposed settlement in Washington. He explained the process by which the general council approved the settlement, including a meeting with the band chiefs, who had in turn discussed the settlement at meetings with their respective bands, in order to obtain the consensus of the bands. Assistant Chief Tom Palmer also testified about the approval process. Corena Mae England testified that she was both the general council secretary and the Seminole Nation secretary, and she confirmed the validity of the council resolutions approving the settlement. The settlement was approved by the Indian Claims Commission on April 27, 1976. The settlement required the United States to compensate the tribes in the amount of $16,000,000, with no offsets.[38]

After the commission's approval of the settlement, the council authorized the principal chief to seek a loan to be used to finance necessary operations and expenses of the Seminole Nation Judgment Fund Committee, composed of representatives of each band. The committee was given the task of working on a plan for allocating the funds between the Seminole Nation and the Seminole Tribe of Florida and for distributing the funds. By the fall of 1976, negotiations between the two tribes were described as being at a "standstill, with the Seminole Nation of Oklahoma requesting a division on a population basis, and the Seminole Tribe of Florida requesting an equal division of the funds." The BIA prepared a supplementary research report dated May 21, 1977, that was approved by the judgment fund committee and by the council. A hearing was set for June 30, 1977, in order to provide the resulting proposal to attending tribal members. The council approved submission of a bill to Congress to request that it proceed with a division of the Florida land claims award but was not successful in these efforts, in part because there were disputes about whether the Seminole Nation of Oklahoma's freedmen members should be considered in calculating the division of the award funds. Sadly, the Oklahoma and Florida Seminoles were not able to access the award until 1991, fifteen years after they succeeded in settling the case with the United States.[39]

The Seminole Nation's lack of success in most of its claims cases was understandably frustrating, particularly in light of language in the nineteenth-century Seminole treaties purporting to protect the Seminole Nation from intruders. Partly as a result of the difficulties with the as-yet-unresolved railroad claims case, a group whose membership called themselves the Seminole Treaty Government, also known as the Seminole Treaty People, became a center of controversy within the Seminole Nation in 1975, just three years after members of the American Indian Movement, known as AIM, had occupied the BIA headquarters in Washington, D.C. The Treaty People, consisting mostly of Seminole members, were strongly influenced by Meredith Quinn, a Santee Sioux member who claimed to serve as their legal advisor. They advocated that the Nation's treaties were controlling over other federal laws and were critical of the Nation's elected officials. In June 1975 the Treaty People sent a letter to Chief Tanyan, informing him that the group intended to seek recognition from the United Nations.[40]

In July 1975 the general council enacted a resolution that dismissed complaints by the Treaty People against the Seminole Nation Housing Authority, the Seminole Nation attorney general, and Chief Tanyan. The council also approved a resolution stating that from time to time private groups of Seminole citizens had attempted to act for the Seminole Nation without authority to do so, most notably the Seminole Treaty group. The resolution provided that only the general council, tribal officials and committees, and other bodies recognized by the council had authority to represent the Seminole Nation. Seminole leaders were concerned that the Treaty People's aggressive stance would threaten the Nation's recovery of its claim pending before the Indian Claims Commission in Docket 247, which involved land takings by railroads under early-twentieth-century federal legislation. In 1974 the Court of Claims had found that it was not fair and honorable for a federal law to vest in municipalities title to the lands that were the sites of abandoned

Treaty People, 1970s. *Kneeling on right*: Tom Ahaisse, later a defendant in federal prosecution; and *middle row, third from left:* Ted Underwood, future Seminole Nation tax commissioner. (Photograph courtesy of Ted Underwood)

railroad stations and remanded the case back to the Indian Claims Commission, where it was still pending.[41]

Undaunted by the general council's efforts to limit the significance of the Treaty People's actions, in November of 1975 the Treaty People focused their attentions on the railroads. They demanded payment from the Santa Fe, Rock Island, and Frisco railroad companies for use of rights of way through the Seminole Nation. These demands resulted in the cancellation of railroad runs between Oklahoma City and Ada for a brief time. In early December, Treaty People member Johnson Warledo met with a Santa Fe Railroad agent and demanded that the railroad pay $217,580, stating that the Treaty People would repossess the railroad if their demands were not met. A few days later a meeting was held with a larger group of Treaty People, the railroad agent, and two FBI agents. Meredith Quinn told the meeting attendees that the Treaty People would stop the trains with barricades and explosives if their demands were not met. In December 1975, the attorney general of the Seminole Nation obtained a state court injunction against Treaty People members. Concerned that the Treaty People were jeopardizing the Nation's railroad claim, the council had authorized the suit in order to prevent the Treaty People from attempting to act on behalf of the Seminole Nation and from attempting to negotiate with railroads or others as to claims that the Seminole people might have against any such organization or company.[42]

A few days later, the FBI arrested five members of the group— Jack Warledo, Johnson Warledo, Tom Ahaisse, Gary Larney, and Ryder Larney—on federal conspiracy charges related to a railroad bridge fire in a county adjacent to Seminole County and a barricade of a railroad track. The five Seminole defendants denied that they had committed the alleged crimes, and their supporters believed that others, possibly federal agents, were responsible for the fire. The five Seminoles, along with Meredith Quinn, who was later arrested, were indicted in Muskogee, Oklahoma, by a federal grand jury in January 1976 on charges of conspiracy, extortion, and possession of an unregistered firearm (an explosive device). That same month, the council enacted a law prohibiting the use of the words "Seminole Nation" and the use of the seal or flag without the consent of the general council.[43]

The trial was held in March 1976, and all of the defendants except Ryder Larney were convicted. However, after a well-known criminal attorney from Minnesota, Kenneth E. Tilsen, assisted by local counsel Barry Benefield, appealed the convictions, the Tenth Circuit Court of Appeals reversed the convictions. The Tenth Circuit found that the U.S. attorney's introduction of an A.R. 15 rifle, which was unrelated to any of the criminal charges, into evidence at trial for the purpose of impeaching the testimony of defendant Thomas Ahaisse could not help but prejudice all of the defendants in the eyes of the jury. On the second day of the retrial of the case, the United States dropped the extortion and conspiracy

charges after the defendants pled guilty to mailing a threat against
the Santa Fe railroad property and to President Gerald Ford; as
a result, the defendants received shorter prison terms than had
been ordered following the earlier convictions.[44]

As Chief Tanyan neared the end of his term of office, federal
court decisions and federal policies continued to promote tribal
self-determination. Federal interference with Five Tribes governments was slowed somewhat by the landmark case of *Harjo v.
Kleppe*, which was decided by the U.S. District Court for the District
of Columbia in 1976 and affirmed by the District of Columbia
Court of Appeals in 1978. Several Muscogee (Creek) citizens
brought the *Harjo* suit against various federal officials, including
the Secretary of the Interior and Claude Cox, who was the Muscogee (Creek) principal chief elected pursuant to procedures devised
under the 1970 act. The central issue was whether the Muscogee
(Creek) Nation's government had survived statutory dismember-
ment, and, if so, whether the federal government was acting
legally in recognizing the principal chief as the sole embodiment
of that government with authority to expend tribal funds without
council involvement in the Creek Nation's financial management.
The court discussed the interaction of federal officials and the
Creeks during the twentieth century, which was remarkably similar to Seminole experiences. The court found that the Department
of the Interior and its BIA engaged in a pattern of action "designed
to prevent any tribal resistance to the Department's methods of
administering those Indian affairs delegated to it by Congress."
The court further characterized this attitude as "bureaucratic
imperialism," manifested in "deliberate attempts to frustrate,
debilitate, and generally prevent from functioning the tribal governments expressly preserved by § 28 of the [1906] act." The court
concluded that the historical record demonstrated that "a competent [Muscogee (Creek)] legislative–executive government has
persisted throughout more than half a century of the most adverse
conditions imaginable."[45]

In the *Harjo* decision the court rejected federal officials' restric-
tive interpretation of several federal law provisions shared in

common by the Five Tribes. The court determined that the 1906 Five Tribes Act allowed federal appointments of the Five Tribes chiefs only under three limited circumstances: the removal, disability, or death of the incumbent. The court rejected the federal government's disingenuous argument that the Act of October 20, 1970, authorizing the popular selection of the chiefs of the Five Tribes, was "a repeal of the tribes' right to constitutional self-government in favor of a one-man elected monarchy." The court examined the legislative history of the 1970 act and found that it showed that "the fundamental congressional judgment underlying the Act was a desire to facilitate tribal self-determination."[46]

In *Harjo* the court also reviewed a provision in the 1906 act concerning the collection and disbursement of tribal funds and ruled that, contrary to the policy and practice of federal officials, it "had no effect on the tribes' authority to manage their financial affairs as long as the tribes were in existence." The court summarized its ruling as having "arrived at the inescapable conclusion" that despite the general intentions of Congress in the late nineteenth century and early twentieth century to ultimately terminate the tribal government of the Creeks, and despite an elaborate statutory scheme implementing numerous intermediate steps toward that end, "the final dissolution of the Creek tribal government created by the Creek Constitution of 1867 was never statutorily accomplished," and "the government was instead explicitly perpetuated." The court ordered relief designed to establish a mechanism to facilitate the Creeks' development and adoption of a new constitution.[47]

Although the *Harjo* decision was a significant victory for all of the Five Tribes, it had slightly less practical impact on the Seminole Nation, which had already been operating under its new 1969 constitution for almost seven years at the time the decision was rendered. However, after the *Harjo* decision, federal officials could no longer require any of the Five Tribes to obtain BIA approval of their elected chiefs. Hence, in 1991 the Seminole Constitution was amended to eliminate an inactive provision allowing the president of the United States to appoint the chief.[48]

As tribal leaders neared the end of the second four-year term of office under the 1969 constitution, the landmark final report by the American Indian Policy Review Commission was issued in May 1977. The policy review commission had been established by federal law in 1975 and was charged with conducting a comprehensive review of the historical and legal developments underlying Native Americans' relationship with the federal government and with determining the nature and scope of necessary revisions in federal Indian programs and policies. The commission dedicated thirty pages of its report to the status of tribes in Oklahoma and their members. The commission explained the different manner in which Congress treated the Five Tribes and the tribes located in western Oklahoma, noting that it was more difficult to define the sovereignty of the Five Tribes. The commission acknowledged the continued existence of the Five Tribes and noted that the relationship of the United States with the Five Tribes "can only be described as a complete breach of faith."[49]

The American Indian Policy Review Commission discussed jurisdiction over Indian lands in Oklahoma at some length in its report. According to the commission, at or shortly after allotment, the tribal police forces "fell into increasing disuse and more or less faded from existence sometimes [sic] in the early 1940's." The commission found "no legislation or administrative authority of any kind to make the disappearance of tribal police an occurrence predicated by law." According to the commission, the state conducted all law enforcement activities on non-Indian land from statehood on, but it was "unclear as to when the State formalized a policy of claiming jurisdiction over Indian lands." The commission found that there appeared to have been a process by which the state claimed some degree of authority, and that federal officials silently acquiesced. The commission mentioned a study that had recently been issued by the Oklahoma Indian Affairs Commission that had concluded that Indian arrests rates were "many times higher" than the ratio of the Indian and non-Indian populations in various counties. The commission also noted that in 1975 the Oklahoma Department of Public Safety had issued a memorandum intended to establish a basic departmental policy to address increasing Indian activism through such organizations as AIM. AIM's activities in Oklahoma were "inconsequential," according to the commission, who went on to state that it was "hard to decide which is more important to Oklahoma: proper police protection for Indian people or the suppression of A.I.M."[50]

The American Indian Policy Review Commission found that many federal programs unfairly based eligibility on the reservation or non-reservation status of potential tribal participants. The commission noted that there was no legislation specifically abolishing the boundaries of eastern Oklahoma reservations or the boundaries of most western Oklahoma reservations. The commission stated that the characterization of Oklahoma tribes as "non-reservation" tribes was "a simple matter of the BIA taking an action for its own convenience." According to the commission, "Oklahoma is Indian Country, and the United States has the same responsibilities toward the tribes that it does to Indian tribes in any other State in the Union." The commission stressed that reservation status should be "returned" to Oklahoma tribes to enable them to be eligible for certain federal assistance benefits, such as programs involving school construction moneys, employment and training funding, and law enforcement funding from the LEAA. There was "absolutely no logical reason" why education and training funds should be withheld from Oklahoma tribes, the commission stated, and "the reasons for withholding of LEAA funds would seem to be based on legal confusion and administrative fiat."[51]

In light of the Indian Policy Review Commission's report, along with the federal legislation and court decisions of the seventies favoring tribal self-government, the legal climate was ripe for change. The increased self-determination of all tribes and their citizens nationwide was on the horizon, as were other exciting developments in Indian law and improvements in the status of Oklahoma tribes. The Seminole Nation was prepared to take advantage of this situation and appeared to be on its way to a more hopeful and promising future for its citizens by the end of Chief Tanyan's first term of office in 1977.

CHAPTER 8

SELF-DETERMINATION AND DISSENT

*Administrations of Chiefs Richmond Tiger (1977–1978),
Tom Palmer (1978–1981), and James Milam (1981–1985)*

The period between 1977 and 1985 was an exciting time for tribes in Oklahoma. The federal government began to recognize that many Oklahoma Indians had retained their cultural identities and were not as assimilated into the mainstream as previously believed. It acknowledged there was error in the view that Oklahoma tribes were "non-reservation" tribes without the need for federal assistance, and it responded by providing funding to Oklahoma tribal governments on a more equal footing with other tribes nationwide. Equally important, court decisions began to expand judicial recognition of the governmental authority of Indian tribes, both on a national scale and at the local level in Oklahoma. Notwithstanding the exercise of state legislative and judicial authority over Indians for decades in Oklahoma, courts began to recognize that this practice was not supported by the law; resulting decisions enabled Oklahoma tribes to truly spread their governmental wings for the first time since statehood.

These positive national developments occurred at the same time that the Seminole Nation was making its own progress, albeit with some severe setbacks. The elections for principal chief, assistant chief, and general council members were held on July 9, 1977. Richmond Tiger, a World War II veteran and a member of the Mekusukey Band, was elected chief. Thomas Palmer, a member of the Tusekia Harjo Band who had served as assistant chief during the first administration of Edwin Tanyan, was reelected to serve as assistant chief in a run-off held on August 13, 1977. New

178

council members were also elected by their bands, including several incumbents, such as Ben Warrior, Tony Palmer, Richard Bemo, Sam Moses, and Thomas Coker, who were elected by their band members for third consecutive terms. J. B. Thurman was also elected for a third term, and he eventually went on to represent the Dosar Barkus Band for at least six consecutive terms. The inauguration ceremony for the new tribal officials was held in September 1977.[1]

After serving as chief for only a little more than a year, Chief Tiger resigned in late 1978 or early 1979 for personal reasons, and Assistant Chief Tom Palmer took over as chief. James Milam was then selected to serve as assistant chief. During the Tiger–Palmer four-year term of office, Lucy Harjo served as council secretary from November 1977 through October 1978, with JoAnna Morris serving as acting secretary for some of the meetings. Corena Mae England resumed serving as council secretary from the March 1979 council meeting through the May 1981 council meeting. During some of this time, Holdenville attorneys James Rodgers and Gordon Allen, a member of the Choctaw Nation, provided legal representation to the Nation.[2]

During Richmond Tiger's term as chief, the council enacted legislation in 1978 specifying eligibility criteria for membership in the Seminole Nation and establishing an enrollment committee responsible for approving or disapproving Seminole membership applications. This legislation was revised less than a year later after Palmer took over as chief. The 1979 version included a general right of appeal to the general council; however, appeals involving membership for purposes of sharing in the distribution of awards from claims against the United States, popularly referred to as "judgment funds," were to be made in accordance with federal regulations. During the brief time that Chief Tiger led the Nation, the council also established a tribal budget committee, which was responsible for assisting with working on all budgetary processes and monitoring the salaries and personal travel expenses of tribal officials, program directors, and employees. The council later amended that law during Tom Palmer's term as chief in order to more specifically describe the duties of the budget committee.[3]

In addition to strengthening the tribal infrastructure in the areas of membership and budget management, one of the highest priorities for the council during the Tiger–Palmer term, which ran from September 1977 until September 1981, was the continuation of federally funded tribal services programs. The council enacted numerous resolutions related to the existing programs, including education programs and elderly programs, and it added a few new programs.[4]

In fiscal years 1977 and 1978 the Nation received grant funding for several essential purposes, including an enrollment committee, a business committee, an accounting department, and an administrative assistant. The Seminole government also obtained funding in fiscal year 1977 to prepare the site for the tribal office building south of Wewoka.[5] Seminole programs from August 1978 to September 1979 included federal grants related to employment, recreation, fuel assistance to the elderly in the winter, economic development, educational needs, housing, and a health management improvement program.[6] The total amount of grants and contracts awarded to the Seminole Nation increased from $110,988.45 for fiscal year 1977 to $946,335 for fiscal year 1980. The most significant increase was attributable to federal contracts, which increased from $10,588 in fiscal year 1977 to $800,985 in fiscal year 1980.[7]

During the late seventies Oklahoma tribes, including the Seminole Nation, made progress in their ongoing fight to obtain the same type of federal assistance provided to other tribes outside Oklahoma. Oklahoma tribes were almost excluded in 1979 from participating in the delivery of food stamp and commodity distribution programs under the 1977 Food Stamp Act. That act allowed tribes to administer food stamp and commodity distribution programs on reservations and defined reservations as "the geographically defined area or areas over which a tribal organization exercises governmental jurisdiction." In 1978 the Department of Agriculture indicated in its proposed regulations for the act that

Oklahoma tribes would not be eligible for participation in the program, expressing the view that many of the "former" Oklahoma reservations did not constitute a legally recognized area subject to tribal governmental jurisdiction. It was only after much opposition from tribes and Indian organizations in Oklahoma that the Department of Agriculture retracted this policy statement from the final regulations and acknowledged that tribes in Oklahoma should be allowed to apply for participation in food stamp and commodity distribution programs.[8]

The Seminole Nation and the other four tribal participants in the Inter-Tribal Council of the Five Tribes recognized the need to educate both federal and state governmental officials about tribal contributions to the general public. The Inter-Tribal Council made efforts to inform the public of the benefits that the Five Tribes brought to Oklahoma. For example, a 1979 survey conducted by the Indian Rights Association of Philadelphia demonstrated the positive effect of funds produced and administered by the Five Tribes on local economies throughout the state. The survey also attempted to dispel the myth that Indians do not have to pay taxes, noting that Indians pay federal, state, and local income and sales taxes. According to the survey report, although tribes were exempt from local property taxes on Indian trust lands, incoming federal funds more than compensated for the loss of funds for local schools caused by nonpayment of real property taxes. For example, there were federal Title IV education program funds coming in as well as Johnson O'Malley (JOM) funds, which were used to pay for counselors in public schools with high enrollment levels of Indian students, teachers for remedial courses, and kindergarten programs.[9]

Another high priority of tribal leaders during the four-year term shared by Chief Tiger and Chief Palmer was the improvement of both health and housing conditions for tribal members. Regarding health issues, the general council enacted a law establishing a Seminole Nation Department of Health and Social Services, which was intended to serve as the primary health planner and coordinator of health services for Indian people within Seminole

County. The council also enacted resolutions supporting a health care recruitment program, supporting the Eastern Oklahoma Indian Health Planning Board, and attempting to improve IHS programs.[10] The council actively worked with the Housing Authority of the Seminole Nation in supporting the housing authority's application for federal funding from HUD for low-rent housing and housing for homeownership.[11] Housing was also important to the Inter-Tribal Council of the Five Civilized Tribes, which sent its delegates with tribal officials to meet with the HUD secretary to discuss allocations of federal housing funds.[12]

During the Tiger–Palmer term of office, the Seminole Nation established an Indian Child Welfare Program. That program was developed after Congress enacted the federal Indian Child Welfare Act in 1978, most of which became effective in April 1979. That law, popularly known as the ICWA, included congressional findings that a high percentage of Indian families were broken up by the (often unwarranted) removal of their children by nontribal public and private agencies and that an alarmingly high percentage of these children were placed in non-Indian foster and adoptive homes and institutions. The ICWA expressly recognized that tribal courts possessed exclusive jurisdiction over cases involving custody of Indian children—except placement of children involved in criminal conduct or award of custody to a parent in divorce proceeding—if the child was domiciled in Indian country. The ICWA also allowed transfers to tribal courts of state cases involving foster care placements of Indian children and termination of parental rights, and it established special requirements for those cases that remained in the state court system. These requirements included notice to the child's tribe and parents and a higher burden of proof for the removal of an Indian child from his home and placement in foster care. It required an even higher burden of proof for termination of parental rights by state courts. The ICWA established placement preferences for children who were removed from their parents or Indian custodians or placed for adoption, with a high priority being given to placements with relatives and members of Indian tribes.[13]

The establishment of the Seminole Indian Child Welfare Program and other such tribal programs throughout the state of Oklahoma was beneficial to the state because it increased the number of workers looking out for the welfare of Indian children, reducing some of the state workers' workload in the process. This effort was supported by the Oklahoma Legislature. In 1982 the state legislature enacted the Oklahoma Indian Child Welfare Act, which was authored by Oklahoma State Rep. Kelly Haney, a member of the Seminole Nation who represented the district in which the Seminole Nation was located. The purpose of the state law, referred to as the OICWA, was to clarify state policies and procedures regarding the state implementation of the ICWA and to require full state cooperation with Oklahoma Indian tribes to ensure that the intent and provisions of the ICWA were enforced. The OICWA also allowed the Oklahoma Department of Human Services to enter into foster home agreements with Indian tribes so that federal funds could be used for foster homes licensed by Indian tribes. The state and Indian tribes were quick to implement these agreements, and they developed a model tribal–state foster care agreement that was routinely used by the state and a number of Oklahoma tribes, including the Seminole Nation. As a result, tribal ICWA programs recruited and licensed Indian foster homes, which were then eligible for financial assistance in the form of foster care payments funded by the federal government and distributed by the state.[14]

Only a few years after enactment of the OICWA, Oklahoma Indian Legal Services, a federally funded legal aid office established in 1981 to provide free legal services to low-income members of Indian tribes, represented a nineteen-year-old Seminole father in an unsuccessful attempt to overturn a state court adoption of his infant child by non-Indians. The child's non-Indian mother had placed the baby boy for adoption by non-Indians, and the child was adopted without notice to the father and without his consent. The case eventually resulted in a 1985 decision by the Oklahoma Supreme Court known as *Matter of Baby Boy D.* In a ruling concurred in by only five of the nine Justices, the court upheld the legality of the adoption, finding that the state court had not been required to follow the ICWA and OICWA because the baby had not been "removed" from the father, who never had physical custody of his newborn child. This judicial exception to application of the ICWA was known as the "Indian family exception."[15]

In 1989 the U.S. Supreme Court rendered a decision that did not specifically address the "Indian family exception" but that nevertheless called into question the soundness of the *Baby Boy D* decision. In that case, *Mississippi Band of Choctaw Indians v. Holyfield*, the Court found that the ICWA applied to newborn twins who had never been in the custody of their parents, and it invalidated the twins' state court adoption based on ICWA requirements. According to that decision, the ICWA was intended to address not only the interests of Indian children and families, but also the impact on Indian tribes of the large numbers of Indian children adopted by non-Indians. Five years after the decision, Seminole member Kelly Haney, by then a state senator, sponsored and secured passage of amendments of the OICWA, clarifying that the OICWA and the ICWA applied to Indian children regardless of whether they were removed from an Indian family. Another decade passed before the Oklahoma Supreme Court finally expressly overruled the *Baby Boy D* case in *Matter of Adoption of Baby Boy L*, a 2004 decision that involved a Muscogee (Creek) child. In the meantime, in 1991 the Oklahoma Supreme Court recognized the importance of tribal involvement in Indian child custody cases. In a case involving a state court guardianship of a Seminole child placed with non-Indian grandparents against the mother's wishes, the court ruled that Indian tribes have the right to intervene under the ICWA at any point in such cases.[16]

At the beginning of the Tiger–Palmer term of office, the Seminole Nation's railroad claims and Florida land claims still had not been finally resolved. The council extended Paul Niebell's attorney contract to continue working on the claims cases and hired an appraiser for the railroad claims case. The council agreed to a settlement of the railroad claim, Docket 247, in the amount of $100,000, and on December 19, 1980, the Court of Claims issued an award in that amount to the Seminole Nation. The council approved a maximum of $10,000 to be paid to Paul Niebell and the estate of Roy St. Lewis for their legal services related to that claim. The council developed a proposed plan for use of the award, subject to approval by the Department of the Interior, as required by the Judgment Fund Act of October 19, 1973, which governed plans for use and distributions of judgment fund awards. The council found that the award was too small for per capita distribution and proposed a plan under which all of the funds were to be invested by the Department of the Interior, with the accrued interest and investment income from that investment to be used for a tribal governmental operations program.[17]

During the Tiger–Palmer term, tribal leaders were involved in trying to secure a final plan for use of the Florida land claims award approved by the Court of Claims in April 1976. Congress appropriated funds for the award by the Act of June 1, 1976, but the 1973 Judgment Fund Act still required the development and approval of a plan to divide the funds among the four designated beneficiaries: the Seminole Tribe of Florida, the Miccosukee Tribe of Indians of Florida, the independent Seminoles of Florida, and the Seminole Nation of Oklahoma. The BIA made various attempts to assist the tribal beneficiaries in developing a use and distribution plan, including a formula for division of the funds. In the meantime, an appeal by the Florida Miccosukee Tribe concerning the settlement of the claim between the tribal beneficiaries and the United States was litigated, resulting in a U.S. Supreme Court decision in late 1977 that the Court lacked jurisdiction to hear the appeal, letting the settlement stand.[18]

The Seminole Nation Judgment Fund Committee was involved in most of the process involving congressional appropriation of funding for payment of the Florida claims award. The committee consisted of a member by blood from each of the Seminole Nation's twelve Indian bands, plus five additional members known as the judgment fund committee planners: the chief, the assistant chief, and three persons selected by the chief, subject to general council's approval. Terms of committee members ran concurrently with the term of each principal chief. The committee's duties included, among other things, negotiating with various federal, state, or tribal agencies; advising and counseling committees about accountability and distribution of judgment fund awards; preparing quarterly reports for the general council; monitoring programs funded with judgment funds; and recommending additional programs to the general council.[19]

In March 1978 the Senate Select Committee on Indian Affairs held a hearing on two bills concerning the distribution of the Florida claims award. The first bill, Senate Bill 2000, was sponsored by Oklahoma senators Dewey Bartlett and Henry Bellmon and was supported by the Seminole Nation of Oklahoma—including the judgment fund committee—and by the Department of the Interior. At the hearing, Chief Richmond Tiger, Assistant Chief Tom Palmer, council member Edwin Tanyan, and Seminole negotiator John Tiger all testified in favor of Senate Bill 2000, which provided for a division of the award giving three-fourths to the Oklahoma Seminoles and one-fourth to the Florida Seminoles. The formula for this proposed distribution was based on populations of the Oklahoma and Florida Seminoles during the period from 1906 to 1914, excluding Seminole freedmen. There were 2,146 Seminoles by blood on the 1906 Seminole rolls, with 90 percent of those members being of one-half Indian blood or more. According to a Florida census, as reconstructed by the BIA, there were 700 Florida Seminoles in 1914. The Department of the Interior supported freedmen exclusion from participation because the Florida lands were taken in 1823, and it was Interior's position that "the Negroes did not become members of the Seminole Nation until 1866." The second bill, Senate Bill 2188, was supported by the Seminole Tribe of Florida and provided for the referral of the division of the award funds to the chief commissioner of the Court of Claims to determine a fair and equitable division based on all relevant factors, including any difference in benefits received by the Oklahoma and Florida Seminoles. According to testimony of tribal leaders, the Oklahoma and Florida Seminoles could not reach an agreement regarding the split.[20]

Neither bill was enacted into law. Instead, on April 24, 1978, the assistant secretary of the Interior sent to Congress the plan supported by the Oklahoma Seminoles. It was believed that the effective date of the plan would be June 19, 1978, under the Judgment Fund Act of 1973, absent House action disapproving the plan. The Seminole Indian Tribe of Florida and Guy Osceola, as spokesman for the independent Seminoles of Florida, joined by the two Oklahoma freedmen bands as intervenors, challenged the validity of the plan in a suit against the Secretary of the Interior. This challenge resulted in a ruling by the U.S. District Court for the District of Columbia finding that the plan was invalid because hearing requirements of the Judgment Fund Act of 1973 had not been met and because the Department of the Interior had failed to meet statutory time limitations established by that act in its submission of the plan to Congress. The Court of Appeals for the District of Columbia affirmed and clarified the decision in 1980, based on the stipulation of the parties.[21]

In December 1979 the general council enacted a resolution requesting the secretary to seek re-implementation of the Oklahoma Seminoles' version of the judgment fund distribution plan for the Florida lands claim. Efforts to secure the necessary federal legislation to achieve a division of the Florida land claim judgment funds among the Oklahoma and Florida Seminoles continued into the eighties, without success. In 1980 there were 800 freedmen members of the Dosar Barkus and Caesar Bruner bands, led by Ben Warrior and Andrew Crockett, who sought to be included in the award benefits. The freedmen band members were also unable to participate in federal Indian programs, which the federal government restricted to the use of Indians. In spite of the efforts of Seminole leaders, no plan for the division of the Florida land claim award was approved by Congress by the end of the Tiger–Palmer term of office in September 1981 or even by the end of Milam's term in September 1985. It took five more years before Congress resolved issues concerning division of the Florida land claim judgment funds among the Oklahoma and Florida Seminoles.[22]

In the late seventies, significant changes began to occur regarding state regulatory and judicial authority over Indian country in western and central Oklahoma. The Seminole Nation and other tribes in eastern Oklahoma were not immediately affected by these changes, but the changes were ground-breaking and enhanced the ability of the eastern Oklahoma tribes to secure similar results many years later. In 1977 Otoe-Missouri member F. Browning Pipestem achieved the first significant victory concerning Oklahoma tribal jurisdictional matters in *United States v. Littlechief*. In that case, the U.S. District Court for the Western District of Oklahoma decided that the state courts had no authority to prosecute an Indian defendant for the murder of another Indian on a Kiowa trust allotment, stating that it was "common ground" that Indian conduct occurring on a trust allotment was beyond the state's jurisdiction and was instead the proper concern of tribal or federal authorities. The court further found that *Ellis v. Page*, a 1963 Oklahoma Court of Criminal Appeals case relied on for many years as authority for the exercise of Oklahoma state jurisdiction over Indians on Indian lands, was not applicable because the *Ellis* case involved ceded Indian lands, not trust allotments. The court also found that although Oklahoma had once had the opportunity to assume jurisdiction over Indian crimes committed in Indian country under Public Law 280, it had failed to exercise that option before Public Law 280 was amended to require tribal consent. The *Littlechief* case was significant because it diminished state authority over Indian trust lands in western Oklahoma, recognized the existence of a geographic area subject to tribal governmental authority, established the need for tribal courts, and resulted in a swift reaction on the part of governmental authorities.[23]

As a result of the *Littlechief* case, the federal government began prosecuting major crimes occurring on Indian country lands in western Oklahoma. In addition, the Department of the Interior advised western Oklahoma tribes that they had no legal impediment to exercising tribal law enforcement over misdemeanors occurring on Indian trust allotments if they had a constitution authorizing tribal exercise of judicial powers. Because most of the western Oklahoma tribes lacked such constitutional provisions, in 1979 the Department of the Interior amended the *Code of Federal Regulations* to establish a "CFR Court," more formally referred to as the "Court of Indian Offenses," for tribes in western Oklahoma served by the BIA Anadarko Area Office (later renamed the Southern Plains Regional Office). The CFR courts had been in existence in many other parts of the United States since 1883. According to a later federal court decision upholding the validity of the amended regulations, CFR courts were established in western Oklahoma because of "an urgent and compelling need for judicial and law enforcement services" on western Oklahoma Indian trust or restricted lands. Although the CFR court retained some characteristics of a federal government agency, it also functioned as a tribal court.[24]

The inclusion of western Oklahoma tribes in the CFR court system did not affect inherent tribal sovereignty to establish tribal courts and exercise jurisdiction under tribal law. Many tribes in western Oklahoma later amended their constitutions and established their own tribal courts. The tribes in eastern Oklahoma, including the Seminole Nation, were not included in the 1979 amendment of the regulations governing CFR courts, because at that time no similar court decisions had been rendered concerning the Indian country status of restricted and trust lands in eastern Oklahoma. The tribes in eastern Oklahoma were eventually included in the CFR court system in the early nineties, after the state and federal courts recognized the Indian country status of Five Tribes restricted allotments and certain other Five Tribes lands.[25]

Another significant court decision arising in central Oklahoma consistent with the *Littlechief* decision soon followed that case. In 1979 the Oklahoma Court of Criminal Appeals ruled in *C.M.G. v. State* that the prosecution of an Indian student for the murder of another Indian student at the Chilocco Indian School in north central Oklahoma was not subject to state jurisdiction, because the crime was committed at a "dependent Indian community," which constituted Indian country under federal law. The court discussed a 1978 U.S. Supreme Court decision in the *C.M.G.*

case, *United States v. John*. In the *John* case, the Court found that in order to determine what constituted Indian country, one had to see whether the fundamental consideration of Congress and the Department of the Interior was the protection of a dependent people. The Court found in *John* that the test for Indian country was whether the land "had been validly set apart for the use of the Indians as such, under the superintendence of the government." The Supreme Court ruled in the *John* decision that land placed in trust for the Mississippi Choctaw Tribe was Indian country, even though the Choctaws residing in Mississippi allegedly had become fully assimilated into the political and social life of Mississippi and even though Mississippi's jurisdiction over Indians and Indian land had gone unchallenged for many years. The cases concerning the Indian country status of lands in central and western Oklahoma were significant with regard to criminal matters only when an Indian was being prosecuted, because in 1978 the U.S. Supreme Court ruled in *Oliphant v. Suquamish Indian Tribe* that tribal courts did not have jurisdiction to try and punish non-Indians in criminal matters. Jurisdiction over crimes by non-Indians in Indian country remained subject to state court prosecution.[26]

The new developments concerning jurisdiction over Indian country in western Oklahoma affected civil cases as well as criminal cases. In 1980 the Tenth Circuit Court of Appeals ruled that Oklahoma hunting and fishing laws did not apply to Indians hunting and fishing on Cheyenne and Arapaho trust allotments or on tribal trust lands, which the court determined constituted Indian country as defined by federal law. In 1983 the Oklahoma Supreme Court held that a dispute between an Indian housing authority and an Indian homebuyer concerning a house on a Kiowa trust allotment was not subject to state civil jurisdiction. The court found that the 1950 Tenth Circuit decision in *Tooisgah v. United States*, a case long used to support the exercise of state jurisdiction over trust allotments, was not applicable. The court noted that the status of Indian trust allotments was not at issue in *Tooisgah*, which involved a federal crime predicated on the commission of certain crimes on Indian reservations. Although these decisions did not have an immediate impact on the Seminole Nation and the other tribes located in eastern Oklahoma within the service area of the BIA Muskogee Area Office, they opened the door to reconsideration of the Indian country status of individual restricted and tribal trust lands in eastern Oklahoma. These cases became even more significant following the U.S. Supreme Court's 1985 decision in *National Farmers Union Insurance Company v. Crow Tribe of Indians*, which recognized the importance of tribal courts in civil matters. That case involved a personal injury suit filed in tribal court against a non-Indian, where the injury of an Indian youth occurred in Indian country. The Supreme Court held that tribal court remedies, including a tribal court determination regarding the tribal court's jurisdiction, must be exhausted before the federal court would entertain the non-Indian's claim for injunctive relief in the case.[27] These cases were all significant for the Five Tribes in eastern Oklahoma after their judicial authority was finally judicially recognized in 1988.

When the cases concerning the jurisdictional status of Indian lands in western and central Oklahoma were being litigated in the late seventies and early eighties, the Seminole Nation was attempting, without success, to secure federal funding for law enforcement through the LEAA. The Muscogee (Creek) Nation was also seeking federal funding for a court system and law enforcement at that time. In the late seventies, Seminole Nation attorney general James Rodgers recommended that the Seminole Nation adopt a constitutional amendment to include a judicial system. Instead, Seminole government leaders contacted the Native American Rights Fund, an Indian advocacy law firm in Boulder, Colorado, about a potential administrative appeal challenging a LEAA determination of the Seminole Nation's ineligibility for LEAA funding. The Seminole leaders wanted to request a reconsideration of the legal basis for the LEAA determination, which was an April 20, 1978, opinion by Thomas W. Fredericks, the associate solicitor of the Division of Indian Affairs, Department of the Interior. The associate solicitor's opinion stated that no tribe in Indian Territory as it existed in 1898 (after the 1890 establishment of Oklahoma

Territory on the western side and the reduction in size of Indian Territory on the eastern side) had the authority to exercise civil or criminal jurisdiction. The 1978 solicitor's opinion cited provisions in the 1898 Curtis Act stating that the courts of the Five Tribes were abolished and concluded that no subsequent legislation had repealed or modified those provisions.[28]

This inexplicable, continuing refusal to afford the Five Tribes the same rights enjoyed by other tribes continued in May 1982 when the deputy assistant secretary of the Interior cited the 1978 associate solicitor opinion in a memorandum to the Muskogee Area Office concerning tribal "security programs" in eastern Oklahoma. According to the memorandum, tribes and the BIA did not have the power to authorize tribal officers to carry firearms or make arrests, and tribal security personnel could do so only if allowed by local law enforcement. The memorandum stated that it was the BIA's "policy" to adhere to the Curtis Act and "to discourage tribal activities which may lead to violation of its provisions."[29]

As it turned out, the Muscogee (Creek) Nation, rather than the Seminole Nation, challenged the BIA's position concerning tribal court authority. In October 1982 Harold M. Shultz, Jr., the Muskogee field solicitor (part of the Department of the Interior Office of the Solicitor, and the predecessor to the Tulsa field solicitor) issued an opinion consistent with the 1978 opinion and the 1982 memorandum. The opinion referenced both the Curtis Act provisions concerning abolishment of Five Tribes courts and provisions in the 1901 Creek allotment agreement stating that nothing contained in it should be construed to revive or reestablish the Muscogee (Creek) courts. The opinion briefly discussed the 1934 IRA and the 1936 OIWA, finding that those acts did not authorize reestablishment of a Muscogee (Creek) tribal court with jurisdiction similar to the jurisdiction exercised by Creek courts before enactment of the Curtis Act. The opinion further stated that the Muscogee (Creek) Nation, which had adopted a federally approved constitution under the OIWA in 1979, did not have "reservation status over lands owned by it, either unallotted or purchased for it by the United States in trust status" and stated that it would take an act of Congress to establish reservation status of those lands.[30]

Notwithstanding federal opposition to Five Tribes courts, the Muscogee (Creek) Nation enacted a law to authorize tribal court jurisdiction over civil and criminal matters. The BIA Muskogee Area director issued a memorandum to agency superintendents, stating that law enforcement and security were not contractable because of the Curtis Act and stating that federal funds should not be programmed for that purpose in the annual budgets. As a result, the BIA Okmulgee Agency superintendent sent a letter to the principal chief of the Muscogee (Creek) Nation, requiring revision of the tribe's budget to eliminate the law enforcement line item. After the Muscogee (Creek) Nation filed an appeal in May 1983, the acting deputy assistant secretary requested the associate solicitor to reevaluate the 1978 opinion for the purpose of assisting the BIA in deciding the appeal. The associate solicitor, Paul T. Baird, issued an opinion in early 1984, again concluding that federal legislation enacted at the turn of the century deprived the Muscogee (Creek) Nation of its law enforcement authority, and that those laws had continued in effect. In July 1985 the Interior Board of Indian Appeals (IBIA) affirmed the BIA's decision to deny funding for the Creek courts and law enforcement. The IBIA's affirmation was not the final word on this issue, though, because the Muscogee (Creek) Nation filed suit in the U.S. District Court for the District of Columbia and, after losing in that court, obtained a favorable decision by the District of Columbia Circuit Court of Appeals.[31]

While these important legal developments were occurring, Seminole members continued their work at the local tribal level. In what would become a regular practice, in the spring of 1981 the council repealed earlier election laws and enacted a new one, which was approved by the BIA Muskogee Area director. That law, which was applicable to the upcoming elections to be held that summer, required the election board to provide three voting precincts where members could vote on election day. Members of the general council attempted to stop the general election set for July 10, 1981, by filing a federal court suit, because only one polling place was set to be open. They were unsuccessful in that endeavor, and James Milam was elected chief in a runoff with Tom Palmer that was held in early August 1981. Chief Milam and the assistant chief, Alan Miller, along with newly elected council members, were installed in office on September 5, 1981. Corena Mae England served as general council secretary in September and October 1981 at the beginning of Chief Milam's term. After that, Mary Ann Emarthale served as council secretary from December 1981 through at least April 1984, which was apparently the last date of the recorded enactment of council legislation until near the end of Chief Milam's term in September 1985.[32]

During the first year of Chief Milam's tenure, the federal government began taking back several programs operated by the Seminole Nation, in part because the Nation failed to pay employee payroll taxes and to meet federal demands for repayments of disallowed costs. Some of these problems were attributable to the Nation's quick growth coupled with inadequate training about financial management and internal financial control standards. The Nation's first debt to the federal government had arisen during Chief Tanyan's first term, when the Seminole's CHR program was found to be in tax arrears in the amount of $18,904 because of an employee payroll tax deficit, plus interest. The Seminole government could have avoided paying penalties if it had been able to make a lump sum payment for the tax liability, but it was unable to do so. The Nation paid $55,000 to the Internal Revenue Service (IRS) in 1981 during Chief Palmer's term, including more than $49,800 from its award in Indian Claims Commission Docket 248 related to the Mekusukey lease claim, but that payment was insufficient to satisfy the Nation's mounting debt to the federal government.[33]

One of the first actions that the general council took after Milam assumed office was to request an audit by the General Accounting Office (GAO) for a five-year period, citing administrative changeover at the Seminole Nation. At the September 1981 council meeting, the council also requested the use of a

1981 training and technical assistance contract to fund audits of 1981 grants and contracts and authorized continuation of numerous federally funded programs, including education, housing, and child welfare programs. Shortly after that, in December 1981, the council enacted a resolution reciting that the BIA Muskogee Area Office director had directed that the Nation receive no funds as of September 30, 1981. According to the resolution, which requested that the area director release carryover funds to the Nation, Milam's new administration had not been able to provide services, and a large number of tribal employees had been terminated. The situation grew worse in June 1982, when the deputy area director notified the Seminole Nation that it owed a large sum to the federal government. Notwithstanding these problems, the council continued to request funding for the operation of various federal programs.[34]

An unstable political situation soon resulted, contributing to the economic turmoil. In June 1982 twenty-three of the forty-two general council members met and signed a petition calling for the impeachment of Chief Milam and Assistant Chief Miller. The BIA Wewoka Agency sanctioned the legality of that meeting, and the council obtained a security blockade of the tribal headquarters south of Wewoka for almost three days, allowing only people working with five federally funded programs to enter the area. The BIA Muskogee Area Office and the BIA headquarters in Washington, D.C., overruled the agency determination within weeks and declared the June meeting concerning Milam's impeachment invalid under the Seminole Nation Constitution. On August 9, 1982, the acting area director of the BIA Muskogee Area Office sent a letter to Milam concerning a plan for repayment of disallowed expenditures of federal funds for programs contracted by the Seminole Nation. The letter stated that a concurring resolution by the general council was needed, and that if the council was not called into emergency session for that purpose, the BIA would have "no other choice" but to reprogram funds intended for the Seminole Nation for use by other tribes in the area.[35]

On September 4, 1982, Chief Milam and a council faction that included his supporters met at the Mekusukey Mission. The other council faction met at the courthouse in Wewoka and voted for the second time to remove Chief Milam and Assistant Chief Miller from office. The removal action was again supported by the BIA Wewoka Agency, which issued letters dated September 9 and 11, 1982, stating that it was freezing funding and that it no longer recognized James Milam and Alan Miller as tribal officials. Milam appealed those agency determinations by letter dated September 14, 1982. In early September, the general council elected Edwin Tanyan to serve as chief. Shortly after that, volunteer armed guards who were supporters of James Milam, stood watch at the tribal headquarters. Milam disputed the removal action and, to the ridicule of some tribal members, challenged Edwin Tanyan to an Indian stickball contest to decide the tribal leadership issue.[36]

In late October 1982 BIA officials in Washington agreed with the agency that the September removal of James Milam as chief was legal. Milam supporters protested the BIA's position, arguing that the BIA was interfering with tribal affairs by taking a position in support of removing tribal officials. Milam continued to maintain offices at the tribal headquarters, and Edwin Tanyan maintained an office at the BIA Wewoka Agency across the road. In November 1982, shots were fired at the tribal headquarters and at the BIA agency, with each side blaming the other. As a result, the BIA dispatched armed guards to the Wewoka Agency office. The U.S. attorney filed suit in the U.S. Court for the Eastern District of Oklahoma in Muskogee on November 24, 1982, stating that there was a continuing trespass that had caused "a complete shutdown" of Seminole tribal operations and seeking an injunction to remove Milam from possession of the tribal headquarters. A hearing was set in that case for November 30, 1982, but it was postponed pending a hearing scheduled for December 8 in a federal suit filed by Milam in Washington, D.C., in which he sought a court ruling that he was validly serving as chief of the Seminole Nation.[37]

On December 23, 1982, the U.S. District Court for the District of Columbia ruled that insufficient notice was provided to the forty-two council members before the council's impeachment of Milam, and it ordered the BIA to recognize James Milam as chief and to not take any action that had the effect of removing him from office. The following month, the Inter-Tribal Council for the Five Civilized Tribes voted to seek the removal of Jack Ellison from the position of area director of the BIA Muskogee Area Office because of delays in getting necessary BIA approval for tribal proposals and alleged BIA interference in internal tribal matters. This action was approved by Milam but criticized by Tanyan.[38] The council faction working with Milam continued to meet in 1982 and 1983 and approved a variety of resolutions seeking the continuance of the Nation's federally funded programs, but these actions were not successful.[39]

During 1983 the council recognized by Chief Milam enacted several resolutions reflecting the seriousness of the dispute that was splitting the Seminole Nation. In February the council faction supporting Milam passed a resolution calling for the termination or transfer of Cecil Shipp, superintendent of the BIA Wewoka Agency. In March 1983 the Milam council approved a resolution stating that there was a continuing controversy within the Seminole Nation and that sixteen listed council members from seven listed bands had been removed—removals that were "reaffirmed and validated." Another resolution was enacted on the same date, stating that twelve listed council members from five other bands had also been removed. These resolutions demonstrated that in the eyes of James Milam and his supporters, twenty-eight members of the council that had originally been elected and seated in September 1981 had been removed from the council. In June the council affiliated with Chief Milam approved a resolution stating that the BIA had refused to release funds because it "used the excuse" that there were two councils; the resolution authorized Chief Milam to hire an attorney to file suit against the BIA for the release of fiscal year 1983 funds.[40]

The controversy continued through 1983 and 1984, during which time James Milam continued to act as the federally recognized chief and two different councils coexisted, each refusing to recognize the legality of the other. In January 1983 the BIA decided that it would not recognize band removal of members of the council as it had existed in June 1982 unless it was approved by the remaining members of the elected council. This decision was based on the BIA's opinion that under the Seminole Constitution, bands had the authority to remove band members under certain circumstances, but such removal was subject to approval of the council. In March 1983 the acting Muskogee Area director notified Milam that in order for the Nation to qualify for federal grants and contracts, the BIA required the council to submit a resolution requesting the grant or contract, provide certification that it had an acceptable financial system in place, and implement a repayment plan for outstanding fiscal year 1981 and 1982 funds that had been provided by the BIA for Seminole programs but had not been properly invoiced or returned.[41]

The Seminole government was unable to demonstrate these qualifications for federal funding, and tribal offices were closed. The BIA Wewoka Agency operated programs that had been operated by the Seminoles, including social services, adult vocational training, and home improvement programs. Edwin Tanyan, Houston Ross, Jennie Ross, Dwayne Miller, Thomas McGeisey, and Tinnie Tiger filed suit in federal court in Muskogee in March 1983 seeking BIA recognition that they were members of the council, but the case was later dismissed. In January and April 1984 letters, the Muskogee Area director confirmed an earlier BIA opinion that the June 5, 1982, council was the last properly constructed council. This opinion did not resolve the Nation's problems, because Milam continued to assert that certain council members had been removed after the June 1982 meeting, and he refused to meet with the council consisting of those council members who were in office on June 5, 1982.[42]

The Seminole government's financial accountability problems continued. On August 28, 1984, members of the council that Milam refused to recognize, including former chiefs Edwin Tanyan and Floyd Harjo, sent a letter to federal officials, requesting that certain revenue sharing funds be put on hold and expressing concern that there would be a lack of accountability if the funds were subject to Milam's oversight. A few months later, the acting area director for the BIA Muskogee Area Office argued the importance of a "duly constituted" general council in a letter to James Milam dated November 2, 1984, noting that the Seminole Nation was "beset with many internal problems." In January 1985 an inspector general audit report concluded that the Seminole government maintained poor accounting records and lacked administrative staff continuity, and it recommended that the BIA recover disallowed costs of $136,853. The tribally operated programs that the Nation had built up in the dozen years since the people had approved the 1969 constitution had essentially vanished before the end of Chief Milam's term.[43]

Adding to this disastrous turn of events, in 1984 former chief Tom Palmer was convicted in the federal district court in Muskogee on three of four federal charges of willful misapplication of tribal funds. The conviction was based on findings that Palmer had paid himself for 760 hours of annual leave, that he had received payment for undocumented travel claims in the amount of $1,676, and that he had approved payments of consultant fees in the amount of $5,200 to the Nation's accountant without a written contract. Palmer was ordered to serve two concurrent terms of two and a half years of imprisonment, remain on probation for an additional year, and pay $8,923.98 in restitution. Palmer appealed the conviction, arguing that the Seminole Nation had exclusive jurisdiction over the alleged crimes, but the Tenth Circuit rejected that argument. The accountant involved in Palmer's case was indicted in March 1984 for misappropriation of $8,000 in tribal funds. In later years Palmer continued to play a role in Seminole government by serving on various committees.[44]

Economic development was a low priority during the Tiger–Palmer and Milam administrations, with the council considering only a few potential projects for economic development, including proposals for construction of a radio tower on tribal land and development of a manufacturing plant for gasohol processing; none of these proposals led to viable projects.[45] However, in the eighties bingo enterprises on tribal trust lands became a new source of tribal income. In 1981, in *Seminole Tribe of Florida v. Butterworth*, a federal appeals court recognized that state gaming laws did not apply to tribal gaming on tribal lands. The court found in that case that Florida state laws governing bingo games were civil–regulatory and could not be applied to the Seminole Tribe of Florida, which had contracted with a private entity to build and operate a bingo hall on the Seminole Reservation in Florida. After that decision the Oklahoma Seminoles conducted bingo games for four months in late 1982, halted them for a brief time, resumed the operations in March 1983, and halted them again in 1984. Several other Oklahoma tribes operated bingo games on trust lands during this time, including the Pawnee Tribe, Ponca Tribe, Citizen Band Potawatomi Tribe, Muscogee (Creek) Nation, Seneca Cayuga, and Quapaw Tribe. The authority of tribes to conduct the bingo games without state regulation was the subject of ongoing suits nationwide, ultimately resulting in decisions favorable to the tribes. Eventually this situation led to the 1988 enactment of the Indian Gaming Regulatory Act (IGRA), which enhanced the Seminole Nation's ability to generate purely tribal funds for use in its governmental activities, economic development, and other purposes authorized by IGRA.[46]

There apparently were few, if any, records of any written council resolutions for all of 1984 and for most of 1985. On March 30, 1985, twenty-two members of the original June 1982 council and six members of the Milam council held a council meeting attended by Chief Milam and approved a new election law, which was approved by the BIA Muskogee Area director. The BIA assisted by allocating funding for the Seminole Election Board, acting as federal employees, to conduct the election.[47]

The eight years during which Tiger, Palmer, and Milam each served as chief of the Seminole Nation was a period in which there was a breakdown in the new government that was exacerbated by tribal inexperience in handling financial affairs, the absence of a tribal court system, and the inconsistent and damaging interference of the BIA. Nonetheless, there were still positive developments during the Tiger and Palmer administrations. The court decisions that affirmed tribal sovereignty nationwide had long-term positive effects on the Seminole Nation, particularly the cases that later contributed to the validation of the judicial and law enforcement authority of the Five Tribes. The Seminole government also demonstrated its ability to generate significant increases in federal funding, which was a positive step for the Nation in the long run, even though the Nation suffered financial setbacks that were, in large part, attributable to tribal officials' inexperience in grant administration and proper recordkeeping. The Seminole government's most notable other achievements included the establishment of the Nation's Indian child welfare program, increased affordable Indian housing, continuing efforts to achieve distribution of the Florida claims case award, and the beginning development of tribal gaming operations, which generated a source of non-federal funding for the Seminole government. Perhaps wiser for the difficulties that the Nation suffered between mid-1977 and mid-1985, the Nation conducted new elections in the summer of 1985, obtained new leadership, and moved forward on a difficult road to recovery.

CHAPTER 9

RECONSTRUCTION AND RESOURCE DEVELOPMENT

Administrations of Chiefs Edwin Tanyan (1985–1989)
and Jerry G. Haney (1989–1993)

The Seminole Nation eventually regained its positive momentum during the second administration of Edwin Tanyan and the first administration of Jerry G. Haney, thanks to the hard work and commitment of those chiefs and many other Seminole leaders who contributed countless hours to rebuild and repair the damage caused by the political strife of the early eighties. Seminole accomplishments during this time included resolving the Nation's dispute with Florida Seminoles over the distribution of the Florida land claims award, creating a plan for use of the Florida claims award, and establishing programs funded by the award. The Oklahoma Seminole government also rebuilt federally funded programs and provided services to tribal members under those programs, improved its governmental infrastructure by developing a codified system of laws, amended its constitution, and expanded its bingo operations.

Edwin Tanyan defeated candidate Kenna Harjo in a runoff election for chief on August 10, 1985.[1] Tanyan began his second, although not consecutive, term as principal chief of the Seminole Nation that year, with Simeon Bemo serving as assistant chief. At the beginning of his second administration, Tanyan had to deal with continued disruption of the Seminole Nation's government by former chief Milam and his supporters. Several tribal members, including James Milam and Alan Miller, contested the validity of the election and requested a federal court ruling that the defendants, BIA officials and Seminole Election Board members, were improperly involved in the 1985 Seminole elections and the internal affairs of the Seminole Nation. During this time, Tanyan was forced to maintain a temporary office at the Seminole Nation Housing Authority. At first Milam continued to occupy the tribal headquarters south of Wewoka, which reportedly had suffered up to $50,000 in damages, but in the spring of 1986 he finally vacated the tribal headquarters and relocated to the Mekusukey Mission grounds south of Seminole, which had also remained under his control.[2]

Former chief Milam and his supporters interfered with the new Tanyan administration to such a great extent that in December 1985 the general council requested the federal government to direct Milam and Alan Miller to cease acting on behalf of the Seminole Nation. The council asked the BIA to initiate a proper accounting of tribal equipment and machinery located at Mekusukey and to prevent any unauthorized disposition of them. In May 1986 the BIA Muskogee Area Office requested that the FBI investigate an incident during which several tribal members, who had been instructed by Chief Tanyan to repair a gate at the Mekusukey Mission grounds, were confronted by a group of armed Milam supporters. Months earlier, in October 1985, Chief Tanyan had requested assistance from the U.S. attorney in removing Milam and his supporters from Mekusukey. The incidents at Mekusukey were later the subject of a federal grand jury investigation.[3]

The U.S. Court for the Eastern District of Oklahoma ended the impasse when it rendered judgment against Milam and the other plaintiffs in October 1986. Three years later, the Tenth Circuit upheld that decision, citing other federal court decisions that recognized that internal tribal disputes ordinarily were matters for tribal resolution under principles of tribal self-determination and were not within the jurisdiction of the federal courts. The court found that although tribal elections were central to a tribe's ability to govern itself, the BIA had the authority to interpret the Seminole Constitution to determine which tribal government to recognize so that it could carry out government relations with the Nation, including distributing "much-needed" federal funds for tribal programs.[4] As recognized in other Tenth Circuit decisions, the BIA would not have had authority to get involved if a tribal forum had existed for resolving the Nation's internal election disputes. Although most Seminole voters did not immediately recognize it, the absence of a tribal court was a major factor in the federal government's ability to insert itself in tribal affairs and contributed to the lengthy and damaging Milam dispute as well as to future internal conflicts.[5]

Because of the Milam controversy, Chief Tanyan did not effectively have a full four-year term to make progress, although progress was indeed made during his tenure. In 1989 Chief Tanyan was defeated by Jerry G. Haney, a bilingual member of the Hichitee Band, in his bid for a third term of office. Haney was the son of Willie Haney, who had served as chief in the forties. He had grown up in a tiny Indian community north of Seminole, was a recently retired Tinker Air Force Base worker, and had raised his family in Shawnee, only a few miles from Seminole County. Consistent with the Nation's history of challenges to the authority of principal chiefs, a group of Seminoles attempted to remove Haney and Assistant Chief Dan Factor from office in 1991, but a majority of council members voted to dismiss the charges against them on grounds of lack of evidence.[6]

General council members who served during the Tanyan and Haney administrations included many persons who provided decades of service on the council. Long-time council members elected at the July 6, 1985, election included incumbents J. B. Thurman, Robert Kernell, Sr., and Sam Moses, who were elected for their fifth consecutive terms. In the 1989 elections, former chief Floyd Harjo was elected to his fifth consecutive council term, Grace Dailey was elected to her fourth consecutive term, and Lawrence Cudjoe and Tinnie Tiger were elected to third consecutive terms. In the 1989 elections, there were no candidates for five of the fourteen bands, and two of the bands selected only one council member. The vacancies were eventually filled after the council passed a resolution requesting that the bands select persons certified eligible by the Nation's election board to act as their council representatives.[7]

Seminole Nation General Council, 1985–1989. *Front row, left to right beginning with fifth from left:* former assistant chief Eula Doonkeen, attorney Charles Grounds, Chief Edwin Tanyan, and Assistant Chief Simeon Bemo; *back row, fifth from right:* former chief Floyd Harjo; *back row, second from right:* future assistant chief Dan Factor. (Photograph courtesy of Ted Underwood)

Several Seminole members served as general council secretary from late 1985 until late 1993, including Corena Mae England, Carol Harjo Hawkins, Madonna Williams, Loisetta Nix, and Loretta (Burgess) Finkenberg. They performed council secretary duties, including attending meetings, preparing minutes, and executing resolutions and ordinances. Several other Seminoles served as treasurer, which was an important position even though it was not established in the Seminole Constitution. Pauline Stewart served as the Nation's treasurer during Chief Tanyan's second term. After Chief Haney took office in September 1989, James Coleman served briefly as interim treasurer, followed by Ardeena Angelo. Near the end of Chief Haney's first term, Thomas McGeisey, Jr., former director of the Nation's judgment fund office, was appointed to serve as treasurer for the next four-year term beginning in September 1993.[8]

Both the Tanyan and the Haney administrations were faced with the challenge of addressing federal disallowed costs and delinquent federal unemployment taxes. In November 1985 the council resolved "to clear the good name of the Seminole Nation." The council pursued a variety of solutions, including seeking forgiveness of some of the disallowed costs, filing administrative appeals, and making payments using trust funds (some of which were made under protest). A significant portion of the indebtedness to the federal government was the Nation's federal unemployment tax debt to the IRS that had accrued over several years. The nonpayment of unemployment taxes was not an uncommon problem for Indian tribes, because tribes did not have the status of states for purposes of tribal employees' unemployment benefits systems. The Nation held funds in escrow for some of the unemployment taxes, hoping that Congress would revise federal unemployment laws to address this problem, including forgiveness of tribal unemployment tax debts. By the early nineties, the Seminole Nation owed a large sum for unpaid unemployment taxes, penalties, and interest, and in 1993 the council approved payment to the IRS for 1989 and 1991 payroll taxes. Years later, in 2000, Congress finally enacted a law to address the problem by allowing tribes to elect to participate in state systems, and in 2002, the Oklahoma State Legislature enacted a law addressing tribal participation in the state system.[9]

Soon after Chief Tanyan took office in late 1985, the general council approved applications for federal funding for Aid to Tribal Government, educational programs, Indian child welfare, and a community health representative program. The council also requested the assistance of the Inter-Tribal Council of the Five Civilized Tribes in obtaining the BIA's release of federal program funds to the Seminole Nation in the fall of 1985. In 1986 and 1987 the council approved applications and the contracting of numerous federal programs, including new elderly service programs and a new nutrition program for women and children. The Seminole government continued to obtain federal grants for operating numerous programs for fiscal years 1989 and 1990, including commodity foods distribution, a Farmers Home Administration program, and housing programs. During the Haney administration, the Seminole government administered millions of dollars in federal funding, tribal bingo revenues, and tribal trust funds.[10]

During Tanyan's second administration (1985–1989), he continued the work he had started during his first administration with regard to the division and distribution of the 1976 award to the Oklahoma and Florida Seminoles in the Florida land claims case, Dockets 73 and 151. The case involved inadequate compensation paid to the Seminoles for the 1823 and 1832 treaty cession of millions of acres of Florida lands. Chief Tanyan and the council spent much of their time and efforts during his second administration working to achieve final resolution of the dispute between the Seminole Nation, the Seminole Tribe of Florida, the Miccosukee Tribe, and the Independent Seminoles concerning division of the award. In October 1985 the council approved a resolution stating support of the plan approved by the Secretary of the Interior that had been contained in earlier proposed federal legislation. The council remained firm that the Seminole Nation should receive seventy-five percent of the award. Tribal leaders continued to meet with members of Congress throughout Chief Tanyan's term to try to obtain federal legislation necessary to resolve the matter. On March 13, 1989, the Wewoka Agency superintendent recommended the Muskogee Area director's approval of a distribution plan that was supported by a general council resolution advocating passage of federal judgment fund legislation. In April 1989 the council hired attorney Ross Swimmer, former chief of the Cherokee Nation and former Department of the Interior assistant secretary, to assist Paul Niebell in seeking congressional approval of the distribution plan.[11]

That summer, two bills were filed in Congress involving the Seminole judgment fund distribution among the Oklahoma Seminoles and the Florida Seminoles. The first of these, Senate Bill 1096, was sponsored by Oklahoma senators David Boren and Don Nickles and supported the Oklahoma Seminoles' desire for a 75–25 percent split. The second bill, House Bill 2838, was filed by Florida congressmen Larry Smith and Tom Lewis in July 1989 and sought a 50–50 split. On September 14 and 15, 1989, tribal officials testified before two congressional committees concerning the judgment fund distribution. Seminole Nation leaders who attended included Chief Jerry Haney, who had begun his first term only two weeks earlier; Frank Alexander, the new executive director; Duane Miller; and state senator Kelly Haney. Chief Haney and claims attorney Paul Niebell, who was eighty-eight years old by then, testified on behalf of the Oklahoma Seminoles. Florida chief James Billie testified on behalf of the Florida Seminoles. At the hearing, Senator Daniel Inouye, the committee chairman, urged the two tribes to resolve the dispute themselves. On October 9, 1989, Chief Haney and other delegates met with Chief Billie in Florida, resulting in a proposal by Chief Billie for a 37.5–62.5 split, but the Oklahoma Seminoles rejected the proposal. On October 14, 1989, the general council approved a resolution requesting Congress to proceed with the approval of Senate Bill 1096 at the earliest possible date. Chief Billie made another effort to settle the matter in November 1989, without success.[12]

The general council held a special meeting on January 20, 1990, and voted to send Floyd Harjo, Wayne Shaw, Tom Palmer, and

Fred Jones as general council representatives to support Chief Haney in presenting the Nation's position to Congress. The Seminole delegation, accompanied by attorney Joe Membrino, attended a joint committee meeting of the Senate Select Committee on Indian Affairs and the House Interior and Insular Affairs Committee regarding the judgment fund bill on March 21, 1990. After resolution of differences between the Senate and House versions of the bill involving the percentages to be allocated among the Oklahoma and Florida Seminoles, the bill was approved in Congress and signed into law by the president on May 1, 1990, as Public Law 101-277.[13]

The 1990 law provided that the Seminole Nation would receive 75.404 percent of the funds appropriated to satisfy the Florida claims award, and the Florida Seminoles would receive 24.596 percent. This was the same percentage split recommended by the Secretary of the Interior as early as 1977 and was based on 1914 Seminole Indian population statistics, excluding Seminole freedmen. Congress apparently agreed with the Secretary of the Interior's determination that use of the 1914 statistics was a more fair method of determining the split than 1990 population statistics. Use of the 1990 statistics would have been problematic, because the number of Florida Seminole tribal members was curtailed by membership eligibility requirements based on a specified minimum degree of Seminole Indian blood, whereas Oklahoma Seminoles who could trace ancestry to the 1906 Seminole Indian rolls by blood could be tribal members regardless of degree of Indian blood. Congress viewed the 1914 statistics as a more fair measure, because in 1914 most Oklahoma Seminoles by blood had one-half or more Indian blood, and the first formal census of the Florida Seminoles was taken between 1913 and 1914.[14]

The 1990 judgment fund distribution law also specified the allocation of the 24.596 percent Florida Seminole share of the award funds among the Seminole Tribe of Florida, the Miccosukee Tribe of Indians of Florida, and the independent Seminole Indians of Florida. Because of accrued interest, the Oklahoma Seminoles' 75.404 percent share of the appropriation for the Florida claims award had increased to approximately $42.2 million at the time that Public Law 101-277 was enacted. After the law was passed, the general council directed payments of $171,126 to Ross Swimmer and $309,837 to Paul Niebell for their legal services related to that effort.[15]

The 1990 law required that the Seminole Nation's governing body prepare a plan for use and distribution of its share of the funds, in consultation with the Secretary of the Interior, within 180 days of the act's passage. It required the plan to provide that not less than 80 percent of the funds be set aside and programmed to serve common tribal needs, educational requirements, and other purposes "as the circumstances of the Seminole Nation of Oklahoma may determine." It prohibited per capita payments to tribal members, with the exception that investment income from no more than 20 percent of the fund could be distributed from time to time at the discretion of the tribal governing body pursuant to its approved distribution plan, subject to certain other requirements.[16]

Chief Haney and other tribal leaders, including judgment fund coordinator Andrew Harjo, members of the judgment fund committee representing the twelve Seminole Indian bands, and general council members, spent a great deal of time and energy conducting surveys, holding public meetings, and working to reach a consensus among tribal members regarding the usage plan. These efforts were successful, as the Nation met the 180-day deadline for approval of the plan. Band leaders involved in the process included former chief Tom Palmer, Houston Ross, Jane McGeisey, Hazel Larney, George Jones, Jim Wise, Ted Underwood, Louis Fife, Kenna Harjo, Jonah Harjo, Lucy Harjo, and Dwayne Miller.

After two series of public meetings, the judgment fund committee recommended a plan for submission to the BIA. In October 1990 the council approved the September 12, 1990, "Plan for the Use and Distribution of the Seminole Nation of Oklahoma's Share of Judgment Funds in Dockets 73 and 151 Before the Indian Claims Commission." The chief forwarded the plan, including supporting documentation, to the BIA Wewoka Agency superintendent, who eventually forwarded it to the BIA Muskogee Area Office. After

review by the Tulsa Field Solicitor's Office, the Muskogee Area
director forwarded the plan to the BIA Central Office in Washington, D.C., on January 10, 1991, requesting review and submission
to Congress.[17]

The approved judgment fund usage plan did not include any
provisions for per capita payments to tribal citizens. Instead, it
provided that all of the funds would be invested by the Secretary
of the Interior, and it also included provisions concerning possible
investment of part or all of the funds by the "tribal governing
body." It made the principal, interest, and investment income
accrued available "for use by the tribal governing body on an
annual budgetary basis for programs and services established in
accordance with priorities determined by the tribal governing body"
in various program areas. The program areas included, but were
not limited to, health, education, social services, needs of the
elderly, housing, general community improvement, economic and
business development, expansion and preservation of the tribal
land base, and tribal government support and development.[18]

The judgment fund plan provided that any budget that would
cause the available principal to fall below $35,000,000 would be
subject to approval of at least two-thirds of the qualified voters
of the tribe voting on a budget referendum in a general or special
election. It also stated that nothing in the plan would preclude
the "tribal governing body" from using a portion of the principal
as collateral for bond obligations issued by the Seminole Nation.
The plan stated that the funds made available under the plan for
programming would not be subject to federal or state income
taxes and would not be considered as income or resources for
purposes of reducing financial assistance or other benefits under
the Social Security Act or any federal or federally assisted program.[19]

In July 1991 the council approved a budget for use of judgment
funds, including judgment fund committee expenses, burial assistance, school clothing assistance, elderly assistance, and higher
education scholarships. The council later added a program called
the Cultural and Recreational Enhancement Assistance Program,
under which it appropriated funding for such purposes as the

Seminole Nation Princess, summer youth camp, and Christmas fruit. Each judgment fund program was governed by a separate tribal law containing eligibility requirements specific to that program, but each program had at least one eligibility requirement in common: that the beneficiary must be an enrolled member of the Seminole Nation of Oklahoma and must be descended from a member of the Seminole Nation as it existed in Florida on September 18, 1823. The Seminole government adhered to the position that only Seminoles by blood met these criteria—a position that was consistent with the congressional exclusion of non-Indian freedmen from the Seminole population statistics used to divide the Florida claim award between the Oklahoma and Florida Seminoles. As a result, tribal members who could not trace descendancy from an ancestor on the Seminole Indian rolls prepared by the Five Tribes Commission in 1906 were not eligible for the judgment fund programs, a situation that was protested by freedmen members. The Seminole government continued appropriating judgment funds for these programs in subsequent years. The budget for 1994 judgment fund programs and operations in 1994 was in excess of two million dollars.[20]

The Seminole Nation was empowered by the 1990 law to make tribal investment decisions, but the law required such investment plans to be approved by the Secretary of the Interior. This situation was somewhat ironic, because on April 22, 1992, the U.S. House of Representatives Committee on Government Operations issued a report entitled "Misplaced Trust: The Bureau of Indian Affairs' Mismanagement of the Indian Trust Fund." The report described the BIA as a "high risk" agency, a "multifaceted monster," and "an organizational nightmare," and it contained a detailed review of attempts to correct problems with BIA mismanagement of Indian trust funds, which it characterized as "a national disgrace." The Seminole government recognized the importance of preserving its judgment funds—which were managed by the BIA—so it began exploring options to protect its trust assets. In late 1993 the council approved a law establishing a Trust Fund Management Board, which was responsible for developing an investment plan for judgment funds and ensuring compliance with applicable federal and tribal law, including the Nation's 1990 Judgment Fund Plan. The first members of that board were Eula Doonkeen, Richard Harjo, Rick Deer, treasurer Tom McGeisey, and principal chief Haney. The board began considering possible options for developing an investment plan that would afford the Seminole Nation a greater measure of oversight and supervision and potentially result in greater investment returns to the Nation.[21]

The Seminole people made significant strides in strengthening their governmental infrastructure during the combined eight years of the second Tanyan administration and the first Haney administration. During the Tanyan administration, the council approved use of Robert's Rules of Order at general council meetings and directed the close-out of old bank accounts. It also reconfirmed the validity of the Nation's previously approved personnel policies, procurement and property management plan, standard accounting procedures, and motor fleet operations policy as well as the use of those documents as "part of the everyday operations of the new administration of the Seminole Nation of Oklahoma." The council also approved several laws related to government operations, including the following: creation of an audit committee responsible for overseeing the accountability and distribution of funds administered by the Seminole government; authorization of meeting stipends of $35 for each full meeting attended by council members; and creation of the Seminole Nation Law Enforcement Division, including provisions for training, code of conduct, and cross-deputation with other law enforcement agencies.[22]

The process for strengthening the Seminole Nation Constitution began as early as 1985, when the Seminole Constitution Revision Committee—including Yvette Harjo, an attorney and daughter of former chief Floyd Harjo—began working on proposed constitutional amendments. The general council decided not to submit to vote of the people a proposed amendment that would have based membership on a minimum of one-quarter Seminole blood, because of the BIA's position that questions of legality needed to be addressed first. Seminole members approved the other proposed amendments in February 1989, except for one that would have expanded council authority over selection of a chief and assistant chief in the event of vacancies in those offices. The approved amendments included an amendment reducing the number of council members from forty-two members to twenty-eight members, so that the council would consist of two members from each of the fourteen bands elected by a plurality of votes cast, instead of three members per band. This amendment became effective before the council elections later that year, so that the new 1989 twenty-eight-member council was significantly smaller than previous councils. The amendments also provided for at-large elections for chief and assistant chief by a majority of votes cast and permitted run-off elections only for candidates for chief. The amendments added election filing requirements, repealed provisions originally governing the conduct of the first elections that had been held after the 1969 approval of the constitution, and deleted references to the Oklahoma Constitution.[23]

During the first administration of Chief Haney, Seminole leaders focused on strengthening the jurisdictional position of the Nation against a backdrop of important federal and state court decisions recognizing the judicial authority of the Five Tribes and the Indian country status of restricted Five Tribes allotments. These decisions included a 1988 landmark decision reestablishing federal acknowledgment of the judicial authority of the Muscogee (Creek) Nation. In August 1985 the Muscogee (Creek) Nation, then represented by Geoffrey M. Standing Bear, an Osage attorney, and George Almerigi, a Creek attorney and general counsel for the Creek Nation, filed suit in the U.S. District Court of the District of Columbia challenging an IBIA decision that the Creek Nation had no judicial authority. In 1987 the federal district court upheld the IBIA decision, finding that Congress explicitly abolished the power of the Muscogee (Creek) Nation to maintain a court system with general civil and criminal jurisdiction and never acted to restore that power. The court stated that the Nation could only maintain a court with authority to make decisions concerning its internal affairs.[24]

The Creek Nation, dissatisfied with this result, then filed an appeal, with legal representation by Choctaw attorney Susan Work, Muscogee (Creek)–Yuchi attorney Leah Harjo Ware, and Muscogee (Creek) attorney Sherrin Watkins. On appeal, the District of Columbia Circuit ruled in 1988 in *Muscogee (Creek) Nation v. Hodel* that provisions in the 1898 Curtis Act abolishing Creek Nation courts had been repealed by the 1936 OIWA, and that the Muscogee (Creek) Nation had the power to establish tribal courts with civil and criminal jurisdiction, subject only to the same limitations imposed by statutes generally applicable to all tribes. In its decision the court implicitly recognized that the Curtis Act provisions concerning tribal courts never applied to the Seminole Nation, which had negotiated its allotment agreement preserving tribal judicial authority prior to the enactment of the Curtis Act, nor did the Curtis Act provisions apply to the Choctaw and Chickasaw Nations, which negotiated allotment agreements preserving their tribal courts after enactment of the Curtis Act. This decision once and for all invalidated the BIA's long-standing position that the Five Tribes could not have tribal courts.[25]

Several other important federal and state cases enhancing Five Tribes sovereignty in the late eighties and early nineties involved the existence of Indian country in eastern Oklahoma and aided in defining the geographic area subject to the Five Tribes governmental authority. The first case involving the Indian country status of lands in eastern Oklahoma was *Indian Country U.S.A. v. Oklahoma Tax Commission*, which was decided by the Tenth Circuit U.S. Court of Appeals in 1987. The court ruled that unallotted land that had been owned in fee by the Muscogee (Creek) Nation since before allotment and statehood was Indian country, and that the state had no authority to regulate or tax bingo enterprises located there. In the 1989 case of *State v. Klindt*, the Oklahoma Court of Criminal Appeals ruled that individual Cherokee trust lands constituted Indian country. In *Klindt* the court found that it had "misinterpreted the statutes and cases upon which it based its opinion" in its 1936 decision in *Ex Parte Nowabbi*, in which the court had determined that Oklahoma courts had criminal jurisdiction over restricted Choctaw allotments.[26]

In 1990 the Oklahoma Supreme Court ruled in *Housing Authority of the Seminole Nation v. Harjo* that a Mutual Help homesite located within a small cluster of other such homesites, occupied by Seminole tribal member Josephine Harjo and administered by the Housing Authority of the Seminole Nation, met the "dependent Indian community" definition of Indian country, and that the state courts had no subject matter jurisdiction of an action by the housing authority seeking recovery of the home's possession. The same year, the Tenth Circuit expressly determined in *Ross v. Neff* that the state had no law enforcement authority over alleged offenses by Indians on Cherokee trust land, implicitly recognizing the Indian country status of that land. In 1992 the Tenth Circuit recognized in *United States v. Sands* that a restricted Creek allotment was Indian country and that a felony by an Indian against another Indian on the allotment was subject to federal prosecution.[27]

Those decisions led to a renewed Seminole effort to develop a tribal court system. In the fall of 1990, the general council enacted a resolution stating that the Seminole Nation recognized the need to establish a judicial system with civil jurisdiction over matters arising in Indian country in the Seminole Nation, including cases in which non-Indians were parties. The resolution also stated that the Seminole Nation desired to exercise criminal jurisdiction over cases arising in Indian country, subject to the limitation that tribal criminal jurisdiction would be exercised only in cases involving Seminole defendants. The resolution referenced that limitation because the Supreme Court had recently ruled in *Duro v. Reina* that tribal courts had no criminal jurisdiction over nonmember Indians—a problem soon corrected by the Indian Law Enforcement Reform Act of 1990, which recognized tribal court jurisdiction over all Indians. The 1990 Seminole resolution further stated that the Nation found it desirable to amend its constitution to clarify its judicial authority and to enact judicial and law enforcement codes. The council authorized the principal chief to seek funding for these purposes and established a Constitution Revision Committee and a Code Development Committee. The following month, in February 1991, the council authorized the chief to submit an application for a tribal court grant from the BIA. The council also approved a special services attorney contract with Susan Work, who was actively involved in the court and code development project and served as the Seminole Nation's attorney general for almost four years, until November 1994.[28]

The Seminole Nation made tremendous progress in 1991 with regard to strengthening of its governmental infrastructure and preparing to secure a tribal court system. In 1991 the general council repealed a 1970 tribal law requiring BIA approval of tribal laws. The council enacted a membership code and an election code, and it instituted laws defining the council secretary's duties; establishing the form and manner of drafting, numbering, enacting, approving, and maintaining ordinances and resolutions; setting the chief's salary at $33,218 and the assistant chief's salary at $26,728; and establishing an Arts and Crafts Committee responsible for registering Seminole artisans.[29]

More significantly, the Seminole Nation's Code Development Project made great progress in 1991. The project was funded by a grant from the Administration for Native Americans. Tribal member Leonard M. Harjo, a graduate of Harvard and Yale and the son of former chief Floyd Harjo, served as project coordinator. Paralegal Leonard Gouge served as research analyst, and Renae Larney performed organizational and clerical work on the project. Separate lists of all available ordinances and resolutions passed by the general council from 1969 through most of 1991 were prepared, and copies were placed in separate ordinance and resolution books. The ordinance and resolution books were distributed to the general council secretary, the executive office, the Seminole Nation Library, the attorney general, and the Code Development Project office.

The attorney general, assisted by the Code Development Project staff, consolidated all ordinances enacted through August 29, 1991, except those that had been repealed, into a comprehensive tribal code, with title numbers assigned to subject areas listed in alphabetical order. All amended ordinances were placed in the code as amended, with a legislative history containing references to the original ordinances and amendments included with each code section. Resolutions that were directed at specific matters within specific time frames were not placed in the tribal code, because they were not intended to be permanent general laws. The codification of tribal laws was provided to the general council in the fall of 1991, and on November 16, 1991, the council approved the code and repealed all other laws not contained in the code. This action enabled the Seminole Nation to identify on an ongoing basis Seminole permanent laws in effect and to move forward in developing additional laws and amending the old laws when necessary. Additional laws incorporated into the code in 1992 and 1993 included amendments involving tribal membership, recreation programs, and establishment of a Tribal Employment Rights Office (TERO). These laws were enacted with reference to title and section numbers in the code, and the code was updated annually by the attorney general.[30]

At the same time the code development project was underway, the Constitution Revision Committee was also working on additional proposed Seminole constitutional amendments. After public meetings were conducted, an election was held on December 14, 1991, and three of the five proposed amendments were approved. The first approved amendment defined the geographical area subject to the governmental powers of the Seminole Nation, making it clear that the Seminole Nation had governmental authority over all Indian country lands, including restricted lands, trust lands, and land owned in fee by the Seminole Nation. The second amendment eliminated the constitution's authorization of the president of the United States to appoint the principal chief, in part because the Act of October 22, 1970, effectively repealed provisions in the Act of April 26, 1906, concerning presidential appointments of the chiefs of the Five Tribes.[31]

The third amendment that was approved eliminated provisions in the constitution that required federal approval of constitutional amendments. Because of that amendment, the Seminole Nation did not request BIA approval of any of the amendments, instead only providing the agency superintendent with a certification of election results. The area director nevertheless sent the amendments to the BIA Central Office in Washington, D.C., for review. The acting director of the BIA Office of Tribal Services approved the first two amendments in July 1992 but disapproved the third amendment. The acting director decided that the Secretary of the Interior could not approve any tribal constitutional amendments that would eliminate secretarial approval "until such time as Congress makes it clear that the Secretary should not be exercising any authority and judgment in approving constitutions and amendments thereto and relieves the Secretary of his responsibility over Indian affairs."[32]

The Seminole Nation appealed the decision to the IBIA. The Nation presented documentation that other tribes, such as the Navajo Nation, operated without a federally approved organizational document and included a detailed analysis of federal laws affecting the issue of federal approval of such documents. On September 23, 1993, the IBIA upheld the decision of the acting director of the BIA Office of Tribal Services. The IBIA found that, because the Seminole Nation Constitution had given the BIA authority to approve or disapprove constitutional amendments without any limitations, the BIA had the discretion to disapprove an amendment that would retract that authority. The IBIA later issued an order clarifying that the 1906 act's provisions concerning federal approval of ordinances did not empower the BIA to approve or disapprove council resolutions proposing constitutional amendments. The Seminole Nation could have appealed the IBIA decision in a federal court action but did not do so. More than a decade later, the Cherokee Nation, which had filed a brief in support of the Seminole position in its IBIA case, succeeded in securing BIA approval of a similar amendment to its constitution that eliminated BIA approval authority over Cherokee constitutional amendments.[33]

Two of the 1991 proposed amendments were not approved by Seminole citizens at the constitutional amendment election. One of the failed proposed amendments involved tribal taxation. The other proposed amendment, which failed by only one vote, would have established a court system for the Seminole Nation and would have enabled Seminole Nation courts to hear a variety of civil cases, including cases filed by and against non-Indians, such as contract disputes, child welfare issues, housing issues, tax issues, and interpretations of the tribal constitution. It would also have enabled Seminole courts to hear criminal charges for misdemeanors committed by Indians on Indian country lands. The United States retained authority to prosecute major felony crimes in cases arising on Indian country and involving Indian offenders and Indian victims.[34]

Less than a year after the failure of the proposed constitutional amendment that would have created Seminole courts, the Secretary of the Interior published final federal regulations on February 26, 1992, to establish a Court of Indian Offenses (CFR court) for the tribes served by the Muskogee Area Office, including the Seminole, Choctaw, and Chickasaw Nations. There was no need for CFR courts for the Muscogee (Creek) and Cherokee Nations, because each already operated its own tribal court. The final rule stated that recent state and federal court decisions had "raised serious questions whether the State of Oklahoma possesses criminal jurisdiction over offenses committed by Indians on certain Indian lands in the former Indian Territory," and that establishment of the CFR court was "immediately necessary" to protect the lives, persons, and property of people residing on Indian country lands until tribal courts were established to exercise criminal jurisdiction.[35]

The general council requested the Wewoka Agency superintendent to take administrative responsibility to establish a CFR court within the boundaries of the Seminole Nation and agreed to provide space for the conduct of the court at the Mekusukey Mission. The council also approved a budget from its special federal grant for court development, for the purpose of assisting in the development of the CFR court. The council later enacted a law setting jurisdictional limitations on the CFR courts, stating that "it would be contrary to the sovereign status of the Seminole Nation for the CFR Court to render decisions involving internal constitutional and governmental affairs of the Seminole Nation."[36]

The council appointed Houston Ross, Russell Coker, and Susie Worcester to serve on the Seminole Nation Judiciary Committee, a committee established in 1992 to assist in developing tribal laws relating to a court system. The committee worked with the Seminole Nation's attorney general to draft laws governing court operations, with the intention that these laws would be followed by the CFR court and would someday be used by Seminole Nation courts, if and when the Nation finally established its own judicial system. Because the federal regulations governing CFR courts required BIA approval of any laws to be applied by the CFR courts other than those contained in the regulations, the Nation's court codes were submitted to the BIA for review and approval. These court codes included provisions concerning the CFR court operation and selection of CFR judges, civil and criminal procedures codes, and an evidence code. Although the codes were fairly consistent with state and federal laws, the Seminole Nation was unable to secure BIA approval; thus, the codes were not implemented by the CFR court. In late 1992 the council approved the BIA's July 1992 appointment of Cherokee attorney Linda Barker to serve as CFR court judge. The council reconfirmed her appointment in the spring of 1993 but expressed its desire that this be a temporary measure, that the position be advertised, and that the judiciary committee participate in the selection process.[37]

At the same time, the Seminole government addressed the need for at least a quasi-judicial body to hear disputes involving internal tribal matters by establishing administrative appeals boards in 1993, including a Membership Appeals Board and a Judgment Fund Appeals Board. Tribal members Lottie Coody, Terri Springer, and Jane McGeisey were the first members of the Membership Appeals Board. The first members of the Judgment Fund Appeals Board included former chief Tom Palmer, Russell Coker, Rick Deer, Don Coker, and Marie Hall. In November 1993 the Seminole government consolidated these boards to form a single Administrative Appeals Board to hear appeals of decisions regarding certain Seminole Nation programs and agencies affecting individuals.

This law allowed a person to appeal a denial of judgment fund program benefits that was based on grounds other than a finding that an applicant was not a member of the Nation. In addition, the law allowed for appeals of enrollment decisions under certain circumstances and appeals involving other internal tribal matters if expressly provided by tribal law. The Administrative Appeals Board consisted of five council members appointed by the chief and confirmed by the council. Decisions of the Administrative Appeals Board were final and not subject to review by any state, tribal, or federal government body or court.[38]

During the terms of chief Tanyan and Haney, the Seminole Nation—like many tribes in Oklahoma and nationwide—began to explore and reap the economic benefits of conducting gaming in Indian country. In December 1985 the general council authorized the executive office to explore the feasibility of a business ventures committee and a tribal bingo operation. The Seminole government began operating a bingo facility on tribal property on Brown Street in Wewoka in the mid-eighties, at first using outside management groups. In 1986 the council approved its first law regulating bingo operations. The following year, the U.S. Supreme Court validated earlier federal court of appeals decisions favoring tribes by ruling in *California v. Cabazon Band of Mission Indians* that a state had no authority to regulate bingo and certain other gaming activities conducted by Indian tribes on reservations, even though the players were predominantly non-Indians coming onto the reservation. This decision led to the enactment of the federal Indian Gaming Regulatory Act (IGRA) in 1988, which established requirements for tribal gaming, including a list of provisions that were required to be included in tribal gaming laws.[39]

In 1991, the general council decided not to renew a 1986 bingo management agreement with an outside management firm for the Seminole's bingo facility in Wewoka. Instead, the council solicited proposals for management of the facility and hired new managers later that year. The council also enacted a new gaming code in 1991 that complied with requirements of the 1988 IGRA and secured National Indian Gaming Commission approval of that new law.

In 1992 the Seminole Nation moved its bingo operations from Wewoka to the Mekusukey Mission, south of Seminole. The council approved a gaming policies and procedures manual in 1993 and took over management of the bingo operation at Mekusukey, saving a substantial sum previously paid to outside management firms.[40] The Seminole Nation and other tribes moved beyond simple paper bingo games and also used gaming machines, which were arguably included in the same "class II gaming" category as bingo. In 1992 and 1993 the chief and attorney general attempted to negotiate a gaming compact with the state of Oklahoma, as required by IGRA, to enable the Nation to operate other types of electronic games categorized as "class III games" but made no progress because of the state's uniform resistance to most types of compacted tribal gaming.[41]

During the Tanyan and Haney administrations, the Seminole Nation operated a business venture called the Seminole Nation Trading Post, located in a building across the highway from the Seminole Nation headquarters. In the summer of 1987, tribal trust funds were used for a loan to the trading post and for purchase of a nine-acre tract adjacent to and just west of the tribal headquarters; this tract was used as the site for construction of a convenience store. In late 1987 the council established the Seminole Economic Development Authority, called "SEDA," for development and management of tribal business enterprises. By 1989 the stability of the SEDA board was questioned by the council, which suspended the authority of the board and transferred responsibility for operation of the trading post to the tribal administration. The council approved a loan from tribal trust funds to help pay for SEDA activities and for the convenience store construction project in 1989, specifying that the loan be repaid from trading post and bingo revenues. The trading post was a successful business, generating more than $51,000 in net income in fiscal year 1991. In 1992 tribal officials learned that the trading post had not filed federal unemployment tax reports for 1989, 1990, and 1991, placing a tax burden on its operations that had to be repaid. Notwithstanding that setback, by 1993 the trading post was still generating sufficient funds to pay off debts of the Nation's small sewing business, called "SNO-ANA." SNO-ANA had been created to provide employment opportunities to tribal members, but it was phased out in 1993 after a few years of operation, following its move from Seminole to Wewoka. The convenience store eventually replaced the trading post, and the old trading post building was used for governmental offices.[42]

In late 1987, during the Tanyan administration, the general council enacted laws that established the Tax Commission of the Seminole Nation and that directed tribal taxation of cigarette and tobacco sales at smoke shops located on Seminole Indian country. Seminole member Ted Underwood, who was instrumental in developing these laws and securing their approval, was selected to serve as the tax commissioner. The council appropriated funds for the operation of the commission and for legal research concerning the Seminole Nation's taxation authority in 1989. The council continued to recognize the importance of the tax commission during the Haney administration, appropriating funds from its tax revenues to support commission operations and to fund a land research project to be administered by the commission. In 1992 the tax commission's name was changed to the Business and Corporate Regulatory (BCR) Commission, and its duties were expanded to include registration of corporations in addition to tax functions.[43]

In the late eighties, state officials in Oklahoma began to recognize that improved tribal–state relations would be beneficial to all of the state's citizens. Hence, in 1988 the Oklahoma Legislature enacted the State–Tribal Relations Act, which promoted tribal–state cooperation. That law was sponsored by future Seminole chief Enoch Kelly Haney, a Seminole member who served in the Oklahoma Legislature for more than twenty years. The law acknowledged that the state of Oklahoma recognized the unique status of Indian tribes and pledged the state's intent to work in a spirit of cooperation with all federally recognized Indian tribes in furtherance of federal policy for the benefit of both the tribes and the state. It allowed the governor of Oklahoma, or his or her designee, to negotiate and enter into cooperative agreements with federally recognized Indian tribes to address issues of mutual interest, subject to approval by the Joint Committee on State–Tribal Relations established by the act.[44]

Although some tribes criticized the State–Tribal Relations Act as an attempt to infringe on tribal sovereignty, passage of the act represented a positive turning point in tribal–state relations, and the act was used to strengthen law enforcement in Oklahoma. On March 1, 1991, Oklahoma attorney general Robert Henry issued an opinion concerning law enforcement in Indian country within Oklahoma; the opinion's author was an assistant attorney general, Diane Hammons, a member of the Cherokee Nation who later became the attorney general of the Cherokee Nation. The opinion found that state and local law enforcement officers had no authority to make arrests for violations of federal law in Indian country, except under a cooperative agreement approved in accordance with the State–Tribal Relations Act. The opinion referenced the federal Indian Law Enforcement Reform Act of 1990, which allowed the Secretary of the Interior to enter into agreements for the use of tribal, state, or other government agency resources to assist in enforcing federal law and tribal laws in Indian country. Soon afterward, many Oklahoma tribes, including several of the Five Tribes, entered into cross-deputization agreements with the state of Oklahoma and the BIA to ensure that all law enforcement officers had authority to enforce federal, state, and tribal laws involving both Indian and non-Indian offenders in Indian country. In early 1992 the BIA and Seminole County entered into a cross-deputization agreement for enforcement of federal laws in Indian country in the Seminole Nation.[45]

The State–Tribal Relations Act also was used to fashion a truce between many Oklahoma tribes and the state with regard to the state's ongoing challenge of tribal taxation authority and the state's attempts to tax various activities in Indian country. In February 1991 the Supreme Court held in *Oklahoma Tax Commission v. Citizen Band Potawatomi Indian Tribe of Oklahoma* that the state of Oklahoma had authority to impose cigarette excise taxes on non-members purchasing cigarettes and tobacco products on trust land but no authority to impose those taxes on sales to tribal members. This ruling posed a dilemma for the Oklahoma Tax Commission, which had no way of distinguishing between sales to members versus non-members. The tax commission had been on a collision course with tribes and individual Indians for many years in its mostly unsuccessful efforts to force payment of certain types of state taxes. The *Potawatomi* decision also presented potential problems for tribes. The tribes feared that the tax commission would stop the wholesalers, before they entered Indian country, from delivering cigarettes and tobacco products to retailers on Indian country, causing a loss in tribal tax revenues.[46]

In April 1992 the general council authorized negotiations for a tribal–state compact for payment in lieu of cigarette taxes to the state, subject to the council's approval of the final compact. The compact and supporting state legislation were developed by a joint tribal and state work group. The work group included counsel for the Cherokee Nation, including Chad Smith, who later became chief of the Cherokee Nation; Susan Work, the Seminole Nation attorney general; Bob Rabon, counsel for the Choctaw Nation; state senate leaders, including Senator Kelly Haney, a member of the Seminole Nation; and Robert Thompson, a senate staff attorney who maintained a good working relationship with tribal leaders over the years. This joint effort resulted in significantly revised language in the proposed state legislation concerning taxation of tobacco products sold on Indian country: HB 759. The bill was satisfactory to both state officials and many tribal officials. Cherokee, Choctaw, and Seminole legal counsel met with an intertribal group at Arrowhead Lodge in April 1992 and a few days later presented an outline of key compact provisions to senate representatives. The tribal–state work group then finalized a model tribal–state compact to be used in implementation of the new legislation, which was enacted into law on May 28, 1992, with the support of some tribes and the opposition of others.[47]

The new tobacco tax law amended the Oklahoma tax code to require the collection of taxes at the rate of 75 percent of the state excise taxes for non-compacting tribes. It provided an incentive to tribes to enter into compacts by authorizing the state to collect payments in lieu of taxes from compacting tribes in the amount of 25 percent of the state excise tax rate. The payments in lieu of taxes were to be made for all cigarettes and tobacco products purchased by a compacting tribe or its licensees for resale in the tribe's Indian country, without reference to the membership or non-membership status of the purchasing public. The percentages established in the new law were favorable even to non-compacting tribes, because the *Potawatomi* case established that the state could collect taxes on sales to non-Indians, who represented much more than 75 percent of the total population.[48]

On May 16, 1992, the general council approved the model compact. The model compact included the Seminole Nation's agreement to purchase cigarettes and tobacco products only from wholesalers licensed by the state. These wholesalers collected the payments in lieu of taxes and verified sales records to the state. The cigarettes were required to bear tribal and state stamps or a single stamp approved by both parties. The Seminole Nation's compact, which was signed by Principal Chief Jerry Haney and Governor David Walters and was filed with the Oklahoma secretary of state on June 4, 1992, was for a ten-year term, running from January 1, 1993, through December 31, 2002. By entering into the compact, the Seminole Nation was able to make significantly smaller payments to the state and impose its own tribal taxes on cigarette and tobacco product sales at a lesser rate than the state taxes, giving it and its licensees a competitive edge. Another benefit was that it eliminated the Oklahoma Tax Commission's attempts to take enforcement action against the Nation; in addition, the use of special stamps that were placed on the cigarette packages by the wholesaler cut overhead costs of Seminole retailers.[49]

The Seminole Nation generated a significant amount of tribal tax revenues from cigarette and tobacco sales in Seminole Indian country during the term of the compact, which was later renewed. In the meantime, the Oklahoma Tax Commission continued its efforts to tax Indian individuals and tribes in Oklahoma with regard to other types of taxes. One such effort resulted in another state loss in *Oklahoma Tax Commission v. Sac and Fox Nation*, a decision by the U.S. Supreme Court finding that Oklahoma could not impose motor vehicle taxes on tribal members who lived in Indian country and could not tax the income of tribal members who lived and worked in Indian country.[50]

The Seminole Nation remained active in the Five Civilized Tribes Inter-Tribal Council during the terms of Chief Tanyan and Chief Haney. At a 1986 Inter-Tribal Council meeting, Chief Tanyan thanked the Inter-Tribal Council for its assistance in obtaining federal recognition of the Seminole Nation as a working tribal government. Jerry Haney was also active on the Inter-Tribal Council, serving as its chairman from time to time. In 1991 the Inter-Tribal Council declared that it was most urgent that a method be developed for preserving a land base for the Five Tribes to the greatest extent possible, and it began to work on proposed reform of the land laws affecting the Five Tribes.[51]

Seminoles were also active in other intertribal organizations. In 1986 the general council empowered Seminole members who were veterans of the Vietnam War to use the name of the "Seminole Nation Chapter of the Inter-Tribal Vietnam Veterans." In 1992 the council approved the Seminole Nation Chapter of the Vietnam Era Veterans Intertribal Association as the official veterans' organization to represent the Nation and conduct Native American veterans' military burial rites; the council also approved funding for the group, which was referred to as the Seminole Nation Color Guard.[52] That same year the council decided to participate in the Intertribal Monitoring Association on Indian Trust Funds, which was involved in oversight of a BIA effort to reconcile and audit Indian trust funds; the Environmental Tribal Council of Oklahoma; and the Central Oklahoma Economic Development District. The Seminole Nation Bingo held a fundraiser in 1992 and raised $1,000 to help the city of Wewoka purchase a "jaws of life."[53] Throughout the terms of Chief Tanyan and Chief Haney, the annual Seminole Nation Days event continued as a celebration enjoyed by both Seminole members and the general public.[54]

Seminole Nation Color Guard, 1990s. (Photograph courtesy of Oklahoma Historical Society, Oklahoma City)

During Chief Edwin Tanyan's second term and Chief Jerry G. Haney's first term, the Seminole Nation had again overcome great obstacles to forge ahead in developing the Nation as a viable, functioning tribal government. On August 7, 1993, Chief Haney was reelected for a second term of office, and James Factor was elected assistant chief. Predictably, the validity of the election was immediately challenged by their opponents, former chief Edwin Tanyan and Dwayne Miller. Fortunately, this time the Seminole Nation's election laws included a workable process for handling election challenges in an expedient matter. Under those laws, an Election Appeals Board was convened and a hearing was held regarding various claimed irregularities in the election. The board upheld the validity of the election, and that decision was appealed to the general council. The general council, which under the election laws had authority to make a final, unappealable decision, ruled on September 20, 1993, that the election was valid. An appeal to the CFR court was dismissed following a hearing on October 15, 1993. In this way, using its own laws, the Seminole Nation was able to avoid BIA interference and protracted litigation concerning the chief's authority.[55]

The year 1993 marked the one-hundred-year anniversary of Congress's establishment of the Five Tribes Commission in 1893 for the purpose of allotting tribal lands of the Five Tribes and dissolving the governments of the Five Tribes—a decision that caused tragic consequences and great hardship for the people of the Five Tribes. Notwithstanding that blow and the federal executive and legislative assaults that followed for decades, by 1993 Seminole leaders had moved forward in their endeavors to achieve a strong government, one with the ability to provide much-needed services for the betterment of the Seminole Nation and its citizens. Life went on, including celebration of the Nation's 25th Annual Seminole Nation Days in early September 1993 and the many other ordinary joys of life that Seminoles had experienced over the years in spite of the harsh treatment that they had suffered. Although there would be other conflicts and controversies along the way, the Nation forged its way toward and into the twenty-first century.

Epilogue

The fifteen years following the end of Chief Jerry G. Haney's first term of office in the fall of 1993 included periods both of great progress and growth and of struggle, including enforcement action by the National Indian Gaming Commission (NIGC), internal conflicts, withdrawal of federal program funding, and litigation concerning governmental and freedmen issues. From late 1993 through 2008, under the leadership of chiefs Jerry Haney, Kenneth Chambers, and Kelly Haney, the Seminole Nation made progress, but that progress was diminished by internal disputes and interference by the Department of the Interior, particularly in the beginning years of the twenty-first century. Although the picture looked bleak at times, the Seminole people recovered and their leaders continued on their determined path. Now, in early 2009, the Nation is enjoying a period of stability and growth, with a stronger government and improved services for tribal members and county citizens.

Jerry G. Haney's second term of office ran from September 1993 through September 1997, and his third term ran from September 1997 through September 2001. However, the BIA continued to recognize Haney's service in office even after the 2001 election, in which Kenneth Chambers was elected principal chief, until early 2003 when Chambers took office (more details below). Chief Chambers served more than two years of the 2001–2005 term. In the summer of 2005, Jerry Haney's nephew, Enoch Kelly Haney, was elected to serve as principal chief, and Larry Harrison was elected to serve as assistant chief. They took office in September 2005.

The Seminole government's conflict with the NIGC began near the end of Jerry Haney's third term of office. By 2000 the Seminole Nation was conducting gaming operations at four locations, including a casino south of Interstate 40 in northern Seminole County. At that time the Seminole Nation Economic Development Authority (SNEDA)—composed of fourteen council members, one from each band—was responsible for the Nation's economic development ventures, including its casino operations. Under the IGRA, tribes could not legally operate devices classified as class III games without tribal–state compacts. Because of state resistance to such gaming compacts, many Oklahoma tribes, including the Seminole Nation, were operating a variety of electronic gaming devices without compacts. After the NIGC ruled that some of these devices were class III games, the SNEDA did not cease use of such devices. As a result, the NIGC ordered temporary closure of Seminole casinos in May and September 2000 and eventually took additional federal court enforcement action, which cost the Seminole Nation millions of dollars in fines. Perhaps the Seminole Nation was used as an example to induce other Oklahoma tribes, which were not as harshly treated for their operation of similar gaming devices, to be more compliant with NIGC orders. In any event, the Nation's finances suffered as a result of SNEDA's resistance to the NIGC.[1]

The Seminole Nation was eventually allowed to reopen its casinos, which were used as a source of revenue for the tribe and also to fund installment payments to the NIGC for its fines. In 2005 the Nation began operating class III games pursuant to a federally approved class III gaming compact with the state of Oklahoma. The compact was in compliance with the IGRA and an Oklahoma law that was approved in a state referendum in 2004. The law authorized the governor to enter into a model tribal–state class III gaming compact that was included as part of that law. The state law and the model compact had been developed by state and tribal leaders over many months of negotiations,

Seminole Nation General Council, 1990s. *Back row, far left:* Chief Jerry G. Haney; *back row, far right:* Assistant Chief Jimmy Factor; *front row, fifth from left:* JoAnna Morris, former council secretary; *front row, sixth from left:* Eula Doonkeen, former assistant chief. (Photograph courtesy of Jerry G. Haney)

and it required tribes to make payments to the state, resulting in a significant revenue source for Oklahoma. The Seminole Nation was among a number of Oklahoma tribes that approved the compacts. As of 2009 the Seminole Nation is still repaying fines to the NIGC.[2]

During Chief Jerry Haney's last few years as chief, a federal suit concerning freedmen claims was litigated. The case involved freedmen claims to benefits of the Seminole judgment fund programs, which were funded by the 1990 law approving distribution of the award in the suit by the Oklahoma and Florida Seminoles against the United States for Florida land taken as a result of the 1823 Camp Moultrie Treaty. Freedmen plaintiffs challenged the validity of the Seminole Nation requirement that a person must provide a certificate of degree of Indian blood (CDIB) as proof that he or she was a descendant of a person on the Seminole Indian rolls (as opposed to freedmen rolls) established during the allotment era, in order to establish eligibility for judgment fund programs. In 1996 freedman band member Sylvia Davis filed the case on behalf of her son, who had been denied Seminole Nation judgment fund program benefits on the basis of his inability to provide a CDIB. The two Seminole freedmen bands, the Dosar-Barkus and Bruner bands, joined Davis as plaintiffs in the suit, which was filed against the United States and other federal defendants, including the BIA and the Secretary of the U.S. Department of the Interior.[3] The district court dismissed the case, but the Tenth Circuit Court of Appeals remanded the case to the district court in 1999 for further consideration and findings.

After the remand, the district court determined in 2002 that the Seminole Nation, which was protected by sovereign immunity from suit, was an indispensable party in the case. The district court found that the case could not be litigated "in equity and good conscience" without the Nation as a party, and it again dismissed the case. In reviewing the case, the court mentioned that the southwest regional field solicitor for the Interior had previously found that the eligibility standards contained in the Seminole Nation's judgment fund laws were acceptable, because the 1990 law approving the Florida land claim judgment fund division, Public Law 101-277, did not express any congressional intent concerning freedmen participation in the judgment fund benefits. The Tenth Circuit Court of Appeals upheld the dismissal of the suit in 2003. The Seminole freedmen currently continue to participate as Seminole Council members and to vote in tribal elections, but freedmen members who cannot prove descendancy from the Indian rolls cannot participate in the Seminole Nation's judgment fund programs funded by the Florida land claim award, and they reportedly receive little, if any, federal program services.[4]

At the time of the 2002 and 2003 federal court rulings in the *Davis* case, the Seminole Nation was undergoing another period of great political turmoil. This turmoil began in earnest after Seminole citizens approved nine proposed amendments to the Seminole Constitution in July 2000. These amendments included provisions to restrict tribal membership eligibility to persons who could establish descendancy from the allotment rolls of Seminole Indians by blood. These membership provisions, had they been implemented, would have resulted in membership ineligibility for those Seminole freedmen members whose ancestry could be traced only to the allotment rolls of freedmen but would not have affected the eligibility of those Seminole members of African American heritage who could trace ancestry to the allotment rolls for Seminole by blood. The Seminole government did not submit the amendments to the BIA for approval; however, the BIA refused to recognize their validity, and they were not implemented. The Nation filed suit in federal court in the District of Columbia, which resulted in a 2001 ruling that the Seminole Constitution authorized the Department of the Interior to approve constitutional amendments. The court also found that the Act of October 22, 1970, afforded some authority to the Interior to approve constitutional amendments involving selection of the chief. The court upheld the BIA's disapproval of the amendments affecting freedmen membership eligibility, but it remanded the remaining six amendments back to the BIA for approval or disapproval.[5] These amendments involved judicial authority, separation of powers, council authority to raise revenue and lay and collect taxes, establishment of a general council chairman, term limits, and establishment of initiative and referendum powers. However, some of these amendments were challenged by the federal government and other parties, and none had been implemented as of August 2009.[6]

In the meantime, the BIA refused to recognize the validity of the July 2001 election of Kenneth Chambers as principal chief and Mary Ann Emarthale as assistant chief, because votes of freedmen were not counted in those elections. The BIA stopped providing federal funding to the Seminole Nation in October 2001. At that time the BIA notified the Seminole government that it would not restore a government-to-government relationship with the general council until the freedmen's representatives were restored to the council, that it would continue to recognize Jerry Haney as principal chief and James Factor as assistant chief, and that it required reinstatement of the general council as it existed before August 10, 2000.

The BIA's stance led to a second suit by the Seminole Nation against the Department of the Interior in the District Court of the District of Columbia as well as suits among Seminole leaders in federal court and in the Court of Indian Offenses. In September 2002 the district court upheld the validity of the BIA's finding that the July 2001 elections for principal chief and assistant chief were unlawful because the votes of the freedmen were not counted. The court found that the BIA had not violated the 1970 act by its recognition of Jerry Haney as principal chief until either a new election with freedmen participation was conducted or Haney was removed by a legally constituted general council. After that decision, the Seminole government continued to be at something of a standstill until February 2003, when nineteen members of the council again voted to remove Jerry Haney as chief. The BIA recognized that action as valid, and Kenneth Chambers was appointed by the council to serve as chief until the end of his term of office in late 2005.[7]

The Seminole Nation's internal conflicts and struggles with the BIA adversely affected its ability to take advantage of 1994 and 2000 amendments of the Indian Self-Determination Act. These amendments allowed eligible tribes to enter into self-governance compacts with the United States. Compacting tribes, known as "self-governance tribes," no longer entered into separate 638 contracts for federal programs but, instead, implemented annual funding agreements approved by tribal officials and the Department of the Interior (or, in the case of health compacts, by Health and Human Services), in accordance with the tribe's self-governance compact. The use of annual funding agreements allowed flexibility in determining and meeting the specific needs of compacting tribes from year to year. Many tribes in Oklahoma became self-governance tribes, including the Cherokee, Choctaw, Chickasaw, and Muscogee (Creek) Nations. Those tribes either no longer had local BIA agencies or had agencies with only a skeleton crew, and they engaged in more direct government-to-government relations with the BIA Eastern Oklahoma Regional Office and the BIA Central Office in Washington, D.C. As of early 2009, the Seminole Nation had not yet achieved eligibility for entry into a self-governance compact, in part because of past financial management issues. As a result, the Nation does not yet have the freedom to set priorities for federal funding use that is enjoyed by self-governance tribes.[8]

Very few of the federal programs previously operated by the Seminole government were regained during Kenneth Chambers's tenure as chief. After Kelly Haney took office as chief, the Nation began a more successful, although sometimes slow, recovery process. By 2008 the Seminole government had regained control of most of the numerous federal programs it had previously operated, including the following: family services, such as a tribal youth program for the provision of in-school, after-school, and summer activities; Indian child welfare; domestic violence prevention; food distribution; social services; emergency family services; and housing assistance through the housing authority. In addition to these programs, the Seminole government also currently operates programs involving employment training and placement, CHRs, diabetes management, and alcohol and substance abuse. The

Seminole people have also continued to make education a high priority through the efforts of an education committee, headed by Seminole council representative Terry Spencer, a retired educator. Tribal students are beneficiaries of scholarships at Seminole State College as a result of the Nation's contributions to a new building, named the Seminole Nation Residential Learning Center. The Seminole Nation's judgment fund programs for higher education, school clothing, and burial assistance also continue to provide economic support to qualifying tribal members.[9]

By 2008 the Seminole Nation's annual budget had grown to more than twenty million dollars, including an annual payroll of six million dollars. In addition, the Seminole Nation had again become a significant source of employment opportunities for area residents, providing jobs for more than 230 persons. The Seminole Nation Department of Commerce—which replaced the SNEDA and is under the oversight of a smaller board composed of persons with practical experience who (with the exception of the non-voting member chief) are not elected officials—employed an additional 350 persons and generated significant revenues for the Nation through gaming and other business ventures.

The Nation is also currently making positive strides in the redevelopment of its governmental operations, including programs related to basic government operations, such as fiscal services, human resources, program development, communications, enrollment, environmental protection, historic preservation, regulation of gaming, taxation, and law enforcement. The general council continues to develop the Nation's laws, including updating and republishing the Code of Laws that was first established in the early 1990s. Seminole leaders, including a Judicial Review Committee, worked to develop the Nation's own court system, using a $200,000 federal grant for that purpose. The establishment of the new court system was approved in the fall of 2008 by Seminole citizens through a constitutional amendment establishing a judicial branch. Attorney William Wantland—the last living member of the committee that developed the 1969 Seminole Nation Constitution, a retired Episcopalian bishop, and chief magistrate for the Seminole Nation Court of Indian Offenses—has been involved in developing the new Seminole court system. However, as of August 2009 the Department of Interior has not approved the constitutional amendment, and the new court system is not yet operational.

In the same constitutional amendment election, the people approved an amendment removing the authority of the Interior to approve Seminole constitutional amendments. As of August 2009, Interior has also failed to act on this amendment. Notwithstanding Interior's slow pace concerning approval action, these constitutional amendments bring hope that the historic BIA interference in internal Seminole disputes will finally end, and that such disputes can finally be resolved by the Seminole people's own court system. Complementing plans for the new court system, the Nation recently secured funding for a number of new patrol cars, a methamphetamine project, and a gang resistance program. The Nation's Lighthorse Police, numbering up to six well-trained officers, has taken over all law enforcement functions for the Nation and has made significant contributions to the safety of all Seminole County citizens.[10]

The Seminole Nation's tax revenues, although small compared with tax revenues generated by other tribes, such as the Muscogee (Creek) Nation, have been an important funding source. According to a report of the BCR Commission, in fiscal year 2006 the Nation collected more than $1.8 million from tax revenues, representing a $298,200 increase over the fiscal year 2005 tax revenues. The largest tax revenue amount came from a motor fuel tax rebate in the amount of $506,933, which was paid to the Nation in accordance with a motor fuel tax compact with the state of Oklahoma. Tobacco tax collections in the amount of $465,395 resulted in the second largest revenue. The commission also collected more than $423,510 for vehicle registrations and car tags in fiscal year 2006.[11]

During Jerry Haney's earlier terms as chief and during Kelly Haney's term, the Seminole Nation successfully expanded its land base, constructed and purchased new buildings, and established outreach facilities for tribal members. The Nation now maintains several facilities in Wewoka, including the housing authority building; a tribal office building; a community building that was constructed in the 1990s for the elderly nutrition program's use, various family-oriented services, and meeting space for tribal functions; a newly constructed casino near the community building; and a convenience store. The Nation also still owns an old warehouse building on trust property on Brown Street in Wewoka that was once used for its first bingo facility, and it continues to lease tribal trust property across the highway from the tribal complex to the IHS for the Wewoka Clinic and to the BIA for the Wewoka Agency.

The Oklahoma Seminoles' facilities also include an area in the southwestern portion of Seminole County, in the areas of Konawa and Sasakwa. Near the southern boundary of the Seminole Nation, not far from Konawa, the Nation purchased property on the highway between Seminole and Ada. A fairly new building there houses a children's Head Start program, which serves citizens in the Konawa area. The Rivermist Casino is also located at that site. In 2007 the Nation constructed a community building on a five-acre tract in Sasakwa, also in the southern portion of the Seminole Nation, which is frequently used by tribal members for meetings and social events.

Between 1993 and 2008, the Seminole Nation also significantly improved and expanded its facilities in the area of Seminole, Oklahoma. At the Mekusukey Mission property south of Seminole, the Nation renovated the council building and attached offices for the Seminole Lighthorse Police and for the BCR Commission. A dialysis center for diabetic patients and a large community building were also constructed. The Mekusukey Mission property is also the site of a food distribution center; an old gymnasium, which is used for fundraisers, powwows, basketball games, and other events; a Head Start program serving preschool children in the Seminole area; and several baseball diamonds. The Seminole Nation also owns two undeveloped sites: forty acres located a few miles south of Mekusukey, where a domestic violence safe house is planned, plus a twenty-nine-acre tract south of Seminole.

The Seminole government purchased seven acres in Seminole in 2008 for records management and a child care center, and it purchased a building at another Seminole location for an alcohol and substance abuse program. The previous year, the Nation purchased an office plaza in Seminole near the hospital; this plaza is used for the Nation's judgment fund programs and for its gaming commission, which maintains regulatory oversight over its gaming operations. The Seminole Nation finished construction of a community building on ten acres near the Strother community in northeast Seminole County in 2006, and that facility is enjoyed by tribal members and other members of the community for various functions. The Nation's Mystic Winds Casino is located north of Seminole on a 3.2-acre tract of land that is part of a larger seventeen-acre tract purchased during Chief Jerry Haney's administration in the nineties.

In sum, between 1969 and 2008, the Nation succeeded in increasing its land base, which at one time after statehood consisted of only the 160-acre Mekusukey tract, to approximately 350 acres. A land acquisition program approved by the council under the administration of Chief Kelly Haney plans to increase the land base even more.

The Seminole people continue to maintain a rich social and cultural life, notwithstanding internal governmental conflicts. For example, recognizing the importance of art, the Seminole government established a new Arts and Culture Committee, which includes Seminole member Dr. Mary Jo Watson, director of the University of Oklahoma School of Art, and Seminole–Creek filmmaker Sterlin Harjo. Tribal social events include an annual Thanksgiving and Christmas dinner for tribal members and wild onion dinners in the spring. Seminoles also maintain Christian and traditional religious practices. There are still a number of Indian churches in the Seminole Nation, where the native tongue is often spoken and sung.[12] There is currently only one ceremonial grounds

Seminole Nation dialysis center, Mekusukey Mission Grounds, 2008. (Photograph by John Hudson Haney)

site, known as Garr Creek, remaining within the Seminole Nation. The Garr Creek ceremonial grounds are used by the more traditional Seminoles as a meeting place and campground for religious purposes, and it is not open to the general public. Garr Creek is probably the only location where Seminole stickball games are still played as a recreational activity.

The Seminole Nation has also become a more visible and positive part of non-Indian communities within Seminole County. In addition to benefiting from employment opportunities, law enforcement protection, and a county-wide public transit system, non-Indian county residents also benefit from Seminole Nation roads programs, its Older American Program, and its Head Start program for preschool children. During the Kelly Haney administration, the Seminole Nation began to place the monthly tribal newspaper, the *Cokv Tvlvme*, on its Internet website and as an insert in the Wewoka and Seminole newspapers, thus providing information about the Nation's activities and services not only to tribal members, but also to non-tribal members.[13] This action has had the effect of educating people about Seminole contributions to the community, the Nation's achievements, and the importance of the Nation to the local economy, which has paved the way to improved community relations. The Fortieth Annual Seminole Nation Days celebration was held in late September 2008, with 15,000 people in attendance. The Forty-first Annual Seminole Nation Days celebration is slated for September 2009, at which time the newly elected Chief, Leonard M. Harjo, and the newly elected Assistant Chief, Ella Colman, will be sworn in, together with the newly elected Council members. More than a century after Oklahoma statehood and after overcoming tremendous obstacles, the Seminole Nation is continuing on its remarkable path to strengthen and stabilize its government for the betterment of tribal members, their communities, and future generations.

Appendix: Seminole Nation General Council Election Results According to Band, 1969–1989

Note: Other individuals also served on the Council. It was not unusual for bands to fill Council vacancies arising during the terms through internal band elections.

Band	1969	1973	1977	1981	1985	1989
Bruner (Freedmen)	Aaron Jackson Harper Osborne Sam Osborne	Aaron Jackson Harper Osborne Sam Osborne	Andrew Crockett Willie Phillips Elmer Crockett	Andrew Crockett Lawrence Cudjoe	Leon Brown Lawrence Cudjoe Lance Cudjoe	Lawrence Cudjoe Lance Cudjoe
Ceyvha	Effie G. Kivett Ishmael Tiger Delmer Wolf	Jennie Rice Houston Ross	Kenneth Tiger Juanita Scott Jennie Scott	Tinnie Tiger Jennie Ross Houston Ross	Tinnie Tiger Jennie Ross Houston Ross	TinnieTiger Tommy Ray Bighead
Dosar Barkus (Freedmen)	George Roberts Ben Warrior J.B. Thurman	Dave Carolina Ben Warrior J.B. Thurman	Dave Carolina Ben Warrior J.B. Thurman	Dave Carolina Ben Warrior J.B. Thurman	J.B. Thurman	
Eufaula	Elmer Larney Amos Tiger Jim Lena	Joe Tiger Amos Tiger Lucy Lena	Anderson Burgess Amos Tiger Lucy Lena	Lucy Lena Leo Tiger Jerome Warledo	Christine B. Harjo	Jane McGreisey
Fuchutche	Tony Palmer Marsey Cully Jackson Tiger	Tony Palmer Marcy Cully Susie Periote	Tony Palmer Roy Wood Ida Harjo	Jackson Tiger	Jackson Tiger	
Hecete	Edwin Tanyan Wesley Tanyan Terry Little	David Little Charles Grounds Terry Little	Mitchell Little Samuel Fixico Terry Little	Mitchell Little Kenneth Fixico Mary A. Jackson	William Yeager Anita Lena	Charles Grounds
Hvteyievlke ("Newcomer")	Jane McGreisey Andrew Harjoche Eastman Factor	Jane McGreisey Corena England Mandy Wise	Velma Roberts Raymond Johnson Virginia Cosar	Virginia Cosar	Marie Hall Charles Johnson	Marie Hall Evan Haney

Band	1969	1973	1977	1981	1985	1989
Mekusukey	William Coker Alice Kernell Solomon Fish	Robert Kernell Jr. Richmond Tiger Enoch Kelly Haney	Grace Dailey Thomas Revas Alvin Harjo	Grace Dailey Joe A. Harjo Robert Kernell Jr.	Grace Dailey Joe A. Harjo Robert Kernell Jr.	Grace Dailey Eula Doonkeen
Nurcup Harjo	Robert Kernell Sr. Bennie F. Johnson Samuel Johnson	Robert Kernell Sr. Raymond Harjo Beulah M. Jones	Robert Kernell Sr. James Milam Beulah M. Jones	Robert Kernell Sr. Beulah M. Jones	Robert Kernell Sr.	
Ocese	Shirley Scott James Spencer Richard Bemo	Simeon Bemo Charles Foster Richard Bemo	Moses Harjo George H. Bemo Richard Bemo	George B. Harjo Alene Miller	George B. Harjo George H. Bemo Leo Fish	Kathleen Coachman Leo Fish
Rewalke	Benny Factor Jonah Harjo Drew Harjo	Benny Factor Franklin Harjo Wayne Shaw	Bennie Factor Jonah Harjo	Carl Lee Harjo Jonah Harjo Jr. Mararet A. Tiger	Carl Lee Harjo Mary L. Tiger Wayne Shaw	
Tallahasse	Sam Moses Robert Lena Elmer Lusty	Sam Moses Robert Lena Sam Tiger	Sam Moses Edmond Harjo Sam Tiger	Sam Moses Lucy M. Harjo Robert Lena	Sam Moses Lucy M. Harjo Robert Lena	
Tom Palmer	Louis Harjo Fred Jones Irene Bemo	Louis Harjo Roy Cosar V.V. Harjo	Joe Pennokee Roy Cosar V.V. Harjo	Edna Lucille Harjo Lina Louise Wood	Fred Jones Roy Yargee Katherine Alexander	Susie Miller Fannie Harjo
Tusekia Harjo	Sampson Cully Russell Coker Thomas Coker	Randy Woods Tom McGreisey Sr. Thomas Coker	Floyd Harjo Tom McGreisey Sr. Thomas Coker	Floyd Harjo Dorsey Nero Jerome Warledo	Floyd Harjo Dorsey Nero Joanna Morris	Floyd Harjo Joanna Morris

NOTES

CHAPTER 1

1. For histories of the Five Tribes in the nineteenth and early twentieth centuries, see Debo, *Rise and Fall of the Choctaw Republic*; Debo, *And Still the Waters Run*; Debo, *Road to Disappearance*; Debo, *Five Civilized Tribes of Oklahoma*; McReynolds, *Seminoles*; Kidwell, *Choctaws in Oklahoma*; and Miller, *Coacoochee's Bones, A Seminole Saga*.

2. *Cherokee Nation v. Georgia*, 30 U.S. (5 Pet.) 1 (1831); and *Worcester v. Georgia*, 31 U.S. (6 Pet.) 515 (1832). See also *Mackey v. Cox*, 59 U.S.100 (1855).

3. Seminole Treaty of Camp Moultrie, Act of Sept. 18, 1823, 7 *Stat.* 224, Seminole Treaty of 1832, Act of May 9, 1832, 7 *Stat.* 368; Creek Treaty of 1833, Act of Feb. 14, 1833, 7 *Stat.* 417; Seminole Treaty of 1833, Act of Mar. 28, 1833, 7 *Stat.* 423; see chapter 4 for discussion of Florida land claim arising from 1823 land loss.

4. McReynolds, *Seminoles*, 156, 236.

5. Seminole Treaty of 1832, 7 *Stat.* 368, Art. 1; Creek and Seminole Treaty of 1845, Act of Jan. 4, 1845, 9 *Stat.* 821, Art. 1; U.S. Dept. of the Interior, Census Office, *Five Civilized Tribes of Indian Territory: Bulletin* (hereafter cited as 1894 Census Bulletin), 24; and McReynolds, *Seminoles*, 222, 234, 250, 259. See also Mulroy, *Seminole Freedmen: A History*.

6. Creek and Seminole Treaty of 1856, Act of Aug. 7, 1856, 11 *Stat.* 699, Art. 1, Art. 3 (Seminoles to hold fee title to the land).

7. Bylaws of the Seminole Tribe, 1856 (unsigned translation dated Feb. 18, 1964), private family collection of papers of Terry Walker (hereafter cited as Terry Walker Papers); and William Wantland, interview with the author, Dec. 3, 2005 (hereafter cited as Wantland interview). But see U.S. Dept. of the Interior, *Annual Report of U.S. Indian Inspector, FY 1900*, 70 (stating that Seminole Nation had never had any written laws).

8. Schmeckebier, *Office of Indian Affairs, Its History*, 127; but see Leupp, *Indian and His Problem*, 332. Seminole legislation enacted from 1886 to 1893 has

been recorded but has not been translated into English. See Acts of National Council, Seminole Nation (vol. 1, 1886–1893), Seminole Documents, Indian Archives, Oklahoma Historical Society.

9. 1894 Census Bulletin, 7; McReynolds, *Seminoles*, 260; and Sattler, "Seminoli Italwa: Socio-Political Change," 300, 348–351.

10. 11 *Stat.* 699, Art. 4 and 15.

11. Seminole Treaty of 1866, Act of Mar. 21, 1866, 14 *Stat.* 755, Art. 7, 9, and 11; see 11 *Stat.* 699, Art. 4 and 15; see McReynolds, *Seminoles*, 289–312, 316–18.

12. 14 *Stat.* 755; Act of Mar. 2, 1889, 25 *Stat.* 980, § 12 (appropriating $1,912,942 to compensate the Nation for 2,037,414 acres ceded under the 1866 treaty); and § 13 (providing that ceded lands would be a part of the public domain). Art. 3 of the 1866 treaty established the boundaries of the new Seminole domain as "Beginning on the Canadian River where the line dividing the Creek lands according to the terms of their sale to the United States by their treaty of Feb. 6, 1866, following said line due north to where said line crosses the north fork of the Canadian River; thence up said north fork of the Canadian River a distance sufficient to make two hundred thousand acres by running due south to the Canadian River; thence down said Canadian River to the place of beginning." See also 1894 Census Bulletin, 2.

13. Cherokee Treaty of 1866, Act of July 19, 1866, 14 *Stat.* 799; Choctaw & Chickasaw Treaty of 1866, Act of Apr. 28, 1866, 14 *Stat.* 769; Creek Treaty of 1866, Act of June 14, 1866, 14 *Stat.* 785; and Seminole Treaty of 1866, 14 *Stat.* 755, Art. 7.

14. W. P. Boudinott, "The Okmulgee Constitution," *Cherokee Advocate* (vol. 2, no. 45-97, Mar. 2, 1872), John F. Brown Collection (folder 3), Seminole Nation Papers, University of Oklahoma Western History Collection (hereafter cited as WHC).

15. Act of Mar. 3, 1871, 16 *Stat.* 566, codified at 25 U.S.C. § 71; *Cherokee Nation v. Hitchcock*, 187 U.S. 294, 305 (1901); and see Rice, "Indian Rights: 25 U.S.C. § 71," 242–43, 248–49, n. 24.

16. Seminole Treaty of 1866, 14 *Stat.* 755, Art. 5 (authorizing railroad rights of way up to three miles on either side); and Cherokee Treaty of 1866, 14 *Stat.* 799, Art. 11 (authorizing railroad right of way "only for such length as may be absolutely necessary" and restricting the width of the right of way for tracks to no more than 200 feet).

17. Act of July 4, 1884, 23 *Stat.* 73 (Southern Kansas Railway Co.); *Cherokee Nation v. Southern Kansas Ry.*, 135 U.S. 641 (1889); 1894 Census Bulletin, 13; and Debo, *Rise and Fall of the Choctaw Republic*, 117.

18. 1894 Census Bulletin, 32–33.

19. Ibid., 10, 23.

20. *Atlantic and Pacific Railroad v. Mingus*, 165 U.S. 413, 437 (1897).

21. Act of Mar. 2, 1899, ch. 374, 30 *Stat.* 990; Act of Feb. 28, 1902, 32 *Stat.* 43, § 13; Morris, Goins, and McReynolds, *Historical Atlas of Oklahoma*, plate 64; and McReynolds, *Seminoles*, 242, 342.

22. General Allotment Act of Feb. 8, 1887, 24 *Stat*.388 (codified as amended at 25 U.S.C. §§ 331–34, 339, 341–42, 348–49, 354, 381).

23. J. F. Brown to editor, *Catholic Columbian*, John F. Brown Collection (box B-38, folder 6), Seminole Nation Papers, WHC.

24. 1894 Census Bulletin, 32, 33.

25. See Creek and Seminole Treaty of 1856, 11 *Stat*. 699, Art. 15 and 18, which state that "The United States shall protect the Creeks and Seminoles from domestic strife, from hostile invasion, and from aggression by other Indians and white persons, not subject to their jurisdiction and laws; and for all injuries resulting from such invasion or aggression, full indemnity is hereby guaranteed to the party or parties injured out of the Treasury of the United States, upon the same principle and according to the same rules upon which white persons are entitled to indemnity for injuries or aggressions upon them, committed by Indians." See also Seminole Treaty of 1866, 14 *Stat*. 755, Art. 1, which states that "the United States guarantee them quiet possession of their country, and protection against hostilities on the part of other tribes; and, in the event of such hostilities, that the tribe commencing and prosecuting the same shall make just reparation therefore. Therefore the Seminoles agree to a military occupation of their country at the option and expense of the United States."

26. Seminole Treaty of 1866, 14 *Stat*. 755, Art. 7, par. 7; Act of Jan. 31, 1877, 19 *Stat*. 230; Act of Jan. 6, 1883, 22 *Stat*. 400; 47th Cong., 2nd sess., 14 *Cong. Rec.* S503 (Dec. 21, 1882) (statement of Sen. Garland); and McReynolds, *Seminoles*, 331.

27. Act of Mar. 3, 1885, § 9, 23 *Stat*. 385, codified at 18 U.S.C. § 1153; and *Ex Parte Crow Dog*, 109 U.S. 556 (1883).

28. *United States v. Kagama*, 118 U.S. 375, 384 (1886); and *Talton v. Mayes*, 163 U.S. 376, 380 (1896).

29. Act of Mar. 1, 1889, 25 *Stat*. 783; and 50th Cong., 2nd sess., 20 *Cong. Rec.* S1709, S1714 (Feb. 9, 1889) (statement of Sen. Morgan).

30. 25 *Stat*. 783, §§ 5, 6, 20, 23, 25, 26.

31. Ibid., § 8.

32. Ibid., §§ 6, 27; 50th Cong., 2nd sess., 20 *Cong. Rec.* S1714 (Feb. 9, 1889) (statement of Sen. Morgan); and 1894 Census Bulletin, 9.

33. 1894 Census Bulletin, 7, 10, 13, 16; and McReynolds, *Seminoles*, 343.

34. Organic Act of May 2, 1890, 26 *Stat*. 81, §§ 2–28; 51st Cong., 1st sess., 21 *Cong. Rec.* S1066 (Feb. 5, 1890) (statement of Sen. Platt); and 21 *Cong. Rec.* H2176 (Mar. 12, 1890) (statement of Rep. Mansur).

35. 51st Cong, 1st sess., H.R. Rep. No. 66 (1890); and 21 *Cong. Rec.* S3719 (Apr. 23, 1890) (statement of Sen. Butler).

36. 26 *Stat*. 81, §§ 29–43; and 1894 Census Bulletin, 21. Also see *Thebo v. Choctaw Tribe*, 66 Fed. 372, 375 (8th Cir.1895) (finding that the 1889 and 1890 acts did not confer jurisdiction on the court in Indian Territory and stating, "It has been the policy of the United States to place and maintain the Choctaw

Nation and the other civilized Indian Nations in the Indian Territory, so far as relates to suits against them, on the plane of independent states.")

37. 26 *Stat.* 81, § 31; 1894 Census Bulletin, 21–22; and Debo, *Rise and Fall of the Choctaw Republic*, 185, 189–91.

38. 26 *Stat.* 81, §§ 25, 31; *Alberty v. United States*, 162 U.S. 499 (1896) (federal court authority over freedmen defendant); and *Raymond v. Raymond*, 83 F. 721 (8th Cir.1897) (Cherokee court authority over divorce action).

39. 51st Cong., 1st sess., H.R. Rep. No. 66 (1890); and 51st Cong., 1st sess., 21 *Cong. Rec.* H3719 (Feb. 11, 1890) and H3628 (Apr. 21, 1890) (statements of Rep. Struble).

40. 51st Cong., 1st sess., 21 *Cong. Rec.* S3719 (Feb. 11, 1890) (statement of Sen. Ingalls); and 21 *Cong. Rec.* S3713 (Apr. 19, 1890) (statement of Sen. Butler).

41. 1894 Census Bulletin, 13; Organic Act, § 43; and Debo, *Rise and Fall of the Choctaw Republic*, 184.

42. 1894 Census Bulletin, 4.

43. Act of Mar. 3, 1893, 27 *Stat.* 612, 645; 52 Cong., 2nd sess., 24 *Cong. Rec.* S270–71(Dec. 21, 1892) (statement of Sen. Perkins); and 24 *Cong. Rec.* S80 (Dec. 12, 1892) (statement of Sen. Berry). Also see 24 *Cong. Rec.* S98 (Dec.13, 1892) (statement of Sen. Jones); and 24 *Cong. Rec.* S102 (Dec.13, 1892) (statement of Sen. Platt).

44. 52nd Cong., 2nd sess., 24 *Cong. Rec.* S100 (Dec. 13, 1892) (statement of Sen. Platt); 24 *Cong. Rec.* S84 (Dec. 12, 1892) (statements of Sen. Vest and Sen. Berry); and 24 *Cong. Rec.* S99 (Dec.13, 1892) (statement of Sen. Jones).

45. 1894 Census Bulletin, 23; and Debo, *And Still the Waters Run*, 22. See also Debo, *Road to Disappearance*.

46. Commissioner Henry Dawes was a Mass. Republican who served in Congress from 1875 until 1893 and was on the Senate Committee on Indian Affairs. He served on the Commission to the Five Civilized Tribes from 1893 until his death in 1903. McReynolds, *Seminoles*, 333–34; and *Stephens v. Cherokee Nation*, 174 U.S. 445, 447–51 (1899), citing Five Tribes Commission Report, Nov. 18, 1895, and citing S. Rep. No. 377, 53rd Cong., 2nd sess. (1896).

47. J. F. Brown to Henry L. Dawes and Gentlemen of the U.S. Commission, John F. Brown Collection (box B-38, folder 9), Seminole Nation Papers, WHC.

48. Act of Mar. 1, 1895, 28 *Stat.* 693, §§ 1, 4, 9, 10.

49. 53rd Cong., 3rd sess., 27 *Cong. Rec.* H950 (Jan. 14, 1895) (statement of Rep. Curtis); and 27 *Cong. Rec.* H949 (Jan. 14, 1895) (statement of Rep. Culberson). See also 27 *Cong. Rec.* H960 (Jan. 14, 1895) (statement of Rep. Little).

50. *In Re Mayfield*, 141 U.S. 107 (1891); *Nofire v. United States*, 164 U.S. 657 (1897); *Talton v. Mayes*, 163 U.S. 376 (1896); and Cherokee Treaty of 1866, 14 *Stat.* 799.

51. Act of June 10, 1896, ch. 398, 29 *Stat.* 321, 339; "News Item of J. F. Brown," *The David (Indian Territory) Progress* (vol. 2, no. 44, July 30, 1896), John F. Brown Collection (box B-38, folder 11), Seminole Nation Papers, WHC.

52. Act of June 7, 1897, 30 *Stat*.62; and 54th Cong., 2nd sess., 29 *Cong. Rec.* S2323–24 (Feb. 26, 1897) (statement of Sen. Berry).

53. 54th Cong., 2nd sess., 29 *Cong. Rec.* S2310 (Feb. 26, 1897) (statement of Sen. Bate).

54. 54th Cong., 2nd sess., 29 *Cong. Rec.* S2246 (Feb. 25, 1897) (statement of Sen. Pettigrew); 29 *Cong. Rec.* S2305 (Feb. 26, 1897) (statement of Sen. Vest); 29 *Cong. Rec.* S2349 (Feb. 26, 1897) (statement of Sen. Teller); 29 *Cong. Rec.* S2351 (Feb. 26, 1897) (statement of Sen. Hoar); 29 *Cong. Rec.* S2309 (Feb. 26, 1897) (statement of Sen. Bate); 29 *Cong. Rec.* S2352 (Feb. 26, 1897) (statement of Sen. Vilas); and Littlefield, *Seminole Burnings*.

55. 29 *Cong. Rec.* S2352 (Feb. 26, 1897) (statement of Sen. Vilas).

56. Act of July 1, 1898, 30 *Stat.* 567; and McReynolds, *Seminoles*, 334.

57. U.S. Dept. of the Interior, *Annual Report of the Commission of the Five Civilized Tribes, FY 1903*, 7.

58. Act of June 28, 1898, 30 *Stat.* 495, §§ 11, 14, 19; 26, 28–30.

59. "The Five Tribes in Congress," *The Claremore (Indian Territory) Progress* (vol. 5, no. 31, Jan. 20, 1898), John F. Brown Collection (box B-38, folders 12.and 15), Seminole Nation Papers, WHC; Act of June 28, 1898, 30 *Stat.* 495; 30 *Stat.* 567; and U.S. Dept. of the Interior, *Annual Report of Commission of Five Civilized Tribes, FY 1898*, 4 (The Seminole Agreement "is now the law which will hereafter control in that nation both its government and property holdings").

60. U.S. Dept. of the Interior, *Annual Report of Commission of Five Civilized Tribes, FY 1898*, 2.

CHAPTER 2

1. Act of May 2, 1890, 26 *Stat.* 81, §§ 2–28; Act of Feb. 8, 1887, 24 *Stat.* 388, (codified as amended, 25 U.S.C. §§ 331–34, 339, 341–42, 348–49, 354, 381).

2. See chapter 1 for a more detailed discussion of 1897 negotiation and congressional approval of the Seminole Allotment Act, Act of July 1, 1898, 30 *Stat.* 567, and the enactment of the 1898 Curtis Act, Act of June 28, 1898, 30 *Stat.* 495 (most of which was inapplicable to the Seminole Nation).

3. 30 *Stat.* 567; Act of June 7, 1897, 30 *Stat*.62; and 55th Cong., 2nd sess., 31 *Cong. Rec.* S5575 (June 6, 1898) (statement of Rep. Curtis) (recognizing that until their government was dissolved, the Seminoles would have the right to enact laws, and that their courts were to have limited jurisdiction). See also U.S. Dept. of the Interior, *Annual Report of Commission of Five Civilized Tribes, FY 1898*, 4.

4. "History of the Seminoles," *New-State Tribune (Muskogee, I.T.)*, May 17, 1906, 12th year, no. 30, Seminole Papers (folder no. 12), WHC; and "Seminole Council Is Now in Session to Select a Tribal Trustee," *Oklahoman*, July 22, 1905.

5. "A Passing Show—Seminole Council Is Gravely Finishing Up Its Business," *Oklahoman*, Oct. 8, 1905.

6. 30 *Stat.* 567; and "Act to Provide for the Appointment of Townsite Commissioners and the Location of a Town and Other Purposes," *Seminole Council Act* (Apr. 23, 1897), Seminole Documents (vol. 4, pp. 1–6), Indian Archives, Oklahoma Historical Society.

7. 30 *Stat.* 567; and see U.S. Dept. of the Interior, *Annual Report of the U.S. Indian Inspector, FY 1900*, 62–63 (description of education in Indian Territory after approval of the Seminole Allotment Act).

8. Act of June 2, 1900, 31 *Stat.* 250; and John F. Brown Collection (box B-38, folders 16, 17), Seminole Nation Papers, WHC.

9. Act of Mar. 1, 1901, 31 *Stat.*, 861, § 36.

10. Act of June 6, 1900, 31 *Stat.* 657. This law was amended in 1903 to allow railroads to use timber and stone on lines outside Indian Territory and to provide that allottees could dispose of timber and stone on their allotments. Act of Jan. 21, 1903, 32 *Stat.* 774.

11. *Maxey v. Wright*, 54 S.W. Rep. 807 (Ind. Terr. Ct. App. 1900), *aff'd*, 105 F. 1003 (8th Cir. 1900), discussed in U.S. Dept. of the Interior, *Annual Report of U.S. Indian Inspector FY 1900*, 148.

12. U.S. Dept. of the Interior, *Annual Report of U.S. Indian Inspector FY 1900*, 45–47, 50, 53, 54, 167–68. See also 59th Cong., 1st sess., 40 *Cong. Rec.* S3273 (Mar. 2, 1906) (statement of Rep. McCumber).

13. "Closing of the Seminole Rolls," *South McAlester Capital*, Aug. 23, 1900, John F. Brown Collection (folder no. 18), WHC; U.S. Dept. of the Interior, *Annual Report Department of Interior FY 1901, Indian Affairs, Part II*, 34–36; U.S. Dept. of Interior, *Annual Report of Commission of Five Civilized Tribes FY 1903*, 33; and "Refuse to Select Homesteads," *Oklahoman*, Sept. 22, 1904.

14. Act of Mar. 3, 1901, 31 *Stat.* 1447, amending 24 *Stat.* 388, § 6 (U.S. citizenship); Act of Feb. 18, 1901, 31 *Stat.* 794, §§ 1, 9 (Arkansas corporations laws); Act of Feb. 19, 1903, 32 *Stat.* 841; and "The Townsite of Wewoka," *Oklahoman*, Oct. 18, 1902.

15. "Criminal Court," *Oklahoman*, Jan. 13, 1904; 58th Cong., 2nd sess., H.R. Rep. No. 1191 (Feb. 23, 1904), 1–2; and 58th Cong., 2nd sess., 38 *Cong. Rec.* H5004, H5006 (Apr. 18, 1904) (statement of Rep. Thomas, chart of statistics, and letter from Judge Raymond, U.S. Dist. Ct., West. Dist., Ind. Ter.).

16. Act of Apr. 28, 1904, 33 *Stat.* 573, §§ 1, 2.

17. "Editorial on Defeat of J. F. Brown," *Holdenville Times*, June 7, 1902, John Brown Collection (folder no. 24), Seminole Nation Papers, WHC; and "Editorial on J. F. Brown," *South McAlester Capital*, Dec. 1, 1904, John Brown Collection (folder no. 30), Seminole Nation Papers, WHC.

18. *Revised Statutes of the Seminole Nation* (1903), chaps.1, 8, 9, 12, 13, 14, 20, 21, 27, 28, 32, 34, 40, 44–47, 51, and 61, and 67, Seminole Documents (vol. 5, translation), Indian Archives, Oklahoma Historical Society; see vol. 12 for the original document in the Mvskoke language.

19. Act of Mar. 1, 1901, 31 *Stat.* 861 (Creek); Act of June 28, 1898, 30 *Stat.* 495 (Choctaw and Chickasaw); Act of Mar. 1, 1901, 31 *Stat.* 848 (Cherokee); and Act of July 1, 1902, 32 *Stat.* 716 (Cherokee).

20. Commissioner of Indian Affairs to Secretary of the Interior, Jan. 20, 1903, referencing a Dec. 23, 1902, letter from Hulbutta Micco, chief of the Seminole Nation, file LB 579, RG 75, National Archives, Natural Resources Division (hereafter cited as NA NRD); and Act of Mar. 3, 1903, 32 *Stat.* 982, § 8.

21. See *Morris v. Hitchcock*, 194 U.S. 384 (1904) (recognizing the constitutionality of a Chickasaw law prescribing permit taxes, and the regulation of the Secretary of the Interior governing the introduction of livestock in the Chickasaw Nation by non-citizens); *Buster v. Wright*, 135 F. 947 (8th Cir. [Ind. Terr.]1905), app. dismissed 203 U.S. 599 (1906) (recognizing the validity of Creek Nation permit tax laws imposed on the conduct of business by noncitizens, and the authority of the Secretary of the Interior to enforce those laws); and *Walker v. McLoud*, 138 F. 394 (8th Cir. 1905), *aff'd* 204 U.S. 302 (1906) (recognizing the duty of the federal government to enforce a Choctaw law requiring noncitizens to sell "their so-called improvements" within the Choctaw Nation to tribal members and stating that if they failed to do so, the improvements would be sold at public sale to the highest bidder). See also *Crabtree v. Madden*, 54 F. 426 (8th Cir. [Ind. Terr.] 1893); and *Maxey v. Wright*, 3 Ind. Terr. 243, 54 S.W. 807 (Ind. Terr. Ct. App.1900), *aff'd*, 105 F. 1003 (8th Cir. 1900).

22. Commissioner of Indian Affairs to Secretary of the Interior, Feb. 20, 1905, file LB 579, RG 75, NA NRD.

23. U.S. Dept. of the Interior, *Annual Report of the U.S. Indian Inspector, FY 1904*, 12–13; and Act of Mar. 3, 1905, 33 *Stat.* 1048. See McReynolds, *Seminoles*, 346–52, for a more detailed discussion of federal concerns regarding John Brown's purchase of lots in the Wewoka Townsite.

24. Acting Commissioner of Indian Affairs to Secretary of the Interior, Feb. 20, 1905, file LB 737, RG 75, NA NRD.

25. "Seminole Council Is Now in Session to Select a Tribal Trustee," *Oklahoman*, July 22, 1905; "Seminole Council Adjournment," *Oklahoman*, Aug. 5, 1905; and "A Passing Show—Seminole Council Is Gravely Finishing Up Its Business," *Oklahoman*, Oct. 8, 1905.

26. Act of March 3, 1905, ch. 1479, 33 *Stat.* 1048; U.S. Dept. of the Interior, *Annual Report, U.S. Indian Superintendant Union Agency FY 1913*, 61; and 60th Cong., 1st sess., H.R. Rep. No. 1454 (Apr. 6, 1908), 3.

27. 59th Cong., 1st sess., S.J. Res. 37 (Pub. Res. No. 7) (Mar. 2, 1906); 40 *Cong. Rec.* H1241 (Jan. 18, 1906) (statement of Rep. Curtis); S2976 (Feb. 26, 1906) (statement of Sen. McCumber); S3054–64 (Feb. 27, 1906) (statements of Sen. McCumber and Sen. Long); S3064 (Feb. 28, 1906) (statement of Sen. Nelson); S3122 (Feb. 28, 1906) (statement of Sen. Teller); and H3221 (Mar. 1, 1906) (statement of Rep. Curtis). See also Commissioner of Indian Affairs to Secretary of

the Interior, Feb. 18, 1905, file LB 736, RG 75, NA NRD. See *Gritts v. Fisher*, 224 U.S. 640 (1912); *Board of County Commissioners of Creek County v. Seber*, 318 U.S. 705 (1943), *reh. denied* 319 U.S. 782 (1943); *Oklahoma Tax Commission v. United States*, 319 U.S. 598 (1943); and *Creek Nation v. United States*, 318 U.S. 629 (1943).

28. Act of Apr. 26, 1906, 34 *Stat.* 137, § 28.

29. 34 *Stat.* 137, § 6; and Exec. Order of June 7, 1951, no 10250, 16 *Fed. Reg.* 5385.

30. "Dawes Commission Has a New Division for Making Patents for the Allotments in Seminole Nation," *Oklahoman*, Sept. 27, 1906.

31. First assistant secretary of the Interior to U.S. Indian Inspector for Indian Territory, Mar. 24, 1906, Seminole Misc. Doc. # 39518-0, Indian Archives, Oklahoma Historical Society; U.S. Indian Agent, Union Agency, Muskogee, Indian Territory to Commissioner of Indian Affairs, May 12, 1905, Seminole Misc. Doc. # 39518-J, Indian Archives, Oklahoma Historical Society; and Op. Assist. Atty. Gen., July 22, 1905, Seminole Misc. Doc. 39518-K, Indian Archives, Oklahoma Historical Society.

32. Act of Oct. 22, 1970, Pub. L. No. 91-495, 84 *Stat.* 1091.

33. *Harjo v. Kleppe*, 420 *F. Supp.* 1110, 1127 (D.D.C. 1976), *aff'd sub nom. Harjo v. Andrus*, 581 F.2d 949 (D.C. Cir. 1978).

34. 34 *Stat.* 137, §§ 1, 2, 3, 4 (enrollment), § 8 (records), § 11 (tribal revenues, taxes), § 17 (per capita distributions), and § 18 (claims); and 59th Cong., 1st sess., 40 *Cong. Rec.* S4653–54 (Apr. 3, 1906) (statement of Rep. Teller).

35. 34 *Stat.* 137, § 12 (purchase of town lots), § 14 (lands reserved from allotments, etc.), § 15 (sale of tribal buildings), § 16 (sale of unallotted lands), and § 27 (reserved tribal lands).

36. 59th Cong., 1st sess., 40 *Cong. Rec.* H1245 (Jan. 18, 1906) (statement of Rep. Stephens).

37. 34 *Stat.* 137, § 10 (schools).

38. 59th Cong., 1st sess., 40 *Cong. Rec.* H1242 (Jan. 18, 1906) (statement of Rep. Curtis).

39. Ibid., H1241 (Jan. 18, 1906) (statement of Rep. Curtis).

40. Ibid., H1243 (Jan. 18, 1906) (statement of Rep. Curtis).

41. 34 *Stat.* 137, § 24 (highways) and § 26 (streets, municipalities).

42. Bonaparte, Charles J. (Dept. of Justice), "Seminole Indians—Modification of Agreement With," Aug. 19, 1907, Letters Received 1881–1907, BIA, RG 75, NA NRD. See *Cherokee Nation v. Hitchcock*, 187 U.S. 294 (1902); and also see *Lone Wolf v. Hitchcock*, 187 U.S. 553 (1903) (power of Congress over sale of lands of Kiowa, Comanche, and Apache Indians in Oklahoma Territory).

43. 59th Cong., 1st sess., 40 *Cong. Rec.* S3213, S4390, and S4392 (Mar. 1 and 28, 1906) (statements of Sen. La Follette); and 34 *Stat.* 137, § 13.

44. U.S. Dept. of Interior, *Annual Report of the U.S. Indian Inspector, FY 1904*, 8; Act of Mar. 11, 1904, 33 *Stat.* 65; Welsh, Townes, and Morris, *History of the*

Greater Seminole Oil Field, 6–7; "Oil Fields Are Best in the World," *Oklahoman*, Mar. 26, 1905; and "Seminole County," *Oklahoman*, Apr. 22, 1910.

45. 59th Cong., 1st sess., 40 *Cong. Rec.* H1243 (Jan. 18, 1906) (statement of Rep. Curtis).

46. U.S. Dept. of the Interior, *Annual Report of Commission to the Five Civilized Tribes* (vol. 21, 1914), 8; and Act of March 3, 1905, ch. 1479, 33 *Stat.* 1048.

47. 59th Cong., 1st sess., 40 *Cong. Rec.* S4655 (Apr. 3, 1906) (statements of Sen. Clark and Sen. Spooner); and S3061 (Feb. 27, 1906) (statement of Sen. Teller).

48. 59th Cong., 1st sess., 40 *Cong. Rec.* H1514–15 (Jan. 24, 1906) (statement of Rep. Beall); H1552 (Jan. 25, 1906) (statement of Rep. Floyd); H1567 (Jan. 25, 1906) (statement of Rep. McGuire); S8399 (June 13, 1906) (statement of Sen. Morgan); and S3386 (Mar. 6, 1906) (statement of Sen. Long).

49. Act of June 16, 1906, 34 *Stat.* 267, §§ 1, 3.

50. Ibid., §§ 1, 3, 13, and 19; and Oklahoma Constitution, Art. 1, § 3.

CHAPTER 3

1. Act of July 1, 1898, 30 *Stat.* 567; and Act of June 2, 1900, 31 *Stat.* 250.

2. See Act of May 27, 1908, 35 *Stat.* 312, § 3 (final rolls "of citizenship and of freedmen" conclusive evidence as to the quantum of Indian blood).

3. Federal laws that validated various types of conveyances included Act of July 2, 1945, 59 *Stat.* 313, §§ 1– 3; Act of Aug. 4, 1947, 61 *Stat.* 731, §§ 7 and 9; Semple, *Oklahoma Indian Land Titles*; Bledsoe, *Indian Land Titles*; Rarick, *Guide to Rarick's Oklahoma Indian Land Titles*; and Rarick, *Cases and Materials.*

4. The decisions of the Oklahoma Supreme Court interpreting federal Five Tribes individual restricted allotted land laws were more numerous during the first half of the twentieth century and decreased with the passage of time. As discussed in the introduction, it is outside the scope of this book to provide an analysis of such state court decisions.

5. Act of Apr. 21, 1904, 33 *Stat.* 180; and see *Moore v. Carter Oil Co.*, 43 F.2d 322 (10th Cir. 1930), *cert. denied*, 282 U.S. 903 (1931) (effect of Seminole Allotment Act on tribal communal title).

6. 59th Cong., 1st sess., 40 *Cong. Rec.* S4395 (Mar. 2, 1906) (statements of Sen. Spooner and Sen. Teller); S3275 (Mar. 2, 1906) (statement of Sen. McCumber); and S4654 (Apr. 3, 1906) (statements of Sen. Spooner and Sen. Teller).

7. 33 *Stat.* 180; 34 *Stat.* 137, § 19 (restrictions on alienation of allotments), § 20 (leases), and § 22 (inherited lands); and see *Brader v. James*, 246 U.S. 88, 95 (1918) (re-imposition of constitutional restrictions).

8. Act of Apr. 26, 1906, 34 *Stat.* 137, § 19 (taxation), § 23 (wills), and § 19 (invalid contracts); see also Act of Aug. 1, 1914, 38 *Stat.* 601, § 17, par. 14, codified

at 25 U.S.C. § 86, as amended by Act of June 25, 1948, 62 *Stat.* 683 (invalid contracts); *Heckman v. United States*, 224 U.S. 413 (1912) (1906 act a lawful exercise
of federal guardianship power); *Davis v. Williford*, 271 U.S. 484 (1926) (purpose
of § 23); and *Blundell v. Wallace*, 267 U.S. 373 (1925) (effect of § 23).

9. 34 *Stat.* 137, § 19 (determination of blood quantum); 35 *Stat.* 312, § 3
(blood quantum); 61 *Stat.* 731, § 2 (blood quantum); see 25 U.S.C. § 355 note;
see *United States v. Wildcat*, 244 U.S. 111 (1917) (Dawes Commission authority
to enroll Five Tribes member who refused to select allotment); *United States v.
Fisher*, 222 U.S. 204 (1911) (upholding secretarial decision to strike names from
freedmen rolls without due process, where there was proof of fraud in securing
enrollment and no proof of entitlement to membership); and *Garfield v. Goldsby*,
211 U.S. 249 (1908) (secretary had no authority to summarily strike Chickasaw
enrollees names from rolls).

10. 60th Cong., 1st sess., H.R. Rep. No. 1454, (Apr. 6, 1908), 3; and "To Sign
6,000 Deeds for Seminole Land," *Oklahoman*, Jan. 12, 1907. According to a later
Indian Claims Commission decision, *Seminole Nation v. United States*, 10 Ind. Cl.
Comm. 450, 486 (Op., Aug. 22, 1962), the final enrollment was slightly different:
a total of 3,128 persons enrolled, 986 of whom were freedmen, not including
five persons later added to the Seminole rolls under the Act of Aug. 1, 1914, ch.
222, 38 *Stat.* 582, 600, § 17, par. 14. For descriptions of the number of allottees
and allotment sizes for the other four tribes, see U.S. Dept. of Interior, *Annual
Report of Commission to Five Civilized Tribes* (vol. 21, 1914), 8–9.

11. 60th Cong., 1st sess., H.R. Rep. No. 1454 (Apr. 6, 1908), 1–2, 4; see also
Sen. Rep. No. 575 (Apr. 28, 1908), 4.

12. 60th Cong., 1st sess., H.R. Rep. No. 1454 (Apr. 6, 1908), 2–3; see also
Sen. Rep. No. 575 (Apr. 28, 1908), 4; and 35 *Stat.* 312.

13. See note 12 above; 35 *Stat.* 312, § 1 (removal of restrictions as to certain
classes of allottees); see *Choate v. Trapp*, 224 U.S. 665 (1912), and *Carpenter v.
Shaw*, 280 U.S. 363 (1930) (constitutionally protected rights established by
allotment agreements).

14. 35 *Stat.* 312, § 4 (restrictions), § 8 (state court approval of wills), § 9
(restrictions for half-blood heirs); and "Want Indian Cases in Federal Courts,"
Oklahoman, Feb. 22, 1908, 7.

15. 35 *Stat.* 312, § 11 (oil and gas leases); 30 *Stat.* 567 (Seminole Allotment
Act);Welsh et al., *History of the Greater Seminole Oil Field*, 16–17; "Many Wildcats
at Holdenville, Eighteen Tests Drilling in Hughes and Seminole Counties,"
Oklahoman, June 27, 1920, 44; and see chapter 4 for discussion of the Seminole
mineral claim against the United States.

16. 34 *Stat.* 137, § 6 (sales by guardians); 35 *Stat.* 312, § 6 (Oklahoma probate court jurisdiction over minor allottees' estates); and *Harris v. Bell*, 254 U.S.
103 (1920) (§ 9 of the 1908 act inapplicable to conveyances of minor heirs'
property pursuant to § 6 of the 1908 act).

17. Mott, *A National Blunder*, 2, 4 (discussing attached Report of M. L. Mott and including "Indian Appropriation Bill Speech") (hereafter cited as Mott Report).

18. Ibid.; see also *Coppedge v. Clinton*, 72 F.2d 531, 532 (10th Cir. 1934) ("This is another of those all too common cases in Creek County where a white guardian has looted the estate of his Indian ward."); "Odd Transfer in Okfuskee County," *Oklahoman*, May 11, 1911; and "Judge Cobb's Memory Bad," *Oklahoman*, May 26, 1911.

19. Mott Report, 46–47.

20. Ibid., 53. See *Mott v. United States*, 283 U.S. 747 (1931) (upholding authority of United States to require M. L. Mott to restore $15,000 paid to Mott by a Creek landowner's wife).

21. Mott Report, 2, 4.

22. 38 *Stat.* 582, 601, § 17.

23. Act of June 14, 1918, 40 *Stat.* 606, §§ 1, 2, codified in 25 U.S.C. § 375; Merriam and Associates, *Problem of Indian Administration*, 801; *Shade v. Downing*, 333 U.S. 586 (1948) (the United States is not a necessary party to Five Tribes heirship cases filed under 1918 act); *United States v. Hellard*, 322 U.S. 363 (1944) (restrictions removed if land sold at partition sale; the United States is a necessary party to partition proceedings filed under 1918 act); *United States v. Bond*, 108 F.2d 504 (10th Cir. 1939) (partition of inherited restricted land in probate proceeding valid); and also see *Armstrong v. Maple Leaf Apartments, Ltd*, 622 F.2d 466 (10th Cir.1979), *cert. denied*, 449 U.S. 901 (1980) (interpretation of 1947 act application to partitioned interests).

24. Mott Report, 2 (containing 1923 Oklahoma Bar Association Committee Resolution).

25. Mott Report, 16–44 (including S. E. Wallen to Charles H. Burke)

26. Ibid.

27. Act of Apr. 12, 1926, 44 *Stat.* 239, §§ 1 and 3, amended, 61 *Stat.* 731, § 3; 69th Cong., 1st sess., H.R. Rep. No. 322 (Feb. 19, 1926), 2, 4, Secretary of Interior to the Chairman of the Committee on Indian Affairs (Feb. 16, 1926); and Sen. Rep. No. 317 (Mar. 9, 1926). Also see *United States v. Rice*, 327 U.S. 742 (1946) (no right to appeal order remanding case to state court).

28. 44 *Stat.* 239, § 2; 12 Okla. Stat. Annot. § 93 (describing time period for statutes of limitations governing real property matters); and 69th Cong., 1st sess., H.R. Rep. No. 322 (Feb. 19, 1926), 3, Secretary of Interior to the Chairman of the Committee on Indian Affairs (Feb. 16, 1926); and Sen. Rep. No. 317 (Mar. 9, 1926). Also see *Armstrong v. Maple Leaf Apartments*, 622 F.2d 466 (10th Cir. 1979), *cert. denied*, 449 U.S. 901 (1980) (applicability of doctrine of laches); *Wolfe v. Phillips*, 172 F.2d 481 (10th Cir. 1949), cert. denied, 336 U.S. 968 (1949) (state statute of limitations applicable as amended, modified or supplemented by state law); and *Stewart v. Keyes*, 295 U.S. 404 (1935).

29. Act of May 10, 1928, 45 *Stat.* 495, § 1; see *Ward v. United States*, 139 F.2d 79 (10th Cir. 1943) (1928 act extension of period of restrictions to inherited allotments); *United States v. Williams*, 139 F.2d 83 (10th Cir. 1943), *cert. denied*, 322 U.S. 727 (1944) (1928 act extension of period of restrictions to lands that became restricted upon purchase with restricted funds).

30. 45 *Stat.* 495, §§ 3, 4 (§ 3 amended by the Act of Feb. 14, 1931, 46 *Stat.* 1108, and amended by Act of Mar. 12, 1936, 49 *Stat.* 1160; § 4 amended by Act of May 24, 1928, 45 *Stat.* 733); see *Oklahoma Tax Commission v. United States*, 319 U.S. 598 (1943) (transfers of restricted lands inherited by half-bloods were exempt from state estate taxes, but restricted cash and securities were not); *Clark v. United States*, 587 F.2d 465 (10th Cir. 1978) (oil and gas lease bonus and delay rentals not taxable under § 3 of 1928 act); *United States v. Daney*, 370 F.2d 791 (10th Cir. 1966) (oil and gas lease bonus not taxable under § 3 of 1928 act); *United States v. Hester*, 137 F.2d 145 (10th Cir. 1943) (sales for delinquent taxes); and *Zweigel v. Webster*, 32 F. Supp. 1015 (E.D. Okla. 1940) (significance of tax exempt certificate).

31. 70th Cong., 1st sess., S. Rep. No. 982 (May 3, 1928), 1.

32. Merriam and Associates, *Problem of Indian Administration*, 798–804.

33. Act of Mar. 2, 1931, 46 *Stat.* 1471, amended by Act of June 30, 1932, 47 *Stat.* 474, codified at 25 U.S.C. § 409a as amended; and Act of May 19, 1937, 50 *Stat.* 188 (lands purchased with restricted funds tax-exempt).

34. Act of Jan. 27, 1933, 47 *Stat.* 777, §§ 1–8, §§ 1 and 8, *repealed*, 61 *Stat.* 731, § 12. For cases interpreting §§ 1 and 8 of the 1933 act, see *United States v. Watashe*, 117 F.2d 947 (10th Cir. 1941); *United States v. Meadors*, 70 F. Supp. 800 (E.D. Okla. 1947) (meaning of term "restricted Indian" under § 1 of 1933 act), *reversed other grounds*, 165 F.2d 215 (10th Cir. 1947); and *Burgess v. Bosen*, 31 F. Supp. 352 (N.D. Okla. 1940).

35. Act of Feb. 11, 1936, 49 *Stat.* 1135; Act of June 20, 1936, 49 *Stat.* 1542, § 1, amended, 50 *Stat.* 188; and *Board of Commissioners v. Seber*, 318 U.S. 705 (1943), *reh. denied*, 319 U.S. 782 (1943) (upholding constitutionality of 1936 act concerning tax-exempt status of lands purchased with restricted funds).

36. Act of June 18, 1934, 48 *Stat.* 985, codified at 25 U.S.C. §§ 465, *et seq.* (IRA); Act of June 26, 1936, 49 *Stat.* 1967, codified at 25 U.S.C. §§ 501, *et seq.* (OIWA).

37. 49 *Stat.* 1967, § 2, codified at 25 U.S.C. § 502; 46 *Stat.* 1471, as amended, 47 *Stat.* 474, codified at 25 U.S.C. § 409a as amended; and 61 *Stat.* 731, § 10 (waivers of secretarial preferential purchase rights).

38. See *Hearings Before House Committee on Indian Affairs*, H.R. 6234, 74th Cong., 1st sess., 69, 71 (Apr. 26, 1935) (statement of Lawrence Lindley, Indian Rights Association); 85–86 (Apr. 25, 1935) (C.H. Drew, attorney, to Committee); 86, 249 (Apr. 29 and May 15, 1935) (written statements of John Caesar, president, Seminole Nation Council, and Harper Burgess); and 94 (Apr. 30, 1935) (statement of Alan G. Harper, secretary, American Indian Defense Association).

39. See *Hearings Before the House Comm. on Indian Affairs, H.R. 6234*, 74th Cong., 1st sess. 186–88, 228, 236 (May 7, 9, and 15, 1935) (statement of Okla. congressman Jack Nichols); 52, 57–59, 63–64, 110 (Apr. 25, 26, and 30, 1935) (statement of Okla. attorney Clark Nichols); 55 (Apr. 25, 1935) (statement of Grady Lewis); and 156 (May 3, 1935) (statement of Wesley Disney).

40. *Hearings Before the House Committee on Indian Affairs, H .R. 6234*, 74th Cong., 1st sess., 196–215 (May 7, 1935) (statement of John Collier).

41. Ibid.

42. Ibid.

43. Ibid., 217–34 (May 9, 1935) (statement of Harold L. Ickes, Secretary of Interior).

44. Ibid.

45. 61 *Stat.* 731, § 13 (repeal); 40 *Stat.* 606; and 44 *Stat.* 239.

46. 61 *Stat.* 731, § 1 (restrictions), § 2 (rolls determinative of blood quantum), § 5 (restricted funds), and § 8 (purchases with restricted funds). Also see 25 U.S.C. § 355 note; 80th Cong., 1st sess., S. Rep. No. 543 (July 14, 1947), 4; *Armstrong v. Maple Leaf Apartments, Ltd.*, 508 F.2d 518 (10th Cir. 1975) (right of Indian owner to object to sale); and *Springer v. Townsend*, 336 F.2d 397 (10th Cir. 1964) (discussion and interpretation of 1947 act).

47. 61 *Stat.* 731, § 3 (exclusive state court jurisdiction over guardianships and probates; notices to superintendent of Five Tribes; removal of certain cases to federal court), § 4 (federal attorneys); and see 25 U.S.C. § 355 note. The Act of Dec. 24, 1942, 56 *Stat.* 1080, which established exclusive secretarial authority over probate of estates limited to restricted funds not exceeding $2,500, remained in effect; see also Act of Aug. 12, 1953, 67 *Stat.* 558 (secretarial distribution of trust funds not exceeding $500).

48. 61 *Stat.* 731, § 6 (tax exemptions and tax records), amended, 67 *Stat.* 558, § 2; see *United States v. Wewoka Creek Water and Soil Conservancy District No. 2 of State of Oklahoma*, 222 F. Supp. 225 (E.D. Okla. 1963) (tax exempt certificates under 1947 Act).

49. 61 *Stat.* 731, § 11 (state oil and gas conservation laws).

50. Act of Aug. 11, 1955, 69 *Stat.* 666, §§ 1–5; and 84th Cong., 1st sess., S. Rep. No. 845 (July 13, 1955) and H.R. Rep. No. 1185 (July 14, 1955).

51. See note 50 above.

52. Act of May 7, 1970, Pub. L. No. 91-240, 84 *Stat.* 203, codified at 25 U.S.C. § 375d.

53. See *Bunch v. Cole*, 263 U.S. 250 (1923) (lease that Congress pronounces absolutely void cannot be validated or given any force in Okla., and an Okla. statute attempting to do so is invalid in that respect); *Parker v. Richard*, 250 U.S. 235 (1919) (even where Congress has conferred jurisdiction on state courts over the disposition of lands of Five Tribes members, they are acting as federal agencies); *Brader v. James*, 246 U.S. 88, 95 (1918) (congressional authority over restricted lands did not terminate when the restrictions expired, and Congress

had the power to impose restrictions on Choctaw lands); and *Tiger v. Western Inv. Co.*, 221 U.S. 286 (1911) (Okla. is without authority to enact or give effect to a local statute that disregards restrictions imposed by Congress on the alienation of Indian lands). Also see *Armstrong v. Maple Leaf Apartments*, 508 F.2d. 518 (10th Cir. 1975); *Springer v. Townsend*, 336 F.2d 397 (10th Cir. 1964); *United States v. Goldfeder*, 112 F.2d. 615 (10th Cir. 1940); and *United States v. Easely*, 33 F. Supp. 442 (W.D. Okla. 1940) (finding that state court acting as federal instrumentality under federal laws governing disposition of restricted lands of Five Tribes members).

54. 35 *Stat.* 312, § 6 (district agents); 38 *Stat.* 582, § 17; and *Walker v. United States*, 663 F. Supp. 258, 263, 267 (E.D. Okla. 1987).

55. *Walker v. United States*, 663 F. Supp. at 263, 267; and see also Vollmann and Blackwell, "State Court Approval of Leases."

56. See *Hearings before the House Committee on Indian Affairs, H.R. 6234*, 74th Cong., 1st sess., 59 (Apr. 26, 1935) (statement of Clark Nichols, Okla. attorney).

57. 61 *Stat.* 731, § 1 (approval proceedings); see also "Procedures and Guidelines for Trial Attorneys Appearing at Conveyance Approval Proceedings in Oklahoma District Courts Pursuant to Section 1 of the Act of Aug. 4, 1947," unpublished guidelines, June 14, 1988, in the author's possession; and Vollmann and Blackwell, "State Court Approval of Leases."

58. See note 57 above.

59. Martin R. Steinmetz, acting field solicitor, Office of Tulsa Field Solicitor, U.S. Dept. of the Interior, to David A. Mullon, Jr., Aug. 19, 1999, including "Inventory of Restricted Lands Held by Members of the Five Civilized Tribes, 1978–1998" (from Annual Reports, Muskogee Area Office/Eastern Oklahoma Regional Office, BIA), in the author's possession.

60. H.R. 5308, 106th Cong., 2nd sess. (2000), and H.R. 2880, 107th Cong., 2nd sess. (2002), available from THOMAS search engine, the Library of Congress, "Search Multiple Congresses," http://thomas.loc.gov/home/multicongress/multicongress.html.

61. See note 60 above.

62. See note 60 above. Also see "Indian Land Bill Aground, Inhofe Says—Concern of Oil–Gas Producers Stall Measure," *Daily Oklahoman*, Oct. 18, 2002.

63. 48 *Stat.* 985, codified at 25 U.S.C. § 465; and 49 *Stat.* 1967, codified at 25 U.S.C. § 501.

64. *Mammoth Oil Co. v. United States*, 275 U.S. 13 (1927) (determination that oil and gas leases had been corruptly obtained and invalidation of leases); *Fall v. United States*, 49 F.2d 506 (D.C. Cir. 1931), *cert. denied*, 283 U.S.867 (1931) (bribery conviction); Indian Land Consolidation Act (ILCA), 25 U.S.C. §§ 2201, *et seq.*, as amended by the American Indian Probate Reform Act of 2004, Act of Oct. 27, 2004, Pub. L. No. 108-374, 118 *Stat.* 1773; and see 25 U.S.C. § 2202 (making ILCA inapplicable to Five Tribes restricted and trust lands by providing that nothing in that section "is intended to supersede any other provision of

Federal law which authorizes, prohibits, or restricts the acquisition of land for Indians with respect to any specific tribe, reservation, or state(s).")

65. *Cobell v. United States*, 455 F.3d 317 (D.C. Cir. 2006), *cert. denied*, 127 S. Ct. 1876, 167 L. Ed. 2d 386 (2007) (including overview of previous numerous trial and appellate rulings in that case involving allegations of federal mismanagement of trust funds).

CHAPTER 4

1. Act of May 20, 1924, 43 *Stat.* 133, §§ 1–7, as amended by Joint Res. of May 19, 1926, 44 *Stat.* 568, Joint Res. of Feb. 19, 1929, 45 *Stat.* 1229; Act of March 4, 1929, 45 *Stat.* 1562; Act of Feb. 14, 1931, 46 *Stat.* 1115; Act of March 2, 1934, 48 *Stat.*362; and Act of Dec. 23, 1943, 57 *Stat.* 611.

2. 43 *Stat.* 133, §§ 1–7, as amended by 44 *Stat.* 568; 45 *Stat.* 1229; and Act of Aug. 16, 1937, 50 *Stat.* 650.

3. Indian Claims Commission Act, Act of Aug. 8, 1946, 60 *Stat.* 939, codified at 25 U.S.C. §§ 70–70n. The Indian Claims Commission terminated on Sept. 30, 1978, in accordance with 25 U.S.C. § 70v. The Indian Claims Commission Act applied to claims accruing before Aug. 13, 1946. The U.S. Court of Federal Claims retained jurisdiction over certain tribal claims accruing after that date under 28 U.S.C. § 1505.

4. Regarding the mineral claim, see the following: Act of May 27, 1908, 35 *Stat.* 312, § 11; "The City of Wewoka and Seminole County," *Oklahoman*, Sept. 25, 1927; "Seminole Indians Launch Effort to Regain Lands in Valuable Oil District," *Oklahoman*, Mar. 31, 1929; and C. J. Rhoades, commissioner of Indian Affairs, to Chili Fish, Sept. 28, 1929, NA, NRD.

5. See note 4 above.

6. *Seminole Nation v. United States* [ICC Docket 204] 17 Indian Claims Comm. 67 (Findings of Fact and Op., June 24, 1966); 28 Ind. Cl. Comm. 117 (Comm. Op.; Order Vacating Commission's Findings of Fact, Opinion, and Interlocutory Order; and Order Dismissing Petition, May 31, 1972); 28 Ind. Cl. Comm. 421 (Order Denying Plaintiff's Motion for Rehearing, Jan. 26, 1973); *Seminole Nation of Oklahoma v. United States*, 204 Ct. Cl. 655, 498 F.2d 1368 (Ct. Cl. 1974), *cert denied*, 420 U.S. 907 (1975), petition for rehearing denied, *Seminole Nation of Oklahoma v. United States*, 420 U.S. 984 (1975); "Seminole Landowners Protest Royalty Bill," *Oklahoman*, Jan. 26, 1930; Roy St. Lewis to John Brown, chairman of Seminole Nation Council, Sept. 29, 1961, Thomas Coker Papers, 1942–1983 (box 11, folder 3), Oklahoma Historical Society (hereafter cited as Thomas Coker Papers); and "Case May Give State Seminole Tribe 'Millions,'" *Oklahoman*, July 2, 1966.

7. See note 6 above.

8. Regarding the tribal annuities claim, see the following: *Seminole Nation v. United States*, 82 Ct. Cl. 135 (Ct. Cl. 1935), *rev'd, United States v. Seminole Nation*, 299 U.S. 417 (1937); *Seminole Nation v. United States*, 93 Ct. Cl. 500 (Ct. Cl. 1941); and *Seminole Nation v. United States*, 93 Ct. Cl. 500 (Ct. Cl. 1941), *aff'd in part and rev'd in part, Seminole Nation v. United States*, 316 U.S. 286, 297 (1942). Also see 50 *Stat.* 650.

9. See note 8 above.

10. *Seminole Nation v. United States*, 102 Ct. Cl. 565 (Ct. Cl. 1944), *cert. denied*, 326 U.S. 719 (1945).

11. Regarding the erroneous survey claim, see *Seminole Nation v. United States*, 316 U.S. 310 (1942); and *Seminole Nation v. United States*, 102 Ct. Cl. 565 (Ct. Cl.1944), *cert. denied*, 326 U.S. 719 (1945).

12. See note 11 above.

13. Regarding the claim for damages arising from distribution of tribal property and funds to freedmen under the 1866 treaty, see the following: Treaty of March 21, 1866, 14 *Stat.* 755; *Seminole Nation v. United States*, 78 Ct. Cl. 455 (1933); and *Seminole Nation v. United States*, 90 Ct. Cl. 151 (1940), *cert. denied*, 310 U.S. 639 (1940).

14. See note 13 above. Also see chapter 3 regarding freedmen allotments.

15. Regarding the claim for damages arising from distribution of tribal property and funds to freedmen under 1866 treaty, see 14 *Stat.* 755; and *Seminole Nation v. United States* [ICC Docket 152], 10 Ind. Cl. Comm. 450, 461, and 501a (Findings of Fact, Opinion, and Final Order, Aug. 22, 1962). Also see 25 U.S.C. §§ 70–70n (Indian Claims Commission Act).

16. Regarding the Wewoka Townsite claim, see the following: *Seminole Nation v. United States*, 92 Ct. Cl. 210 (1940), *cert. denied*, 313 U.S. 563 (1941); *Seminole Nation v. United States* [ICC Docket 53], 2 Ind. Cl. Com. 115 (Findings, Apr. 22, 1952) 2 Ind. Cl. Com. 122 (Opinion, Apr. 22, 1952); and Act of March 3, 1905, 33 *Stat.* 1048.

17. Regarding the loyal Seminole claim, see the following: *Burden, et al. v. United States*, [ICC Docket 121], 6 Ind. Cl. Comm. 127 (Op., Feb. 27, 1958); *Seminole Nation v. United States* [ICC Docket 205], 12 Ind. Cl. Comm. 798 (Findings, Nov. 7, 1963); *Seminole Nation v. United States*, 12 Ind. Cl. Comm. 809 (Op., Nov. 7, 1963), *aff'd, Seminole Nation v. United States*, 171 Ct. Cl. 477 (1965) [ICC Docket 205]; Treaty of March 21, 1866, 14 *Stat.* 755; and Act of May 31, 1900, 31 *Stat.* 221, 240. Also see Act of Apr. 26, 1906, 34 *Stat.* 140, § 11.

18. Regarding the railroad claim, see the following: *Creek Nation v. United States*, 75 Ct. Cl. 873 (Ct. Cl. 1932); *Creek Nation v. United States*, 97 Ct. Cl. 591 (Ct. Cl. 1942); and *Seminole Nation v. United States*, 97 Ct. Cl. 723 (1942), *aff'd Creek Nation v. United States*, and *Seminole Nation v. United States*, 318 U.S. 629, 634, 637–39 (1943), *rehearing denied* 319 U.S. 780 (1943).

19. Regarding the railroad claim, see the following: *Seminole Nation v. United States* [ICC Docket 247], 27 Ind. Cl. Comm. 141 (Findings of Fact, March 24, 1972); 27 Ind. Cl. Comm. 157 (Opinion, March 24, 1972), *rehearing denied*, 29 Ind. Cl. Comm. 422 (Jan. 26, 1973), *aff'd in part, rev'd in part, and remanded, Seminole Nation of Oklahoma v. United States*, 203 Ct. Cl. 637, 492 F.2d 811 (Ct. Cl. 1974); *Seminole Nation v. United States*, 40 Ind. Cl. Comm. 231 (Order Rejecting Plaintiff's Offer of Proof, June 22, 1977); 40 Ind. Cl. Comm. 231 (Opinion, June 22, 1977); and 40 Ind. Cl. Comm. 247 (Order Certifying and Transferring Cases to United States Court of Claims, July 13, 1978) (transfer of case that was attributable to the dissolution of the Indian Claims Commission prior to final adjudication). Also see *Seminole Nation v. White*, 224 F.2d 173 (10th Cir. 1955), *cert. denied*, 350 U.S. 895 (1955) (suit against individual landowner, finding no tribal right to railroad right of way adjacent to allotted lands); S.N. Res. 81-8 (Mar. 7, 1981) (railroad claim settlement); and S.N. Res. 81-16 (May 1, 1981) (railroad claim settlement) (all citations of Seminole Nation [S.N.] resolutions are from *Resolutions of the Seminole Nation of Oklahoma*, available from the General Council Office, Seminole Nation of Oklahoma, Wewoka, Okla.).

20. Regarding the Emahaka claim, see the following: *Seminole Nation v. United States* [ICC Docket 150], 6 Ind. Cl. Comm. 335a (Conclusions of Law and Final Award, June 4, 1958); 6 Ind. Cl. Comm. 336 (Additional Findings of Fact, June 4, 1958); 6 Ind. Cl. Comm. 345 (Opinion, June 4, 1958); *United States v. Seminole Nation*, 146 Ct. Cl. 171,173 F. Supp. 784 (Ct. Cl. 1959); and Act of Sept. 28, 1959, Pub. L. No. 86-383, 73 *Stat.* 717 (Emahaka award). Also see Act of Oct. 17, 1968, Pub. Law No. 90-585, 82 *Stat.* 1148 (law specifying permissible uses of awards funds appropriated in 1959 and 1966).

21. Regarding the Mekusukey claim, see the following: *Seminole Nation v. United States* [I.C.C. Docket 248], 14 Ind. Cl. Comm. 484 (Findings of Fact, Dec. 23, 1964); 14 Ind. Cl. Comm. 505 (Opinion, Dec. 23, 1964); 14 Ind. Cl. Comm. 517a (Final Award, Dec. 23, 1964); Act of May 13, 1966, Pub. L. No. 89-426, 80 *Stat.* 141 (Mekusukey award); and Act of Oct. 17, 1968, Pub. L. No. 90-585, 82 *Stat.* 1148 (law specifying permissible uses of awards funds appropriated in 1959 and 1966).

22. Regarding the Florida lands claim, see *Seminole Indians of the State of Florida and the Seminole Nation of Oklahoma v. United States* [ICC Dockets 73, 151, 73-A], 13 Ind. Cl. Comm. 326 (Ind. Cl. Comm. 1964), *aff'd, United States v. the Seminole Indians of State of Florida and the Seminole Nation of Oklahoma*, 180 Ct. Cl. 375 (Ct. Cl. 1967).

23. *Seminole Indians of State of Florida and the Seminole Nation of Oklahoma v. United States*, 23 Comm. 108 (Ind. Cl. Comm. 1970) and 24 Ind. Cl. Comm. 1 (Ind. Cl. Comm. 1970), *rev'd*, 197 Ct. Cl. 350 (Ct. Cl. 1972).

24. *Seminole Indians of State of Florida and the Seminole Nation of Oklahoma v. United States*, 38 Comm. 62 (Ind. Cl. Comm. 1976); Act of June 1, 1976, 90 *Stat.*

597, 629; Act of Apr. 30, 1990, Pub. Law No. 101-277, 104 *Stat.* 143; 101st Cong., 2nd sess., H.R. Rep. No. 101-399, *Providing for the Use and Distribution of Funds* (Feb. 6, 1990), 11 (report together with supplemental views to Accompany S. 1096); "Seminoles Finally Near U.S. Settlement," *Tulsa Tribune,* March 22, 1990; and "Congress Votes 75/25%!!!" *Seminole Nation Cokv Tvlvme,* March 1990, 1. See chapter 9 for a more detailed discussion of the 1990 judgment fund law, the judgment fund plan, and other issues concerning the Florida land claims award; see also Gross, *What Blood Won't Tell,* 172; and Mulroy, *Seminole Freedmen: A History,* 314–16.

CHAPTER 5

1. "Seminole Has Old Splendors in Memories," *Oklahoman,* June 26, 1927.

2. *United States Express Co. v. Friedman,* 191 F. 673 (8th Cir. 1911); *Gritts v. Fisher,* 224 U.S. 640,644 (1912); but see *Turner v. United States,* 248 U.S. 354, 358 (1919) (affirming Court of Claims dismissal of claim for mob destruction of fence in the Creek Nation in suit against the United States and the Creek Nation, and stating that the "tribal government had been dissolved").

3. Frank L. Campbell, assistant attorney general, to Secretary of the Interior, July 22, 1905, NA NRD; "Governor Brown was 'Moses' for Seminole Tribe," *Oklahoman,* Aug. 8, 1920; George Jones to F. E. Leupp, commissioner of Indian Affairs, July 26, 1907, NA NRD; F. E. Leupp, commissioner of Indian Affairs, to the Secretary of the Interior, Aug. 26, 1907, NA NRD; G. W. Woodruss, acting Secretary of Interior, to F. E. Leupp, commissioner of Indian Affairs, Sept. 5, 1907, NA NRD; commissioner of Indian Affairs to the Secretary of the Interior, Jan. 28, 1908, NA NRD; and Kvasnicka and Viola, *Commissioners of Indian Affairs, 1824–1977,* 221–32. According to news accounts, Jacob Harrison had become chief following the death of Hulputta Micco, was impeached, and was replaced by special election of John Brown in 1905. "Editorial on Jacob Harrison," *South McAlester (Indian Territory) Capital,* May 11, 1905; and "Impeachment of Jacob Harrison," *Holdenville (Indian Territory) Tribune,* May 18, 1905, Jacob Harrison (box 1, folders 2 and 3), Seminole Nation Papers, WHC.

4. Cato Sells, commissioner of Indian Affairs, to John Brown, Dec. 2, 1915, NA NRD; and Kvasnicka and Viola, *Commissioners of Indian Affairs, 1824–1977,* 243–50.

5. Act of May 18, 1916, 39 *Stat.* 123, 148; Act of Feb. 14, 1920, 41 *Stat.* 408; Act of May 24, 1922, 42 *Stat.* 552, 575, codified at 25 U.S.C. § 124 ("No money shall be expended from tribal funds belonging to the Five Civilized Tribes without specific appropriation by Congress.").

6. Act of May 27, 1908, 35 *Stat.* 312, § 11; Act of June 30, 1913, 38 *Stat.* 77, § 18; Act of May 18, 1916, 39 *Stat.* 123; Act of March 2, 1917, 39 *Stat.* 969; Act of

May 25, 1918, 40 *Stat.* 561; Act of June 30, 1919, 41 *Stat.* 3; and "Indian Payment Due this Week," *Oklahoman*, July 15, 1917.

7. Act of Nov. 2, 1921, 42 *Stat.* 208, amended Act of Oct. 12, 1976, Pub. L. No. 94-482, 90 *Stat.* 2233, and Act of Oct. 7, 1998, Pub. L. No. 105-244, 112 *Stat.* 1619, codified at 25 U.S.C. § 13.

8. *Harjo v. Kleppe*, 420 F. *Supp.* 1110, 1130 (D.D.C. 1976), *aff'd sub nom. Harjo v. Andrus*, 581 F.2d 949 (D.C. Cir. 1978).

9. Miller, *Coacoochee's Bones, A Seminole Saga*, 118, 149, 152, 173–77, 188–92; "Seminoles Begin Trip to Claim Mexican Reservation," *Oklahoman*, Jan. 16, 1921; "Friendly Mexicans Help Seminoles to Find Lands Claimed as Reservation," *Oklahoman*, Jan. 30, 1921; "Mexico to Study Seminoles in State," *Oklahoman*, July 13, 1938; and "Seminole Colony for Mexico Fades," *Oklahoman*, Nov. 1, 1938.

10. Thomas McGeisey to commissioner of Indian Affairs, Apr. 11, 1922, NA NRD; Petition from Seminole citizens to Secretary of the Interior and commissioner of Indian Affairs, Apr. 15, 1922, NA NRD; Kvasnicka and Viola, *Commissioners of Indian Affairs, 1824–1977*, 251; and Welsh et al., *History of the Greater Seminole Oil Field*, 103.

11. Hubert Work, Secretary of the Interior, to the commissioner of Indian Affairs, Dec. 30, 1922, NA NRD; Hubert Work, Secretary of the Interior, to the president, May 22, 1923, NA NRD; Thomas McGeisey and Chili Fish to Charles H. Burke, commissioner of Indian Affairs, June 21, 1923, NA NRD; and Alice B. Davis to acting superintendant, June 26, 1923, NA NRD. Also see "Mrs. Davis of 'Royal Clan,'" *Oklahoman*, Jan. 14, 1923; and "Woman Chief Gets Commission Soon," *Oklahoman*, June 6, 1923.

12. John Burgess to Sen. Robert L. Owen, Nov. 20, 1923, NA NRD; John Burgess to Sen. Robert L. Owen, Dec. 3, 1923, NA NRD; George Jones to the Secretary of the Interior, Aug. 1, 1924, NA NRD; Charles H. Burke, commissioner of Indian Affairs, to George Jones, Sept. 17, 1924, NA NRD; "Minutes, Seminole Meeting," Dec. 28, 1925, NA NRD; acting superintendant to commissioner of Indian Affairs, Jan. 18, 1926, NA NRD; Harry Tiger to commissioner of Indian Affairs, July 3, 1926, NA NRD; E. B. Meritt, assistant commissioner of Indian Affairs, to Nina Tanyan, Nelia Tanyan, and Isaac Jones, March 16, 1928, NA NRD; "Mystery Fire Destroys Emahaka Mission," *Oklahoman*, June 8, 1927; and *United States v. Seminole Nation*, 146 Ct. Cl. 171, 173 F. *Supp.* 784 (Ct. Cl. 1959) (final Emahaka claims decision). See chapter 4 for a detailed summary of the claims cases.

13. Act of June 2, 1924, 43 *Stat.* 253, codified at 8 U.S.C. § 1401(b); Act of March 3, 1901, 31 *Stat.* 1447, amending Act of Feb. 8, 1887, 24 *Stat.* 388, § 6; and *United States v. Nice*, 241 U.S. 591, 598 (1916), overruling *In re Heff*, 197 U.S. 488 (1905).

14. Harry Hully Tiger to the Secretary of the Interior, July 26, 1927, NA NRD; Charles H. Burke, commissioner of Indian Affairs, to Harry Tiger, July 26, 1927, NA NRD; memo from the commissioner of Indian Affairs to the Secretary of

the Interior, Sept. 14, 1927, NA NRD; and E. B. Meritt, assistant commissioner of Indian Affairs, to Harry Hully Tiger, Aug. 26, 1927, NA NRD.

15. Meriam, *Problem of Indian Administration*; "Minutes, Seminole Council," Oct. 16, 1928, NA NRD; Chili Fish, June Factor, and Charles H. Brown to commissioner of Indian Affairs, Nov. 24, 1928, NA NRD; Chili Fish to Frank Boudinot, Dec. 14, 1928, NA NRD; Chili Fish, Allan Crain, and Louis Fife to the Secretary of the Interior, May 25, 1929, NA NRD; Jos. M. Dixon, acting Secretary of the Interior, to Frank J. Boudinot, June 29, 1929, NA NRD; Jos. M. Dixon, acting Secretary of the Interior, to Thomas B. Latham, June 29, 1929, NA NRD, citing 35 A.G. Op. 421 (March 22, 1928); C. J. Rhoads, commissioner of Indian Affairs, to Chili Fish, Sept. 28, 1929, NA NRD; and Kvasnicka and Viola, *Commissioners of Indian Affairs, 1824–1977*, 263–72.

16. "Stage is Set for Seminole Tribe Reunion," *Oklahoman*, July 3, 1931; and "Throng Views Seminoles in Tribal Buffalo Dance," *Oklahoman*, July 4, 1931.

17. C. J. Rhoads, Commissioner of Indian Affairs, to W. E. Tiger, Apr. 10, 1931, NA NRD; Act of May 18, 1916, 39 *Stat.* 123, 148; Act of May 24, 1922, 42 *Stat.* 552, 575, codified at 25 U.S.C. § 124; see also *Harjo v. Kleppe*, 420 *F. Supp.* 1110, 1134 (D.D.C. 1976), *aff'd sub nom. Harjo v. Andrus*, 581 F.2d 949 (D.C. Cir. 1978).

18. Chili Fish to A. M. Landhan, superintendant of the Five Tribes Agency, May 4, 1931, NA NRD.

19. "Indians Plan Petition for Federal Suit," *Oklahoman*, July 22, 1931; and "Lawmakers Invited to Indian Meeting," *Oklahoman*, Aug. 6, 1931.

20. "Seminole Protest Lodged at Capital," *Oklahoman*, Jan. 7, 1932; "Chili Fish Leads March of Indians in Call on Hoover," *Oklahoman*, Jan. 30, 1932; *Seminole Nation v. United States* [I.C.C. Docket 248], 14 Ind. Cl. Comm. 484 (Findings of Fact, Dec. 23, 1964); 14 Ind. Cl. Comm. 505 (Opinion, Dec. 23, 1964); and 14 Ind. Cl. Comm. 517a (Final Award, Dec. 23, 1964). See chapter 4 for additional discussion of the Mekusukey lease claim.

21. Act of Apr. 27, 1932, 47 *Stat.* 140; and C. J. Rhoades, commissioner of Indian Affairs, to John Burgess, July 26, 1932, NA NRD.

22. "Seminole Groups to Hold Elections," *Oklahoman*, June 5, 1932; and "Indians Hosts to All Today," *Oklahoman*, July 19, 1932.

23. Act of June 15, 1933, 48 *Stat.* 146; and "Indian Council to Study Cash Offer," *Oklahoman*, Dec. 3, 1933. Congress approved a few more per capita payments in the fifties. Act of July 2, 1942, 56 *Stat.* 506; Act of Dec. 24, 1942, 56 *Stat.* 1080 ($50 per capita); and Act of March 24, 1948, 62 *Stat.* 84.

24. *Cook v. United States*, 288 U.S. 102 (1933).

25. Margold, *Powers of Indian Tribes*, 55 I.D. 14 (Oct. 25, 1934).

26. 73rd Cong., 2nd sess., 78 *Cong. Rec.* H11727–29 (June 15, 1934) (Statement of Rep. Howard).

27. *A Bill to Promote the General Welfare: Hearings on H.R. 6234 Before the House Comm. on Indian Affairs*, 74th Cong., 1st. sess. (1935), 11–12; *A Bill to Promote the General Welfare: Hearings on S. 2047 before the Senate Comm. on Indian Affairs,*

74th Cong., 1st. sess. (1935), 9; IRA, Act of June 18, 1934, 48 *Stat.* 985, codified at 25 U.S.C. § 461, et seq. The following IRA sections applied to the listed Oklahoma tribes: §§ 1, 3, 5, 6, 8–15, and 19 (codified at 25 U.S.C. §§ 461, 463, 465, 466, 468–475, and 479). Section 13 of the IRA, codified at 25 U.S.C. 473, provided that the following sections of the IRA did not apply to the listed Oklahoma tribes: §§ 2, 4, 7, 16, 17, and 18 (codified at 25 U.S.C. §§ 462, 464, 467, 476, 477, and 478); and 73rd Cong., 2nd sess., 78 *Cong. Rec.* S11126 (June 12, 1934) (statement of Sen. Thomas).

28. "Constitution and By-Laws of the Executive Committee of the Seminole Nation," June 12, 1934, William Wantland [former attorney general for the Seminole Nation] Constitution Files, Seminole Nation Museum.

29. OIWA, Act of June 26, 1936, 49 *Stat.* 1967, codified at 25 U.S.C. §§ 501, et seq. Section 8 of the OIWA, codified at 25 U.S.C. § 508, expressly made the OIWA inapplicable to Osage County. See chapter 3 of this book for a more detailed of discussions of the legislative history of the OIWA regarding Indian lands in Oklahoma.

30. OIWA, 25 U.S.C. §§ 501, et seq.; see also *A Bill to Promote the General Welfare of the Indians of the State of Oklahoma and for Other Purposes: Hearings on H.R. 6234 before the House Comm. on Indian Affairs, ,* 74th Cong., 1st sess. (Apr. 22, 23, and 26; May 2, 3, 6, 7, 9, and 15, 1935); and *A Bill to Promote the General Welfare of the Indians of the State of Oklahoma and for Other Purposes: Hearings on S. 2047 Before the Senate Comm. on Indian Affairs,* 74th Cong., 1st sess. (Apr. 8–11, 1935) (see specifically pp. 25–29, testimony of John Collier, commissioner of Indian Affairs, Apr. 9, 1935); Kvasnicka and Viola, *Commissioners of Indian Affairs, 1824–1977,* 260, 273; and also see 74th Cong., 2nd sess., H.R. Rep. No. 2408, to accompany S. 2047, (Apr. 5, 1936).

31. OIWA, 25 U.S.C. §§ 503, 507, and 509.

32. "Council Re-Elects Chief of Seminoles," *Oklahoman,* July 10, 1937; and "Seminole Marshal Urged by Tribe," *Oklahoman,* Oct. 19, 1937.

33. A. M. Landham, superintendent, to commissioner of Indian Affairs, Dec. 21, 1938, NA NRD.

34. "Minutes of Seminole Council Meetings," Oct. 5, Nov. 2, Nov. 18, and Nov. 30, 1938 (forwarded to Dept. of Interior on Dec. 21, 1938), NA NRD; "Minutes of Seminole Council Meetings," Mar. 1 and June 19, 1939 (forwarded to the Dept. of Interior July 1, 1939), NA NRD; "Minutes of Seminole Council Meetings," Apr. 6 and July 5, 1939, Charles Grounds (attorney, Seminole, Okla.) private files, in author's possession and also at Seminole Nation Museum (hereafter cited as Grounds Files); and Eugene Wheeler, assistant superintendent, to commissioner of Indian Affairs, enclosing minutes of Seminole Council meeting dated July 5, 1939 (sent on July 18, 1939), NA NRD.

35. Act of May 10, 1939, 53 *Stat.* 685. Also see Act of June 18, 1940, 54 *Stat.* 40; and Act of June 28, 1941, 55 *Stat.* 303.

36. See Act of Sept. 1, 1937, 50 *Stat.* 888, codified as amended at 42 U.S.C. §§ 1437, et seq.; and Oklahoma Housing Authority Act, 1965 Okla. Leg., codified at 63 Okla. *Stat.* Annot. § 1051, et seq.

37. "Seminole Indian Tribe in Oklahoma to Settle Third Term Issue of Its Own in June Election," *Oklahoman*, May 26, 1940; and "Movie Star Rules over Five Tribes," *Oklahoman*, Oct. 15, 1948 (mentioning Jeffie Brown as Seminole chief).

38. "Minutes of Seminole Council Meetings," Oct. 27 and Nov. 29, 1944 (forwarded to Dept. of Interior on May 2, 1945), NA NRD; "Resolution of the Seminole General Council," June 22, 1948, NA NRD; "Minutes of Seminole Council Meetings," Sept. 29, 1944; Aug. 21, 1945; Feb., Apr. 23, May 7, June 18, July 16, Oct. 15, and Dec. 10, 1946; Jan. 21, and Apr. 15, 1947; June 22, and July 5, 1948; and Apr. 19, July 19, Aug. 26, and Oct. 18, 1949, Grounds Files.

39. "Resolution of the Seminole General Council," Nov. 29, 1944, Grounds Files.

40. "Railroad and Attorneys Committee Meeting Minutes," March 23, 1946, Thomas Coker Papers (box 9, folder 5).

41. "Indian Creditors Set Board Meet," *Oklahoman*, July 21, 1946.

42. Heard, Norris, and Westmoreland, *History of the Inter-Tribal Council*, 40.

43. Act of May 4, 1948, 62 *Stat.* 211, codified at 18 U.S.C. § 1151; see also Major Crimes Act, 18 U.S.C. § 1153.

44. *Donnelly v. United States*, 228 U.S. 243, 269 (1913) (involving the murder of an Indian on an Indian reservation, and the basis for 18 U.S.C. § 1151[a]); *United States v. Pelican*, 232 U.S. 442, 449 (1914) (involving an Indian victim of a crime on a trust allotment, and the basis for 18 U.S.C. § 1151(c); *United States v. Sandoval*, 231 U.S. 28 (1913) (involving federal offense for the introduction of liquor onto Pueblo communally owned fee lands found to constitute Indian Country, and the basis for 18 U.S.C. § 1151(b)); and *United States v. McGowan*, 302 U.S. 535 (1938) (involving federal offense for the introduction of liquor at Reno Indian Colony on lands owned by the United States found to constitute Indian Country, and a basis for 18 U.S.C. § 1151(c). See also *United States v. John*, 437 U.S. 634, 648–49 (1978), and *Oklahoma Tax Commission v. Sac and Fox Nation*, 508 U.S. 114, 125 (1993) ("[T]he intent of Congress, as elucidated by [court] decisions, was to designate as Indian country all lands set aside by whatever means for the residence of tribal Indians under federal protection, together with trust and restricted Indian allotments.").

45. As defined by 18 U.S.C. § 1151(a), a reservation is "all land within the limits of any Indian reservation under the jurisdiction of the United States government, *notwithstanding the issuance of any patent*, and including rights-of-way running through the reservation" (emphasis added).

46. *Williams v. Lee*, 358 U.S. 217, 223 (1959).

47. *United States Express Co. v. Friedman*, 191 F. 673 (8th Cir. 1911); *Ex Parte Webb*, 225 U.S. 663 (1912) (Cherokee who had taken liquor into Indian Country

in eastern Oklahoma was subject to prosecution in federal courts for violating federal law); *United States v. Wright*, 229 U.S. 226 (1913); Act of March 5, 1934, 48 *Stat.* 396; *Southern Surety Co. v. State of Oklahoma*, 241 U.S. 582, 584 (1916) (declining to decide whether adultery offense involving Indians was punishable in state courts); *Jefferson v. Fink*, 247 U.S. 288, 290–91 (1918) ("A territorial government never was established in the Indian Territory and it never had a territorial Legislature. Apart from the tribal laws of the Indians, among which were laws relating to descent and distribution, the only laws which became operative there were such as Congress enacted or put in force.").

48. *Ex Parte Nowabbi*, 61 P.2d 1139 (Okla. Cr. 1936), *overruled, State v. Klindt*, 782 P.2d 401 (Okla. Cr. 1989); *United States v. Ramsey*, 271 U.S. 467 (1926); *Ellis v. Page*, 351 F.2d. 250 (10th Cir. 1965) (no federal jurisdiction over prosecution of Indian for murder of another Indian within original boundaries of lands set aside for the tribe, because there was no claim that crime arose in Indian Country as defined by federal law); and *Ellis v. State*, 386 P.2d 326 (Okla. Crim. App. 1963), *cert. denied*, 376 U.S. 945 (1964) (murder of Indian by another Indian in same matter was subject to state court jurisdiction); *Tooisgah v. United States*, 186 F.2d 93 (10th Cir. 1950) (murder of an Indian by another Indian on a trust allotment before enactment of 18 U.S.C. § 1151, which included trust allotments within the definition of Indian Country for purposes of the Major Crimes Act, 18 U.S.C. § 1153, was not subject to federal prosecution, based on the court's finding that the Kiowa, Comanche, and Apache reservation had been disestablished); and also see *In re: Yates*, 349 P.2d 45 (Okla. Crim. App. 1960) (citing *Tooisgah* as controlling in manslaughter case involving an Indian victim in Comanche County). See chapters 8 and 9 for a more detailed discussion of the development of the law regarding jurisdiction over Indian Country lands in Oklahoma.

49. National American Indian Court Judges Association Long Range Planning Project, *Indian Courts and the Future.*

50. Act of July 3, 1952, 66 *Stat.* 323, amending § 28 of the Act of Apr. 26, 1906, 34 *Stat.* 137; and "BIA Operating Statement, Muskogee Area, Five Civilized Tribes Agency, Seminole Tribal Budget, 1953 Program," Grounds Files.

51. *Muskogee Daily Phoenix,* July 15, 1954.

52. "Minutes of the Seminole Executive Board Meeting," May 9, 1953, Grounds Files; "Creek Indian Chief's Removal Is Being Sought by Petitions," *Oklahoman*, May 17, 1953; Resolution of the General Council, May 22, 1954, Grounds Files (requesting the secretary to extend the certificate to July 1956 when Cully's term was to expire under tribal law);"McKay Orders Probe of Tribal Chief's Election," *Oklahoman*, Aug. 6, 1954; F. M. Haverland, acting Muskogee Area director, BIA, to Jeffie Brown and Phillip Walker, Nov. 17, 1954, Grounds Files; Paul Fickinger, area director, to Charles Grounds, Dec. 21, 1954, Grounds Files; Charles Grounds to Arthur Jones, Mar. 25, 1955, Grounds Files; and Paul Fickinger, area director, to Thomas Coker, March 25, 1955, Grounds Files.

53. "Minutes of the Meeting of a Committee for Reorganization," May 24, 1958, Grounds Files; and "Meeting of Seminole Indian Comm.," Sept. 23, 1961, Grounds Files.

54. Act of Aug. 15, 1953, 67 *Stat.* 588, amended by Pub. L. No. 90-284, Act of Apr. 11, 1968, 82 *Stat.* 80, codified at 25 U.S.C. §§ 1321–26.

55. Ibid.

56. See Act of June 17, 1954, 68 *Stat.* 250, 25 U.S.C. §§ 891–902, repealed by Act of Dec. 22, 1973, Pub. L. No. 93-197, 87 *Stat.* 770, 25 U.S.C. 903–903f (Menominee Tribe). See also Act of Aug. 2, 1956, 70 *Stat.* 938, 25 U.S.C. §§ 821–26 (Peoria Tribe); Act of Aug. 1, 1956, 70 *Stat.* 893, 25 U.S.C. §§ 791–807 (Wyandotte Tribe); and Act of Aug. 3, 1956, 70 *Stat.* 963, 25 U.S.C. §§ 841–53 (Ottawa Tribe). The Peoria, Wyandotte, and Ottawa termination acts were all repealed by Act of May 15, 1978, Pub. L. No. 95-281, 92 *Stat.* 246, 25 U.S.C. §§ 861–861c (Restoration of Wyandotte, Ottawa and Peoria Tribes).

57. Economic Opportunity Act, Act of Aug. 20, 1964, Pub. L. No. 88-452, 78 *Stat.* 519, title II, §§ 210, 211, codified as amended at 42 U.S.C. §§ 2790, 2791, repealed by Act of Aug. 13, 1981, Pub. L. No. 97-35, 95 *Stat.* 519, title VI § 638(a); and Public Works and Economic Development Act of 1965, Act of Aug. 26, 1965, Pub. L. No. 89-136, 79 *Stat.* 552, codified, as amended, at 42 U.S.C. § 3131, repealed by Act of Nov. 13, 1998, Pub. L. No. 105-393, 112 *Stat.* 360, §§ 102(a), and codified, as amended, by 42 U.S.C. §§ 3161, et seq.

58. "Indians to Get Job Training at Muskogee," *Oklahoman*, Jan. 10, 1962; "Wewoka Plastics Now SEE, Inc., Out of Trouble," *Oklahoman*, Mar. 28, 1965; and "Many Indians Need Jobs but Won't Go Where the Work Is," *Oklahoman*, Sept. 19, 1966.

59. "Indians Whoop at Muskogee," *Oklahoman*, Oct. 14, 1948; "'Green Corn' Dance Slated by Seminoles," *Oklahoman*, July 8, 1949; and "Agency Again Is Five Tribes Hub," *Oklahoman*, July 25, 1965.

60. Act of Sept. 28, 1959, Pub. L. No. 86-383, 73 *Stat.* 717 (Emahaka award); Act of May 13, 1966, Pub. L. No. 89-426, 80 *Stat.* 141 (Mekusukey mineral lease award); Act of Oct. 17, 1968, Pub. L. No. 90-585, 82 *Stat.* 1148 (permissible uses of 1959 and 1966 appropriation for claims awards identified as ICC Dockets 150 and 248); and also see "Indian Claims Bills Pass, Go to LBJ," *Oklahoman*, Sept. 17, 1968. The claims award for the taking of Florida lands from the Seminoles is discussed in more detail in chapter 4, and the use and distribution of that award is discussed in chapter 9.

CHAPTER 6

1. Const. of the Cherokee Nation, June 26, 1976, amended June 20, 1987, revised July 26, 2003; Const. of the Muscogee (Creek), Aug. 17, 1979, amended

Dec. 7, 1991, amended Feb. 18, 2006; Const. of the Chickasaw Nation, Aug. 27, 1983, amended eff. June 21, 2002; and Const. of the Choctaw Nation, June 9, 1983. The Cherokee Nation was the only other of the Five Tribes that declined to rely on the OIWA as authority for its constitution.

2. Act of June 28, 1898, 30 *Stat.* 495; and *Harjo v. Kleppe*, 420 F. *Supp.* 1110 (1976), *aff'd sub nom. Harjo v. Andrus*, 581 F.2d 949 (D.C. Cir. 1978).

3. Bylaws of the Seminole Intra-Tribal Business Association, Inc. (SITBA), Art. III, IX, and XVI, Terry Walker Papers; "List, Board of Directors," May 9, 1964, Terry Walker Papers; Mary McCormick, interview with the author, March 26, 2006 (hereafter cited as McCormick interview); and Wantland interview.

4. "Minutes of Mass Meeting," Feb. 1, 1964, Thomas Coker Papers (box 9, folder 5).

5. "Minutes of SITBA Annual Meeting," May 9, 1964, Terry Walker Papers; "Minutes of SITBA Board Meetings," May 14 and 26, 1964; June 24, 1964; July 3, 1964; and Aug. 19, 1964, Terry Walker Papers; "Res. of SITBA Board," May 14, 1964, Terry Walker Papers; letter from C. C. Carshall, acting BIA area dir., Muskogee area office, May 22, 1964, Terry Walker Papers; and Floyd Harjo, president, SITBA, to Virgil Harrington, BIA Muskogee area dir., July 7 and Aug. 20, 1964, Terry Walker Papers.

6. Also attending these meetings were other representatives of the BIA, including Henry McGahey, field representative of the Wewoka Indian Office, and the following employees of the BIA Muskogee Area Office: Virgil Harrington, area director; Marie Wadley, tribal relations officer; and Frank Sokolik, assistant tribal relations officer. "Minutes of the First, Adjourned (Second), Third, and Sixth Meetings of the Constitution Comm. of the Seminole Nation of Oklahoma," June 8, 10, 12, and 17, 1964, Terry Walker Papers; "Minutes of the Fourth Meeting of the Constitution Comm. of the Seminole Nation of Oklahoma," June 15, 1964, Thomas Coker Papers (folder 11); and "Tribal Constitution Revision Underway," June 14, 1964, Thomas Coker Papers (box 7, folder 16).

7. "Five Civilized Tribes—Status of Freedmen—Organization Under Oklahoma Indian Welfare Act," 1 Sol. Op. 1077, Oct. 1, 1941, Memorandum of commissioner of Indian Affairs, U.S. Dept. of the Interior; "Minutes of SITBA Board Meetings," June 24, 1964, Terry Walker Papers; Virgil Harrington to John Brown, June 29, 1964, Thomas Coker Papers (box 7, folder 14), also referenced in "Minutes of SITBA Board Meeting," July 28, 1964, Terry Walker Papers,.

8. "Minutes of SITBA Board Meetings," June 24, 1964, Terry Walker Papers.

9. "Draft Constitution and Bylaws of the Seminole Tribe of Oklahoma," June 19, 1964, William Wantland Constitution Files, Seminole Nation Museum.

10. John Brown to council members, Nov. 4, 1964, Thomas Coker Papers (box 7, folder 14).

11. "Report of Visit to Muskogee Office," March 19, 1965, Terry Walker Papers; John Brown to council members, Apr. 8, 1965, and Virgil Harrington to Charles

Grounds, Apr. 12, 1965, Terry Walker Papers; "Minutes of SITBA Board Meetings," Dec. 14, 1964; Jan. 7 and 21, 1965; Feb. 8 and 16, 1965; March 9 and 23, 1965; Apr. 6, 20, and 27, 1965; and Sept. 7, 1965, Terry Walker Papers.

12. "Minutes of SITBA Board Meetings," May 25, 1965; and Wantland interview.

13. "Minutes of SITBA Board Meeting," June 1 and 22, 1965, Terry Walker Papers.

14. Ibid., June 8, 1965, Terry Walker Papers.

15. Ibid., July 20, 1965, Terry Walker Papers; and Wantland interview.

16. "Minutes of Meeting of Members of the Seminole Tribe, Sponsored by the SITBA," Sept. 14, 1965, Terry Walker Papers.

17. Ibid.

18. *Harjo v. Kleppe*, 420 F. Supp. 1110 (1976), *aff'd sub nom. Harjo v. Andrus*, 581 F.2d 949 (D.C. Cir. 1978).

19. 1964 draft, Art. III, § 4, and Art. VII, § 1; see also May and Dec. 1968 drafts and 1969 approved constitution, Art. IV, § 3, and Art. XII, § 1.

20. "Minutes of Informal Meeting of Members of the Seminole Tribe, Sponsored by the SITBA," Nov. 16, 1965, Terry Walker Papers.

21. Wantland interview. The first Native American commissioner of Indian Affairs was Ely S. Parker, a member of the Seneca Nation, who served between 1869 and 1871. Kvasnicka and Viola, *Commissioners of Indian Affairs*, 123–31 (Parker), 320 (Nash), and 325 (Bennett).

22. "Report of Meeting Held in W. C. Wantland's Office, Seminole, Okla., Saturday P.M., Jan. 7, 1967," Terry Walker Papers.

23. "Minutes of SITBA Member Meeting," Jan. 12, 1967; and Wantland interview.

24. Draft constitution, signed on Feb. 25, 1967, by Terry Walker, acting chairman, Constitutional Comm. of the Seminole Nation, and Effie Kivett, secretary of Constitutional Comm. ("1967 draft const."), William Wantland Constitution Files; as amended by May 3, 1968, draft constitution signed by John Brown, chairman, Seminole General Council, and Wisey Cully, secretary, Seminole General Council ("May 1968 draft const."), William Wantland Constitution Files; as amended by Dec. 9, 1968, draft constitution ("Dec. 1968 draft const."), William Wantland Constitution Files; as amended by Jan. 10, 1969, draft constitution, entitled "Final Draft to Be Voted on at the Seminole Tribal Elections on March 8, 1969" ("Constitution"), William Wantland Constitution Files (hereafter collectively referred to as "Draft const. and Seminole Const.").

25. William E. Friole to Terry Walker, May 9, 1967, Terry Walker Papers.

26. "Summary of Meeting in BIA Muskogee Area Dir.'s Office, Muskogee, Okla.," Oct. 20, 1957, Terry Walker Papers.

27. Associate solicitor to commissioner of Indian Affairs (memorandum) Nov. 2, 1967, Thomas Coker Papers (box 7, folder 12); and National Congress of American Indians, "History," http://www.ncai.org/History.14.0.html.

28. "Minutes of SITBA annual meeting," Nov. 21, 1967, and "Board Meeting," Nov. 28, 1967, Terry Walker Papers.

29. "Minutes of SITBA Board Meeting," Feb. 27, 1968, Terry Walker Papers; "Resolution," dated Mar. 2, 1968, signed by John Brown, chairman, general council, attested by Wisey Cully, secretary, William Wantland Constitution Files; and May 3, 1968, draft constitution, William Wantland Constitution Files.

30. *Harjo v. Kleppe*, 420 F. *Supp.* 1110 (D. D.C. 1976), *aff'd sub nom. Harjo v. Andrus*, 581 F.2d 949 (D.C. Cir. 1978) (expenditures of tribal funds); Act of Apr. 26, 1906, 34 *Stat.* 137, § 6; and Wantland interview.

31. Clyde Busey, tribal operations officer, BIA Muskogee area office, Sept. 16, 1968, William Wantland Constitution Files; Wantland interview; and Dec. 1968 draft const., William Wantland Constitution Files

32. "Minutes of Election Comm. Meetings," Sept. 30, 1968; Oct. 14 and 21, 1968; and Nov. 1 and 4, 1968, Terry Walker Papers.

33. "Seminoles to Vote on Constitution Adoption Saturday," *Seminole Producer*, March 6, 1969; "Indians to Vote on Constitution," *Seminole Producer*, March 8, 1969; "Seminoles Adopt New Constitution," *Seminole Producer*, March 9, 1969; Constitution of the Seminole Nation of Oklahoma ("Constitution"), Art. XIV, "Adoption," and certificate of adoption executed by John Brown, general council chairman, Bennie F. Johnson, the chairman of the Seminole Election Commission, and Effie G. Kivett, the general council secretary, on March 12, 1969, William Wantland Constitution Files. The constitution was approved by the commissioner of Indian Affairs, Robert L. Bennet, on Apr. 15, 1969.

34. McCormick interview; "1st Annual Seminole Nation Days Program," private collection of Mary McCormick (in author's possession); and Wantland interview.

35. McCormick interview.

36. Draft const. and Seminole Const., preamble; Art. I, "Name."

37. Draft const. and Seminole Const., Art. II, "Membership."

38. *Muscogee (Creek) Nation v. Hodel*, 851 F.2d 1439 (D.C. Cir. 1988), *cert. denied, Hodel v. Muscogee (Creek) Nation*, 488 U.S. 1010 (1989).

39. Draft const. and Seminole Constitution, Art. III, "Chief and Assistant Chief."

40. Ibid., and Art. IX, "Removal and Filling of Vacancies."

41. Draft const. and Seminole Constitution, Art. IV, "General Council," and Art. X, "Elections."

42. Draft const. and Seminole Constitution, Art. V, "General Council Powers"; Art. VI, "General Council Meetings"; Art. VII, "Order of Business"; and Art. VIII, "Duties of Officers."

43. Draft const. and Seminole Constitution, Art. IX, "Removal and Filling of Vacancies."

44. Draft const. and Seminole Constitution, Art. X, "Elections."

45. 25 U.S.C. § 1302; and draft const. and Constitution, Art. XII, "Bill of Rights."

46. Draft const. and Seminole Constitution, Art. XIII, "Amendment"; see chapter 9 for discussion of constitutional amendment elections in 1989 and 1991; see epilogue for discussion of constitutional amendment elections in 2000 and 2008.

CHAPTER 7

1. "President's Indian Bureau 'Chief' Choice is Applauded," *Tulsa (Okla.) World,* June 11, 1970; and Kvasnicka and Viola, *Commissioners of Indian Affairs,* 333–40.

2. Indian Financing Act of Apr. 12, 1974, Pub. L. No. 93-262, 88 *Stat.* 77 (codified as amended at 25 U.S.C. §§ 1451–1543) .

3. Indian Self-Determination and Education Assistance Act of Jan. 4, 1975, Pub. L. No. 96-638, 88 *Stat.* 2203, codified as amended at 25 U.S.C. §§ 450–450n, 455–458e, 458aa–458hh; 458aaa–458aaa-18.

4. *McClanahan v. Arizona State Tax Commission,* 411 U.S. 164, 172, 174 (1973).

5. *Morton v. Mancari,* 417 U.S. 535, 543, 553–54, 302, note 24 (1974). Other decisions supportive of tribal self-government in the seventies included *Kennerly v. District Court of Ninth Judicial Dist. of Montana,* 400 U.S. 423 (1971); *United States v. Mazurie,* 419 U.S. 544 (1975); and *Fisher v. District Court of Sixteenth Judicial District of Montana,* 424 U.S. 382 (1976).

6. The acreage of restricted lands decreased from 35,763 acres to 32,068 acres between 1971 and 1975—a loss of 3,695 acres in a five-year period; "Seminole Nation of Oklahoma Comprehensive Base Studies," June 30, 1975 (hereafter cited as 1975 Base Studies), 3, 32–33, private collection of Enoch Kelly Haney (hereafter cited as Enoch Kelly Haney Collection); "Interim Comprehensive Plan of the Seminole Nation, Seminole Nation Planning Dept.," June 30, 1975 (hereafter cited as 1975 Interim Comp. Plan), 1–3, Enoch Kelly Haney Collection.

7. See note 6 and see American Indian Policy Review Commission, *Final Report of the American Indian Policy Review Commission,* vol. 1, pp. 432, 437.

8. "Colorful Activities Mark Seminole Nation Day," *Daily Times, Wewoka, Oklahoma,* Sept. 7, 1969; "Second Annual Seminole Nation Days Program," Thomas Coker Papers (box 9, folder 1); and "S. N. General Council Minutes," Sept. 20, 1969, 1; Sept. 18, 1971, 1; Dec. 4, 1971, 1; and Mar. 4, 1972, 1, Eula Narcomey Doonkeen Collection (replacement of council members).

9. Act of Oct. 22, 1970, Pub. L. No. 91-495, 84 *Stat.* 1091.

10. Ibid.; S.N. Res. No. 70-12 (Dec. 5, 1970) (chief); S.N. Res. No. 71-16 (Apr. 17, 1971) (chief); Mitchell Melich, solicitor, U.S. Dept. of the Interior, to William Wantland, May 4, 1971, Terry Walker Papers; Harrison Loesch, assistant secretary of the Interior, to Terry Walker, May 7, 1971, Terry Walker Papers.

11. S.N. Res. No. 70-3 (May 9, 1970) (confirming James Rodgers and Charles Grounds as claims attorneys); S.N. Res. No. 71-5 (Dec. 4, 1971) (Niebell contract confirmation); George Scott, acting commissioner of Indian Affairs, to Terry Walker, principal chief, June 18, 1970 (disapproval of Grounds and Rodgers attorney contracts), Eula Narcomey Doonkeen Collection; and Paul Niebell to delegates of the general council (memorandum), Nov. 4, 1971, and "Memorandum on Resolution 70-3 (1970) Approving Contract with Grounds and Rodgers," Nov. 23, 1971, Thomas Coker Papers. See "S.N. General Council Minutes," Sept. 18, 1971, 3, and Dec. 4, 1971, 3–4, Eula Narcomey Doonkeen Collection; "Report on Trip to Washington, D.C.," Oct. 25–27, 1971, Eula Narcomey Doonkeen Collection; and Billie Palmer, chairman mass meeting group, to Terry Walker, Jan. 4, 1972, Terry Walker Papers.

12. S.N. Res. No. 72-1 (Feb. 12, 1972) (Walker); and "S.N. General Council Minutes," Jan. 15, 1972, 1–2, Eula Narcomey Doonkeen Collection.

13. S.N. Res. No. 72-5 (Apr. 22, 1972) (Walker); "S.N. General Council Minutes," Apr. 22, 1972, 1–3, Eula Narcomey Doonkeen Collection; S.N. Res. No. 72-4 (March 4, 1972) (signed by Floyd Harjo as council chairman); S.N. Res. No. 72-5 (Apr. 22, 1972) (seeking BIA recognition of Floyd Harjo as acting chief); S.N. Res. No. 72-6 (June 3, 1972) (signed by Floyd Harjo as acting chief); S.N. Res. No. 72-7 (July 1, 1972) (signed by Floyd Harjo as chief); and *Walker v. Harjo*, Seminole County Case No. S-C-72-30, Thomas Coker Papers (box 11, folder 8).

14. "Seminoles Seek Tribal Positions," *Oklahoman*, Aug. 1, 1973; "Seminole Runoff Vote Set," *Oklahoman*, Aug. 7, 1973; "Annual Report," Sept. 1, 1975, Thomas Coker Papers (box 7, folder 2) (list of council members); and see *Seminole Intra-Tribal Business Association v. Tanyan and Palmer*, Seminole County Case No. S-C-76-131, Thomas Coker Papers (box 11, folder 10) (suit against Chief Tanyan and Assistant Chief Palmer, seeking an accounting for payment of salaries for Community Health Representative [CHR] personnel); notice from Floyd Harjo, Thomas Coker Papers (box 7, folder 19); memo from Seminole Nation Election Board, Sept. 4, 1973, Thomas Coker Papers (box 7, folder 18); "Annual Report," Sept. 1, 1975, Thomas Coker Papers (box 7, folder 2); Kelly Haney, interview with the author, Jan. 1, 2006 (hereafter cited as Kelly Haney interview). See the appendix for list of council members elected at general elections from 1969 through 1989.

15. *Resolutions of the Seminole Nation of Oklahoma* (1969–1977), available from the Office of General Council Secretary, Seminole Nation of Oklahoma; and Wantland interview.

16. Kelly Haney interview; see Howard and Lena, *Oklahoma Seminoles*, 84.

17. See note 16.

18. *Seminole Indians of the State of Florida and the Seminole Nation of Oklahoma v. United States*, 38 Comm. 62, 78 (Ind. Cl. Comm. 1976) (describing band system as an effective method of communication with tribal membership).

19. S.N. Ord. No. 70-1 (Mar. 7, 1970) (form of laws and resolutions).

20. S.N. Res. No. 69-10 (Oct. 4, 1969) (salaries); and S.N. Ord. No. 74-1 (Mar. 30, 1974) (salaries).

21. S.N. Ord. No. 70-2 (June 6, 1970) (treasurer); S.N. Ord. No. 70-6 (Dec. 5, 1970) (treasurer); S.N. Res. No. 70-13 (Dec. 5, 1970) (treasurer); S.N. Ord. No. 72-3 (Sept. 2, 1972) (elections); and S.N. Ord. No. 73-1 (May 5, 1973) (elections). See also S.N. Ord. No. 73-2 (July 10, 1973) (elections); S.N. Ord. No. 77-2 (Mar. 29, 1977) (elections); S.N. Res. No. 74-8 (Apr. 20, 1974) (personnel board); S.N. Ord. No. 74-2 (June 8, 1974) (personnel board); S.N. Ord. No. 76-1 (July 17, 1976) (personnel board); S.N. Ord. No. 77-4 (Aug. 20, 1977) (enrollment office); and "Annual Report," Sept. 1, 1975, Thomas Coker Papers (box 7, folder 2).

22. S.N. Res. No. 69-11 (Dec. 6, 1969) (attorney general); S.N. Ord. No. 70-5 (June 6, 1970) (attorney general); S.N. Res. No. 72-9 (July 1, 1972) (attorney general); S.N. Res. No. 75-23 (July 31, 1975) (attorney general); and S.N. Res. No. 75-25 (Aug. 16, 1975) (attorney general).

23. S. Res. No. 70-4 (May 9, 1970) (Albert); "Seminoles to Host Meet of Inter-Tribal Council," *Seminole Producer*, Oct. 7, 1971; S.N. Res. No. 73-7, 73-8, and 73-9 (Sept. 22, 1973) (delegate and board appointments); "Indian Advisory Panel Picks New Officers at Meeting," *Oklahoman*, Feb. 9, 1975; "Big Seminole Nation Fest Slated Today," *Oklahoman*, Aug. 25, 1973; S.N. Res. No. 75-24 (Aug. 16, 1975) (county commissioners); "1973 Membership List of the Inter-Tribal Council of the Five Civilized Tribes" and "Report on Trip to Washington, D.C.," June 19 and 20, 1973 (Housing and Urban Development), Eula Narcomey Doonkeen Collection; and "First Elected Chief Dies," *Seminole Producer*, Oct. 18, 1988.

24. Act of Oct. 17, 1968, Pub. L. No. 90-585, 82 *Stat.* 1148; *Providing for the Disposition of Funds*, 90th Cong., 2nd sess., S. Rep. No. 1594 (Sept. 24, 1968), 6, 9; S.N. Res. No. 74-14 (Aug. 8, 1974) (use of claims funds); and 1975 Interim Comp. Plan, 3, Enoch Kelly Haney Collection.

25. "S.N. General Council Minutes," Sept. 20, 1969, 3, Eula Narcomey Doonkeen Collection (BIA position regarding freedmen eligibility for federal programs); S.N. Res. No. 72-7 (July 1, 1972) (Indian action team); S.N. Res. No. 74-4 (Mar. 30, 1974) (Indian Action Team); "Interim Economic Development Plan for the Seminole Nation," June 12, 1975 (hereafter cited as 1975 Interim Econ. Dev. Plan) at 3, 4, and table I, Enoch Kelly Haney Collection; S.N. Res. No. 70-10 (Aug. 22, 1970) (education); S.N. Res. No. 70-5 (May 9, 1970) (housing); S.N. Ord. 72-2 (June 13, 1972) (CHR Program); S.N. Res. No. 73-5 (June 2, 1973) (continuation of CHR Program); S.N. Res. No. 75-8 (March 1, 1975) (CHR Program); S.N. Res. No. 74-9 (Apr. 20, 1974) (Five Tribes Foundation as conduit for 1975 fiscal year funds under the Comprehensive Employment and Training Act [CETA] of Dec. 28, 1973, Pub. L. No. 93-203, 87 *Stat.* 882); S.N. Res. No. 74-12 (July 13, 1974) (HEW funding); S.N. Res. No. 75-2 (Jan. 25, 1975) (Indian Action Team); S.N. Res. No. 75-40 (Dec. 6, 1975) (continuation of federal contracts); S.N. Res.

No. 75-41 (Dec. 6, 1975) (Alcohol and Drug Abuse Program); S.N. Res. No. 77-2 (Jan. 15, 1977) (additional tribal programs); S.N. Res. No. 76-8 (June 5, 1976) (Indian Action Team); S.N. Res. No. 76-9 (June 5, 1976) (Indian Action Program); S.N. Res. No. 76-10 (June 5, 1976) (Indian Action Program); S.N. Res. No. 77-1 (Jan. 15, 1977) (Indian Action Program); S.N. Res. No. 76-12 (July 17, 1976) (additional funding sources); and S.N. Res. No. 76-14 (Sept. 4, 1976) (other BIA programs).

26. S.N. Res. No. 74-17 (Jan. 26, 1974) (planning department); S.N. Res. No. 75-9 (Mar. 1, 1975) (planning department); 1975 Interim Comp. Plan, acknowledgments, Enoch Kelly Haney Collection; and 1975 Interim Econ. Dev. Plan, Enoch Kelly Haney Collection.

27. 1975 Interim Comp. Plan, 1, 4, 7, 47, Enoch Kelly Haney Collection; 1975 Interim Econ. Dev. Plan, Enoch Kelly Haney Collection; and S.N. Res. No. 75-41 (Dec. 6, 1975) (tribal planning commission).

28. S.N. Res. No. 70-1 (Mar. 7, 1970) (business lease); S.N. Res. No. 70-6 (May 9, 1970) (oil and gas lease); S.N. Res. No. 70-7 (May 9, 1970) (oil and gas lease); and S.N. Res. No. 70-9 (June 6, 1970) (grazing lease).

29. Fred Jones letter, Thomas Coker Papers (box 11, folder 24); S.N. Ord. No. 72-1 (Apr. 22, 1972) (recreation areas); amended S.N. Ord. No. 75-2 (Sept. 6, 1975) (recreation areas); S.N. Res. No. 72-12 (Oct. 28, 1972) (building committee); S.N. Res. No. 73-3 (March 3, 1973) (community building); S.N. Res. No. 74-21 (Jan. 26, 1974) (Mekusukey building); 1975 Base Studies, 17, 23, 33–34 (Mekusukey building), Enoch Kelly Haney Collection; S.N. Res. No. 76-5 (Apr. 10, 1976) (Mekusukey sanitation system); and Wantland interview.

30. 1975 Interim Comp. Plan, 40–43, Enoch Kelly Haney Collection; and *Providing for the Disposition of Funds*, 90th Cong., 2nd sess., S. Rep. No. 1594 (Sept. 24, 1968), 8.

31. S.N. Res. No. 73-14 (Nov. 17, 1973) (health); S.N. Res. No. 73-15 (Nov. 8, 1973) (health); S.N. Res. No. 74-38 (Jan. 23, 1974) (health); S.N. Res. No. 75-20 (Sept. 27, 1975) (establishment of non-profit and profit corporations); S.N. Res. No. 76-17 (Dec. 4, 1976) (construction); S.N. Res. No. 76-11 (July 17, 1976) (clinic); see also S.N. Res. No. 76-16 (Sept. 4, 1976) (supporting wishes of the Shawnee IHS Advisory Board to contract for the Community Development Program under Public Law 93-638); 1975 Interim Comp. Plan, 42–46, Enoch Kelly Haney Collection; "Annual Report," Sept. 1, 1975, Thomas Coker Papers (box 7, folder 2); and Kelly Haney interview.

32. S.N. Res. No. 75-16 (June 7, 1975) (Wewoka Agency).

33. S.N. Res. No. 75-30 (Sept. 27, 1975) (tribal corporations); "Non-Profit Certificate of Incorporation for Seminole Nation Enterprise," Oct. 7, 1975, in author's possession; S.N. Res. No. 77-3 (March 29, 1977) (bid on construction of tribal headquarters); 1975 Interim Comp. Plan, 9, 33, Enoch Kelly Haney Collection; letter from Tom Palmer, principal chief, Seminole Nation, May 14, 1979, Thomas Coker Papers (box 11, folder 24); and Kelly Haney interview.

34. 63 O.S. § 1057; 1975 Interim Comp. Plan, 22–24, Enoch Kelly Haney Collection; 1975 Interim Econ. Dev. Plan, 3, 4, and table I, Enoch Kelly Haney Collection; S.N. Res. No. 74-3 (Mar. 30, 1974) (housing); S.N. Res. No. 75-6 (Mar. 1, 1975) (housing); S.N. Res. No. 75-37 (Dec. 6, 1975) (housing); S.N. Res. No. 76-2 (Feb. 14, 1976) (housing); and "S.N. General Council Minutes," Sept. 20, 1969, 5, and Aug. 12, 1972, 1–2, Eula Narcomey Doonkeen Collection.

35. 1975 Interim Comp. Plan, 1, 31, Enoch Kelly Haney Collection; see Cohen, *Handbook of Federal Indian Law*, 146–47, 192–95 (summarizing in some detail federal education legislation in the seventies, including the Johnson O'Malley Act, 48 *Stat.* 596, codified as amended at 25 U.S.C. §§ 452–54, and the Indian Education Act, Pub. L. No. 92-318, §§ 401–53, 86 *Stat.* 335–45, codified as amended at 20 U.S.C. §§ 241aa–241ff, 1211a, 1221f–1221h, 3385–3385b, but *repealed*, Pub. L. No. 100-297, Act of Apr. 28, 1988, 102 *Stat.* 414); 1975 Base Studies, 9, 11, Enoch Kelly Haney Collection; S.N. Res. No. 73-13 (Nov. 17, 1973) (education committee); S.N. Res. No. 74-2 (Mar. 30, 1974) (Johnson O'Malley Program [JOM]); and "HEW Awards Indians Funds for Training," *Oklahoman*, Nov. 13, 1976.

36. Act of June 19, 1968, Pub. L. No. 90-351, §§ 101–601, 82 *Stat.* 197; "S.N. General Council Minutes," June 2, 1973, Eula Narcomey Doonkeen Collection; "Dispute Over Police Chief Heats up Seminole," *Oklahoman*, May 15, 1974; 1975 Base studies, 22, 23, 26, Enoch Kelly Haney Collection; and also see S.N. Ord. No. 77-3 (Apr. 30, 1977) (firearms prohibition).

37. *Seminole Indians of State of Florida and the Seminole Nation of Oklahoma v. United States*, 23 Comm. 108 (Ind. Cl. Comm. 1970) and 24 Ind. Cl. Comm. 1 (Ind. Cl. Comm. 1970), *rev'd*, 197 Ct. Cl. 350 (Ct. Cl. 1972); *Seminole Indians of State of Florida and the Seminole Nation of Oklahoma v. United States*, 38 Comm. 62 (Ind. Cl. Comm. 1976); and S.N. Res. No. 70-8 (June 6, 1970) (Florida trip).

38. *Seminole Indians of State of Florida and the Seminole Nation of Oklahoma v. United States*, 23 Comm. 108 (Ind. Cl. Comm. 1970) and 24 Ind. Cl. Comm. 1 (Ind. Cl. Comm. 1970), *rev'd*, 197 Ct. Cl. 350 (Ct. Cl. 1972); *Seminole Indians of State of Florida and the Seminole Nation of Oklahoma v. United States*, 38 Comm. 62 (Ind. Cl. Comm. 1976); S.N. Res. No. 75-22 (July 31, 1975) (Florida claims settlement); S.N. Res. No. 75-31 (Sept. 27, 1975) (Florida claims settlement); S.N. Res. No. 71-5 (Dec. 4, 1971) (Niebell contract confirmation); S.N. Res. No. 72-3 (March 4, 1972) (Niebell contract); and Wantland interview. See chapter 4 for additional discussion of the Florida land claim litigation.

39. "S.N. General Council Minutes," Jan. 15, 1972, 2, and March 4, 1972, 2, Eula Narcomey Doonkeen Collection (judgment fund committee); S.N. Res. No. 76-3 (Mar. 16, 1976) (judgment fund committee); S.N. Res. No. 76-17 (Oct. 2, 1976) (Fla. claims settlement negotiations); S.N. Res. No. 77-7 (June 4, 1977) (BIA Fla. claim research report); S.N. Res. No. 77-9 (July 16, 1977) (Fla. claims bill).

40. Kvasnicka and Viola, *Commissioners of Indian Affairs*, 338; and Johnson Warledo to Chief Edwin Tanyan, June 11, 1975, Private collection of Jerry G.

Haney, former chief of the Seminole Nation, loaned to author (hereafter cited as Jerry G. Haney Papers).

41. S.N. Res. No. 75-20 (July 19, 1975) (Treaty People); S.N. Res. No. 75-21 (July 19, 1975) (private groups claiming to represent Nation); see *Seminole Nation of Oklahoma v. United States,* 203 Ct. Cl. 637, 492 F.2d 811 (Ct. Cl. 1974). Also see chapter 4 for a more detailed discussion of the Nation's railroad claims.

42. S.N. Res. No. 75-38 (Dec. 6, 1975) (Treaty People); "Seminoles Sue Own Dissidents," *Oklahoman,* Dec. 16, 1975; "Indians Hit by Extension of Injunction," *Oklahoman,* Jan. 7, 1976; and *United States v. Warledo,* 557 F.2d 721 (10th Cir. 1977).

43. S.N. Ord. No. 76-1 (Jan. 17, 1976) (Seminole name and seal); *United States v. Warledo,* 557 F.2d 721 (10th Cir. 1977); Ted Underwood, interview with author, Jan. 16, 2008; "5 Arrested over Threats to Railroads," *Oklahoman,* Dec. 19, 1975; "6 Seminoles Released," *Oklahoman,* Dec. 23, 1975; and "Jury Indicts Six Indians in Dispute," *Oklahoman,* Jan. 16, 1976.

44. See note 43. Also see "Seminole Denies Railway Violence," *Oklahoman,* Mar. 4, 1976; "Both Sides Rest in Indians' Trial," *Oklahoman,* Mar. 11, 1976; "Five Convicted in Conspiracy," *Oklahoman,* Mar. 12, 1976; and "U.S. Drops Threat Count," *Oklahoman,* Dec. 7, 1977.

45. *Harjo v. Kleppe,* 420 F. Supp. 1110, 1118, 1127–28, 1130–42 (D.D.C. 1976), *aff'd sub nom. Harjo v. Andrus,* 581 F.2d 949 (D.C. Cir. 1978).

46. Ibid.; and Act of Oct. 22, 1970, Pub. L. No. 91-495, 84 *Stat.* 1091.

47. *Harjo v. Kleppe,* 1123; and Act of Apr. 26, 1906, 34 *Stat.* 137, § 19.

48. See chapter 9 for a discussion of the 1991 constitutional amendments.

49. Act of Jan. 2, 1975, Pub. L. No. 93-580, 88 *Stat.* 1910 (not codified, but described as amended at 25 U.S.C. § 174 note); and *Final Report of the American Indian Policy Review Commission, 1977,* vol. 1, p. III (James Abourezk, chairman, to vice president Walter Mondale, May 17, 1977) and pp. 503–33 (chap. 12, part B, "Oklahoma").

50. *Final Report of the American Indian Policy Review Commission, 1977,* vol. 1, pp. 517–18.

51. Ibid.

CHAPTER 8

1. See the appendix for a list of council members elected in 1977; also see memo from Robert Kernell, Jr., Thomas Coker Papers (box 7, folder 19); "Chief Picked by Seminoles," *Oklahoman,* July 11, 1977; "Indians Elect Tiger as Chief," *Seminole Producer,* July 12, 1977; "Agenda for Inauguration of R. J. Tiger as Principal Chief and Tom Palmer as Assist. Chief, with Welcome by Outgoing Chief Edwin Tanyan," Thomas Coker Papers (box 11, folder 24).

2. S.N. Res. No. 78-21 (Dec. 15, 1978) (Rodgers attorney contract); and S.N. Res. No. 80-23 (June 7, 1980) (approval of special services contract with James Rodgers and Gordon Allen).

3. S.N. Ord. No. 78-1 (June 3, 1978) (enrollment committee); S.N. Ord. No. 78-2 (June 3, 1978) (membership criteria); S.N. Ord. No. 78-17 (Oct. 28, 1978) (budget committee); S.N. Ord. No. 79-2 (Feb. 23, 1979); and S.N. Ord. No. 80-4 (June 7, 1980) (budget committee).

4. S.N. Res. No. 77-20 (Oct. 1, 1977) (renewals of federal programs, FY 1978); S.N. Res. No. 77-23 (Dec. 3, 1977) (Indian Action Team program); S.N. Res. No. 78-15 (July 15, 1978) (soil and moisture program); S.N. Res. No. 79-4 (Mar. 20, 1979) (JOM); S.N. Res. No. 79-7 (June 2, 1979) (federal grants and contracts, FY 1980); S.N. Res. No. 79-19 (Oct. 26, 1979) (U.S. Dept. of Commerce funding for construction of commodities warehouse); S.N. Res. No. 79-21 (Oct. 26, 1979) (special needs children proposal); S.N. Res. No. 79-22 (Oct. 26, 1979) (Seminole language project); S.N. Res. No. 79-28 (Dec. 1, 1979) (emergency crisis assistance program); S.N. Res. No. 80-6 (Mar. 8, 1980) (early childhood development program, FY 1980–83); S.N. Res. No. 80-7 (Mar. 8, 1980) (support of adult education program); S.N. Res. No. 80-8 (Mar. 8, 1980) (higher education program); S.N. Res. No. 80-14 (June 7, 1980) (BIA 638 programs); S.N. Res. No. 80-17 (June 7, 1980) (Older American Act program); S.N. Res. No. 80-27 (Sept. 6, 1980) (BIA contract for training and technical assistance); S.N. Res. No. 81-4 (Jan. 10, 1981) (administration for Native Americans application); and S.N. Res. No. 81-17 (May 1, 1981) (older American program).

5. "Seminole Nation Annual Report" submitted by Emil Farve, Jr., tribal planner, Sept. 1, 1978, pp. 6–8, Thomas Coker Papers (box 7, folder 3).

6. "Annual Report," Aug. 1978–Sept. 1979, p. 18, Thomas Coker Papers (box 7, folder 4).

7. "Annual Report," Sept. 1, 1978, Exhibit IV, Thomas Coker Papers (box 7, folder 3).

8. Food Stamp Act of Sept. 29, 1977, Pub. L. No. 95-113, title XIII, §§ 1301, 1302(a) (1), 91 *Stat.* 958, 979 (amendment of food stamp act to add definition of "reservation"), codified as amended, 7 U.S.C. §§ 2011, et seq.; and see 7 U.S.C. § 2012(j) (definition of "reservation").

9. Heard, Norris, and Westmoreland, *History of the Inter-Tribal Council,* 2, 22–24.

10. S.N. Res. No. 78-1A (Jan. 7, 1978) (contract related to developing a tribal-specific health plan); S.N. Res. No. 78-7 (Mar. 11, 1978) (supporting Eastern Oklahoma Indian Health Planning Board); S.N. Res. No. 78-12 (June 3, 1978) (Health Care Recruitment Program, FY 1979); S.N. Res. No. 79-5 (March 20, 1979) (supporting Eastern Oklahoma Indian Health Planning Board Proposal); S.N. Res. No. 79-8 (June 2, 1979) (Seminole Nation Health Careers Recruitment Program, FY 1979, FY1980); S.N. Res. No. 79-15 (Sept. 1, 1979) (Public Health Service Project documents); S.N. Ord. No. 80-1 (Mar. 8, 1980) (Seminole Nation Health Dept.); S.N. Res. No. 80-9 (Mar. 8, 1980) (health department and services development program); S.N. Res. No. 80-15 (June 7, 1980) (CHR program); S.N. Res. No. 80-16 (June 7, 1980) (IHS grant for Seminole Nation Health Dept.

and Services Development Program); S.N. Res. No. 81-6 (Mar. 7, 1981) (authorizing chief to propose and administer a health care management services program funded by IHS); S.N. Res. No. 81-7 (Mar. 7, 1981) (CHR program, FY 1982); and S.N. Res. No. 81-18 (May 1, 1981) (Dept. of Health and Social Services and 638 contract for training program).

11. S.N. Res. No. 78-8 (May 6, 1978) (housing); S.N. Res. No. 79-9 (June 2, 1979) (low rent housing); S.N. Res. No. 79-12 (Aug. 10, 1979) (HUD Community Development Block Grant); S.N. Res. No. 79-13 (Sept. 1, 1979) (mutual help housing); S.N. Res. No. 81-9 (Apr.10, 1981) (application for low-income housing funding); S.N. Res. No. 81-10 (Apr.10, 1981) (housing authority application for loan for low-rent housing project surveys and planning).

12. Heard, Norris, and Westmoreland, *History of the Inter-Tribal Council*, 21.

13. Act of Nov. 8, 1978, Pub. L. No. 95-608, 92 *Stat.* 3069, codified at 25 U.S.C. §§ 1901, et seq.; S.N. Res. No. 79-30 (Dec. 1, 1979) (grant for development and operation of child welfare program); S.N. Res. No. 80-3 (Jan. 19, 1980) (establishment of administrative body to coordinate activities related to implementation of ICWA); and S.N. Res. No. 81-5 (Mar. 7, 1981) (ICW program proposal).

14. Oklahoma Indian Child Welfare Act, 10 O.S. §§ 40.1, et seq.; S.N. Ord. No. 83-2 (Mar. 12, 1983) (Indian foster care licenses); and S.N. Res. No. 83-18a (Mar. 12, 1983) (Indian foster care standards).

15. *Matter of Adoption of Baby Boy D*, 742 P.2d 1059 (Okla. 1985), *cert. denied, Harjo v. Duello*, 484 U.S. 1072 (1988), *overruled, In the Matter of Adoption of Baby Boy L*, 103 P.3d 1099 (Okla. 2004).

16. *Mississippi Band of Choctaw Indians v. Holyfield*, 490 U.S. 30 (1989); *Matter of Adoption of Baby Boy D*, 742 P.2d 1059 (Okla. 1985), *cert. denied, Harjo v. Duello*, 484 U.S. 1072 (1988), *overruled, In the Matter of Adoption of Baby Boy L*, 103 P.3d 1099 (Ok. 2004); *Guardianship of QGM*, 808 P.2d 604 (Ok. 1991); and 10 O.S. §§ 40.1, et seq., as amended.

17. Act of Oct. 19, 1973, Pub. L. No. 93-134, 87 *Stat.* 466, codified as amended, 25 U.S.C. §§ 1401, et seq.; S.N. Res. No. 77-21 (Nov. 19, 1977) (extended Niebell attorney contract); S.N. Res. No. 78-1 (Oct. 1, 1977) (railroad claims appraiser); S.N. Res. No. 79-16 (Sept. 1, 1979) (railroad claims appraiser); S.N. Res. No. 81-8 (March 7, 1981) (railroad claim); and S.N. Res. No. 81-16 (May 1, 1981) (railroad claim award).

18. Pub. L. No. 93-134, codified as amended at 25 U.S.C. §§ 1401, et seq.; Act of June 1, 1976, 90 *Stat.* 597, 629; *Seminole Indians of the State of Florida and the Seminole Nation of Oklahoma v. United States*, 38 Ind. Cl. Comm. 62 (Ind. Cl. Comm. 1976); "Court OKs Indian Pact," *Oklahoman*, Nov. 1, 1977; and Eddie F. Brown, assistant secretary of the Interior, to Sen. Daniel K. Inouye, Feb. 7, 1990, Jerry G. Haney Papers.

19. S.N. Res. No. 79-27 (Dec. 1, 1979) (judgment fund committee); S.N. Res. No. 79-32 (Dec. 1, 1979) (Florida claims award investments); and S.N. Ord. No. 80-5, June 7, 1980 (judgment fund committee).

20. Assistant secretary of the Interior to President George Bush, Aug. 27, 1981, citing Pub. L. No. 93-134 (Indian Judgment Funds Act) and citing *Seminole Indian Tribe of Florida v. Andrus*, D.D.C., Civil No. 78-994 (Order and Memorandum Opinion, July 9, 1979), Jerry G. Haney Papers; 101st Cong., 2nd sess., H.R. Rep. No. 101-399 (Feb. 6, 1990); 95th Cong., 2nd sess., *Distribution of Seminole Judgment Funds: Hearing before the U.S. Senate Select Committee on Indian Affairs on S. 2000, "To Provide for Use and Distribution of Funds of the Judgment Awarded to the Seminole Indians," and on S. 2188, "To Provide for Use and Distribution of the Award Granted to the Seminole Nation,"* 1–3 (Mar. 2, 1978) (statement of Sen. Dewey F. Bartlett), 5–9 (S. 2000 text), 10–15 (S. 2188 text), 18–23 (testimony of Seminole Nation of Oklahoma chief Richmond Tiger, assist. chief Tom Palmer, Ed Tanyan, and John Tiger), and 24 (testimony of Howard Tommie, tribal council chairman, Seminole Indian Tribe of Florida); and "Bill Favoring State's Seminoles Wins Administration's Support," *Oklahoman*, Mar. 3, 1978.

21. Assistant secretary of the Interior to President George Bush, Aug. 27, 1981, citing *Seminole Indian Tribe of Florida v. Andrus*, D. D.C., Civil No. 78-994 (order and memorandum opinion, July 9, 1979) and stating that it was affirmed by the District of Columbia Circuit in 1980, Jerry G. Haney Papers; and *Indian Judgment Funds Use or Distribution Plans: Hearings Before the Select Committee on Indian Affairs, U.S. Senate, on S.J. Res. 108*, 96th Cong., 1st sess., 10–15 (Nov. 5, 1979), containing *Seminole Indian Tribe of Florida v. Andrus*, D.D.C. Civil Action No. 78-994 (order and memorandum opinion, July 9, 1979).

22. S.N. Res. No. 79-26 (Dec. 1, 1979) (supporting secretarial plan for use and distribution of Seminole Judgment Funds); "'Brothers' Fighting over Indian Money," *Oklahoman*, Oct. 6, 1980; "Seminoles Reach Tentative Accord in Funds Dispute," *Oklahoman*, June 8, 1983; and "Oklahoma Seminoles Agree with Florida Tribe on Award," *Oklahoman*, June 9, 1983.

23. Act of Apr. 11, 1968, Pub. L. No. 90-284, 82 *Stat.* 78, codified as amended, 25 U.S.C. §§ 1321, et seq.; *State v. Littlechief*, 573 P.2d 263 (Okla. Cr. 1977), citing *United States v. Littlechief*, Case No. CR-76-207-D (slip op. Nov. 7, 1977, W.D. Okla.); and *Ellis v. Page*, 351 F.2d 250 (10th Cir. 1965).

24. *Tillett v. Lujan*, 931 F.2d 636, 640, 641 (10th Cir. 1991); see 44 *Fed. Reg.* 37,502 (June 22, 1979) (final rule amending 25 C.F.R. Part 11 ("Courts of Indian Offenses and Law and Order Code") to include western Oklahoma tribes in CFR court system), codified in 25 C.F.R. § 11.100(a); 44 *Fed. Reg.* 24,305 (Apr. 25, 1979) (proposed rule amending regulations to include western Oklahoma tribes in CFR court system); and National American Indian Court Judges Association Long Range Planning Project, *Indian Courts and the Future.*

25. 57 *Fed. Reg.* 3270 (Jan. 28, 1992) (final rule including Muskogee area tribes, Okla., within Court of Indian Offenses system), codified in 25 C.F.R. § 11.100(a). See chapter 9 for discussion of cases determining that Five Tribes restricted lands and certain other types of lands were Indian country.

26. *United States v. John,* 437 U.S. 634 (1978); *C.M.G. v. State,* 594 P.2d 798, 803 (Okla. Cr. 1979); and *Oliphant v. Suquamish Indian Tribe,* 435 U.S. 191 (1978), 8.

27. *National Farmer's Union Insurance Co. v. Crow Tribe of Indians,* 471 U.S. 845 (1985); *Cheyenne–Arapaho Tribes of Oklahoma v. Oklahoma,* 618 F.2d 665 (10th Cir. 1980) and *Cheyenne–Arapaho Tribes of Oklahoma v. State of Oklahoma,* 681 F.2d 705 (10th Cir. 1982); *Ahboah v. Housing Authority of the Kiowa Tribe,* 660 P.2d 625, 660 (Okla. 1983); and *Tooisgah v. State,* 186 F.2d 93 (10th Cir. 1950).

28. "Annual Report," Aug. 1978–Sept. 1979, pp. 9–12, 18, Thomas Coker Papers (box 7, folder 4); S.N. Res. No. 79-29 (Dec. 1, 1979) (seeking secretarial certification of eligibility to participate in the LEAA programs); S.N. Res. No. 80-33 (Dec. 6, 1980) (concerning request for a new opinion from the Dept. of Interior's solicitor regarding the jurisdictional status of the Seminole Nation); see also S.N. Res. No. 80-34 (Dec. 6, 1980) (effect of 1978 solicitor's opinion on the Nation's eligibility to provide a commodity distribution program); *Muscogee (Creek) Nation v. Hodel,* Civ. No. 87-5377 (D.C. Circuit), memorandum to chief administrative judge, Board of Indian Appeals, with appendix submitted by Appellant Muscogee (Creek) Nation (hereafter cited as Muscogee appendix), Mar. 9, 1984, p. 32, Exhibit 3, Doc. #1, associate solicitor, Division of Indian Affairs, to chief, Division of Law Enforcement Services (memorandum), Apr. 20, 1978; and Curtis Act of June 28, 1898, 30 *Stat.* 495.

29. Muscogee appendix, p. 34, Exhibit 3, Doc. # 3, deputy assistant secretary of the Interior (Operations) to Muskogee Area director (memorandum), May 3, 1982.

30. Muscogee appendix, p. 39, Exhibit 3, Doc. # 5, field solicitor, Muskogee, to Muskogee Area director (memorandum), Oct. 13, 1982.

31. Muscogee appendix, p. 41, Doc. # 6, acting area tribal operations officer to Okmulgee Agency superintendent (memorandum), Oct. 20, 1982; Muscogee appendix, p. 43, Exhibit 3, Doc. # 7, acting Muskogee Area director to agency superintendent (memorandum), Mar. 18, 1983; Muscogee appendix, p. 44, Exhibit 3, Doc. # 8, field representative, Okmulgee Agency, to Claude Cox, principal chief, Apr. 6, 1983; see also Muscogee appendix, p. 50, Exhibit 3, Doc. #10, acting Muskogee Area director to deputy assistant secretary of the Interior (Operations) (memorandum), June 1, 1983; Muscogee appendix, p. 52, Exhibit 3, Doc. #11, acting deputy assistant secretary of the Interior (Operations), to associate solicitor, Division of Indian Affairs (memorandum), July 22, 1983; Muscogee appendix, p. 54, Exhibit 3, Doc. #13, associate solicitor, Division of Indian Affairs, to deputy assistant secretary of the Interior (Operations) (memorandum), Jan. 12, 1984; 30 *Stat.* 495 (Curtis Act); and *Muscogee (Creek) Nation v. Acting Area Director, Muskogee Area Office, BIA,* 13 IBIA 211 (1985), *aff'd, Muscogee (Creek) Nation v. Hodel,* 670 F. *Supp.* 434, 444 (D.D.C. 1987), *rev'd, Muscogee (Creek) Nation v. Hodel,* 851 F.2d 1439 (D.C. 1988), *cert. denied, Hodel v. Muscogee (Creek) Nation,* 488 U.S. 1010 (1989). See chapter 9 for discussion of the *Hodel* federal court litigation.

32. S.N. Ord. No. 81-2 (May 16, 1981) (elections), § 10; "Tribal Council Files Lawsuit," *Oklahoman*, July 9, 1981; "Voters Oust Tribal Chief," *Oklahoman*, Aug. 15, 1981; "Palmer, Milam Gain Runoff for Chief," *Seminole Producer*, July 14, 1981; see appendix, which lists council members elected at the 1981 general elections and other general elections from 1969 through 1989.

33. S.N. Res. No. 80-30 (Sept. 20, 1980); S.N. Res. No. 81-2 (Mar. 7, 1981) (IRS indebtedness); S.N. Res. No. 81-3 (Mar. 7, 1981) (legal representation for IRS payroll tax matters, FY 1979, FY 1980, and FY 1981); S.N. Res. No. 81-11 (Apr. 10, 1981) (use of lease proceeds for payment on IRS debt); S.N. Res. No. 81-12 (Apr. 10, 1981) (assignment of tribal oil royalty income for repayment of a bank loan made to Seminole Nation Enterprises, Inc., for use in repaying federal indebtedness); S.N. Res. No. 81-13 (Apr.10, 1981) (authorizing Seminole Nation Enterprises to obtain a loan for payment of IRS debt); and S.N. Res. No. 81-14 (Apr.10, 1981) (transfer of $55,000 of tribal trust funds to IRS for debt).

34. Affidavit of Dennis Springwater, tribal operations officer, BIA Muskogee Area Office, July 31, 1981, Terry Walker Papers; acting assistant secretary of the Interior to James Milam, Jan. 29, 1986, with attached findings of facts and conclusions of law, Jerry G. Haney Papers; S.N. Res. No. 82-5 (Sept. 15, 1981) (audit of 1981 grants and contracts); S.N. Res. No. 82-9 (Sept. 15, 1981) (request for GAO audit); S.N. Res. No. 82-2 (Sept. 15, 1981) (CETA); S.N. Res. No. 82-3 (Sept. 15, 1981) (CHR contract); S.N. Res. No. 82-4 (Sept. 15, 1981) (HUD application for housing funding); S.N. Res. No. 82-6 (Sept. 15, 1981) (administration for Native Americans Program); S.N. Res. No. 82-7 (Sept. 15, 1981) (Community Food and Nutrition Program); S.N. Res. No. 82-8 (Sept. 15, 1981) (Head Start and Title IV education programs); S.N. Res. No. 82-12 (Dec. 5, 1981) (Low Income Home Energy Assistance Act of 1981); S.N. Res. No. 82-13 (Dec. 5, 1981) (Community Services Block Grant Act); S.N. Res. No. 82-14 (Dec. 5, 1981) (nutrition program); S.N. Res. No. 82-15 (Dec. 5, 1981) (community development block grant); S.N. Res. No. 82-16 (Dec. 5, 1981) (housing); S.N. Res. No. 82-18 (Dec. 5, 1981) (vocational training); S.N. Res. No. 82-22 (Dec. 5, 1981) (child welfare); S.N. Res. No. 82-24 (Jan. 9, 1982) (alcoholism treatment and rehabilitation); S.N. Res. No. 82-24A (Jan. 9, 1982) (alcohol and drug education); S.N. Res. No. 82-30 (Mar. 20, 1982) (tribal government grant); S.N. Res. No. 82-28 (Dec. 5, 1981) (Oklahomans for Indian Opportunity); S.N. Res. No. 82-11 (Dec. 5, 1981) (request for federal program carryover funds); S.N. Res. No. 82-40 (Sept. 30, 1982) ($207,983 debt to federal government); S.N. Res. No. 83-7 (Jan. 15, 1983) (misappropriation of funds); and "Seminoles to Hold Financial Meeting," *Oklahoman*, Jan. 18, 1981.

35. Acting director, BIA Muskogee Area Office, to James Milam, principal chief, Seminole Nation, Aug. 9, 1982, Jerry G. Haney Papers; affidavit of Dennis Springwater, tribal operations officer, BIA Muskogee Area Office, July 31, 1981, Terry Walker Papers; and acting assistant secretary of the Interior to James

Milam, Jan. 29, 1986, with attached findings of fact and conclusions of law, Jerry G. Haney Papers.

36. James Milam, principal chief, to Kenneth L. Smith, assistant secretary of the Interior, BIA, Sept. 14, 1982, Jerry G. Haney Papers; acting assistant secretary of the Interior to James Milam, Jan. 29, 1986, with attached findings of fact, Jerry G. Haney Papers; "Chief Claims Impeachment by Seminole Council Illegal," *Oklahoman*, June 26, 1982; "Seminole Offices Guarded in Dispute Over Chief's Ouster," *Oklahoman*, Sept. 14, 1982; "Unpaid Volunteers Guarding Headquarters, Seminole Says," *Oklahoman*, Sept. 15, 1982; "Ousted Chief Asks Duel," *Oklahoman*, Sept. 25, 1982; "Game to Solve Seminole Tiff Inappropriate, BIA Boss Says," *Oklahoman*, Oct. 1, 1982; and "BIA Upholds Tribal Ouster of Seminole Nation's Chief," *Oklahoman*, Oct. 26, 1982.

37. *Milam v. U.S. Department of the Interior*, Case No. 82-C-3099, Slip Op. (D.C.C. Dec. 23, 1982), 10 Ind. L. Rep. 3013 (American Indian Law Training Program); *Milam v. Hodel*, Case No. 86-61-C, E.D. Okla., Judgment, Findings of Fact and Conclusions of Law, Oct. 23, 1986, *aff'd Milam v. Hodel*, Case No. 86-2755, Order and Judgment (10th Cir. Jan. 6, 1989); acting assistant secretary of the Interior to James Milam, Jan. 29, 1986, with attached findings of fact and conclusions of law, Jerry G. Haney Papers; "Seminoles Protest BIA Naming Principal Chief," *Oklahoman*, Oct. 30, 1982; "Seminole Factions Fighting Over Leaders," *Oklahoman*, Nov. 13, 1982; "Evictions of Indians Requested," *Oklahoman*, Nov. 25, 1982; "Seminoles Summoned for Hearing," *Oklahoman*, Nov. 30, 1982; "Chief Ouster Ruling Made," *Oklahoman*, Dec. 29, 1982; and "Impeachment Squabble Has Split Seminoles, Chief Says," *Oklahoman*, Dec. 30, 1982.

38. "Five Civilized Tribes Chiefs Seek Ouster of BIA Area Boss," *Oklahoman*, Jan. 21, 1983; "Former Chief Criticizes Call for Area BIA Ouster," *Oklahoman*, Jan. 26, 1983; and Heard, Norris, and Westmoreland, *History of the Inter-Tribal Council*, 30.

39. S.N. Res. No. 82-34 (Sept. 30, 1982) (housing); S.N. Res. No. 82-35 (Sept. 30, 1982) (alternative energy projects); S.N. Res. No. 82-36 (Sept. 30, 1982) (CHR program, FY 1983); S.N. Res. No. 82-37 (Sept. 30, 1982) (community services block grant); S.N. Res. No. 82-38 (Sept. 30, 1982) (administration for Native Americans); S.N. Res. No. 82-39 (Sept. 30, 1982) (CETA); S.N. Res. No. 82-41 (Sept. 30, 1982) (aid to tribal government for law enforcement); S.N. Res. No. 82-43 (Sept. 30, 1982) (Head Start); S.N. Res. No. 83-2 (Jan. 15, 1983) (BIA housing funds); S.N. Res. No. 83-3 (Jan. 15, 1983) (CHR program); S.N. Res. No. 83-4 (Jan. 15, 1983) (BIA agricultural and land management); S.N. Res. No. 83-5 (Jan. 15, 1983) (aid to tribal government); S.N. Res. No. 83-16 (Mar. 12, 1983) (tribal alcohol and drug education); S.N. Res. No. 83-18 (Mar. 12, 1983) (Indian child welfare program); S.N. Res. No. 83-21 (Mar. 12, 1983) (JOM); S.N. Res. No. 83-27 (June 4, 1983) (employment assistance and other programs); S.N. Res. No. 83-29 (June 4, 1983) (Title VI of Older American Act); S.N. Res. No. 83-31

(June 4, 1983) (BIA scholarship program); S.N. Res. No. 83-32 (June 4, 1983) (adult education); S.N. Res. No. 83-33 (June 4, 1983) (early childhood); S.N. Res. No. 83-34 (June 4, 1983) (JOM); S.N. Res. No. 83-40 (Aug. 4, 1983) (CHR); S.N. Res. No. 83-41 (Aug. 4, 1983) (emergency medical training); S.N. Res. No. 83-43 (Aug. 4, 1983) (community service block grant); S.N. Res. No. 83-44 (Aug. 4, 1983) (law enforcement); and S.N. Res. No. 83-45 (Aug. 4, 1983) (HUD housing funding).

40. S.N. Res. No. 83-12 (Feb. 12, 1983) (request for termination of agency superintendent); S.N. Res. No. 83-24 (Mar. 12, 1983) (council member removal); S.N. Res. No. 83-25 (Mar. 12, 1983) (council member removal); and S.N. Res. No. 83-37 (June 4, 1983) (suit against BIA).

41. *Milam v. Hodel*, Case No. 86-61-C, E.D. Okla., Judgment, Findings of Fact and Conclusions of Law, Slip Op., Oct. 23, 1986, *aff'd Milam v. Hodel*, Case No. 86-2755, Order and Judgment (10th Cir. Jan. 6, 1989); acting assistant secretary of the Interior to James Milam, Jan. 29, 1986, with attached findings of fact, Jerry G. Haney Papers; "Milam Seeking Federal Suit," *Seminole Producer*, Feb. 8, 1983; "Dissident Council Ousts Milam Again," *Seminole Producer*, Feb. 15, 1983; and "Judge Suggests Another Tribal Election," *Seminole Producer*, Feb. 24, 1983.

42. *Tanyan v. Ellison*, Case No. 83-189-C, Complaint, Mar. 20, 1983; "Tanyan Gets 20 Days to Answer," *Seminole Producer*, May 4, 1983; "Milam Will Offer New BIA Attack," *Seminole Producer*, June 2, 1983; "Milam Rebuts 'Playing Politics' Charges," *Seminole Producer*, Nov. 25, 1983; "Seminole Chief Might Not Run," *Seminole Producer*, Jan. 12, 1984; "Seminoles Not Going on Warpath," *Oklahoman*, June 3, 1983; "Seminole Nation Chief Earns Controversial Reputation," *Oklahoman*, June 12, 1983; "Seminole Chief Claims Readiness to Bury Tomahawk with Rival," *Oklahoman*, Aug. 5, 1983; "Seminole Tribe Members Seek End to Bureaucratic Suicide," *Oklahoman*, Apr. 22, 1984; and "Feuding Tribe Warned," *Oklahoman*, June 22, 1984.

43. Acting assistant secretary of the Interior to James Milam, Jan. 29, 1986, with attached findings of fact, Jerry G. Haney Papers; Edwin Tanyan to Carl Thorpe, acting Muskogee Area director, Aug. 28, 1984, Jerry G. Haney Papers; and Donald Moon, acting area director, BIA Muskogee Area Office, to James Milam, principal chief, Seminole Nation, Nov. 2, 1984, Jerry G. Haney Papers.

44. *United States v. Palmer*, 766 F.2d 1441 (10th Cir. 1985); "Ex-Tribal Accountant Accused," *Oklahoman*, March 22, 1984; and "Former Chief Resentenced," *Oklahoman*, Apr. 18, 1984.

45. S.N. Res. No. 79-18 (Oct. 26, 1979) (gasohol project); S.N. Res. No. 80-4 (Jan. 19, 1980) (construction of radio tower); and S.N. Res. No. 80-11 (March 8, 1980) (gasohol project).

46. *Seminole Tribe of Florida v. Butterworth*, 658 F.2d 310 (5th Cir. 1981), *cert. denied, Butterworth v. Seminole Tribe*, 455 U.S. 1020 (1982); S.N. Res. No. 82-42 (Sept. 30, 1982) (bingo management contract); S.N. Res. No. 83-15 (Feb. 12,

1983) (bingo contract); "Bingo Parlor Being Opposed," *Oklahoman*, Feb. 22, 1983; "Tribe to Resume Games Despite Legal Challenge," Mar. 15, 1983; "Ruling Upholding Tribal Bingo Games No Surprise to State Indian Leaders," *Oklahoman*, May 17, 1983; "Indian Reservations Luring Gamblers," *Oklahoman*, Sept. 3, 1983; and "Tribes Bingo Games Halted," *Seminole Producer*, Mar. 22, 1984.

47. Acting assistant secretary of the Interior to James Milam, Jan. 29, 1986, with attached findings of fact, Jerry G. Haney Papers; *Milam v. Hodel*; S.N. Ord. No. 85-1 (Mar. 30, 1985) (election law); and "Seminoles Seek Election Board," *Oklahoman*, Nov. 29, 1984.

CHAPTER 9

1. See the appendix, which lists general council members elected at general elections from 1969 through 1989; Merritt Youngdeer, acting area director, to Edwin Tanyan, principal chief, Seminole Nation, Sept. 17, 1985, Jerry G. Haney Papers; Merritt Youngdeer, acting area director, to Edwin Tanyan, principal chief, Seminole Nation, Oct. 18, 1985, Jerry G. Haney Papers; "Seminoles Face Runoff Vote," *Oklahoman*, July 9, 1985; "Two Seminoles Continue Battle for Office of Chief," *Oklahoman*, Nov. 13, 1985; and "Chief, Assistant Chief Runoff Election Slated," *Seminole Producer*, July 9, 1985.

2. *Milam v. Hodel*; and "Legal Woes Impacting Seminoles," *Seminole Producer*, Oct. 10, 1985.

3. S.N. Res. No. 85-26 (Dec. 7, 1985) (regarding James Milam and Alan Miller); S.N. Res. No. 85-34 (Dec. 21, 1985) (equipment protection); S.N. Res. No. 85-34A (Dec. 21, 1985) (equipment protection); Edwin Tanyan, principal chief, Seminole Nation, to Roger Hilfiger, U.S. attorney, Oct. 31, 1985, Jerry G. Haney Papers; acting assistant secretary of the Interior to James Milam, Jan. 29, 1986, Jerry G. Haney Papers; Zane Browning, acting director, BIA Muskogee Area Office, to Thomas H. George, FBI, May 19, 1986, Jerry G. Haney Papers; and Roger Hilfiger, U.S. attorney, Eastern District of Okla., to Edwin Tanyan, chief, Seminole Nation, May 23, 1986.

4. *Milam v. Hodel*; and Joe M. Parker, BIA Muskogee Area director, to Edwin Tanyan, principal chief, Seminole Nation, Nov. 6, 1986, Jerry G. Haney Papers.

5. *Wheeler v. United States Department of the Interior*, 811 F.2d 549, 553 (10th Cir. 1987); and see also *Nero v. Cherokee Nation of Oklahoma*, 892 F.2d 1457, 1165 (10th Cir. 1989).

6. "Tanyan, Bemo Upset in Seminole Election," *Seminole Producer*, July 18, 1989; and S.N. Res. No. 93-85 (Sept. 4, 1993) (Dan Factor severance pay).

7. "Tanyan, Bemo Upset in Seminole Election," *Seminole Producer*, July 18, 1989; and S.N. Res. No. 89-23 (Aug. 19, 1989) (shortfall in number of elected

council members). See the appendix for a list of council members elected from 1969 through 1989. Other persons not on that list also served on the council, as it was not unusual for bands to fill council vacancies arising during the terms through internal band elections.

8. S.N. Res. No. 85-10 (Oct. 5, 1985) (treasurer appointment); S.N. Res. No. 89-24 (Sept. 2, 1989) (treasurer appointment); and S.N. Res. No. 93-84 (Sept. 4, 1993) (treasurer appointment).

9. S.N. Res. No. 85-21 (Nov. 23, 1985) (partial payment for disallowed costs); S.N. Res. No. 85-24 (Oct. 7, 1985) (accountability of persons responsible for debts to federal government); S.N. Res. No. 86-38 (Jan. 18, 1986) (repayment plan); S.N. Res. No. 90-10 (Mar. 31, 1990) (BIA disallowed costs); S.N. Res. No. 91-01 (Jan. 26, 1991) (payment to U.S. Dept. of Health and Human Services [HHS]); S.N. Res. No. 91-08 (Apr. 16, 1991) (U.S. Dept. of Labor repayment plan); S.N. Res. No. 93-100 (Sept. 24, 1993) (payment to HHS); Act of Dec. 21, 2000, Pub. L. No. 106-554, Sec. 1(a) (7) [title I, Sec. 166(a), (d)], Dec. 21, 2000, 114 *Stat.* 2763, 2763A-627 (amendment of Federal Unemployment Tax Act concerning Indian tribes), codified in 26 U.S.C. § 3306; and Okla. Sess. Laws 2002, SB 1404, c. 452, 1, June 5, 2002, codified in 40 O.S. §§ 1–108.

10. *Resolutions of the Seminole Nation of Oklahoma*, Office of General Council Secretary, Seminole Nation of Oklahoma.

11. S.N. Res. No. 85-18 (Oct. 22, 1985) (award distribution); S.N. Res. No. 85-21 (Oct. 22, 1985) (Niebell attorney contract); S.N. Res. No. 86-64 (July 26, 1986) (award distribution); S.N. Res. No. 86-84 (Nov. 8, 1986) (award distribution); S.N. Res. No. 87-100 (Mar. 7, 1987) (award distribution); S.N. Res. No. 87-137B (Nov. 12, 1987) (award distribution); S.N. Res. No. 88-16 (June 27, 1988) (award distribution); S.N. Res. No. 89-7 (Mar. 9, 1989) (award distribution); S.N. Res. No. 89-7 (Mar. 9, 1989) (seeking Representative Watkins's support); S.N. Res. No. 89-8 (Mar. 9, 1989) (seeking Senator Nickles's support); (S.N. Res. No. 89-15 (Apr. 22, 1989) (Niebell and Swimmer attorney contract); and George Goodner, Wewoka Agency superintendent, to Muskogee Area director (memorandum), Mar. 13, 1989, Jerry G. Haney Papers.

12. S. 1096, 101st Cong., 1st sess., 135 *Cong. Rec.* S5988 (introduced June 1, 1989); H.R. 2838, 101st Cong., 1st sess., 135 *Cong. Rec.* H3520 (introduced June 29, 1989); and S.N. Res. No. 89-29 (Oct. 14, 1989) (request for legislation concerning Fla. claims award distribution). From Jerry G. Haney Papers, see the following: "General Council Meeting Minutes," Oct. 14, 1989; James Billie to Jerry Haney, Oct. 20, 1989; Jerry Haney to James Billie, Oct. 23, 1989; James Billie to Jerry Haney, Oct. 31, 1989; and James Billie to Jerry Haney, Nov. 20, 1989. Also see "Plan May Resolve Seminole Indians' 19th-Century Fuss," *Oklahoman*, June 13, 1989; "Florida Congressmen Call for 50–50 Seminole Split," *Seminole Producer*, July 6, 1989; "Tribes' Skirmish over $47 Million Lands in Capitol," *Oklahoman*,

Sept. 15, 1989; and "Seminoles Assigned Deadline to Settle Judgment Dispute," Sept. 17, 1989, *Seminole Producer*.

13. Act of Apr. 30, 1990, Pub. L. No. 101-277, 104 *Stat.* 143; S.N. Res. No.90-05 (Jan. 20, 1990) (award distribution); S.N. Res. No. 90-06 (Jan. 20, 1990) (award distribution); S.N. Res. No. 90-07 (Jan. 27, 1990) (rescinding S.N. Res. No. 90-5); "Seminole Settlement Protested," *Oklahoman*, Feb. 15, 1990;"Congress Votes 75/25%," *Seminole Nation Cokv Tvlvme*, March 1990; and "State Seminoles Get $37 Million from Federal Bill," *Oklahoman*, May 1, 1990.

14. Pub. L. No. 101-277, § 2(a) (Oklahoma–Florida allocation). See H.R. 2838, 101st Cong., 1st sess., and from the 101st Cong., 2nd sess., see the following: S. 1096; H.R. Rep. No. 101-399 (Feb. 6, 1990), 7; H.R. Rep. No. 101-39 (Mar. 29, 1990); and 136 *Cong. Rec.* H1414 (H.R. Conf. Rep. on S. 1096, Apr. 3, 1990), S4350 (S. Conf. Rep. on S. 1096, Apr. 5, 1990), and S4566 (S. 1096, enrolled bill presented Apr. 19, 1990).

15. Pub. L. No. 101-277, § 2 (b) (allocation among Florida tribes); S.N. Res. No.90-28 (Oct. 20, 1990) (Swimmer's fees); and S.N. Res. No.90-36 (Dec. 1, 1990) (Niebell's fees).

16. Pub. L. No. 101-277, § 4 (plan requirements).

17. Pub. L. No. 101-277, §§ 3, 4; S.N. Res. No.90-27 (Oct. 20, 1990) (judgment fund use and distribution plan), codified at 18A *S.N. Code of Laws* § 109; and Jerry G. Haney, principal chief, Seminole Nation, to Jim Fields, superintendent, BIA Wewoka Agency, with attachments, Oct. 25, 1990, Jerry G. Haney Papers.

18. S.N. Res. No. 90-27.

19. Ibid.

20. S.N. Ord. No. 91-4 (July 27, 1991) (burial assistance); S.N. Ord. No. 91-5 (July 27, 1991) (school clothing); S.N. Law No. 91-10 (Nov. 16, 1991) (elderly assistance); S.N. Law No. 91-11 (Nov. 16, 1991) (higher education); S.N. Law. No. 92-9 (June 27, 1992) (Community Cultural and Recreational Enhancement Assistance Program); and S.N. Law. No. 92-12 (Sept. 5, 1992) (Household Economic Assistance Program). Regarding appropriations for judgment fund programs, see S.N. Res. No. 91-18 (July 27, 1991); S.N. Res. No. 91-18b (July 27, 1991); S.N. Res. No. 92-52 (June 27, 1992); S.N. Res. No. 93-64 (June 5, 1993); S.N. Res. No. 93-65 (June 5, 1993); S.N. Res. No. 93-124 (Nov. 6, 1993); S.N. Res. No. 93-148 (Dec. 4, 1993); "Tribe's Freedmen Seek Share," *Oklahoman*, Feb. 21, 1992; and Mulroy, *Seminole Freedmen: A History*, 316–19.

21. Pub. L. No. 101-277, § 4(e); 102nd Cong., 2nd sess., H.R. Rep. No. 102-499 (Apr. 22, 1992); S.N. Law No. 93-21 (Nov. 6, 1993) (Title 14, finance) (Trust Fund Management Board); 18-A *S.N. Code of Laws* § 109 (1990 plan for the use and distribution of judgment funds), enacted by S.N. Law No. 92-16 (Dec. 5, 1992); S.N. Res. No. 93-118 (Oct. 16, 1993) (Trust Fund Advisory Board appointments); and S.N. Res. No. 93-120 (Nov. 6, 1993) (Trust Fund Advisory Board appointments).

22. S.N. Res. No. 85-1 (Nov. 23, 1985) (Robert's Rules of Order); S.N. Res. No. 85-24 (Oct. 22, 1985) (bank accounts); S.N. Res. No. 85-27 (Dec. 7, 1985) (policies and procedures); S.N. Ord. No. 86-1 (Mar. 27, 1986) (Audit Committee); S.N. Ord. No. 87-1 (Feb. 21, 1987) (council stipends and travel regulations); S.N. Ord. No. 87-2 (Sept. 19, 1987) (law enforcement division); and S.N. Ord. No. 88-3 (Apr. 15, 1988) (personnel policies).

23. S.N. Res. No. 85-36 (Dec. 21, 1985) (constitution revision); S.N. Res. No. 88-17 (July 30, 1988) (submission of constitutional amendments to tribal member vote); S.N. Res. No. 88-32 (Nov. 5, 1988) (removing Proposed Amendment E); S.N. Res. No. 88-33 (Dec. 3, 1988); S.N. Res. No. 88-35 (Dec. 17, 1988); and "Certificate of Adoption of Amendments Signed by Robert Kernell, Jr., Chairman of the Seminole Nation Election Board, and Edwin Tanyan, Principal Chief, on Feb. 27, 1989, and Approval Executed by Merritt E. Youngdeer, BIA Muskogee Area Director," Mar. 10, 1989, William Wantland Constitution Files.

24. *Muscogee (Creek) Nation v. Acting Area Director, Muskogee Area Office, BIA,* 13 IBIA 211 (1985), *aff'd, Muscogee (Creek) Nation v. Hodel,* 670 F. Supp. 434, 444 (D.D.C. 1987), *rev'd, Muscogee (Creek) Nation v. Hodel,* 851 F.2d 1439 (D.C. 1988), *cert. denied, Hodel v. Muscogee (Creek) Nation,* 488 U.S. 1010 (1989).

25. Ibid.

26. *Indian Country U.S.A. v. Oklahoma Tax Commission,* 829 F.2d 967 (10th Cir. 1987), *cert. denied, Oklahoma Tax Commission v. Muscogee (Creek) Nation,* 487 U.S. 1218 (1988) (Indian country status of unallotted lands owned by Muscogee [Creek] Nation); and *Ex Parte Nowabbi,* 61 P.2d 1139 (Okla. Cr. 1936) (Indian versus Indian crime on Choctaw restricted allotment subject to state jurisdiction), *overruled, State v. Klindt,* 782 P.2d 401 (Okla. Cr. 1989).

27. *Housing Authority of the Seminole Nation v. Harjo,* 790 P. 2d 1098 (Okla. 1990) (Indian Country status of certain housing authority lands); *United States v. Sands,* 968 F.2d 1058 (10th Cir. 1992), *cert. denied, Sands v. United States,* 506 U.S. 1056 (1993) (Indian Country status of restricted Creek allotment); *Ross v. Neff,* 905 F.2d 1349 (10th Cir. 1990) (Indian Country status of Cherokee tribal trust lands); but see *Eaves v. State,* 800 P.2d 251 (Okla. Cr. 1990) (Mutual Help homes located in Pawhuska not part of dependent Indian community).

28. S.N. Res. No.90-37 (Sept. 29, 1990) (tribal court development funding); S.N. Res. No. 91-05(Feb. 14, 1991) (attorney contract); S.N. Res. No. 91-6 (Feb. 14, 1991) (application for court grant); S.N. Res. No. 91-12 (Apr. 13, 1991) (attorney general contract); S.N. Res. No. 92-06 (Feb. 8, 1992) (attorney contract); and S.N. Res. No. 93-134 (Dec. 4, 1993) (attorney general contract).

29. S.N. Ord. No. 91-03 (Apr. 13, 1991) (BIA approval of tribal law not required); S.N. Ord. No. 91-03A (Apr. 13, 1991) (membership); S.N. Ord. No. 91-6 (Aug. 24, 1991) (election code); S.N. Ord. No. 91-7 (Aug. 29, 1991) (council secretary duties); S.N. Ord. No. 91-9 (Aug. 29, 1991) (form of laws and resolutions); S.N. Law No. 91-16 (Dec. 7, 1991) (officer salaries); and S.N. Law No. 91-17 (Dec. 7, 1991) (Arts and Crafts Committee).

30. S.N. Law No. 91-12 (Nov. 16, 1991) (codification of laws); and *Code of Laws of the Seminole Nation of Oklahoma*. By the time this book is published, an original copy of the first *Seminole Nation Code of Laws* as approved in 1991 will be placed with the Oklahoma History Museum for public reference. S.N. Law No. 93-05 (Jan. 23, 1993) (Tribal Employment Rights Office); S.N. Law No. 93-04 (Jan. 23, 1993) (Title 22, membership code); and S.N. Law No. 92-13 (Sept. 5, 1992) (Title 26, recreation).

31. S.N. Res. No. 91-19(July 27, 1991) (proposed constitutional amendments); S.N. Res. No. 91-19A (Aug. 29, 1991) (proposed constitutional amendments); and S.N. Res. No. 91-19B (Oct. 5, 1991) (proposed constitutional amendments).

32. Act of Oct. 22, 1970, Pub. L. No. 91-495, 84 *Stat.* 1091 (chiefs of Seminole, Creek, Choctaw, and Cherokee Nations and governor of Chickasaw Nation); S.N. Res. No. 91-19(July 27, 1991) (proposed constitutional amendments); S.N. Res. No. 91-19A (Aug. 29, 1991) (proposed constitutional amendments); S.N. Res. No. 91-19B(Oct. 5, 1991) (proposed constitutional amendments); *Harjo v. Kleppe*, 420 F. *Supp.* 1110 (1976), *aff'd sub nom. Harjo v. Andrus*, 581 F.2d 949 (D.C. Cir. 1978); *Seminole Nation of Oklahoma v. Acting Director, Office of Tribal Services, BIA*, 24 IBIA 209 (Sept. 23, 1993); and *Seminole Nation of Oklahoma v. Acting Director, Office of Tribal Services, BIA* (Supplemental Op. IBIA 1993).

33. See note 32.

34. See note 32.

35. 57 *Fed. Reg.* 3270 (Jan. 28, 1992) (final rule including Muskogee area tribes, Okla., within Court of Indian Offenses system).

36. 5 *S.N. Code of Laws* §§ 107-A, 208(c)), enacted by S.N. Law No. 92-5 (June 6, 1992); S.N. Res. No. 92-15 (Mar. 7, 1992) (CFR court authorization); and see *Miller v. Jerry G. Haney, Principal Chief, and Billy Joe Harjo*, Court of Indian Offenses, Wewoka Agency, Case No. CIV-W84-93 (amended order of dismissal, Jan. 20, 1994) (case involving internal band dispute).

37. S.N. Law No. 92-3 (Mar. 7, 1992) (Title 5, CFR courts); S.N. Law No. 92-5 (June 6, 1992) (Title 5, CFR courts; Title 7, criminal procedure; and Title 13, evidence); S.N. Law No. 93-24 (Dec. 4, 1993) (Title 6, criminal offenses code); S.N. Law No. 92-8 (July 27, 1992) (Title 3, civil procedure); BIA Muskogee Area director to BIA Wewoka Agency superintendent (memorandum), July 31, 1992, in author's possession; S.N. Res. No. 92-70–92-72 (Sept. 5, 1992) (judiciary committee appointments); S.N. Res. No. 92-101 (Dec. 5, 1992) (CFR court judge appointment); and S.N. Res. No. 93-27 (Apr. 3, 1993) (CFR court judge reappointment).

38. S.N. Res. No. 93-41– 93-43 (Apr. 22, 1993) (Membership Appeals Board appointments); S.N. Res. No. 93-44–93-48 (Apr. 22, 1993) (Judgment Fund Appeals Board appointment); S.N. Res. No. 93-119 (Oct. 16, 1993) (Administrative Appeals Board appointments); S.N. Law No. 93-22 (Nov. 6, 1993) (Title 16, general council, Administrative Appeals Board).

39. *California v. Cabazon Band of Mission Indians,* 480 U.S. 202 (1987); S.N. Res. No. 85-37 (Dec. 21, 1985) (business ventures and bingo); S.N. Res. No. 86-54 (June 28, 1986) (bingo management contract); S.N. Res. No. 86-76 (Sept. 27, 1986) (LMWR, Inc., bingo management contract); S.N. Res. No. 87-101B (June 6, 1987) (bingo monitoring); and S.N. Ord. No. 86-2 (May 10, 1986) (regulation of bingo).

40. S.N. Res. No. 91-11 (Apr. 13, 1991) (non-renewal of management contract); S.N. Res. No. 91-20 (Aug. 29, 1991) (bingo management); S.N. Res. No. 91-22 (Aug. 29, 1991) (option to purchase property); S.N. Res. No. 91-26 (Dec. 7, 1991) (bingo management contract); S.N. Res. No. 91-27 (Dec. 12, 1991) (bingo enterprise start-up costs); S.N. Res. No. 92-1 (Jan. 3, 1992) (moving bingo operation from Wewoka to Mekusukey); S.N. Res. No. 93-25 (Apr. 3, 1993) (bingo); S.N. Res. No. 933-24 (May 17, 1993) (approval of gaming operations manual); and S.N. Ord. No. 91-8 (Aug. 29, 1991) (gaming code) (later amended by S.N. Law No. 94-2 [Feb. 24, 1994] [gaming code]), as approved by NIGC letter dated May 31, 1994, in author's possession.

41. S.N. Res. No. 92-10 (Mar. 7, 1992); and S.N. Res. No. 92-69 (Sept. 5, 1992) (seeking compact).

42. S.N. Ord. No. 87-4 (Nov. 7, 1987) (SEDA); S.N. Law No. 93-14 (Apr. 3, 1993) (Economic Development Code amendment); S.N. Res. No. 87-99 (Mar. 7, 1987) (store site purchase); S.N. Res. No. 87-105 (June 6, 1987) (trust fund loan for trading post and land purchase); S.N. Res. No. 88-6 (Apr. 15, 1988) (convenience store construction); S.N. Res. No. 89-13 (Mar. 9, 1989) (use of bingo revenues for enterprise loan); S.N. Res. No. 89-14 (Apr. 22, 1989) (loan from tribal trust funds for convenience store construction costs); S.N. Res. No. 89-18 (June 3, 1989) (convenience store construction loan); S.N. Res. No. 89-20 (June 17, 1989) (SEDA Board suspension); S.N. Res. No. 89-21 (June 17, 1989) (trading post management); S.N. Res. No. 89-25 (Sept. 30, 1989) (trust fund loan for SEDA and convenience store); S.N. Res. No. 89-26 (Sept. 30, 1989) (repayment of trust fund loan); S.N. Res. No. 90-40 (Oct. 9, 1990) (SNO-ANA); S.N. Res. No. 92-4 (Feb. 8, 1992) (trading post revenues); S.N. Res. No. 92-11 (Mar. 7, 1992) (trading post federal unemployment tax); S.N. Res. No. 92-36 (May 16, 1992) (SNO-ANA federal withholding taxes); and S.N. Res. No. 93-13 (Jan. 29, 1993) (trading post and SNO-ANA).

43. Tax commission: S.N. Law No. 92-25 (Nov. 14, 1992) (Title 3-A, BCR Commission code); S.N. Res. No. 89-11 (Mar. 9, 1989) (research); S.N. Res. No. 89-12 (Mar. 9, 1989) (funding); S.N. Res. No. 89-19 (June 3, 1989) (research); S.N. Ord. No. 87-3 (Nov. 7, 1987) (tax commission establishment); S.N. Ord. No. 87-5 (Sept. 19, 1987) (tobacco taxes); S.N. Ord. No. 88-1 (Sept. 6, 1988) (General Revenue and Tax Act); S.N. Res. No.89-30 (Nov. 4, 1989) (tax commission operations funding); S.N. Res. No.90-14(June 2, 1990) (research); S.N. Res. No. 91-23 (Oct. 5, 1991) (tax commission operations funding); and S.N. Res. No. 92-95 (Nov. 14, 1992) (BCR Commission funding).

44. State–Tribal Relations Act, 74 O.S. §§ 1221, 1222; and Heard, Norris, and Westmoreland, *History of the Inter-Tribal Council* 38–39.

45. OAG Op. No. 90-32 (Mar. 1, 1991); *United States v. McBratney*, 104 U.S. 621 (1881) (no federal jurisdiction over crime by non-Indian against non-Indian in Indian Country); Tim Vollmann, southwest regional solicitor, to Teresa Black, assistant U.S. Attorney, Western District of Okla., Dec. 20, 1991, in author's possession; Indian Law Enforcement Reform Act of Aug. 18, 1990, Pub. L. No. 101-379, 104 *Stat.* 473, codified as amended, 25 U.S.C. §§ 2501, et seq.; *Duro v. Reina*, 495 U.S. 676 (1990); and James Fields, BIA Wewoka Agency superintendant, to Susan Work, June 5, 1992, in author's possession.

46. *Oklahoma Tax Commission v. Citizen Band Potawatomi Indian Tribe of Oklahoma*, 498 U.S. 505 (1991); "Tribe Declares War Over Cigarette Taxes," *Oklahoman*, Feb. 20, 1987; and "Indians Protest State Taxes," *Oklahoman*, Feb. 20, 1987.

47. Okla. Sess. Laws 1992, ch. 339, May 28, 1992, pp. 1643–56, codified as amended at 68 O.S. §§ 301, 309, 321, 346–52, 401, 403.1, 413, 419, 424–29, and 1355; S.N. Res. No. 92-31 (Apr. 25, 1992) (tobacco compact negotiations); "Tribal, State Leaders Discuss Smoke Shop Taxation Issue," *Oklahoman*, Apr. 11, 1991; "Smoke Shop Tax Bill Nears Completion," *Oklahoman*, May 20, 1992; "Walters, Tribes Sign Pact," *Oklahoman*, June 9, 1992; and "Tribal Heads Assail Smoke Shop Fee," *Oklahoman*, June 10, 1992.

48. Okla. Sess. Laws 1992, ch. 339, May 28, 1992, pp. 1643–56, codified as amended at 68 O.S. §§ 301, 309, 321, 346–52, 401, 403.1, 413, 419, 424–29, and 1355.

49. S.N. Res. No. 92-37 (May 16, 1992) (approval of tobacco compact); and S.N. Law No. 92-15 (Nov. 14, 1992) (Title 28, tobacco retailers and wholesalers code).

50. *Oklahoma Tax Commission v. Sac and Fox Nation*, 508 U.S. 114 (1993).

51. Heard, Norris, and Westmoreland, *History of the Inter-Tribal Council*, 41, 46–47, 49.

52. S.N. Res. No. 86- 87 (Dec. 6, 1986) (Seminole Nation Chapter of the Inter-Tribal Vietnam Veterans); and S.N. Res. No. 92-05 (Feb. 8, 1992) (Seminole Vietnam Veterans).

53. S.N. Res. No. 92-14 (Mar. 7, 1992) (Intertribal Monitoring Association); S.N. Res. No. 92-53 (June 27, 1992) (Environmental Tribal Council); S.N. Res. No. 92-90 (Nov. 14, 1992) ("jaws of life" contribution); S.N. Res. No. 92-99 (Dec. 5, 1992) (Central Okla. Economic Development District membership); S.N. Res. No. 93-22 (Apr. 3, 1993) ("jaws of life" contribution); and S.N. Res. No. 93-141 (Dec. 4, 1993) (Inter-Tribal Council).

54. S.N. Res. No. 86-63 (July 26, 1986) (Seminole Nation Days); and S.N. Res. 87-117 (Aug. 15, 1987) (funds for Seminole Nation Days).

55. S.N. Res. No. 93-32–92-36 (Apr. 22, 1993) (Election Appeals Board appointments);"Haney and Factor Win Run Off," *Cokv Tvlvme*, Aug. 1993; *Tanyan v. Seminole Nation Election Board*, Court of Indian Offenses, Wewoka Agency, Case No. CIV-W113-93 (Order, Oct. 15, 1993); and "Seminole Tribe Plans Celebration," *Oklahoman*, Sept. 7, 1993.

EPILOGUE

1. Indian Gaming Regulatory Act, 25 U.S.C. § 2710(d); *United States v. Seminole Nation*, 321 F.3d 939 (10th Cir. 2002). See the following NIGC enforcements actions at www.nigc.gov: CFA-00-06, Aug. 17, 2000; NIGC NOV-CO-00-06, May 30, 2000; NIGC NOV-01-02, May 18, 2001; NIGC CFA-01-02, Apr. 26, 2002; NIGC CFA-00-10, Aug. 13, 2002; and NIGC RO-03-04, March 5, 2004.

2. Okla. Laws 2004, S. 1252, c. 316, State Question No. 712, Legis. Ref. No. 335, approved at general election held on Nov. 2, 2004, codified at 3A O.S. §§ 261, et seq. (Tribal Gaming Act), see 3A O.S. § 261 (Model Gaming Compact); and Mike Olsen, acting principal deputy assistant secretary of the Interior, to Kenneth Chambers, principal chief, Seminole Nation, Apr. 11, 2005, www .nigc.gov/Reading Room/compacts (U.S. Dept. of Interior approval of gaming compact between Seminole Nation and State of Oklahoma).

3. *Davis v. United States*, 192 F.3d 951 (10th Cir. 1999); "Black Seminoles Urged to Fight for Share of Funds," *Oklahoman*, Feb. 19, 1995; and "Seminole Freedmen Apply for Benefits, Expect Denial," *Oklahoman*, Feb. 24, 1995.

4. *Davis v. United States*, 199 F. Supp.2d 1164 (W.D. Ok. 2002), *aff'd Davis v. United States*, 343 F.3d 1282 (10th Cir. 2003), *cert. denied*, 542 U.S. 937 (2003); for discussions demonstrating different perspectives on freedmen claims concerning the Seminole Nation, see Mulroy, *Seminole Freedmen: A History*, 315–20; and Miller, *Coacoochee's Bones, A Seminole Saga*, 183–88.

5. *Seminole Nation v. Norton*, 206 F.R.D. 1 (U.S. D.C. 2001), *app. dismissed*, *Seminole Nation v. Norton*, No. 01-5418, unpublished order, May 24, 2002, WL 1364249; and Act of Sept. 22, 1970, Pub. L. No. 91-495, 84 *Stat.* 1091 (chiefs of Seminole, Creek, Choctaw, and Cherokee Nations and governor of Chickasaw Nation).

6. See *Seminole Nation v. Norton*, 206 F.R.D. 1 (U.S. D.C. 2001), *app. dismissed*, *Seminole Nation v. Norton*, No. 01-5418, unpublished order, May 24, 2002, WL 1364249; *Seminole Nation of Oklahoma v. Norton*, 223 F. Supp. 2d 122 (U.S. D.C. 2002); and *Haney v. United States*, Case No. 01-679 (U.S. E.D. Okla.).

7. *Seminole Nation of Oklahoma v. Norton*, 223 F. Supp. 2d 122 (U.S. D.C. 2002); *Haney v. United States*, Case No. 01-679 (U.S. E.D. Okla.); and *Haney v. Chambers*, Case No. CIV-02-W40 (Court of Indian Offenses for the Wewoka Agency for the Seminole Nation).

8. Act of Oct. 25, 1994, Pub. L. No. 103-413, title II, § 204, 108 *Stat.* 4271, codified at 25 U.S.C. §§ 458aa, et seq. (Interior self-governance compacts); Act of Dec. 27, 2000, Pub. L. No. 106-568, title XIII, § 1302, 114 *Stat.* 2936, codified at 25 U.S.C. §§ 458aaa, et seq. (HHS self-governance compacts).

9. Enoch Kelly Haney, interview with author and written summary provided by Haney, 2008.

10. Ibid.

11. Okla. Sess. Laws 1996, H.R. 2208, c. 345, § 63, codified at 68 O.S. § 500.63 (motor fuel tribal/state contract).

12. Schultz, *Seminole Baptist Churches of Oklahoma*.

13. See the Seminole Nation's website at http://www.seminolenation.com.

BIBLIOGRAPHY

The bibliography is organized in sections as follows: federal treaties (in chronological order); federal statutes (in chronological order); Seminole Nation constitutional and legislative documents; other tribal constitutions; state constitution, laws, and attorney general opinions (in chronological order); cases; archival and manuscript collections; other government documents and publications (in chronological order); and books and articles. Treaties and statutes cited to Kappler's are from Charles J. Kappler, *Indian Affairs: Laws and Treaties*, 7 vols., Washington, D.C.: GPO, 1904–1970.

TREATIES (IN CHRONOLOGICAL ORDER)

Seminole Treaty of Camp Moultrie, Act of Sept. 18, 1823, 7 *Stat.* 224, 2 Kappler's 203.
Seminole Treaty of 1832, Act of May 9, 1832, 7 *Stat.* 368, 2 Kappler's 344–45.
Creek Treaty of 1833, Act of Feb. 14, 1833, 7 *Stat.* 417, 2 Kappler's 388–91.
Seminole Treaty of 1833, Act of Mar. 28, 1833, 7 *Stat.* 423, 2 Kappler's 394–95.
Creek and Seminole Treaty of 1845, Act of Jan. 4, 1845, 9 *Stat.* 821, 2 Kappler's 550–52.
Creek and Seminole Treaty of 1856, Act of Aug. 7, 1856, 11 *Stat.* 699, 2 Kappler's 756–63.
Seminole Treaty of 1866, Act of Mar. 21, 1866, 14 *Stat.* 755, 2 Kappler's 910–15.
Choctaw & Chickasaw Treaty of 1866, Act of Apr. 28, 1866, 14 *Stat.* 769, 2 Kappler's 918–31.
Creek Treaty of 1866, Act of June 14, 1866, 14 *Stat.* 785, 2 Kappler's 931–37.
Cherokee Treaty of 1866, Act of July 19, 1866, 14 *Stat.* 799, 2 Kappler's 942–50.

FEDERAL STATUTES (IN CHRONOLOGICAL ORDER)

Act of Mar. 3, 1871, ch.120, 16 *Stat.* 566, 1 Kappler's 8, codified at 25 U.S.C. § 71.

Act of Jan. 31, 1877, 19 *Stat.* 230.

Act of Aug. 2, 1882, ch. 371, 22 *Stat.* 181, 1 Kappler's 206–209 (St. Louis and San Francisco Railway Company).

Act of Jan. 6, 1883, 22 *Stat.* 400.

Act of July 4, 1884, ch. 177, 23 *Stat.* 69, 1 Kappler's 217–20 (Gulf, Colorado and Santa Fe Railway Company).

Act of July 4, 1884, ch. 179, 23 *Stat.* 73, 1 Kappler's 220–23 (Southern Kansas Railway Co.

Act of Mar. 3, 1885, ch. 341, 23 *Stat.* 385, 1 Kappler's 32.

Act of June 1, 1886, ch. 395, 24 *Stat.* 73, 1 Kappler's 231–35 (Kansas and Arkansas Valley Railway).

Act of July 1, 1886, ch. 601, 24 *Stat.* 117, 1 Kappler's 235–39 (Denison and Washita Valley Railway Company).

General Allotment Act of Feb. 8, 1887, ch. 119, 24 *Stat.*388, 1 Kappler's 33–36 (codified as amended at 25 U.S.C. §§ 331–34, 339, 341–42, 348–49, 354, 381) (1887).

Act of Feb. 24, 1887, ch. 254, 24 *Stat.* 419, 1 Kappler's 247–50 (Fort Worth and Denver City Railway Company).

Act of Mar. 2, 1887, ch. 319, 24 *Stat.* 446, 1 Kappler's 250–53 (Chicago, Kansas and Nebraska Railway).

Act of Feb. 18, 1888, ch. 13, 25 *Stat.* 39, 1 Kappler's 256–60 (Choctaw Coal and Railway Company).

Act of May 14, 1888, ch. 248, 25 *Stat.* 140, 1 Kappler's 267–70 (Kansas City and Pacific Railroad Company).

Act of May 30, 1888, ch. 337, 25 *Stat.* 162, 1 Kappler's 274–77 (Fort Smith and El Paso Railway Company).

Act of June 26, 1888, ch. 494, 25 *Stat.* 205, 1 Kappler's 281–84 (Paris, Choctaw and Little Rock Railway Company).

Act of Mar. 1, 1889, ch. 333, 25 *Stat.* 783, 1 Kappler's 39–44.

Act of Mar. 2, 1889, ch. 412, 25 *Stat.* 980, 1 Kappler's 340–42.

Organic Act of May 2, 1890, ch. 182, 26 *Stat.* 81, 1 Kappler's 45–54.

Act of Mar. 3, 1893, ch. 209, 27 *Stat.* 612, 645, S16, 1 Kappler's 484, 498.

Act of Mar. 1, 1895, ch. 145, 28 *Stat.* 693, §§ 1, 4, 9–10, 1 Kappler's 70.

Act of June 10, 1896, c. 398, 29 *Stat.* 321, 339.

Act of June 7, 1897, ch. 3, 30 *Stat.* 62, 1 Kappler's 619.

Curtis Act of June 28, 1898, ch. 517, 30 *Stat.* 495, 1 Kappler's 646.

Seminole Allotment Act of July 1, 1898, ch. 545, 30 *Stat.* 567, 1 Kappler's 665.

Act of Mar. 2, 1899, ch. 374, 30 *Stat.* 990.

Act of May 31, 1900, ch. 598, 31 *Stat.* 240, 1 Kappler's 700.

Seminole Supplemental Allotment Act of June 2, 1900, ch. 610, 31 *Stat.* 250, 1 Kappler's 702–703.

Act of June 6, 1900, ch. 795, 31 *Stat.* 657, 1 Kappler's 108.

Act of June 6, 1900, ch. 802, 31 *Stat.* 660, 1 Kappler's 108.

Act of Feb. 18, 1901, ch. 379, 31 *Stat.* 794, 1 Kappler's 110.

Cherokee Allotment Act of July 1, 1902, ch. 1375, 32 Stat. 716, 1 Kappler's 787 (ratified); Cherokee Allotment Act of March 1, 1901, ch. 675, 21 *Stat.* 848, 1 Kappler's 716–29 (unratified).

Stat. Creek Allotment Act of March 1, 1901, ch. 676, 31 *Stat.* 861, 1 Kappler's 729–39.

Act of Mar. 3, 1901, ch. 868, 31 *Stat.* 1447, 1 Kappler's 114, amending Act of Feb. 8, 1887, 24 *Stat.* 388, ch. 119, 1 Kappler's 33–36.

Act of Feb. 28, 1902, ch. 134, 32 *Stat.* 43, 1 Kappler's 744–48.

Cherokee Supplemental Allotment Act of July 1, 1902, ch. 1375, 32 *Stat.* 716, 1 Kappler's 787–98 (1902).

Act of Jan. 21, 1903, ch. 195, 32 *Stat.* 774, 2 Kappler's 5.

Act of Feb. 19, 1903, ch. 707, 32 *Stat.* 841, 3 Kappler's 8–9, 11.

Act of Mar. 3, 1903, ch. 994, 32 *Stat.* 982, 3 Kappler's 14, 24.

Act of Mar. 11, 1904, ch. 505, 33 *Stat.* 65, 3 Kappler's 33.

Act of Apr. 21, 1904, ch. 1402, 33 *Stat.* 180, 3 Kappler's 50–52.

Act of Apr. 28, 1904, ch. 1824, 33 *Stat.* 573, 3 Kappler's 109.

Act of Mar. 3, 1905, ch. 1479, 33 *Stat.* 1048, 3 Kappler's 124, 148.

Five Tribes Act of Apr. 26, 1906, ch. 1876, 34 *Stat.* 137, 3 Kappler's 169–81.

Oklahoma Enabling Act of June 16, 1906, ch.3335, 34 *Stat.* 267, 3 Kappler's 186–92.

Act of May 27, 1908, ch. 199, 35 *Stat.* 312, 3 Kappler's 351–56.

Act of June 30, 1913, ch. 4, 38 *Stat.* 77, § 18, 3 Kappler's 561, 579–81.

Act of Aug. 1, 1914, ch. 222, 38 *Stat.* 582, 600, § 17, par. 14, 4 Kappler's 7, 27, codified at 25 U.S.C. § 86, as amended by Act of June 25, 1948, ch. 645, 62 *Stat.* 683, 6 Kappler's 400.

Act of May 18, 1916, ch. 125, 39 *Stat.* 123, 148, 4 Kappler's 53, 77–78.

Act of Mar. 2, 1917, ch. 146, 39 *Stat.* 969, 4 Kappler's 107, 122.

Act of May 25, 1918, ch. 86, 40 *Stat.* 561, 4 Kappler's 146, 166.

Act of June 14, 1918, ch. 101, 40 *Stat.* 606, §§ 1 and 2, 4 Kappler's 179, codified in 25 U.S.C. §§ 375, 355.

Stat. Act of June 30, 1919, ch. 4, 41 *Stat.* 3, 4 Kappler's 194, 215.

Act of Feb. 14, 1920, ch. 75, 41 *Stat.* 408, 4 Kappler's 235.

Act of Nov. 2, 1921, ch. 115, 42 *Stat.* 208, 4 Kappler's 330, amended Act of Oct. 12, 1976, Pub. L. No. 94-482, 90 *Stat.* 2233, and Act of Oct. 7, 1998, Pub. L. No. 105-244, 112 *Stat.* 1619, codified at 25 U.S.C. § 13.

Act of May 24, 1922, ch. 199, 42 *Stat.* 552, 575, 4 Kappler's 337, codified at 25 U.S.C. § 124.

Act of May 20, 1924, ch. 162, 43 *Stat.* 133, §§ 1–7, 4 Kappler's 414–15, as amended by Joint Res. of May 19, 1926, ch. 341, 44 Stat. 568, 5 Kappler's 550, and Joint Res. of Feb. 19, 1929, ch. 268, 45 Stat. 1229, 6 Kappler's 78.

Act of June 2, 1924, ch. 233, 43 *Stat.* 253, 4 Kappler's 420, codified at 8 U.S.C.
§ 1401(b).

Act of Apr. 12, 1926, ch.115, 44 *Stat.* 239, 4 Kappler's 518–20, amended by Act
of Aug. 4, 1947, ch. 458, 61 *Stat.* 731, 6 Kappler's 361–64.

Act of May 10, 1928, ch. 517, 45 *Stat.* 495, §§ 3, 4, 5 Kappler's 44–46 (§ 3
amended by Act of Feb. 14, 1931, ch. 179, 46 *Stat.* 1108, 5 Kappler's 201,
and amended by Act of Mar. 12, 1936, ch. 138, 49 *Stat.* 1160, 5 Kappler's
463) (§ 4 amended by Act of May 24, 1928, ch. 733, 45 *Stat.* 733).

Act of Mar. 4, 1929, ch. 705, 45 *Stat.* 1562, 5 Kappler's 92, 113.

Act of Feb. 14, 1931, ch. 187, 46 *Stat.* 1115, 5 Kappler's 203, 225.

Act of Mar. 2, 1931, ch. 374, 46 *Stat.* 1471, 5 Kappler's 234; amended by Act of
June 30, 1932, ch. 333, 47 *Stat.* 474, 5 Kappler's 290, codified at 25 U.S.C.
§ 409a as amended.

Act of Apr. 27, 1932, ch. 149, 47 *Stat.* 140, 5 Kappler's 280.

Act of Jan. 27, 1933, ch. 23, 47 *Stat.* 777, §§ 1–8, 5 Kappler's 298–300, §§ 1 and 8
repealed by Act of Aug. 4, 1947, ch. 458, 61 *Stat.* 731, § 12, 6 Kappler's
361, 364.

Act of June 15, 1933, ch. 76, 48 *Stat.* 146, 5 Kappler's 340.

Act of Mar. 2, 1934, ch. 38, 48 *Stat.*362, 5 Kappler's 344, 356.

Act of Mar. 5, 1934, ch. 43, 48 *Stat.* 396, 5 Kappler's 358.

Johnson O'Malley Act of April 16, 1934, ch. 147, 48 *Stat.* 596, codified as
amended at 25 U.S.C. §§ 452–54, 5 Kappler's 364).

Indian Reorganization Act of June 18, 1934, ch. 576, 48 *Stat.* 984, codified at 25
U.S.C. § 465 (IRA), 5 Kappler's 378–83.

Act of Feb. 11, 1936, ch. 50, 49 *Stat.* 1135, 5 Kappler's 462.

Act of June 20, 1936, ch. 622, 49 *Stat.* 1542, § 1, 5 Kappler's 471, amended by
Act of May 19, 1937, ch. 227, 50 *Stat.* 188, 5 Kappler's 513.

Oklahoma Indian Welfare Act of June 26, 1936, ch. 831, 49 *Stat.* 1967, 5 Kappler's 498–500, codified at 25 U.S.C. §§ 501, et seq.

Act of May 19, 1937, ch. 227, 50 *Stat.* 188, 5 Kappler's 513.

Act of Aug. 16, 1937, ch. 651, 50 *Stat.* 650, 5 Kappler's 544.

Act of Sept. 1, 1937, ch. 896, 50 *Stat.*888, codified as amended at 42 U.S.C.
§§ 1437, et seq.

Act of May 10, 1939, ch. 119, 53 *Stat.* 685, 6 Kappler's 7, 22.

Act of June 18, 1940, ch. 395, 54 *Stat.* 40, 6 Kappler's 61, 75.

Act of June 28, 1941, ch. 259, 55 *Stat.* 303, 6 Kappler's 113.

Act of July 2, 1942, ch. 473, 56 *Stat.* 506, 6 Kappler's 154, 169.

Act of Dec. 24, 1942, ch. 813, 56 *Stat.* 1080, 6 Kappler's 180.

Act of Dec. 23, 1943, ch. 380, 57 *Stat.* 611, 6 Kappler's 216–17.

Act of July 2, 1945, ch. 223, 59 *Stat.* 313, §§ 1–3, 6 Kappler's 267–68.

Indian Claims Commission Act of Aug. 8, 1946, ch. 907, 60 *Stat.* 939, 6 Kappler's 318, codified at 25 U.S.C. §§ 70–70n.

Act of Aug. 4, 1947, ch. 458, 61 *Stat.* 731, § 2, 6 Kappler's 361–64.

Act of Mar. 24, 1948, ch. 142, 62 *Stat.* 84, 6 Kappler's 381–82.

Act of May 4, 1948, ch. 258, 62 *Stat.* 211, 6 Kappler's 386.

Act of June 25, 1948, ch. 645, 62 *Stat.* 758; May 24, 1949, ch. 139, § 26, 63 *Stat.* 94; Pub. L. No. 89-707, § 1, Nov. 2, 1966, 80 *Stat.* 1100; Pub. L. No. 90-284, title V, § 501, Apr. 11, 1968, 82 *Stat.* 80; Pub. L. No. 94-297, § 2, May 29, 1976, 90 *Stat.* 585; Pub. L. No. 98-473, title II, § 1009, Oct. 12, 1984, 98 *Stat.* 2141; Pub. L. No. 99-303, May 15, 1986, 100 *Stat.* 438; Pub. L. No. 99-646, § 87(c)(5), Nov. 10, 1986, 100 *Stat.* 3623; Pub. L. No. 99-654, § 3(a)(5), Nov. 14, 1986, 100 *Stat.* 3363; Pub. L. No. 100-690, title VII, § 7027, Nov. 18, 1988, 102 *Stat.* 4397; Pub. L. No. 103-322, title XVII, § 170201(e), title XXXIII, § 330021(1), Sept. 13, 1994, 108 *Stat.* 2043, 2150; Pub. L. No. 109-248, title II, § 215, July 27, 2006, 120 *Stat.* 617, codified as amended 25 U.S.C. §§ 1151 et seq.

Act of May 24, 1949, ch. 139, 63 *Stat.* 102; amended Pub. L. No. 97-164, Apr. 2, 1982, 96 *Stat.* 41; Pub. L. 102-572, Oct. 29, 1992, 106 *Stat.* 4516, codified at 25 U.S.C. § 1505.

Act of July 3, 1952, ch. 549, 66 *Stat.* 323, amending § 28 of the Act of Apr. 26, 1906, ch. 1876, 34 *Stat.* 137, 6 Kappler's 569.

Act of Aug. 12, 1953, ch. 409, 67 *Stat.* 558, 6 Kappler's 590.

Public Law 280 of Aug. 15, 1953, ch. 505, 67 *Stat.* 588, § 7, 6 Kappler's 591, repealed by Pub. L. No. 90-284, Act of Apr. 11, 1968, 82 *Stat.* 79, codified at 25 U.S.C. § 1323.

Act of June 17, 1954, ch. 303, 68 *Stat.* 250, 6 Kappler's 620, codified at 25 U.S.C. §§ 891–902; repealed by Act of Dec. 22, 1973, Pub. L. No. 93-197, 87 *Stat.* 770, 25 U.S.C. 903–903f (Menominee Tribe).

Act of Aug. 11, 1955, ch. 786, 69 *Stat.* 666, §§ 1–5, 6 Kappler's 717–18; see 25 U.S.C. § 355 note.

Act of Aug. 1, 1956, ch. 843, 70 *Stat.* 893, 6 Kappler's 758, 25 U.S.C. §§ 791–807 (Wyandotte Tribe), repealed by Act of May 15, 1978, Pub. L. No. 95-281, 92 *Stat.* 246, 25 U.S.C. §§ 861–861c.

Act of Aug. 2, 1956, ch. 881, 70 *Stat.* 938, 6 Kappler's 764, 25 U.S.C. §§ 821–26 (Peoria Tribe), repealed by Act of May 15, 1978, Pub. L. No. 95-281, 92 *Stat.* 246, 25 U.S.C. §§ 861–861c.

Act of Aug. 3, 1956, ch. 907, 70 *Stat.* 963, 6 Kappler's 767, 25 U.S.C. §§ 841–53 (Ottawa Tribe), repealed by Act of May 15, 1978, Pub. L. No. 95-281, 92 *Stat.* 246, 25 U.S.C. §§ 861–861c.

Act of Sept. 28, 1959, Pub. L. No. 86-383, 73 *Stat.* 717, 6 Kappler's 898.

Economic Opportunity Act of Aug. 20, 1964, Pub. L. No. 88-452, 78 *Stat.* 519, title II, §§ 210, 211, codified as amended at 42 U.S.C. §§ 2790, 2791 (1964), repealed by Act of Aug. 13, 1981, Pub. L. No. 97-35, 95 *Stat.* 519, title VI, § 638(a).

Public Works and Economic Development Act of 1965, Pub. L. No. 89-136, 79 *Stat.* 552, codified, as amended, at 42 U.S.C. § 3131, repealed by Act of Nov. 13, 1998, Pub. L. No. 105-393, 112 *Stat.* 360, § 102(a), and codified, as amended, by 42 U.S.C. §§ 3161, et seq.

Act of May 13, 1966, Pub. L. No. 89-426, 80 *Stat.* 141, 6 Kappler's 1058.

Act of Aug. 29, 1967, Pub. L. No. 90-76, 81 *Stat.* 177, § 3, 6 Kappler's 1103.

Indian Civil Rights Act of Apr. 11, 1968, Pub. L. No. 90-284, 82 *Stat.* 77, 6 Kappler's 1124, codified as amended, 25 U.S.C. §§ 1301, et seq.

Act of June 19, 1968, Pub. L. No. 90-351, §§ 101–601, 82 *Stat.* 197, 6 Kappler's 1133.

Act of Oct. 17, 1968, Pub. L. No. 90-585, 82 *Stat.* 1148, 6 Kappler's 1165.

Act of May 7, 1970, Pub. L. No. 91-240, 84 *Stat.* 203, 6 Kappler's 1187, codified at 25 U.S.C. § 375d.

Act of Oct. 22, 1970, Pub. L. No. 91-495, 84 *Stat.*1091, 6 Kappler's 1208.

Indian Education Act of June 23, 1972, Pub. L. No. 92-318, §§ 401–53, 86 *Stat.* 335–45 (codified as amended at 20 U.S.C. §§ 241aa–241ff, 1211a, 1221f–1221h, 3385–3385b [1972], but repealed, Pub. L. No. 100-297, Act of Apr. 28, 1988, 102 *Stat.* 414).

Indian Tribal Judgment Funds Use or Distribution Act of Oct. 19, 1973, Pub. L. No. 93-134, 87 *Stat.* 466, codified as amended, 25 U.S.C. §§ 1401, et seq.

Comprehensive Employment and Training Act (CETA) of Dec. 28, 1973, Pub. L. No. 93-203, 87 *Stat.* 882, codified at 29 U.S.C. § 991, et seq., but repealed by Act of Oct. 13, 1982, Pub. L. No. 97-300, 96 *Stat.* 1357.

Indian Financing Act, Pub. L. No. 93-262, 88 *Stat.* 77 (codified as amended at 25 U.S.C. §§ 1451–1543) (1974).

Act of Jan. 2, 1975, Pub. L. No. 93-580, 88 *Stat.* 1910, as amended by Act of Aug. 9, 1975, Pub. L. No. 94-80, §§ 1–4, 89 *Stat.* 415, 416; Act of Feb. 17, 1977, Pub. L. No. 95-5, 91 *Stat.* 13 (not codified, but described as amended at 25 U.S.C. § 174 note).

Indian Self-Determination and Education Assistance Act, Pub. L. No. 96-638, 88 *Stat.* 2203, codified as amended at 25 U.S.C. §§ 450–450n, 455–458e, 458aa–458hh, 458aaa–458aaa-18 (1975).

Act of June 1, 1976, 90 *Stat.* 597, 629.

Food Stamp Act of Sept. 29, 1977, Pub. L. No. 95-113, title XIII, §§ 1301, 1302(a)(1), 91 *Stat.* 958, 979, codified at 7 U.S.C. §§ 2011, et seq.

Indian Child Welfare Act of Nov. 8, 1978, Pub. L. No. 95-608, 92 *Stat.* 3069, codified at 25 U.S.C. §§ 1901, et seq.

Indian Land Consolidation Act of Jan. 12, 1983, Pub. L. No. 97-459, 96 *Stat.* 2517, as amended by Pub. L. No. 106-462, Act of Nov. 7, 2000, 114 *Stat.* 1992, as amended by the American Indian Probate Reform Act of 2004, Act of Oct. 27, 2004, Pub. L. No. 108-374, 118 *Stat.* 1773, codified at 25 U.S.C. §§ 2201, et seq.

Indian Gaming Regulatory Act of Oct. 17, 1988, Pub. L. No. 100-497, 102 *Stat.* 2467, codified at 25 U.S.C. §§ 2701, et seq.

An Act To provide for the use and distribution of funds awarded the Seminole Indians, Act of Apr. 30, 1990, Pub. L. No. 101-277, 104 *Stat.* 143.

Indian Law Enforcement Reform Act of Aug. 18, 1990, Pub. L. No. 101-379, 104 *Stat.* 473, codified as amended, 25 U.S.C. §§ 2801, et seq.

Act of Oct. 25, 1994, Pub. L. No. 103-413, title II, § 204, 108 *Stat.* 4271, codified at 25 U.S.C. §§ 458aa, et seq. (Interior self-governance compacts).

Act of Dec. 21, 2000, Pub. L. No. 106-554, Sec. 1(a)(7) [title I, Sec. 166(a), (d)], 114 *Stat.* 2763, 2763A-627 (amendment of Federal Unemployment Tax Act concerning Indian tribes), codified in 26 U.S.C. § 3306.

Act of Dec. 27, 2000, Pub. L. No. 106-568, title XIII, § 1302, 114 *Stat.* 2936, codified at 25 U.S.C. §§ 458aaa, et seq. (HHS self-governance compacts).

Federal Regulations

44 *Fed. Reg.* 24,305 (Apr. 25, 1979) (proposed rule amending regulations to include western Okla. tribes in CFR Court system).

44 *Fed. Reg.* 37,502 (June 22, 1979) (final rule amending regulations to include western Okla. Tribes in CFR Court system), codified in 25 C.F.R. § 11.100(a).

57 *Fed. Reg.* 3270 (Jan. 28, 1992) (final rule including Muskogee area tribes, Okla., within Court of Indian Offenses system), codified in 25 C.F.R. § 11.100(a).

25 C.F.R. § 11.100 (2009) ("Courts of Indian Offenses and Law and Order Code").

Federal Executive Documents

Margold, Nathan. *Powers of Indian Tribes.* 55 I.D. 14 (Oct. 25, 1934).

Exec. Order of June 7, 1951, no 10250, 16 *Fed. Reg.* 5385.

SEMINOLE NATION OF OKLAHOMA
CONSTITUTIONAL AND LEGISLATIVE DOCUMENTS

Seminole Nation Constitution

1903 Revised Statutes of the Seminole Nation (see Archival and Manuscript Collection section below).

Seminole Nation (S.N.) Laws (in Chronological Order)

The *Code of Laws of the Seminole Nation of Oklahoma,* the *Resolutions of the Seminole Nation of Oklahoma,* and the *Ordinances and Laws of the Seminole Nation of Oklahoma* are all available from the Office of General Council Secretary, Seminole Nation of Oklahoma, P.O. Box 1498, Wewoka, Okla. 74884.

S.N. Ord. No. 70-1 (Mar. 7, 1970) (form of laws and resolutions).
S.N. Ord. No. 70-2 (June 6, 1970) (treasurer).
S.N. Ord. No. 70-4 (June 6, 1970) (council meetings).
S.N. Ord. No. 70-5 (June 6, 1970) (attorney general).
S.N. Ord. No. 70-6 (Dec. 5, 1970) (treasurer).
S.N. Ord. No. 72-1 (Apr. 22, 1972) (recreation areas).
S.N. Ord. No. 72-2 (June 13, 1972) (CHR program).
S.N. Ord. No. 72-3 (Sept. 2, 1972) (elections).
S.N. Ord. No. 73-1 (May 5, 1973) (elections).
S.N. Ord. No. 73-2 (July 10, 1973) (elections).
S.N. Ord. No. 74-1 (Mar. 30, 1974) (salaries).
S.N. Ord. No. 74-2 (June 8, 1974) (personnel board).
S.N. Ord. No. 75-2 (Sept. 6, 1975) (recreation areas).
S.N. Ord. No. 76-1 (duplicate numbering) (Jan. 17, 1976) (Seminole name and seal).
S.N. Ord. No. 76-1 (duplicate numbering) (July 17, 1976) (personnel board).
S.N. Ord. No. 77-2 (Mar. 29, 1977) (elections).
S.N. Ord. No. 77-3 (Apr. 30, 1977) (firearms prohibition).
S.N. Ord. No. 77-4 (Aug. 20, 1977) (enrollment office).
S.N. Ord. No. 78-1 (June 3, 1978) (enrollment committee).
S.N. Ord. No. 78-2(June 3, 1978) (membership criteria).
S.N. Ord. No. 78-17 (Oct. 28, 1978) (budget committee).
S.N. Ord. No. 79-2 (Feb. 23, 1979)
S.N. Ord. No. 80-4 (June 7, 1980) (Budget Committee).
S.N. Ord. No. 80-1 (Mar. 8, 1980) (Seminole Nation Health Department).
S.N. Ord. No. 80-5 (June 7, 1980) (judgment fund committee).
S.N. Ord. No. 81-2 (May 16, 1981) (elections).
S.N. Ord. No. 83-2 (Mar. 12, 1983) (Indian foster care licenses).
S.N. Ord. No. 85-1 (Mar. 30, 1985) (election law).
S.N. Ord. No. 86-1 (Mar. 27, 1986) (audit committee).
S.N. Ord. No. 86-2 (May 10, 1986) (regulation of bingo).
S.N. Ord. No. 87-1 (Feb. 21, 1987) (council stipends and travel regulations).
S.N. Ord. No. 87-2 (Sept. 19, 1987) (law enforcement division).
S.N. Ord. No. 87-3 (Nov. 7, 1987) (establishment of tax commission).
S.N. Ord. No. 87-4 (Nov. 7, 1987) (establishment of SEDA).

S.N. Ord. No. 87-5 (Sept. 19, 1987) (tobacco taxes).
S.N. Ord. No. 88-1 (Sept. 6, 1988) (General Revenue and Tax Act).
S.N. Ord. No. 88-3 (Apr. 15, 1988) (personnel policies).
S.N. Ord. No. 88-2 (Dec. 17, 1988) (elections).
S.N. Ord. No. 89-02 (Mar. 27, 1989) (elections).
S.N. Ord. No. 91-03 (Apr. 13, 1991) (BIA approval of tribal law not required).
S.N. Ord. No. 91-03A (Apr. 13, 1991) (membership).
S.N. Ord. No. 91-4 (July 27, 1991) (burial assistance).
S.N. Ord. No. 91-5 (July 27, 1991) (school clothing).
S.N. Ord. No. 91-6 (Aug. 24, 1991) (elections).
S.N. Ord. No. 91-7 (Aug. 29, 1991) (council secretary duties).
S.N. Ord. No. 91-8 (Aug. 29, 1991) (gaming).
S.N. Ord. No. 91-9 (Aug. 29, 1991) (form of laws and resolutions).
S.N. Law No. 91-10 (Nov. 16, 1991) (elderly assistance).
S.N. Law No. 91-11 (Nov. 16, 1991) (higher education).
S.N. Law No. 91-12 (Nov. 16, 1991) (codification of laws).
S.N. Law No. 91-16 (Dec. 7, 1991) (officer salaries).
S.N. Law No. 91-17 (Dec. 7, 1991) (arts and crafts committee).
S.N. Law No. 92-3 (Mar. 7, 1992) (Title 5, CFR courts).
S.N. Law No. 92-5 (June 6, 1992) (Title 5, CFR courts; Title 7, criminal procedure; and Title 13, evidence).
S.N. Law No. 92-8 (July 27, 1992) (Title 3, civil procedure).
S.N. Law. No. 92-9 (June 27, 1992) (community cultural and recreational enhancement).
S.N. Law. No. 92-12 (Sept. 5, 1992) (household economic assistance).
S.N. Law No. 92-13(Sept. 5, 1992) (Title 26, recreation).
S.N. Law No. 92-15 (Nov. 14, 1992) (Title 28, taxes, tobacco retailers, and wholesalers).
S.N. Law No. 92-16 (Dec. 5, 1992) (Title 18-A, judgment funds)
S.N. Law No. 92-25 (Nov. 14, 1992) (Title 3-A, Business and Corporate Regulatory Commission).
S.N. Law No. 93-04 (Jan. 23, 1993) (Title 22, membership).
S.N. Law No. 93-05 (Jan. 23, 1993) (Tribal Employment Rights Office).
S.N. Law No. 93-14 (Apr. 3, 1993) (amendment of Economic Development Code).
S.N. Law No. 93-21 (Nov. 6, 1993) (Title 14, finance, Trust Fund Management Board).
S.N. Law No. 93-22 (Nov. 6, 1993) (Title 16, general council, Administrative Appeals Board).
S.N. Law No. 93-24 (Dec. 4, 1993) (Title 6, criminal offenses)
S.N. Law No. 94-2 (Feb. 24, 1994) (Title 15, gaming).

OTHER TRIBAL CONSTITUTIONS

Constitution of the Cherokee Nation, June 26, 1976, amended June 20, 1987, revised July 26, 2003.
Constitution of the Chickasaw Nation, Aug. 27, 1983, amended eff. June 21, 2002.
Constitution of the Choctaw Nation, June 9, 1983.
Constitution of the Muscogee (Creek), Aug. 17, 1979, amended Dec. 7, 1991, amended Feb. 18, 2006.

STATE CONSTITUTION, LAWS, AND ATTORNEY GENERAL OPINIONS (IN CHRONOLOGICAL ORDER)

Oklahoma Constitution.
"Limitations of Real Actions," Okla. State Leg., R.L. 1910, § 4655; Laws 1945, p. 37; Laws 1949, p. 95; Laws 1961, p. 59, emerg. eff. July 26, 1961, codified at 12 Okla. Stat. Annot. § 93.
Oklahoma Housing Authorities Act, Okla. State Leg., Laws 1965 ch. 251, emerg. eff. June 18, 1965, codified at 63 Okla. Stat. Annot. §§ 1051, et seq.
Oklahoma Indian Child Welfare Act, Okla. State Leg., Laws 1982, HB 1922, ch. 107, emerg. eff. Apr. 6, 1982; *amended by* Laws 1994, HB 1905, ch. 30, eff. Sept. 1, 1994; a*mended by* Laws 2006, HB 2561, ch. 136, § 2, eff. Nov. 1, 2006; *amended by* Laws 1997, ch. 293, eff. July 1, 1997; codified at 10 Okla. Stat. Annot. §§ 40.1, et seq.
State Tribal Relations Act, Okla. State Leg., Laws 1988, S. 210, ch. 160; *amended by* Laws 1989, S. 144, ch. 296, emerg. eff. May 24, 1989; *amended by* Laws 1991, H. 1409, ch. 202, emerg. eff. May 17, 1991; *amended by* Laws 1994, H. 2640, ch. 290; a*mended by* Laws 2000, S. 1246, ch. 240 eff. Nov. 1, 2000; *amended by* Laws 2002, S. 1410, ch. 485, emerg. eff. June 6, 2002; *amended by* Laws 2009, H. 2029, ch. 234, emerg. eff. May 21, 2009, codified at 74 Okla. Stat. Annot. §§ 1221, et seq.
Off. of Att'y Gen. Op. No. 90-32 (Mar. 1, 1991).
Okla. Sess. Laws 1992, ch. 339, May 28, 1992, 1643–56, codified as amended at 68 Okla. *Stat.* Annot. §§ 301, 309, 321, 346–52, 401, 403.1, 413, 419, 424–29, and 1355.
Okla. Sess. Laws 1996, H.. 2208, ch. 345, § 63, codified at 68 Okla. Stat. Annot. § 500.63 (motor fuel tribal–state contract).
Okla. Sess. Laws 2002, S. 1404, ch. 452, § 1, June 5, 2002, *amended by* Laws 2008, S. 1531, ch. 132, § 1, codified in 40 Okla. Stat. Annot. §§ 1–108 (Indian tribes, employer requirements, benefits).
Tribal Gaming Act, Okla. Laws 2004, S. 1252, c. 316, State Question No. 712, Legis. Ref. No. 335, approved at general election held on Nov. 2, 2004,

codified at 3A Okla. *Stat.* Annot. §§ 261, et seq.; see 3A Okla. Stat. Annot. § 261 (Model Gaming Compact).

CASES

U.S. Supreme Court

Alberty v. United States, 162 U.S. 499 (1896).
Atlantic and Pacific Railroad v. Mingus, 165 U.S. 413, 437 (1897).
Blundell v. Wallace, 267 U.S. 373 (1925).
Board of County Commissioners v. Seber, 318 U.S. 705 (1943).
Brader v. James, 246 U.S. 88 (1918).
Bunch v. Cole, 263 U.S. 250 (1923).
California v. Cabazon Band of Mission Indians, 480 U.S. 202 (1987)
Carpenter v. Shaw, 280 U.S. 363 (1930).
Cherokee Nation v. Georgia, 30 U.S. (5 Pet.) 1 (1831).
Cherokee Nation v. Hitchcock, 187 U.S. 294 (1902).
Cherokee Nation v. Southern Kansas Ry., 135 U.S. 641 (1889).
Choate v. Trapp, 224 U.S. 665 (1912).
Cook v. United States, 288 U.S. 102 (1933).
Creek Nation v. United States, 318 U.S. 629 (1943).
Davis v. Williford, 271 U.S. 484 (1926).
Donnelly v. United States, 228 U.S. 243 (1913).
Duro v. Reina, 495 U.S. 676 (1990).
Ex parte Crow Dog, 109 U.S. 556 (1883).
Ex parte Webb, 225 U.S. 663 (1912).
Fisher v. District Court of Sixteenth Judicial District of Montana, 424 U.S. 382 (1976)
Garfield v. Goldsby, 211 U.S. 249 (1908).
Gritts v. Fisher, 224 U.S. 640 (1912).
Harris v. Bell, 254 U.S. 103 (1920).
Heckman v. United States, 224 U.S. 413 (1912).
In re Heff, 197 U.S. 488 (1905).
In re Mayfield, 141 U.S. 107 (1891).
Jefferson v. Fink, 247 U.S. 288, 290–91 (1918).
Kennerly v. Dist. Court of Ninth Judicial Dist. of Montana, 400 U.S. 423 (1971)
Lone Wolf v. Hitchcock, 187 U.S. 553 (1903).
Mackey v. Cox, 59 U.S.100 (1855).
Mammoth Oil Co. v. United States, 275 U.S. 13 (1927).
McClanahan v. Arizona State Tax Commission, 411 U.S. 164, 172, 174 (1973).
Mississippi Band of Choctaw Indians v. Holyfield, 490 U.S. 30 (1989).
Morris v. Hitchcock, 194 U.S. 384 (1904).

Morton v. Mancari, 417 U.S. 535 (1974).

Mott v. United States, 283 U.S. 747 (1931).

National Farmer's Union Insurance Co. v. Crow Tribe of Indians, 471 U.S. 845 (1985).

Nofire v. United States, 164 U.S. 657 (1897).

Oklahoma Tax Commission v. Citizen Band Potawatomi Indian Tribe of Oklahoma, 498 U.S. 505 (1991).

Oklahoma Tax Commission v. Sac and Fox Nation, 508 U.S. 114 (1993).

Oklahoma Tax Commission v. United States, 319 U.S. 598 (1943).

Oliphant v. Suquamish Indian Tribe, 435 U.S. 191 (1978).

Parker v. Richard, 250 U.S. 235 (1919).

Seminole Nation v. United States, 316 U.S. 286, 297 (1942).

Seminole Nation v. United States, 318 U.S. 629 (1943).

Shade v. Downing, 333 U.S. 586 (1948).

Southern Surety Co. v. State of Oklahoma, 241 U.S. 582 (1916).

Stephens v. Cherokee Nation, 174 U.S. 445 (1899).

Stewart v. Keyes, 295 U.S. 404 (1935).

Talton v. Mayes, 163 U.S. 376 (1896).

Tiger v. Western Inv. Co., 221 U.S. 286 (1911).

Turner v. United States, 248 U.S. 354 (1919).

United States v. Fisher, 222 U.S. 204 (1911).

United States v. Hellard, 322 U.S. 363 (1944).

United States v. John, 437 U.S. 634 (1978).

United States v. Kagama, 118 U.S. 375 (1886).

United States v. Mazurie, 419 U.S. 544 (1975).

United States v. McBratney, 104 U.S. 621 (1881).

United States v. McGowan, 302 U.S. 535 (1938).

United States v. Nice, 241 U.S. 591 (1916).

United States v. Pelican, 232 U.S. 442, 449 (1914).

United States v. Ramsey, 271 U.S. 467 (1926).

United States v. Rice, 327 U.S. 742 (1946).

United States v. Sandoval, 231 U.S. 28 (1913).

United States v. Seminole Nation, 299 U.S. 417 (1937).

United States v. Wildcat, 244 U.S. 111 (1917).

United States v. Wright, 229 U.S. 226 (1913).

Williams v. Lee, 358 U.S. 217, 223 (1959).

Worcester v. Georgia, 31 U.S. (6 Pet.) 515 (1832).

U.S. Court of Appeals

Armstrong v. Maple Leaf Apartments, Ltd., 508 F.2d 518 (10th Cir. 1975).

Armstrong v. Maple Leaf Apartments, Ltd., 622 F.2d 466 (10th Cir.1979), *cert. denied*, 449 U.S. 901 (1980).

Buster v. Wright, 135 F. 947 (8th Cir. [Ind. Terr.]1905), *app. dismissed*, 203 U.S. 599 (1906).

Cheyenne–Arapaho Tribes of Oklahoma v. State of Oklahoma, 618 F.2d 665 (10th Cir. 1980).

Cheyenne–Arapaho Tribes of Oklahoma v. State of Oklahoma, 681 F.2d 705 (10th Cir. 1982).

Clark v. United States, 587 F.2d 465 (10th Cir. 1978).

Cobell v. United States, 455 F.3d 317 (D.C. Cir. 2006), *cert. denied*, 127 S. Ct. 1876, 167 L. Ed. 2d 386 (2007).

Coppedge v. Clinton, 72 F.2d 531 (10th Cir. 1934).

Crabtree v. Madden, 54 F. 426 (8th Cir. [Ind. Terr.] 1893).

Davis v. United States, 192 F.3d 951 (10th Cir. 1999).

Davis v. United States, 343 F.3d 1282 (10th Cir. 2003), *cert. denied*, 542 U.S. 937 (2003).

Ellis v. Page, 351 F.2d 250 (10th Cir. 1965).

Fall v. United States, 49 F.2d 506 (D.C. Cir. 1931), *cert. denied*, 283 U.S.867 (1931).

Indian Country U.S.A. v. Oklahoma Tax Commission, 829 F.2d 967 (10th Cir. 1987), *cert. denied*, Oklahoma Tax Commission v. Muscogee (Creek) Nation, 487 U.S. 1218 (1988).

Maxey v. Wright, 3 Ind Terr. 243, 54 S.W. 807 (Ind. Terr. Ct. App.1900), *aff'd*, 105 F. 1003 (8th Cir. 1900).

Moore v. Carter Oil Co., 43 F.2d 322 (10th Cir. 1930), *cert. denied*, 282 U.S. 903 (1931).

Muscogee (Creek) Nation v. Hodel, 851 F.2d 1439 (D.C. Cir. 1988), *cert. denied*, Hodel v. Muscogee (Creek) Nation, 488 U.S. 1010 (1989).

Nero v. Cherokee Nation of Oklahoma, 892 F.2d 1457 (10th Cir. 1989).

Raymond v. Raymond, 83 F. 721 (8th Cir. 1897).

Ross v. Neff, 905 F.2d 1349 (10th Cir. 1990).

Seminole Indian Tribe of Florida v. Andrus, Civil Action No. 78-994 (D. D.C. Order and Memorandum Opinion, July 9, 1979, unpublished).

Seminole Nation v. White, 224 F.2d 173 (10th Cir. 1955), *cert. denied*, 350 U.S. 895 (1955). *Seminole Tribe of Florida v. Butterworth*, 658 F.2d 310 (5th Cir. 1981), *cert. denied*, Butterworth v. Seminole Tribe, 455 U.S. 1020 (1982).

Springer v. Townsend, 336 F.2d 397 (10th Cir. 1964).

Thebo v. Choctaw Tribe, 66 F. 372 (8th Cir.1895).

Tillett v. Lujan, 931 F.2d 636, 640, 641 (10th Cir. 1991).

Tooisgah v. United States, 186 F.2d 93 (10th Cir. 1950).

United States Express Co. v. Friedman, 191 F. 673 (8th Cir. 1911).

United States v. Bond, 108 F.2d 504 (10th Cir. 1939).

United States v. Daney, 370 F.2d 791 (10th Cir. 1966).

United States v. Goldfeder, 112 F.2d. 615 (10th Cir. 1940).

United States v. Hester, 137 F.2d 145 (10th Cir. 1943).

United States v. Littlechief, Case No. CR-76-207-D (slip op. Nov. 1977, W.D. Okla.)

United States v. Palmer, 766 F.2d 1441 (10th Cir. 1985).

United States v. Sands, 968 F.2d 1058 (10th Cir. 1992), *cert. denied, Sands v. United States*, 506 U.S. 1056 (1993).

United States v. Seminole Nation, 321 F.3d 939 (10th Cir. 2002).

United States v. Warledo, 557 F.2d 721 (10th Cir. 1977).

United States v. Watashe, 117 F.2d 947 (10th Cir. 1941).

United States v. Williams, 139 F.2d 83 (10th Cir. 1943), *cert. denied*, 322 U.S. 727 (1944).

Walker v. McLoud, 138 F. 394 (8th Cir. 1905), *aff'd* 204 U.S. 302 (1907).

Ward v. United States, 139 F.2d 79 (10th Cir. 1943).

Wheeler v. United States Department of the Interior, 811 F.2d 549 (10th Cir. 1987).

Wolfe v. Phillips, 172 F. 2d 481 (10th Cir. 1949), *cert. denied*, 336 U.S. 968 (1949).

U.S. District Court

Burgess v. Bosen, 31 F. Supp. 352 (N.D. Okla. 1940).

Davis v. United States, 199 F. Supp.2d 1164 (W.D. Okla. 2002), *aff'd Davis v. United States*, 343 F.3d 1282 (10th Cir. 2003), *cert. denied*, 542 U.S. 937 (2003).

Haney v. United States, Case No. 01-679 (U.S. E.D. Okla.).

Harjo v. Kleppe, 420 F. Supp. 1110 (D. D.C.1976), *aff'd sub nom. Harjo v. Andrus*, 581 F.2d 949 (D.C. Cir. 1978).

Milam v. Hodel, Case No. 86-61-C, E.D. Okla., Judgment, Findings of Fact and Conclusions of Law, Oct. 23, 1986, *aff'd Milam v. Hodel*, Case No. 86-2755, Order and Judgment (10th Cir. Jan. 6, 1989)(unpublished).

Milam v. U.S. Department of the Interior, Case No. 82-C-3099, slip op. (D.C.C. Dec. 23, 1982), 10 Ind. L. Rep. 3013 (American Indian Law Training Program).

Muscogee (Creek) Nation v. Hodel, 670 F. Supp. 434 (D.D.C. 1987), *rev'd Muscogee (Creek) Nation v. Hodel*, 851 F.2d 1439 (D.C. 1988), *cert. denied, Hodel v. Muscogee (Creek) Nation*, 488 U.S. 1010 (1989).

Seminole Nation of Oklahoma v. Norton, 223 F. Supp. 2d 122 (U.S. D.C. 2002).

Seminole Nation v. Norton, 206 F.R.D. 1 (U.S. D.C. 2001); *app. dismissed, Seminole Nation v. Norton*, No. 01-5418, unpublished order, May 24, 2002, WL 1364249.

Tanyan v. Ellison, Case No. 83-189-C, Complaint, Mar. 20, 1983.

United States v. Easely, 33 F. Supp. 442 (W.D. Okla. 1940).

United States v. Littlechief, Case No. CR-76-207-D (slip op. Nov. 7, 1977, W.D. Okla.).

United States v. Meadors, 70 F. Supp. 800 (E.D. Okla. 1947), *reversed*, 165 F.2d 215 (10th Cir. 1947).

United States v. Wewoka Creek Water and Soil Conservancy District No. 2 of State of Oklahoma, 222 F. Supp. 225 (E.D. Okla. 1963).

Walker v. United States, 663 F. Supp. 258 (E.D. Okla. 1987).

Zweigel v. Webster, 32 F. Supp. 1015 (E.D. Okla. 1940).

Indian Claims Commission and U.S. Court of Claims (in Chronological Order)

Mineral Claim
Seminole Nation v. United States [ICC Docket 204], 17 Ind. Cl. Comm. 67 (Findings of Fact and Opinion, June 24, 1966).
Seminole Nation v. United States, 28 Ind. Cl. Comm. 117 (Opinion of the Commission; Order Vacating Commission's Findings of Fact, Opinion, and Interlocutory Order; and Order Dismissing Petition, May 31, 1972).
Seminole Nation v. United States, 28 Ind. Cl. Comm. 421 (Order Denying Plaintiff's Motion for Rehearing, Jan. 26, 1973).
Seminole Nation of Oklahoma v. United States, 204 Ct. Cl. 655, 498 F.2d 1368 (Ct. Cl. 1974), *cert denied*, 420 U.S. 907 (1975), *petition for rehearing denied*, *Seminole Nation of Oklahoma v. United States*, 420 U.S. 984 (1975).

Tribal Annuities Claim
Seminole Nation v. United States, 82 Ct. Cl. 135 (Ct. Cl. 1935), *rev'd, United States v. Seminole Nation*, 299 U.S. 417 (1937).
Seminole Nation v. United States, 93 Ct. Cl. 500 (Ct. Cl. 1941), *aff'd in part and rev'd in part, Seminole Nation v. United States*, 316 U.S. 286, 297 (1942).
Seminole Nation v. United States, 102 Ct. Cl. 565 (Ct. Cl.1944), *cert. denied*, 326 U.S. 719 (1945).

Erroneous Survey Claim
Seminole Nation v. United States, 316 U.S. 310 (1942).
Seminole Nation v. United States, 102 Ct. Cl. 565 (Ct. Cl.1944), *cert. denied*, 326 U.S. 719 (1945).

Claim for Damages Arising from Distribution of Tribal Property to Freedmen under 1866 Treaty
Seminole Nation v. United States, 78 Ct. Cl. 455 (1933).
Seminole Nation v. United States, 90 Ct. Cl. 151 (1940), *cert. denied*, 310 U.S. 639 (1940).
Seminole Nation v. United States [ICC Docket 152], 10 Ind. Cl. Comm. 450, 461 and 501a (Findings of Fact, Opinion, and Final Order, Aug. 22, 1962).

Wewoka Townsite Claim
Seminole Nation v. United States, 92 Ct. Cl. 210 (1940), *cert. denied*, 313 U.S. 563 (1941).
Seminole Nation v. United States [ICC Docket 53], 2 Ind. Cl. Comm. 115 (Findings, Apr. 22, 1952).
Seminole Nation v. United States, 2 Ind. Cl. Comm. 122 (Opinion, Apr. 22, 1952).

Loyal Seminole Claim
Burden, et al. v. United States, [ICC Docket 121], 6 Ind. Cl. Comm. 127 (Opinion, Feb. 27, 1958).

Seminole Nation v. United States [ICC Docket 205], 12 Ind. Cl. Comm. 798 (Findings, Nov. 7, 1963).

Seminole Nation v. United States, 12 Ind. Cl. Comm. 809 (Opinion, Nov. 7, 1963), *aff'd, Seminole Nation v. United States*, 171 Ct. Cl. 477 (1965) [ICC Docket 205].

Railroad Claim

Creek Nation v. United States, 75 Ct. Cl. 873 (Ct. Cl. 1932).

Creek Nation v. United States, 97 Ct. Cl. 591 (Ct. Cl. 1942).

Seminole Nation v. United States, 97 Ct. Cl. 723 (1942), *aff'd Seminole Nation v. United States*, 318 U.S. 629 (1943).

Seminole Nation v. United States [ICC Docket 247], 27 Ind. Cl. Comm. 141 (Findings of Fact, Mar. 24, 1972).

Seminole Nation v. United States, 27 Ind. Cl. Comm. 157 (Opinion, Mar. 24, 1972), *rehearing denied*, 29 Ind. Cl. Comm. 422 (Jan. 26, 1973), *aff'd in part, reversed in part, and remanded, Seminole Nation of Oklahoma v. United States*, 203 Ct. Cl. 637, 492 F.2d 811 (Ct. Cl. 1974).

Seminole Nation v. United States, 40 Ind. Cl. Comm. 231 (Order Rejecting Plaintiff's Offer of Proof, June 22, 1977).

Seminole Nation v. United States, 40 Ind. Cl. Comm. 231 (Opinion, June 22, 1977).

Seminole Nation v. United States, 40 Ind. Cl. Comm. 247 (Order Certifying and Transferring Cases to U.S. Court of Claims, July 13, 1978).

Emahaka Claim

Seminole Nation v. United States [ICC Docket 150], 6 Ind. Cl. Comm. 335a (Conclusions of Law and Final Award, June 4, 1958).

Seminole Nation v. United States, 6 Ind. Cl. Comm. 336 (Additional Findings of Fact, June 4, 1958).

Seminole Nation v. United States, 6 Ind. Cl. Comm. 345 (Opinion, June 4, 1958).

United States v. Seminole Nation, 146 Ct. Cl. 171,173 F. Supp. 784 (Ct. Cl. 1959).

Mekusukey Claim

Seminole Nation v. United States [I.C.C. Docket 248], 14 Ind. Cl. Comm. 484 (Findings of Fact, Dec. 23, 1964).

Seminole Nation v. United States 14 Ind. Cl. Comm. 505 (Opinion, Dec. 23, 1964).

Seminole Nation v. United States 14 Ind. Cl. Comm. 517a (Final Award, Dec. 23, 1964).

Florida Lands Claim

Seminole Indians of the State of Florida and the Seminole Nation of Oklahoma v. United States, [ICC Dockets 73, 151, 73-A] 13 Ind. Cl. Comm. 326 (Ind. Cl. Comm. 1964), *aff'd, United States v. the Seminole Indians of State of Florida and the Seminole Nation of Oklahoma*, 180 Ct. Cl. 375 (Ct. Cl. 1967).

Seminole Indians of the State of Florida and the Seminole Nation of Oklahoma v. United States, 23 Comm. 108 (Ind. Cl. Comm. 1970) and 24 Ind. Cl. Comm. 1 (Ind. Cl. Comm. 1970), *rev'd,* 197 Ct. Cl. 350 (Ct. Cl. 1972).

Seminole Indians of State of Florida and Seminole Nation of Oklahoma v. United States, 38 Comm. 62 (Ind. Cl. Comm. 1976).

Interior Board of Indian Appeals Decisions

Muscogee (Creek) Nation v. Acting Area Director, Muskogee Area Office, BIA, 13 IBIA 211 (1985), *aff'd, Muscogee (Creek) Nation v. Hodel,* 670 F. Supp. 434 (D.D.C. 1987), *rev'd, Muscogee (Creek) Nation v. Hodel,* 851 F.2d 1439 (D.C. 1988), *cert. denied, Hodel v. Muscogee (Creek) Nation,* 488 U.S. 1010 (1989).

Seminole Nation of Oklahoma v. Acting Director, Office of Tribal Services, Bureau of Indian Affairs, 24 IBIA 209 (Sept. 23, 1993).

Seminole Nation of Oklahoma v. Acting Director, Office of Tribal Services, Bureau of Indian Affairs (Supplemental Opinion IBIA 1993).

Court of Indian Offenses, Wewoka Agency

Haney v. Chambers, Case No. CIV-02-W40, Court of Indian Offenses for the Wewoka Agency for the Seminole Nation.

Miller v. Jerry G. Haney, Principal Chief, and Billy Joe Harjo, Court of Indian Offenses, Wewoka Agency, Case No. CIV-W84-93 (Amended Order of Dismissal, Jan. 20, 1994).

Tanyan v. Seminole Nation Election Board, Court of Indian Offenses, Wewoka Agency, Case No. CIV-W113-93 (Order, Oct. 15, 1993).

State

Ahboah v. Housing Authority of the Kiowa Tribe of Indians, 660 P.2d 625 (Okla. 1983).

C.M.G. v. State, 594 P.2d 798, 803 (Okla. Cr. 1979).

Eaves v. State, 795 P.2d 1060 (Okla. Cr. 1990), *rehearing denied,* 800 P.2d 251 (Okla. Cr. 1990), *cert. denied,* 522 U.S. 1149 (1998).

Ellis v. State, 386 P.2d 326 (Okla. Crim. App. 1963), *cert. denied,* 376 U.S. 945 (1964).

Ex parte Nowabbi, 61 P.2d 1139 (Okla. Cr. 1936), *overruled, State v. Klindt,* 782 P.2d 401 (Okla. Cr. 1989).

Guardianship of QGM, 808 P.2d 604 (Okla. 1991).

Housing Authority of the Seminole Nation v. Harjo, 790 P.2d 1098 (Okla. 1990).

In re. Yates, 349 P.2d 45 (Okla. Crim. App. 1960).

Matter of Adoption of Baby Boy D, 742 P.2d 1059 (Okla. 1985), *cert. denied, Harjo v. Duello,* 484 U.S. 1072 (1988), *overruled, In the Matter of Adoption of Baby Boy L,* 103 P.3d 1099 (Okla. 2004).

Seminole Intra-Tribal Business Association v. Tanyan and Palmer, Seminole County
    Case No. S-C-76-131, Thomas Coker Papers, 1942–1983 (box 11, folder
    10), Oklahoma Historical Society [2202.1.4].
State v. Klindt, 782 P.2d 401 (Okla. Cr. App. 1989).
State v. Littlechief, 573 P.2d 263 (Okla. Cr. 1978).
Walker v. Harjo, Seminole County Case No. S-C-72-30, Thomas Coker Papers,
    1942–1983 (box 11, folder 8), Oklahoma Historical Society [2202.1.4].

ARCHIVAL AND MANUSCRIPT COLLECTIONS

Brown, John F., Collection. Seminole Nation Papers. University of Oklahoma
    Western History Collection, Norman.
Grounds, Charles, Files (copies of private files in author's possession and also
    located at Seminole Nation Museum, Wewoka, Okla.).
Haney, Enoch Kelly (private collection).
Haney, Jerry G., Papers (private collection loaned to author).
National Archives, Washington, D.C. Natural Resources Division. RG 75.
Oklahoma Historical Society, Oklahoma City
    Coker, Thomas, Papers, 1942–1983 [2002.14].
    Doonkeen, Eula Narcomey, Collection, 1972–1973 [97.23].
    Seminole Documents, Indian Archives.
Seminole Nation Museum, Wewoka, Okla.
Grounds, Charles, Private files (copies also in author's possession).
Wantland, William, Constitution files.
Walker, Terry, Papers (private family collection).

OTHER GOVERNMENT DOCUMENTS AND PUBLICATIONS
(IN CHRONOLOGICAL ORDER)

47th Cong., 2nd sess., 14 *Cong. Rec.* S503 (Dec. 21, 1882) (statement of Sen. Garland).
50th Cong., 2nd sess., 20 *Cong. Rec.* S1709, S1714 (Feb. 9, 1889) (statement of
    Sen. Morgan).
H.R. Rep. No. 66, 51st Cong., 1st sess. (1890).
51st Cong., 1st sess., 21 *Cong. Rec.* S1066 (Feb. 5, 1890) (statement of Sen. Platt).
51st Cong., 1st sess., 21 *Cong. Rec.* H3719 (Feb. 11, 1890) (statements of Rep.
    Struble and Rep. Ingalls).
51st Cong., 1st sess., 21 *Cong. Rec.* H2176 (Mar. 12, 1890) (statement of Rep.
    Mansur).
51st Cong., 1st sess., 21 *Cong. Rec.* S3713 (Apr. 19, 1890) (statement of Sen. Butler).
51st Cong., 1st sess., 21 *Cong. Rec.* H3628 (Apr. 21, 1890) (statement of Rep. Struble).

51st Cong, 1st sess., 21 *Cong. Rec.* S3719 (Apr. 23, 1890) (statement of Sen. Butler).

52nd Cong., 2nd sess., 24 *Cong. Rec.* S80 (Dec. 12, 1892) (statement of Sen. Berry).

52nd Cong., 2nd sess., 24 *Cong. Rec.* S84 (Dec. 12, 1892).

52nd Cong., 2nd sess., 24 *Cong. Rec.* S98–99 (Dec.13, 1892) (statement of Sen. Jones).

52nd Cong., 2nd sess., 24 *Cong. Rec.* S100, 102 (Dec.13, 1892) (statements of Sen. Platt).

52nd Cong., 2nd sess., 24 *Cong. Rec.* S270–71 (Dec. 21, 1892) (statement of Sen. Perkins).

U.S. Department of the Interior. Census Office. *The Five Civilized Tribes of Indian Territory: Bulletin* (11th Census, 1890, report). Washington, D.C.: Aug. 25, 1894.

53rd Cong., 3rd sess., 27 *Cong. Rec.* H949 (Jan. 14, 1895) (statement of Rep. Culberson).

53rd Cong., 3rd sess., 27 *Cong. Rec.* H950 (Jan. 14, 1895) (statement of Rep. Curtis).

53rd Cong., 3rd sess., 27 *Cong. Rec.* H960 (Jan. 14, 1895) (statement of Rep. Little).

S. Rep. No. 377, 53rd Cong., 2nd Sess. (1896).

54th Cong., 2nd sess., 29 *Cong. Rec.* S2246 (Feb. 25, 1897) (statement of Sen. Pettigrew).

54th Cong., 2nd sess., 29 *Cong. Rec.* S2305 (Feb. 26, 1897) (statement of Sen. Vest).

54th Cong., 2nd sess., 29 *Cong. Rec.* S2309–10 (Feb. 26, 1897) (statements of Sen. Bate).

54th Cong., 2nd sess., 29 *Cong. Rec.* S2323–24 (Feb. 26, 1897) (statement of Sen. Berry).

54th Cong., 2nd sess., 29 *Cong. Rec.* S2349 (Feb. 26, 1897) (statement of Sen. Teller).

54th Cong., 2nd sess., 29 *Cong. Rec.* S2351 (Feb. 26, 1897) (statement of Sen. Hoar).

54th Cong., 2nd sess., 29 *Cong. Rec.* S2352 (Feb. 26, 1897) (statement of Sen. Vilas).

U.S. Department of the Interior. *Annual Report of the Commission to the Five Civilized Tribes, FY 1898.* Location: Washington, D.C.: GPO, 1898.

55th Cong., 2nd sess., 31 *Cong. Rec.* H5575 (June 6, 1898) (statement of Rep. Curtis).

U.S. Bureau of Census. *1899 Census Report.* Washington, D.C.: GPO, 1899.

U.S. Department of the Interior. Indian Affairs. *Annual Report of the U.S. Indian Inspector for the Indian Territory to the Secretary of the Interior, for the Fiscal Year Ended June 30, 1900,* by J. George Wright. Washington, D.C.: GPO, 1900.

U.S. Department of the Interior. Indian Affairs. *Annual Reports of the Department of the Interior for the Fiscal Year Ended June 30, 1901, Indian Affairs, Part II, Report of Commission to Five Civilized Tribes.* Washington, D.C.: GPO, 1901.

U.S. Department of the Interior. *Annual Report of the Commission to the Five Civilized Tribes, FY 1902.* Washington, D.C.: GPO, 1902.

U.S. Department of the Interior. *Annual Report of the Commission to the Five Civilized Tribes, FY 1903.* Washington, D.C.: GPO, 1903.

U.S. Department of the Interior. Indian Affairs. *Annual Report of the U.S. Indian Inspector for the Indian Territory to the Secretary of the Interior, for the Fiscal Year Ended June 30, 1904,* by J. George Wright. Washington, D.C.: GPO, 1904.

H.R. Rep. No. 1191, 58th Cong., 2nd sess. (Feb. 23, 1904).

58th Cong., 2nd sess., 38 *Cong. Rec.* H5004, H5006 (April 18, 1904) (statement of Rep. Thomas and accompanying chart of statistics and Letter from Judge Raymond, United States District Court, Western District, Indian Territory).

59th Cong., 1st sess., 40 *Cong. Rec.* H1241–43 (Jan. 18, 1906) (statements of Rep. Curtis).

59th Cong, 1st sess., 40 *Cong. Rec.* H1245 (Jan. 18, 1906) (statement of Rep. Stephens).

59th Cong., 1st sess., 40 *Cong. Rec.* H1514–15 (Jan. 24, 1906) (statement of Rep. Beall).

59th Cong., 1st sess., 40 *Cong. Rec.* H1552 (Jan. 25, 1906) (statements of Rep. Floyd).

59th Cong., 1st sess., 40 *Cong. Rec.* H1567 (Jan. 25, 1906) (statement of Rep. McGuire).

59th Cong., 1st sess., 40 *Cong. Rec.* S2976 (Feb. 26, 1906) (statement of Sen. McCumber).

59th Cong., 1st sess., 40 *Cong. Rec.* S3054–55 (Feb. 27, 1906) (statements of Sen. McCumber and Sen. Long).

59th Cong., 1st sess., 40 *Cong. Rec.* S3061 (Feb. 27, 1906) (statement of Sen. Teller).

59th Cong., 1st sess.; 40 *Cong. Rec.* S3064 (Feb. 27, 1906) (statement of Sen. Nelson).

59th Cong., 1st sess., 40 *Cong. Rec.* S3122 (Feb. 28, 1906) (statement of Sen. Teller).

59th Cong., 1st sess., 40 *Cong. Rec.* H3221 (Mar. 1, 1906) (statement of Rep. Curtis).

59th Cong., 1st sess., 40 *Cong. Rec.* S3213, S4390, S4392 (Mar. 1 and 28, 1906) (statements of Rep. La Follette).

59th Cong., 1st sess., 40 *Cong. Rec.* S3273 and S3275 (Mar. 2, 1906) (statements of Sen. McCumber).

59th Cong., 1st sess., 40 *Cong. Rec.* S4395 (Mar. 2, 1906) (statements of Sen. Spooner and Sen. Teller).

S.J. Res. 37 (Pub. Res. No. 7), 59th Cong., 1st sess. (Mar. 2, 1906), 34 *Stat.* 822, 3 Kappler's 262.

59th Cong., 1st sess., 40 *Cong. Rec.* S3386 (Mar. 6, 1906) (statement of Sen. Long).

59th Cong., 1st sess., 40 *Cong. Rec.* S4653–54 (Apr. 3, 1906) (statements of Sen. Teller and Sen. Spooner).

59th Cong., 1st sess., 40 *Cong. Rec.* S4655 (Apr. 3, 1906) (statements of Sen. Clark and Sen. Spooner).

59th Cong., 1st sess., 40 *Cong. Rec.* S8399 (June 13, 1906) (statement of Sen. Morgan).

H.R. Rep. No. 1454, "To Accompany H.R. 15641 for the Removal of the Restrictions from Part of the Lands of Allottees of the Five Civilized Tribes, and for Other Purposes," 60th Cong., 1st sess. (Apr. 6, 1908).

S. Rep. No. 575, "To Accompany H.R. 15641 for the Removal of the Restrictions from Part of the Lands of Allottees of the Five Civilized Tribes, and for Other Purposes," 60th Cong., 1st sess. (Apr. 28, 1908).

U.S. Department of the Interior. *Annual Report of the U.S. Indian Superintendent, Union Agency, FY 1913.* Washington, D.C.: GPO, 1913.

U.S. Department of the Interior. *Annual Report of the Commission to the Five Civilized Tribes, FY 1914*. Washington, D.C.: GPO, 1914.

Mott, Marshall L. *The Act of May 27, 1908, Placing in Probate Court of Oklahoma Indian Jurisdiction: A National Blunder*. Report to the U.S. Senate and House of Representatives, with following attachments: Report of M .L. Mott to the Secretary of the Interior (Nov. 21, 1912); the "Indian Appropriation Bill Speech of Hon. Charles H. Burke of S.Dak. on the Mott Report Relative to Indian Guardianships in the Probate Courts of Oklahoma in the House of Representatives" (Dec. 13, 1912); 1923 Oklahoma Bar Association Committee Resolution submitted by John H. Mosier and C. F. Dyer for the committee; and S. E. Wallen, superintendent, U.S. Indian Service, Five Civilized Tribes, to Charles H. Burke, commissioner of Indian Affairs (Dec. 31, 1923). Washington, D.C.: 1925. (Available at WHC.)

H.R. Rep. No. 322, "To Accompany H.R. 4761 'Putting in Force the Statute of Limitations of the State of Oklahoma in Reference to Suits Involving Indian Titles, etc.,'" 69th Cong., 1st sess. (Feb. 19, 1926).

S. Rep. No. 317, "To Accompany S. 1225 'Titles to Indian Lands in Oklahoma,'" 69th Cong., 1st sess. (Mar. 9, 1926).

S. Rep. No. 982, "To Accompany S. 3594 "Extend Period of Restrictions on Lands of Certain Members of the Five Civilized Tribes,'" 70th Cong., 1st sess. (May 3, 1928).

73rd Cong., 2nd sess., 78 *Cong. Rec.* S11126 (June 12, 1934) (statement of Sen. Thomas).

73rd Cong., 2nd sess., 78 *Cong. Rec.* H11727–29 (June 15, 1934) (statement of Rep. Howard).

A Bill to Promote the General Welfare of the Indians of the State of Oklahoma and for Other Purposes: Hearings on H.R. 6234 before the House Comm. on Indian Affairs, 74th Cong., 1st sess. (1935).

A Bill to Promote the General Welfare of the Indians of the State of Oklahoma and for Other Purposes: Hearings on S. 2047 before the Senate Comm. on Indian Affairs, 74th Cong., 1st. sess. (1935).

H.R. Rep. No. 2408, to accompany S. 2047, 74th Cong., 2nd sess. (Apr. 5, 1936).

U.S. Department of the Interior. Indian Affairs. "Five Civilized Tribes—Status of Freedmen—Organization under Oklahoma Indian Welfare Act" (memorandum for commissioner), 1 Sol. Op. 1077, Oct. 1, 1941.

S. Rep. No. 543, 80th Cong., 1st sess. (July 14, 1947).

S. Rep. No. 845, to accompany S. 2198, 84th Cong., 1st sess. (July 13, 1955) and H.R. Rep. No. 1185 to accompany H.R. 7218, 84th Cong., 1st sess. (July 14, 1955), 1955 U.S. Code Cong. Admin. News 2970–73.

S. Rep. No. 1594, "Providing for the Disposition of Funds Appropriated to Pay Judgments in Favor of the Seminole Tribe of Oklahoma in Docket No.s 150 and 248 of the Indian Claims Commission and for Other Purposes," 90th Cong., 2nd sess. (Sept. 24, 1968).

American Indian Policy Review Commission. *Final Report of the American Indian Policy Review Commission*, vol. 1 (submitted to Congress May 17, 1977). Washington, D.C.: GPO, 1977.

Distribution of Seminole Judgment Funds: Hearing before the U.S. Senate Select Committee on Indian Affairs on S. 2000, "To Provide for the Use and Distribution of Funds Appropriated in Satisfaction of the Judgment Awarded to the Seminole Indians in Dockets 73 and 151 Before the Indian Claims Commission, and for Other Purposes," and on S. 2188, "To Provide for the Use and Distribution of the Award Granted by the Indian Claims Commission to the Seminole Nation as it Existed in Florida on Sept. 18, 1823, and for Other Purposes," 95th Cong., 2nd sess. (Mar. 2, 1978).

Indian Judgment Funds Use or Distribution Plans: Hearings Before the Senate Select Committee on Indian Affairs on S.J. Res. 108, "To Validate the Effectiveness of Certain Plans for the Use or Distribution of Funds Appropriated to Pay Judgments Awarded to Indian Tribes or Groups," 96th Cong., 1st sess. (Nov. 5, 1979).

Muscogee (Creek) Nation v. Hodel, Civ. No. 87-5377 (D.C. Circuit), Appendix submitted by Appellant Muscogee (Creek Nation), Ex. 3, Mar. 9, 1984, memorandum to chief administrative judge, Board of Indian Appeals, 32, with memorandums and letters enclosed.

S. 1096, 101st Cong., 1st sess., 135 *Cong. Rec.* S5988 (introduced June 1, 1989) (enacted).

H.R. 2838, 101st Cong., 1st sess., 135 *Cong. Rec.* H3520 (introduced June 29, 1989).

S. 1096, 101st Cong., 2nd sess., 136 *Cong. Rec.*

H.R. Rep. No. 101-399, "Providing for the Use and Distribution of Funds Awarded the Seminole Indian in Dockets 73, 151, and 73-A of the Indian Claims Commission" (with supplemental views to accompany S. 1096), 101st Cong., 2nd sess. (Feb. 6, 1990).

H.R. Rep. No. 101-39, 101st Cong., 2nd sess. (Mar. 29, 1990).

H.R. Conf. Rep. on S. 1096, 101st Cong., 2nd sess., 136 *Cong. Rec.* H1414 (Apr. 3, 1990).

S. Conf. Rep. on S. 1096, 101st Cong., 2nd sess., 136 *Cong. Rec.* S4350 (Apr. 5, 1990).

S. 1096, 101st Cong., 2nd sess., 136 *Cong. Rec.* S4566 (enrolled bill presented Apr. 19, 1990) (enacted).

H.R. Rep. No. 102-499, 102nd Cong., 2nd sess. (Apr. 22, 1992).

Olsen, Mike, acting deputy assistant secretary of the Interior, Indian Affairs, to Kenneth Chambers, principal chief of Seminole Nation, Apr. 11, 2005 (Interior approval of gaming compact between Seminole Nation and State of Oklahoma). U.S. Department of Interior.

National Indian Gaming Regulatory Commission. "Enforcement Actions." NIGS. http://*www.nigc.gov*.

BOOKS AND ARTICLES

Bledsoe, Samuel T. *Indian Land Titles*. 2nd ed. Kansas City, Mo.: Vernon Law Book, 1913.

Cohen, Felix. *Handbook of Federal Indian Law*. Charlottesville, Va.: Michie Co., 1982.

Debo, Angie. *And Still the Waters Run*. Princeton, N.J.: Princeton University Press, 1940. Reprinted Norman: University of Oklahoma Press, 1984.

———. *The Five Civilized Tribes of Oklahoma*. Philadelphia: Indian Rights Association, 1951.

———. *The Rise and Fall of the Choctaw Republic*. Norman: University of Oklahoma Press, 1934.

———. *The Road to Disappearance: A History of the Creek Indians*. Norman: University of Oklahoma Press, 1941.

Gross, Ariela J. *What Blood Won't Tell*. Cambridge, Mass.: Harvard University Press, 2008.

Heard, Suzanne, David Norris, and Ingrid Westmoreland, *A History of the Inter-Tribal Council of the Five Civilized Tribes 1976–1991*. Booklet printed by Publication Committee of the Inter-Tribal Council of the Five Civilized Tribes, 1991.

Howard, James H., and Willie Lena. *Oklahoma Seminoles: Medicines, Magic, and Religion*. Norman: University of Oklahoma Press, 1984.

Kidwell, Clara Sue. *The Choctaws in Oklahoma: From Tribe to Nation, 1855–1970*. Norman: University of Oklahoma Press, 2007.

Kvasnicka, Robert M., and Herman J. Viola. *The Commissioners of Indian Affairs, 1824–1977*. Lincoln: University of Nebraska Press, 1979.

Leupp, Francis E. *The Indian and His Problem*. New York: Charles Scribner's Sons, 1910.

Littlefield, Daniel F. *Seminole Burnings: A Story of Racial Vengeance*. Jackson: University Press of Mississippi, 1996.

McReynolds, Edwin C. *The Seminoles*. Norman: University of Oklahoma Press, 1957, 1972.

Merriam and Associates. *The Problem of Indian Administration*. Baltimore: Johns Hopkins University Press, 1928.

Miller, Susan A. *Coacoochee's Bones, A Seminole Saga*. Lawrence: University Press of Kansas, 2003.

Morris, John W., Charles R. Goins, and Edwin C. McReynolds. *Historical Atlas of Oklahoma*. Norman: University of Oklahoma Press, 1976.

Mulroy, Kevin. *The Seminole Freedmen: A History*. Norman: University of Oklahoma Press, 2007.

National American Indian Court Judges Association Long Range Planning Project. *Indian Courts and the Future* (report; BIA Ind. Aff. Contract no. K51C14201023). Washington, D.C.: GPO 1978.

Rarick, Joseph F. *Cases and Materials on Problems in Lands Allotted to American Indians.* Rev. 1st perm. ed. Norman, Okla., 1950, 1952.

———. *A Guide to Rarick's Oklahoma Indian Land Titles.* 1st ed. Norman, Okla., 1988.

Rice, George William. "Indian Rights: 25 U.S.C. § 71: The End of Indian Sovereignty or a Self-Limitation on Contractual Ability? (note)." *Indian Law Review* 5 (1977): 239–53.

Sattler, Richard A. "Remnants, Renegades, and Runaways: Seminole Ethnogenesis Reconsidered." In *History, Power, and Identity,* edited by Jonathan D. Hill, 36–69. Iowa City: University of Iowa Press, 1996.

———. "Seminoli Italwa: Socio-Political Change among the Oklahoma Seminoles between Removal and Allotment, 1836–1905." PhD diss., University of Oklahoma, 1987.

Schmeckebier, Laurence Frederick. *The Office of Indian Affairs, Its History, Activities and Organization.* Baltimore: Johns Hopkins University Press, 1927.

Schultz, Jack M. *The Seminole Baptist Churches of Oklahoma: Maintaining a Traditional Community.* Norman: University of Oklahoma Press, 1999.

Semple, William F. *Oklahoma Indian Land Titles.* St. Louis, Mo.: Thomas Law Book, 1952.

Vollmann, Tim, and Sharon Blackwell. "State Court Approval of Leases and Conveyances by Indians of the Five Civilized Tribes: Time for Legislative Reform." *Tulsa Law Journal* 25 (1989): 101–156.

Welsh, Louise, Willa May Townes, and John W. Morris. *A History of the Greater Seminole Oil Field.* Oklahoma City: Oklahoma Heritage Association, 1981.

INDEX

Native American Rights Fund, 191
Navajo Nation, 124, 151, 219
New Mexico, 16
Nichols, Jack, 76
Nickles, Sen. Don, 208
Niebell, Paul M., 92, 123, 155, 169, 184–85, 208, 210
Nix, Loisetta, 206
Nofire v. United States, 33
Northcutt, Jane, 158
Nurcup Harjo Band, 135

Ocese Band, 135
Office of Native American Programs, 163
Oil and gas, 42, 45, 54, 56, 63–65, 67, 70, 72, 77–78, 81–85, 94–95, 103–104, 111, 115, 121, 164; Greater Seminole Area, 104; Oklahoma oil and gas conservation laws, 81, 83
Oil and gas royalties (Seminole Nation), 42, 64–65, 77, 82, 94–96, 115, 121, 162
Okfuskee Band, 136
Oklahoma Bar Association, 69, 89
Oklahoma City, Okla. Terr., 17; Oklahoma, 17, 92, 144, 157–58, 172
Oklahoma City Area Indian Health Board, 162
Oklahoma Constitution. *See* Constitution, Oklahoma
Oklahoma Corporation Commission, 81
Oklahoma Department of Human Services, 183
Oklahoma Department of Public Safety, 176
Oklahoma Enabling Act, 55–57, 124
Oklahoma Independent Petroleum Association, 89
Oklahoma Indian Affairs Commission, 163, 176
Oklahoma Indian Child Welfare Act, 183–84

Oklahoma Indian Legal Services, 183
Oklahoma Indian Rights Association, 161
Oklahoma Indian Welfare Act (Thomas Rogers Act), 74–79, 119–21, 133, 137, 192, 215
Oklahoman, The, 54
Oklahoma Organic Act, 23, 25–28, 32
Oklahoma Tax Commission, 215, 225–28
Oklahoma Tax Commission v. Citizen Band Potawatomi Indian Tribe of Oklahoma, 225–27
Oklahoma Tax Commission v. Sac and Fox Nation, 228
Oklahoma Territory, 25, 27, 56, 191–92
Okmulgee, I.T., 45
Okmulgee, Okla., 193
Okmulgee Agency, BIA, 193
Okmulgee Constitution, 12
Older American Program, 243
Oliphant v. Suquamish Indian Tribe, 190
Osceola, Guy, 187

Palmer, Billie, 134
Palmer, Thomas, 157–58, 170, 178–82, 184–87, 194, 199–200, 208, 210, 221
Palmer, Tony, 179
Parker, Ely S., 140
Pars-co-fer, 9
Pawnee, Okla., 165, 200
Pawnee Tribe, 200
Pennokee, Ella Mae, 158
Per capita payments, 109–10, 116, 131, 185, 210–11
Periote, Susie, 157
Perkins, Sen. Bishop, 29
Pipestem, F. Browning, 188
Planning department (Seminole Nation), 163–65
Plasteck Central Manufacturing, 130
Platt, Sen. Orville, 29

www.ingramcontent.com/pod-product-compliance
Lightning Source LLC
Chambersburg PA
CBHW020603270326
41927CB00005B/155